# Architecting Modern Java EE Applications

Designing lightweight, business-oriented enterprise applications in the age of cloud, containers, and Java EE 8

**Sebastian Daschner**

BIRMINGHAM - MUMBAI

# Architecting Modern Java EE Applications

First published: October 2017

Production reference: 1051017

Published by Packt Publishing Ltd.
Livery Place
35 Livery Street
Birmingham
B3 2PB, UK.

ISBN 978-1-78839-385-0

www.packtpub.com

# Credits

**Author**
Sebastian Daschner

**Reviewer**
Melissa McKay

**Commissioning Editor**
Aaron Lazar

**Acquisition Editor**
Alok Dhuri

**Content Development Editor**
Rohit Kumar Singh

**Technical Editor**
Pavan Ramchandani

**Copy Editor**
Safis Editing

**Project Coordinator**
Vaidehi Sawant

**Proofreader**
Safis Editing

**Indexer**
Aishwarya Gangawane

**Graphics**
Abhinash Sahu

**Production Coordinator**
Nilesh Mohite

# Foreword

Languages in our industry come and go, and the pace at which hip new languages come out only seems to increase. Every year, new languages come out and each has the colossal job of building an entire ecosystem around itself before the next new darling language comes and steals all the fickle early adopters. As each trend waxes and wanes, so do the ecosystems built around them.

Those of us who invest heavily in these trending ecosystems are often bitten by a common set of problems that lead to failures at the business level, losing project momentum due to the inability to find and hire developers. The new solutions presented are often the same old idea, but with a youthful misunderstanding of the problem space that leads to real performance and reliability problems. As the ecosystem matures, the act of recognizing and realigning to the true complexity of systems often results in severe incompatibilities. Tooling choices are often narrow or buggy, or they simply never materialize.

The unbeatable source of strength of the Java ecosystem over the last 20 years has been its standards, Java EE being chief among them. There have been 53 Java Specification Requests (JSRs) completed under the Java EE umbrella, ranging from XML parsing to JSON parsing, Servlets to JAX-RS, binary protocols to RESTful protocols, front-end technologies such as JSF or MVC, APIs for marshaling data to XML (JAX-B) or JSON (JSON-B). The breadth of specifications is so wide that even if you do not think of yourself as a Java EE user, if you are a Java developer, you are definitely leveraging it in some way. With an estimate of 9 million Java developers worldwide, this is a stable and experienced talent pool.

Major deployments of Java EE range from Walmart, the world's largest retailer and third largest employer, to NASA's SOFIA program, scanning space at 40,000 feet. While the developer community is large and the corporations that use it are larger, the modern Java EE runtimes are incredibly small. Walmart and NASA, for example, use Apache TomEE, an implementation that is 35 MB on disk, boots in a second and consumes less that 30 MB of memory. This low profile is indicative of all modern implementations including WildFly, Payara, and LibertyProfile. The Java EE tools, cloud and IDE landscape is filled with competitive choices, almost too many to track. The 200+ person company ZeroTurnaround, for example, is built on a product that added instant deploy options to Java EE servers.

With such an expansive ecosystem that has almost 20 years of history, truly getting to the essence of what makes Java EE great today and how to put it into practice for today's Microservices world can be a challenge. It's all too easy to find very informed, but ultimately dated information from 2, 5, and 10 years back. The authoritative tone of one article one date can directly conflict with equally authoritative, but ultimately contrarian perspective of another author on a different year. In fact, a challenge almost unique to Java EE is its history. Few technologies last long enough and evolve so much.

This book, like the author himself, represents a new generation of Java EE. The chapters in this book guide the reader through the journey of leveraging Java EE in the context of today's Microservice and Containerized world. Less of a reference manual for API syntax, the perspectives and techniques in this book reflect real-world experience from someone who has recently gone through the journey themselves, meticulously annotated the obstacles, and has them ready to share. From packaging to testing to cloud usage, this book is an ideal companion to both new and more experienced developers who are looking for an earned insight bigger than an API to help them realign their thinking to architect modern applications in Java EE.

**David Blevins**
Founder and CEO, Tomitribe

# About the Author

**Sebastian Daschner** is a Java freelancer working as a consultant and trainer and is enthusiastic about programming and Java (EE). He participates in the JCP, helping to form future Java EE standards, serving in the JSR 370 and 374 Expert Groups, and collaborating on various open source projects. For his contributions to the Java community and ecosystem, he was recognized with the titles Java Champion and Oracle Developer Champion.

Sebastian is a regular speaker at international IT conferences, such as JavaLand, JavaOne, and Jfokus. He won the JavaOne Rockstar award at JavaOne 2016. Together with Java community manager, Steve Chin, he has traveled to dozens of conferences and Java User Groups on motorbike. Steve and Sebastian have launched JOnsen, a Java unconference held at a hot spring in the countryside of Japan.

# Acknowledgments

There are many people whom I had the privilege to meet during my career, and who had a great impact not only on my work but also this book and without whom this would not have been possible. This list of people grows and grows every year. All of them are indirectly helped shaping this book, which I immensely appreciate.

There are a few friends who had a direct impact on this book and whom I particularly want to thank.

Kirk Pepperdine, for his tireless aspiration to myth-bust the world of software performance and for the permission to use jPDM. His invaluable experience not only vastly improved the quality of this book but also greatly educated me personally.

Melissa McKay, for her tireless reviews, being eager (and crazy) enough to review this whole book, what greatly improved the quality, for sharing her experience in Enterprise Java, and not least for inspiration and motivation.

David Blevins, for sharing the passion in the topic of Java EE and writing the foreword to this book.

Andy Gumbrecht, for help not only in the topic of enterprise testing but also the English language.

Markus Eisele, for igniting the spark of this work.

Philipp Brunenberg, for creating constructive inspiration and not least, tons of motivation through weeks of writing.

# About the Reviewer

**Melissa McKay** has been a software developer, for the last 15 years in the private sector working with various types of applications, both in a contracting capacity for external clients and on enterprise products. Her current focus is on creating Java server applications used in the communications and video industry. Her interests include clustered systems, and she has a particular passion for solving issues with concurrency and multithreaded applications.

Melissa regularly attends the JCrete unconference in Crete, Greece, and had the pleasure of attending the initial launch of the JOnsen unconference in Japan. She enjoys volunteering for technology events for kids including JavaOne4Kids and JCrete4Kids. She is a member of the Content Committee for JavaOne 2017 and an active member of the Denver Java User Group.

# www.PacktPub.com

For support files and downloads related to your book, please visit www.PacktPub.com.

Did you know that Packt offers eBook versions of every book published, with PDF and ePub files available? You can upgrade to the eBook version at www.PacktPub.comand as a print book customer, you are entitled to a discount on the eBook copy. Get in touch with us at service@packtpub.com for more details.

At www.PacktPub.com, you can also read a collection of free technical articles, sign up for a range of free newsletters and receive exclusive discounts and offers on Packt books and eBooks.

https://www.packtpub.com/mapt

Get the most in-demand software skills with Mapt. Mapt gives you full access to all Packt books and video courses, as well as industry-leading tools to help you plan your personal development and advance your career.

# Why subscribe?

- Fully searchable across every book published by Packt
- Copy and paste, print, and bookmark content
- On demand and accessible via a web browser

# Customer Feedback

Thanks for purchasing this Packt book. At Packt, quality is at the heart of our editorial process. To help us improve, please leave us an honest review on this book's Amazon page at https://www.amazon.com/dp/1788393856.

If you'd like to join our team of regular reviewers, you can e-mail us at customerreviews@packtpub.com. We award our regular reviewers with free eBooks and videos in exchange for their valuable feedback. Help us be relentless in improving our products!

*A Cyrine Ben Ayed, pour ta compréhension, ton indéfectible soutien et ton infinie patience. Ce livre t'est dédié.*

# Table of Contents

**Preface**                                                                1

**Chapter 1: Introduction**                                                7
    **New demands in enterprise systems**                  7
    **Modern way of realizing enterprise systems**         8
    **Relevance of Java EE in modern systems**             9
    **Java EE 8 update and roadmap**                       10
    **Java Community Process**                             11
    **What to expect in the book**                         12

**Chapter 2: Designing and Structuring Java Enterprise Applications**      15
    **The purpose of enterprise applications**             15
        What developers should focus on     16
        Meeting customer's demands          16
    **Outer enterprise project structure**                 18
        Business and team structures        18
        Software projects contents          19
            Application source code     19
            Software structures         19
            Version control systems     21
            Binaries                    22
            Build systems               23
        Single versus multi-module projects  23
        Illusion of reusability             24
            Technical dependencies      24
            Organizational challenges   25
            Reusability considerations  25
        Project artifacts                   26
        One project per artifact            26
        Build systems for Java EE           27
            Apache Maven                28
            Gradle                      30
        Structuring for modern frontend technologies   33
            Enter JavaScript frameworks  33
            Organizing modern frontends  34
    **Enterprise project code structure**                  35
        Situation in enterprise projects    36
        Horizontal versus vertical layering  36

| | |
|---|---|
| Business-driven structure | 37 |
| Designing reasonable modules | 38 |
| Realizing package structures | 40 |
| Package contents | 40 |
| Horizontal package layering | 41 |
| Flat module package | 42 |
| Entity Control Boundary | 43 |
| Packages | 44 |
| Package access | 45 |
| Don't over-enforce architecture | 46 |
| **Summary** | 47 |
| **Chapter 3: Implementing Modern Java Enterprise Applications** | 49 |
| **Use case boundaries** | 49 |
| **Core domain components of modern Java EE** | 50 |
| EJB and CDI - differentiation and integration | 51 |
| CDI producers | 53 |
| Emitting domain events | 53 |
| Scopes | 55 |
| **Patterns in Java EE** | 56 |
| Design patterns revisited | 56 |
| Singleton | 56 |
| Abstract factory | 59 |
| Factory method | 62 |
| Object pool | 63 |
| Decorator | 64 |
| Facade | 68 |
| Proxy | 70 |
| Observer | 70 |
| Strategy | 71 |
| Further patterns | 73 |
| Domain-Driven Design | 74 |
| Services | 74 |
| Entities | 75 |
| Value objects | 75 |
| Aggregates | 76 |
| Repositories | 76 |
| Factories | 77 |
| Domain event | 77 |
| **External and cross-cutting concerns in enterprise applications** | 78 |
| Communication with external systems | 78 |
| How to choose communication technology | 78 |
| Synchronous HTTP communication | 81 |
| Representational State Transfer | 82 |
| Java API for RESTful web services | 85 |

| | |
|---|---|
| Mapping HTTP content types | 88 |
| Validating requests | 95 |
| Mapping errors | 101 |
| Accessing external systems | 102 |
| Stability when consuming HTTP | 103 |
| Accessing Hypermedia REST services | 106 |
| Asynchronous communication and messaging | 108 |
| Asynchronous HTTP communication | 108 |
| Message-oriented communication | 109 |
| Server-sent events | 110 |
| WebSocket | 114 |
| Connecting enterprise technology | 116 |
| **Database systems** | 116 |
| Integrating RDBMS systems | 117 |
| Mapping domain models | 118 |
| Integrating database systems | 121 |
| Transactions | 124 |
| Relational databases versus NoSQL | 125 |
| **Cross-cutting concerns** | 126 |
| **Configuring applications** | 129 |
| **Caching** | 131 |
| **Flow of execution** | 133 |
| Synchronous execution | 134 |
| Asynchronous execution | 134 |
| Asynchronous EJB methods | 135 |
| Managed Executor Service | 135 |
| Asynchronous CDI events | 136 |
| Scopes in asynchronicity | 137 |
| Timed execution | 137 |
| Asynchronous and reactive JAX-RS | 139 |
| **Concepts and design principles of modern Java EE** | 143 |
| **Preserving maintainable code with high quality** | 144 |
| **Summary** | 146 |
| **Chapter 4: Lightweight Java EE** | 149 |
| **Lightweight enterprise technology** | 149 |
| **Why Java EE standards?** | 150 |
| **Convention over configuration** | 151 |
| **Dependency management of Java EE projects** | 152 |
| **Lightweight way of packaging applications** | 154 |
| **Java EE application servers** | 158 |
| **One application per application server** | 159 |
| **Summary** | 160 |
| **Chapter 5: Container and Cloud Environments with Java EE** | 163 |

**Motivations and goals**    163
   Infrastructure as code    165
   Stability and production readiness    166
**Containers**    167
**Java EE in the container**    169
**Container orchestration frameworks**    171
**Realizing container orchestration**    173
**Java EE in orchestrated containers**    179
   Connecting external services    179
   Configuring orchestrated applications    180
**12-factor applications and Java EE**    182
   Have one codebase tracked in revision control, many deploys    182
   Explicitly declare and isolate dependencies    183
   Store config in the environment    184
   Treat backing services as attached resources    184
   Strictly separate build and run stages    185
   Execute the app as one or more stateless processes    185
   Export services via port binding    186
   Scale out via the process model    186
   Maximize robustness with fast startup and graceful shutdown    187
   Keep development, staging, and production as similar as possible    188
   Treat logs as event streams    189
   Run admin/management tasks as one-off processes    190
**Cloud, Cloud native, and their benefits**    191
   Cloud native    192
**Summary**    193
**Chapter 6: Application Development Workflows**    195
**Motivation and goals of productive development workflows**    196
**Realizing development workflows**    197
   Version control everything    198
   Building binaries    199
     Java artifacts    199
     Artifact versions    200
     Building containers    201
   Quality assurance    202
   Deployment    204
     Configuration    206
     Credentials    208
   Data migration    209
     Adding database structures    210

Changing database structures                          211
Removing database structures                          212
Implementing migration                                212
Testing                                               215
Build metadata                                        216
Going to production                                   218
Branching models                                      218
Technology                                            220
Pipeline-as-code                                      220
**Workflows with Java EE**                            224
**Continuous Delivery culture and team habits**       225
Responsibility                                        225
Check in early and often                              226
Immediately fixing issues                             227
Visibility                                            227
Improve continuously                                  228
**Summary**                                           229

**Chapter 7: Testing**                                231
**The necessity of tests**                            231
**Requirements of well-crafted tests**               232
Predictability                                        233
Isolation                                             233
Reliability                                           234
Fast execution                                        234
Automation                                            234
Maintainability                                       235
**What to test**                                      235
**Definition of test scopes**                         236
Unit tests                                            237
Component tests                                       237
Integration tests                                     237
System tests                                          238
Performance tests                                     238
Stress tests                                          239
**Implementing tests**                                239
Unit tests                                            240
Implementation                                        240
Technology                                            244
Component tests                                       245
Motivation                                            245

| | |
|---|---|
| Implementation | 245 |
| Delegating test components | 248 |
| Technology | 250 |
| Integration tests | 251 |
| Embedded containers | 251 |
| Embedded databases | 253 |
| Running integration tests | 256 |
| Code level integration tests versus system tests | 257 |
| Shortcomings of integration tests | 257 |
| Shortcomings of system tests | 258 |
| Conclusion | 258 |
| System tests | 259 |
| Managing test scenarios | 260 |
| Simulating external concerns | 261 |
| Designing system tests | 262 |
| Deploying and controlling external mocks | 266 |
| Performance tests | 268 |
| Motivation | 269 |
| Key performance indicators | 269 |
| Developing performance tests | 270 |
| Insights | 273 |
| **Running tests locally** | 273 |
| **Maintaining test data and scenarios** | 276 |
| Importance of maintainable tests | 276 |
| Signs of lack of test quality | 277 |
| Test code quality | 277 |
| Test technology support | 280 |
| **Summary** | 282 |
| **Chapter 8: Microservices and System Architecture** | 285 |
| **Motivations behind distributed systems** | 286 |
| **Challenges of distribution** | 286 |
| Communication overhead | 287 |
| Performance overhead | 287 |
| Organizational overhead | 287 |
| **How to design systems landscapes** | 288 |
| Context maps and bounded contexts | 288 |
| Separation of concerns | 289 |
| Teams | 289 |
| Project life cycles | 290 |
| **How to design system interfaces** | 290 |
| API considerations | 291 |
| Interface management | 291 |

Change-resilient APIs                                      292
Breaking the business logic                               292
Hypermedia REST and versioning                            292
Documenting boundaries                                    293
Consistency versus scalability                            295
**Event sourcing, event-driven architectures, and CQRS**  296
Shortcomings of CRUD-based systems                        297
Scalability                                               297
Competing transactions                                    297
Reproducibility                                           298
Event sourcing                                            298
Benefits                                                  299
Eventually consistent real world                          300
Event-driven architectures                                301
Eventual consistency in event-driven architectures        303
Enter CQRS                                                303
Principles                                                304
Design                                                    304
Benefits                                                  308
Shortcomings                                              309
**Communication**                                         310
**Microservice architectures**                            310
Sharing data and technology in enterprises                311
Shared-nothing architectures                              312
Interdependent systems                                    312
12-factor and cloud native applications                   313
When to use and when not to use microservices             314
**Implementing microservices with Java EE**               314
Zero-dependency applications                              315
Application servers                                       315
Implementing application boundaries                       316
Implementing CQRS                                         316
System interfaces                                         317
Example scenario using Apache Kafka                       317
Integrating Java EE                                       318
CDI events                                                319
Event handlers                                            320
State representation                                      321
Consuming Kafka messages                                  322
Producing Kafka messages                                  325
Application boundaries                                    326
Integrating further CQRS concepts                         328
Java EE in the age of distribution                        329

| | |
|---|---|
| Discovering services | 329 |
| Communicating resiliently | 330 |
| Validating responses | 330 |
| Breaking timeouts and circuits | 330 |
| Bulkheads | 332 |
| Shaking hands and pushing back | 333 |
| More on being resilient | 335 |
| **Summary** | 335 |

## Chapter 9: Monitoring, Performance, and Logging — 337

| | |
|---|---|
| **Business metrics** | 338 |
| Collecting business metrics | 339 |
| Emitting metrics | 340 |
| Enter Prometheus | 341 |
| Realization with Java EE | 343 |
| Integrating the environment | 344 |
| **Meeting performance requirements in distributed systems** | 345 |
| Service level agreements | 345 |
| Achieving SLAs in distributed systems | 345 |
| **Tackling performance issues** | 346 |
| Theory of constraints | 347 |
| Identifying performance regression with jPDM | 348 |
| Subsystems | 348 |
| Actors | 349 |
| Application | 350 |
| JVM | 350 |
| Operating system and hardware | 350 |
| jPDM instances - production situations | 350 |
| Analyzing the jPDM instances | 351 |
| Dominating consumer - OS | 353 |
| Dominating consumer - none | 354 |
| Dominating consumer - JVM | 354 |
| Dominating consumer - application | 355 |
| Conclusion | 355 |
| **Technical metrics** | 356 |
| Types of technical metrics | 356 |
| High frequency monitoring versus sampling | 357 |
| Collecting technical metrics | 357 |
| Boundary metrics | 358 |
| **Logging and tracing** | 359 |
| Shortcomings of traditional logging | 359 |
| Performance | 360 |
| Log levels | 360 |
| Log format | 361 |

| | |
|---|---|
| Amounts of data | 361 |
| Obfuscation | 362 |
| The concerns of applications | 362 |
| Wrong choice of technology | 362 |
| Logging in a containerized world | 364 |
| **Journaling** | 366 |
| **Tracing** | 366 |
| Tracing in a modern world | 369 |
| **Typical performance issues** | 371 |
| Logging and memory consumption | 371 |
| Premature optimization | 372 |
| Relational databases | 373 |
| Communication | 374 |
| Threading and pooling | 375 |
| **Performance testing** | 375 |
| **Summary** | 376 |
| **Chapter 10: Security** | 379 |
| **Lessons learned from the past** | 379 |
| **Security in a modern world** | 380 |
| Security principles | 381 |
| Encrypt communication | 381 |
| Delegate security concerns | 381 |
| Treat user credentials properly | 382 |
| Avoid storing credentials in version control | 382 |
| Include tests | 382 |
| Possibilities and solutions | 383 |
| Encrypted communication | 383 |
| Protocol-based authentication | 383 |
| Decentralized security | 384 |
| Proxies | 385 |
| Integration in modern environments | 385 |
| **Implementing security in Java EE applications** | 386 |
| Transparent security | 386 |
| Servlets | 386 |
| Java principals and roles | 386 |
| JASPIC | 387 |
| Security API | 388 |
| Authentication mechanisms | 388 |
| Identity stores | 388 |
| Custom security | 389 |
| Accessing security information | 391 |
| **Summary** | 392 |

## Chapter 11: Conclusion                                            395
    **Motivations in enterprise development**              395
    **Cloud and Continuous Delivery**                       396
    **Relevance of Java EE**                                396
    **API updates introduced in Java EE 8**                 397
        CDI 2.0                                 397
        JAX-RS 2.1                              398
        JSON-B 1.0                              399
        JSON-P 1.1                              400
        Bean Validation 2.0                     400
        JPA 2.2                                 401
        Security 1.0                            401
        Servlet 4.0                             402
        JSF 2.3                                 403
    **JCP and participation**                               403
    **MicroProfile**                                        404
    **Eclipse Enterprise for Java**                         404
## Appendix: Links and further resources                             405
## Index                                                             409

# Preface

Java EE 8 brings with it a load of features, mainly targeting newer architectures such as microservices, modernized security APIs, and cloud deployments. This book will teach you to design and develop modern, business-oriented applications using Java EE 8. It shows how to structure systems and applications, and how design patterns and Domain-Driven Design aspects are realized in the age of Java EE 8. You will learn about the concepts and principles behind Java EE applications and how they affect communication, persistence, technical and cross-cutting concerns, and asynchronous behavior.

This book focuses on solving business problems and meeting customer demands in the enterprise world. It covers how to create enterprise applications with reasonable technology choices, free of cargo-cult and over-engineering. The aspects shown in this book not only demonstrate how to realize a certain solution, but also explain its motivation and reasoning.

With the help of this book, you will understand the principles of modern Java EE and how to realize effective architectures. You will gain knowledge of how to design enterprise software in the age of automation, Continuous Delivery, and cloud platforms. You will also learn about the reasoning and motivation behind state-of-the-art enterprise Java technology, which focuses on business.

## What this book covers

Chapter 1, *Introduction*, introduces Java EE enterprise applications and why Java EE is (still) relevant in modern systems.

Chapter 2, *Designing and Structuring Java Enterprise Applications*, shows how to design the structure of an enterprise application using examples, keeping design enterprise applications with business use cases in mind.

Chapter 3, *Implementing Modern Java Enterprise Applications*, covers how to implement modern Java EE applications and why that technology choice is still relevant today.

Chapter 4, *Lightweight Java EE*, teaches you how to realize lightweight Java EE applications with a small footprint and minimal third-party dependencies.

Chapter 5, *Container and Cloud Environments with Java EE*, explains how to leverage the benefits of containers and modern environments, how to integrate enterprise applications, and how this movement encourages productive development workflows.

Chapter 6, *Application Development Workflows*, covers the key points for fast development pipelines and high software quality, from Continuous Delivery to automated testing and DevOps.

Chapter 7, *Testing*, as the name suggests, covers the topic of testing, which helps enable you to ensure high quality in software development automated testing with reasonable coverage.

Chapter 8, *Microservices and System Architecture*, shows the key points of how to design systems after the project and company circumstances, how to construct applications and their interfaces, and when microservice architectures make sense.

Chapter 9, *Security*, covers how to realize and integrate security concerns in today's environments.

Chapter 10, *Monitoring, Performance, and Logging*, covers why traditional logging is harmful, how to investigate performance issues, and how to monitor the business and technical aspects of an application.

Appendix, *Conclusion*, recapitulates and summarizes the contents of the book, including giving advice and motivation.

# What you need for this book

To execute and perform the code examples given in the book, you will require the following tools configured in your system:

- NetBeans, IntelliJ or Eclipse IDE
- GlassFish Server
- Apache Maven
- Docker
- Jenkins
- Gradle

# Who this book is for

This book is for experienced Java EE developers who aspire to become the architects of enterprise-grade applications, or for software architects who would like to leverage Java EE to create effective blueprints of applications.

# Conventions

In this book, you will find a number of text styles that distinguish between different kinds of information. Here are some examples of these styles and an explanation of their meaning.

Code words in text, database table names, folder names, filenames, file extensions, pathnames, dummy URLs, user input, and Twitter handles are shown as follows: "The EJB is annotated using `@Startup`."

A block of code is set as follows:

```
@PreDestroy
public void closeClient() {
    client.close();
}
```

When we wish to draw your attention to a particular part of a code block, the relevant lines or items are set in bold:

```
private Client client;
private List<WebTarget> targets;

@Resource
ManagedExecutorService mes;
```

In order to increase simplicity and readability, some code examples are shortened to their essence. Java `import` statements are only included for new types and code parts that are insignificant to the example are omitted using three dots ( . . . ).

Any command-line input or output is written as follows:

```
mvn -v
```

**New terms** and **important words** are shown in bold.

# Reader feedback

Feedback from our readers is always welcome. Let us know what you think about this book-what you liked or disliked. Reader feedback is important for us as it helps us develop titles that you will really get the most out of.

To send us general feedback, simply e-mail feedback@packtpub.com, and mention the book's title in the subject of your message.

If there is a topic that you have expertise in and you are interested in either writing or contributing to a book, see our author guide at www.packtpub.com/authors.

# Customer support

Now that you are the proud owner of a Packt book, we have a number of things to help you to get the most from your purchase.

# Downloading the example code

You can download the example code files for this book from your account at http://www.packtpub.com. If you purchased this book elsewhere, you can visit http://www.packtpub.com/support and register to have the files e-mailed directly to you. You can download the code files by following these steps:

1. Log in or register to our website using your e-mail address and password.
2. Hover the mouse pointer on the **SUPPORT** tab at the top.
3. Click on **Code Downloads & Errata**.
4. Enter the name of the book in the **Search** box.
5. Select the book for which you're looking to download the code files.
6. Choose from the drop-down menu where you purchased this book from.
7. Click on **Code Download**.

Once the file is downloaded, please make sure that you unzip or extract the folder using the latest version of:

- WinRAR / 7-Zip for Windows
- Zipeg / iZip / UnRarX for Mac
- 7-Zip / PeaZip for Linux

The code bundle for the book is also hosted on GitHub at `https://github.com/PacktPublishing/Architecting-Modern-Java-EE-Applications`. We also have other code bundles from our rich catalog of books and videos available at `https://github.com/PacktPublishing/`. Check them out!

# Errata

Although we have taken every care to ensure the accuracy of our content, mistakes do happen. If you find a mistake in one of our books-maybe a mistake in the text or the code-we would be grateful if you could report this to us. By doing so, you can save other readers from frustration and help us improve subsequent versions of this book. If you find any errata, please report them by visiting `http://www.packtpub.com/submit-errata`, selecting your book, clicking on the **Errata Submission Form** link, and entering the details of your errata. Once your errata are verified, your submission will be accepted and the errata will be uploaded to our website or added to any list of existing errata under the Errata section of that title.

To view the previously submitted errata, go to `https://www.packtpub.com/books/content/support` and enter the name of the book in the search field. The required information will appear under the **Errata** section.

# Piracy

Piracy of copyrighted material on the Internet is an ongoing problem across all media. At Packt, we take the protection of our copyright and licenses very seriously. If you come across any illegal copies of our works in any form on the Internet, please provide us with the location address or website name immediately so that we can pursue a remedy.

Please contact us at `copyright@packtpub.com` with a link to the suspected pirated material.

We appreciate your help in protecting our authors and our ability to bring you valuable content.

# Questions

If you have a problem with any aspect of this book, you can contact us at `questions@packtpub.com`, and we will do our best to address the problem.

# 1
# Introduction

Compared to the past, we see a lot of new demands in enterprise software. It is no longer sufficient to just develop some piece of software and deploy it to an application server. Or maybe it never was.

## New demands in enterprise systems

The world moves faster than ever. And *moving fast* is one of the most important criteria of today's IT companies. We see companies that can adapt to the real world and the customer's needs with high velocity. The expected time to market of features has shrunk from years and months to weeks and less. In order to cope with this, companies not only need to introduce new technology or *throw more money* at their business problem, but also rethink and refactor the way they operate at the core of their IT.

What does *move fast* mean in this context? What aspect does this include? And which methods and technology support this?

Moving fast is all about quickly adapting to the needs of the market and customers. If a new feature is desired or looks promising, how long does it take to get from the initial idea to the feature being in the user's hands? If new infrastructure is required, how long does it take from that decision to the running hardware? And do not forget, if a certain piece of software is developed with all that velocity, is there automated quality control in place that ensures everything will work as expected and not break the existing functionality?

In software development, most of these questions lead to Continuous Delivery and automation. Software that is being developed needs to be built, tested, and shipped in an automated, fast, reliable, and reproducible way. A reliable, automated process not only leads to quicker turnarounds but ultimately higher quality. Automated quality control, such as software tests, are part of the process. In modern software development, Continuous

Delivery, automation, and proper testing are some of the most important principles.

Traditionally, infrastructure was a big bottleneck in most companies. Smaller companies often struggled to provide new infrastructure with a limited budget. Bigger companies mostly fail to implement fast and productive processes. For big corporations, in most of the cases the issue is not the budget but the implementation of the processes. It is not untypical to wait days and weeks for new infrastructure, due to approvals and overly complex processes that technically could have been finished in a matter of minutes.

Therefore, application infrastructure and how it is designed is an important aspect. Chapter 5, *Container and Cloud Environments with Java EE*, will show you the topic of modern cloud environments. Actually, we will see that it's not so much about whether cloud service providers are being used. Fast and productive processes certainly can be implemented with on-premises hardware. Rather, it is more a question of whether processes are implemented properly, using well-suited technologies.

Modern infrastructure needs to be set up in a matter of minutes, in an automated, fast, reproducible, and reliable way. It should adapt to changing demands without great effort. To meet this criterion, infrastructure should be defined as code, either with procedural scripts or in declarative descriptors. We will see how infrastructure as code impacts software development workflows and which technologies support it.

These demands will impact the way teams operate. It is no longer sufficient for development teams to *just develop* and let the operational teams deal with running the software and facing potential issues on production. This practice always leads to tensions and finger pointing once critical errors occurred in production. Instead, the common goal should be to deliver software that fulfills a purpose. By defining the required infrastructure and configuration as code, development and operations teams will naturally move together. This **DevOps** movement, a compound of development and operations, aims toward accountability of the software team as a whole. Everybody involved is responsible for customers being able to use proper software. This is more an organizational challenge than a technical one.

On a technical aspect, Continuous Delivery, as well as the **12-factor** and **cloud native** *buzzwords* attempted to meet these demands. The 12-factor and cloud native approaches describe how modern enterprise applications should be developed. They define requirements, not only for the development processes but also for the way applications are run. We will look into these approaches, modern cloud environments, and where Java EE supports us, later in this book.

# Modern way of realizing enterprise systems

Now we will look at how enterprise software projects are being developed.

Following the approach of meeting the needs of real-world customers, we will face the question of the purpose of the application that we want to develop. The motivations and purposes of the enterprise systems need to be clear before immediately going into technology details. Otherwise, software is just being developed for the sake of developing software. Sadly, this is the case way too often. By focusing on business logic and the principles of *Domain-Driven Design*, as wonderfully described in the book by *Eric Evans*, we will ensure that the software we are building will meet the business demands.

Only after the application's purpose and responsibility is clear to the stakeholders, can we focus on the technological aspects. Teams should favor technologies that can not only implement the business use cases appropriately but also reduce the amount of work and overhead. Developers should be able to focus on the business, not the framework and technology. Good frameworks support solving business problems in a lean way and don't want the developer's attention themselves.

The chosen technology should also support productive development workflows as much as possible. This not only includes automation and fast development turnarounds but also the ability to embrace modern infrastructure, such as Linux containers. In Chapter 4, *Lightweight Java EE*, and Chapter 5, *Container and Cloud Environments with Java EE*, we will have a closer look into the nuts and bolts of modern environments and how Java EE supports them.

# Relevance of Java EE in modern systems

Let's talk about Java EE since this is the topic of this book and it is relevant in enterprise systems.

Java EE and J2EE are being used heavily, especially in bigger companies. One of the advantages was always that the platform consists of standards that guarantee to be backwards compatible with older versions. Even old J2EE applications are guaranteed to still function in the future. This was always a big benefit for companies that are planning for the long term. Applications that are developed against the Java EE API can run on all Java EE application servers. Vendor-independent applications enable companies to build future-proof software that doesn't lock it into a specific solution. This turned out to be a sound decision that ultimately led to a mindset of the enterprise industry that standards, or de facto standards which everybody agrees upon, improve the overall situation.

Compared to the J2EE world, a lot has changed in Java EE. The programming model is totally different, much leaner, and more productive. This was drastically changed when the name switched from J2EE to Java EE 5, and especially since EE 6. We will have a look at the modern way of developing Java enterprise in Chapter 3, *Implementing Modern Java Enterprise Applications*. We will see what architectural approaches and programming models are being used and how the platform leverages development productivity much more than in the past. Hopefully, the idea of why Java EE now provides a modern solution to develop enterprise applications will become clear.

Right now, bringing this message out to the industry is actually more of a marketing and political challenge than a technical one. We still see tons of developers and architects who still consider Java EE to be the cumbersome, heavyweight enterprise solution of the J2EE age, which required a lot of time, effort, and XML. **Enterprise JavaBeans** (EJB), as well as application servers, have a particularly bad reputation due to their past. This is why a lot of engineers are biased toward that technology. Compared to other enterprise solutions, Java EE never saw much marketing targeted at developers.

In Chapter 4, *Lightweight Java EE*, we will see why modern Java EE is actually one of the most lightweight enterprise solutions. We will define the term *lightweight* aspects and see why the Java EE platform is more relevant than ever, especially in modern cloud and container environments. The impression the IT industry has of a particular technology is important for its success. I hope this chapter will shed some light into this topic.

Companies have usually chosen Java EE mostly because of its reliability and backwards compatibility. I personally favor Java EE because of its productivity and ease of use. In Chapter 4, *Lightweight Java EE*, and Chapter 5, *Container and Cloud Environments with Java EE*, we will cover more about this. In this book, I would like to show the readers why Java EE is a solution well-suited to today's enterprise demands. I will also show the technologies and standards, not in every detail, but rather how they are integrated with each other. I believe that focusing on the integrational part leads to a better understanding in how to effectively craft enterprise applications.

# Java EE 8 update and roadmap

Let's have a very high-level overview of what has happened in Java EE version 8. The goal of this version is to improve the developer's experience even more, to streamline the API usage further, and to make Java EE ready for new demands in cloud environments. We saw two completely new JSRs, **JSON-B** (Java API for JSON Binding) and **Security**, together with improvements in existing standards. In particular, introducing JSON-B simplifies the integration of JSON HTTP APIs in a vendor-independent way.

The direction of Java EE is to improve the development of enterprise applications in regard to modern environments and circumstances. It turns out that modern environments are not only compatible with Java EE but encourage approaches that have been part of the platform for years. Examples are the separation of the API from the implementation, or application server monitoring.

On the long-term roadmap, there is better support for modern monitoring, health-checks, and resilience. Currently, these aspects have to be integrated in a few lines of codes, as we will see in later chapters. The long-term goal is to make that integration more straightforward. Java EE aims to let developers focus on what they should focus on - solving business problems.

# Java Community Process

What makes Java EE platform unique is the process of how it is specified. The standards of Java EE are developed as part of the **Java Community Process** (**JCP**). The JCP is a prime example of an industry that actively encourages participation in defining standards, not only from the few engineers involved but anybody interested in that technology. The platform comprises standards in the form of **Java Specification Requests** (**JSR**). These JSRs are not only relevant for Java and Java EE but also for technologies that build upon them, such as the Spring framework. Ultimately, the real world experience of these other technologies then again help shaping new JSRs.

During application development, and especially when encountering potential issues, the written specifications that emerge from the JSRs are extremely beneficial. The vendors who support the enterprise platform are required to provide the implementation in the way it's specified in these standards. That said, the specification documents inform both the vendors and developers as to how the technology will work. If some functionality is not met, the vendors are required to fix these issues in their implementations. This also means that developers, in theory, only have to learn and know these technologies, no vendor-specific details.

Every developer can participate in the Java Community Process to help in shaping the future of Java and Java EE. The **Expert Groups** who define the specific standards welcome constructive feedback from anybody interested in the topic, even if they're not active members of the JCP. Other than this, you're able to have a peek into the next versions of the standards even before they're released. These two facts are very interesting for architects and companies. There is not only insight into where the direction will go but also the possibility to contribute and make an impact.

These motivations were also two of the reasons why I personally specialized in Java EE. I have a background of enterprise development with the Spring framework. Besides the fact that both technologies are very similar in terms of the programming model, I especially valued the power of the CDI standard as well as the possibility to seamlessly use all of the technologies within the platform. I started to look into the specific JSRs that are part of the enterprise platform and started to contribute and provide feedback on features that were standardized back then. At the time of writing this book, I'm part of two Expert Groups, JAX-RS 2.1 and JSON-P 1.1. Helping to define these standards improved my knowledge in enterprise systems a lot. You are naturally obliged to dive deep into the topics, motivations, and solutions of the specific technology that you help standardize. And of course, it is somewhat satisfying to know that you helped in working on standards in the IT industry. I can only encourage developers to participate in the JCP, looking into what's currently developed, and to contribute and provide feedback to the Expert Groups.

# What to expect in the book

I've decided to write this book about the things I learned in the past working on Java enterprise systems of all kinds. My motivation is to show you what a modern Java EE approach looks like. This, of course, first of all aims toward developing enterprise applications themselves, and modern programming models. I try to build up an impression as to how Java EE is used in the age of EE 8 and where the platform shines. There are new design patterns and paradigms being used that have emerged from modern framework approaches. If you were familiar with the J2EE world, you will hopefully see the advantage of modern Java EE. I try to show which of the old paradigms, constraints, and considerations that made J2EE sometimes being disliked among developers are not true anymore and can be discarded. Besides this, the book is an attempt to spread some enthusiasm and explain why I am convinced that Java Enterprise serves the purpose of realizing enterprise applications well.

That said, you, the reader, don't need prior knowledge of the J2EE world and patterns and best practices thereof. In particular, the programming model so different that I'm convinced it makes sense to showcase today's approach from a green field.

It you have built and designed J2EE applications, this is great. You will see what the challenges with past J2EE design patterns were, particularly when in the modern world, our domain can focus on business demands first and not the technology used to implement it. This is especially true when we follow the approaches of *Domain-Driven Design*. You will notice how many cumbersome and painful aspects of J2EE systems in the past can be eradicated in modern Java EE. The simplicity and power of the Java EE platform may inspire you to rethink certain approaches that we have done so far. Maybe you can try to take a mental step back to have a fresh, unbiased view on the technology.

This book is meant for software engineers, developers and architects who design and build enterprise applications. In the book, I will mostly use the term developers or engineers. That said, I am convinced that architects should also, from time to time, the more the better, touch source code and *get their hands dirty* with technology. This is not only to support other developers in the team but also important for themselves to get more real-world experience. In the same way all developers should have at least a basic understanding of the system's architecture and the reasoning for the architectural choices. Again, the better this mutual understanding is, the better will the communication and development function in the projects.

Modern enterprise application development touches much more than just the sole development. As we are seeing, new demands of enterprise applications, engineers care about development workflows, cloud environments, containers, and container orchestration frameworks. We will cover whether and how Java Enterprise fits into this world and what approaches and best practices there are that support this. This will tackle the topics of Continuous Delivery and automated testing, why they have such importance, and how they integrate with Java EE. We will also cover container technologies, such as Docker, and orchestration frameworks such as Kubernetes. In today's enterprise world it's important to show how a technology such as Java EE supports these areas.

Microservice architecture is a big topic, another of today's hypes. We will look at what microservices are about, and if and how they can be realized with Java EE. The topics of security, logging, performance, and monitoring will also be covered later in this book. I will point out what architects should know and be aware of in today's enterprise software world. The used choices of technology, especially when it comes to modern solutions that support applications; for example, in the areas of 12-factor or cloud native applications, serve as examples as to what would be chosen as of today. However, it is much more important to understand what the concepts and motivations behind these technologies are. Used technology changes day by day, principles and concepts or computer science live much longer.

For all of the subjects that I cover in this book, my approach is to show the motivations and reasoning behind solutions first, and then how they are applied and implemented in Java EE second. I believe that simply teaching a certain technology may certainly help developers in their daily jobs but they will not fully embrace the solution until the motivations behind it are completely understood. This is why I will also start with the motivations behind enterprise applications in general.

There is a lot of functionality included in Java EE, even more if you look into the past. This book does not aim to represent a full Java EE reference work. Rather, it is intended to provide real world experience as well as recommendations, call them *best practices*, tackling typical scenarios with pragmatic solutions. Now, please lean back and enjoy the journey through a modern enterprise software world.

# 2
# Designing and Structuring Java Enterprise Applications

Every piece of software is designed in a certain way. The design includes the architecture of the system, structure of the projects, and structure and quality of the code. It can either communicate the intentions well or obfuscate them. Engineers need to design an enterprise application or system, before it is implemented. In order to do that, the purpose and motivations of the software need to be clear.

This chapter will cover:

- What aspects to focus on when developing software
- Project build structures and Java EE build systems
- How to structure enterprise projects modules
- How to realize module package structures

## The purpose of enterprise applications

Behind every action, be it in daily life, big organizations, or software projects, there should be a reason. We humans need reasons why we are doing things. In enterprise software development, there is no difference.

When we build software applications, the first question asked should be *why?*. Why is this piece of software needed? Why is it reasonable or required to spend time and effort to develop a solution? And why should the company care about developing that solution itself?

In other words, what is the application's purpose? What problem is this piece of software trying to solve? Do we want the application to implement an important business process? Will it generate revenue? Is it going to gather revenue directly, for example by selling products, or indirectly by marketing, supporting customers, or business processes? Are there other possibilities to support customers, employees, or business processes?

These and other questions target the application's business goals. Generally speaking, every piece of software needs a justification in the overall picture before we invest time and effort into it.

The most obvious legitimization is to implement necessary business use cases. These use cases bring certain value for the overall business and will sooner or later realize features and generate revenue. At the end of the day, the software should achieve the goal of implementing the business use cases as best as possible.

# What developers should focus on

Therefore, software developers as well as project managers should first focus on meeting the business concerns and implementing the use cases.

This clearly sounds obvious, but too often the focus of enterprise projects starts drifting away into other concerns. Developer effort is spent on implementation details or features that have little benefit for solving the actual problem. How many logging implementations, home-grown enterprise frameworks, or over-engineered levels of abstractions have we seen in the past?

Non-functional requirements, quality of software, and so-called cross-cutting concerns are in fact an important aspect of software development. But the first and main focus of all engineering effort should be directed to meeting the business requirements and developing software that actually has a purpose.

# Meeting customer's demands

We have the following questions:

- What is the application's business purpose?
- What are the most important features that users care about?
- Which aspects will generate revenue?

The answers to these questions should be known to the stakeholders. If not, then the correct way would be to take a step back, look at the overall picture of the software landscape, and reconsider the software's right to exist. Not in all cases the motivation will be purely business-driven. There are, in fact, a lot of cases where we will implement solutions that do not directly generate revenue but do so indirectly, by supporting others. These cases are certainly necessary and we will cover them and the general topic of how to construct reasonable system landscapes in Chapter 8, *Microservices and System Architecture*.

Besides these supporting software systems, we focus on business aspects. Having this main goal in mind, the first thing to address is how to model the business use cases and transform them into software. Only after that, the use cases are implemented using certain technologies.

These priorities will also reflect the customer demands. The application's stakeholders care about software that fulfills its purpose.

Software engineers tend to see this differently. They care about implementation details and the elegance of solutions. Engineers are often passionate about certain technologies and spend much time and effort choosing the right solutions as well as implementing them well. This includes a lot of technical cross-cutting concerns, such as logging, and so-called over-engineering, which is not mandatory for the business domain. Embracing software craftsmanship certainly has its importance and is essential for writing better software, but many times it is orthogonal to the client's motivations. Before spending time and effort with implementation details, engineers should be aware of the client's demands first.

Project timeline requirements are another aspect to consider. Software teams weigh business use cases against the quality of technical solutions. They tend to postpone required software tests or quality measures in order to meet deadlines. The technology used to implement the business application should support effective and pragmatic development.

When seeing the enterprise world through the eyes of a paying customer or a manager with limited time and budget, software engineers will likely understand their priorities. Caring about revenue-generating use cases first is mandatory. Technical necessities beyond these are seen by customers and managers as a *necessary evil*.

The rest of this book will show you how to meet and balance these two motivations with Java EE.

# Outer enterprise project structure

Having the goal of business use cases in mind, let's move our focus a bit more down to earth to real-world enterprise projects. In later chapters, we will see what methods are there to help us reflecting the business domains in the architecture in a suitable way.

# Business and team structures

Software projects are usually developed by a team of engineers, software developers, or architects. For simplicity, we will call them developers. Software developers, architects, testers, and all kind of engineers should arguably program from time to time.

However, in most situations we have several people working simultaneously on a software project. This already requires us to take a few things into account, mainly communication and organizational overhead. When we look at the structure within organizations with several teams working on multiple projects, or temporarily even the same project, we deal with even more challenges.

The Conway's law claims that:

> *Organizations which design systems [...] are constrained to produce designs which are copies of the communication structures of these organizations.*

> *- Melvin Conway*

That being said, the way in which the teams are organized and communicate with each other will inevitably leak into software design. The organization chart of developers and their effective communication structures has to be considered when constructing software projects. We will have a detailed look into how to construct several distributed systems and more specific microservices in Chapter 8, *Microservices and System Architecture*.

Even in a single project owned by a team of few developers, there will likely be multiple features and bug fixes being developed simultaneously. This fact impacts how we plan the iterations, organize, and integrate source code, and build and deploy runnable software. In particular Chapter 6, *Application Development Workflows* and Chapter 7, *Testing* will cover this topic.

# Software projects contents

Enterprise software projects include several artifacts necessary to build and ship applications. Let's have a closer look at them.

## Application source code

First of all, all enterprise applications, like probably any application, are written in source code. The source code is arguably the most important part of our software project. It represents the application and all its functionality at its core and can be seen as the single source of truth of software behavior.

The project's sources are separated into code that runs on production and test code to verify the application's behavior. The technologies as well as the quality demands will vary for test and production code. In `Chapter 7`, *Testing*, we will deeply cover the technologies and structures of software tests. Apart from that chapter, the focus of this book lies on production code, which is shipped and which handles the business logic.

## Software structures

The software project organizes the source code in certain structures. In Java projects, we have the possibility to cluster components and responsibilities into Java packages and project modules, respectively:

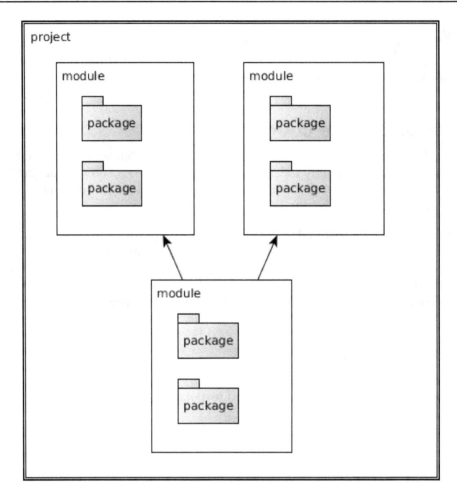

Structuring these components is obviously less a technical rather than an architectural necessity. Code that is packaged arbitrarily would technically run equally well. However, this structure helps engineers understanding the software and its responsibilities. By clustering software components that fulfill coherent features, we increase cohesion and achieve a better organization of the source code.

This and the next chapter will discuss the benefits of *Domain-Driven Design*, described in the book by Eric Evans, and the why and how to organize code in business-driven packages. For now, let's record that we group coherent components that form logical features into logical packages or project modules.

Java SE 9 comes with the possibility of shipping modules as Java 9 modules. These modules are, in essence, similar to the JAR files with the ability to declare dependencies and usages restrictions of other modules. Since this book is targeted for Java EE 8 and since the fact that the usage of Java 9 modules hasn't spread yet in real-world projects, we will cover only Java packages and project modules.

Breaking the structure of software projects further down, the next smaller unit of software components is a Java class. Classes and the responsibilities thereof encapsulate single functionalities in the domain. They are ideally loosely coupled and show a high cohesion.

A lot has been written about clean code practices and representing functionality in source code. The book *Clean Code* by Robert C. Martin, for example, explains methods such as proper naming or refactoring, that help achieve well-crafted source code in packages, classes and methods.

# Version control systems

The source code is kept under version control, since most software projects require coordination of simultaneous code changes, made by multiple developers. **Version control systems** (**VCS**) have established themselves as mandatory to reliably coordinate, track, and comprehend changes in software systems.

There are a lot of choices of version control systems, such as Git, Subversion, Mercurial or CVS. In the last years, **distributed revision control** systems, particularly **Git**, have been widely accepted as the state-of-the-art tools. They use a so-called *hash tree*, or *Merkle tree* to store and resolve individual commits, which enables efficient *diffs* and *merges*.

Distributed VCS enables developers to work with project repositories in distributed ways, without constantly requiring a network connection. Every workstation has its own repository, which includes the full history and is eventually synchronized with the central project repository.

As of writing this book, the vast majority of software projects use Git as version control system.

# Binaries

The VCS project repository should only contain the sources that are produced and maintained by developers. Certainly, enterprise applications will have to be deployed as some kind of binary artifacts. Only these shippable binaries can be executed as runnable software. The binaries are ultimately the outcome of the development and build process.

In the Java world this means that the Java source code is compiled to portable bytecode and is usually packaged as **Web Application Archive** (**WAR**) or **Java Archive** (**JAR**), respectively. WAR or JAR files comprise all classes and files required to ship an application, framework dependency, or library. The **Java Virtual Machine** (**JVM**) finally executes the bytecode and together with that, our business functionality.

In enterprise projects the deployment artifacts, the WAR or JAR files, are either deployed to an application container or already ship the container themselves. The application container is needed, since beside their distilled business logic, enterprise applications will have to integrate additional concerns, such as application life cycle or communication in various forms. For example, a web application that implements certain logic but is not addressable over HTTP communication has little value. In Java Enterprise, the application container is responsible for providing this integration. The packaged application contains the distilled business logic and is deployed to a server, which takes care of the rest.

In recent years, more Linux container technologies such as Docker have emerged. This carries the ideas of shippable binaries even further. The *binary* then not only contains the packaged Java application, but all components required to run the application. This, for examples, includes an application server, the Java Virtual Machine, and required operating system binaries. We will discuss the topic of shipping and deploying enterprise applications, especially regarding container technology, in `Chapter 4`, *Lightweight Java EE*.

The binaries are produced as part of the software build process. It enables to reliably recreate all binaries from the repository's sources. Therefore, the binaries should not be kept under version control. The same is true for generated source code. In the past, for example, JAX-WS classes which are required for SOAP communication were usually generated from descriptor files. Generated source code is created during the build process and should also not be kept under version control. The idea is to keep only the distilled source code in the repository and no artifacts that can be derived from it.

# Build systems

The build process is first of all responsible for compiling the sources of a Java software project into bytecode. This happens every time changes have been made to the project. All modern build systems ship with useful conventions to minimize the required configuration.

In the enterprise world, with all its different frameworks and libraries, an important step is to organize and define all dependencies on APIs and implementations. Build tools such as **Apache Maven** or **Gradle** support developers by including powerful dependency resolution mechanisms. The build tool adds all the dependencies with the corresponding versions required to compile or run the application, respectively. This simplyfies to setup the project among multiple developers. It also enables repeatable builds.

Packaging the compiled classes and their dependencies into deployment artifacts is also part of the build process. Depending on the used technology the artifacts are packaged as WAR or JAR files. Chapter 4, *Lightweight Java EE* will discuss the different ways of packaging Java enterprise applications together with their pros and cons.

The topics, *Gradle* and *Apache Maven*, will discuss the implementation and differences of the two main build systems in more depth.

# Single versus multi-module projects

As said before, we can organize the application's source code in Java packages and project modules, respectively. Project modules group related functionality together into separately buildable sub-projects. They are usually specified by the build systems.

At first, the motivations behind splitting up project modules are quite understandable. Grouping Java code and packages into related modules creates a clearer view for the developers, enables a better structure, and increases cohesion.

Another reason for multi-modules is build time performance. The more complex our software project becomes the longer it will take to compile and package it into artifacts. Developers mostly touch few locations in the projects at a time. Therefore, the idea is to not always rebuild the whole project, but only the modules necessary in order to apply the desired changes. This is an advertised advantage of the Gradle build system, to save time by rebuilding only what has changed.

Another argument for this practice is the possibility of reusing certain sub-modules in several projects. By building sub-projects into self-sufficient artifacts we could possibly take and include a sub-artifact in another software project. For example, a common practice is to design a *model* module that contains the entities of the business domain, usually as standalone **plain old Java objects** (**POJOs**). This model would be packaged to a JAR file and reused as a dependency in other enterprise projects.

There are, however, some drawbacks, or rather, illusions to this practice.

# Illusion of reusability

We have to remind ourselves that software projects are built by teams of developers and the project structure will therefore adhere to their communication structures. Reusing certain modules within several projects requires quite a bit of coordination.

## Technical dependencies

A project's module that is subject to be reused has to meet specific criteria. First of all the technology of the shared modules has to match the target project. This sounds obvious, but has quite some implications on the implementation details. Especially used libraries and frameworks will inevitably cause the involved modules to be coupled and dependent on the specific technology. For example, model classes in Java EE typically contain annotations from APIs such as JPA that need to be available in all dependent modules.

Third-party dependencies with specific versions that are required for a shared module to function correctly have even more technical impact. These dependencies then have to be available at runtime and must not collide with other dependencies or versions thereof. This can cause a lot of headache with colliding dependencies that are already available on the server. The same holds true for implementation details that contain implicit dependencies.

A typical example of this is JSON mapping libraries such as Jackson or Gson. A lot of third-party dependencies use these libraries in specific versions that might collide with other dependencies or versions at runtime. Another example is logging implementations such as **Logback** or **Log4j**.

In general, shared models should be as self-sufficient as possible or at least contain only stable dependencies that won't likely drift into these issues. A good example for a very stable dependency is the Java EE API. Because of the backwards-compatible nature of the Enterprise Edition, usage of the API and resulting functionality won't break if a newer version is introduced.

But even if the Java EE API is the only dependency of shared modules, it will bind the model to a specific version and reduce the freedom to change.

# Organizational challenges

Shared technology and dependencies come with organizational challenges. The greater the number of developers and teams, respectively, the bigger the impact of used technology and dependencies. Teams have to agree upon certain technology, used frameworks and libraries and versions thereof.

If a single teams want to change something in this graph of dependencies or some of the used technologies, this change requires a lot of coordination and overhead. Chapter 8, *Microservices and System Architecture*, covers this topic of sharing code and artifacts within several systems and whether this is advisable or not.

# Reusability considerations

The trade-off is always reusability and having to deal with these issues versus simplicity and potential duplication. Depending on the level of self-sufficiency, the choice will be made toward one or the other. Generally speaking, the cost of coordinating dependencies, versions, and technology, outweighs the benefits of avoiding redundancy.

An important question to be asked, however, is how the projects modules are layered either vertically or horizontally. An example for horizontal layering is the typical three-tier architecture of clustering into a *presentation*, *business* and *data layer*. Vertical layering means to group functionality based on their business domain. Examples would be modules for accounts, orders or articles, including all technical requirements such as HTTP endpoints or database access. Both types of modules can potentially be reused.

In reality horizontal layered modules like models are more likely subject to be shared among other projects. These types of modules naturally have a smaller variety of dependencies, ideally zero. On the contrary, vertical layered modules will contain implementation details and expect certain circumstances, for example, how the container is configured. And again, it depends a lot on the technology being used within the modules that are subject to share.

# Project artifacts

Let's take a step back and look at the deployment artifacts of our enterprise application. Typically, an application results in a single artifact that will run our software. Even with several multi-modules being used at the end of the day, these will boil down to a single or few artifacts. So, in most of the cases all of this structure is flattened again into single JAR or WAR files. Looking at the reusability of modules, which is not necessarily being given, this raises the question of whether we need several modules per project at all. At the end of the day, introducing and managing sub-projects, vertical or horizontal, will require certain developer effort.

It is true that splitting up the code base can improve build performance if only sub-projects that have been changed are rebuilt. However, in the sub-chapters *Apache Maven* and *Gradle* and Chapter 4, *Lightweight Java EE* we will see that building a single reasonably designed project into a single artifact is sufficiently fast and that there are usually other aspects responsible for making builds slow.

# One project per artifact

It is advisable to package the enterprise project into a single deployment artifact that emerges from a single project module. The number and structure of deployment artifacts then maps the structure of the software projects. If other artifacts emerge from the project, they are organized in separate project modules as well. This enables an understandable and lightweight project structure.

Usually, an enterprise project will result in a shippable JAR or WAR file, originating from a single project module. Yet sometimes, we do have good reasons to create modules that are shared among projects. These are then sensibly crafted as own project modules that build own artifacts, for example JAR files.

There are still other motivations for multi-module projects. System tests that verify a deployed enterprise application from the *outside* don't necessarily have dependencies on the production code. It makes sense, in some situations, to organize these tests in separate project modules that are part of a multi-module project.

Another example is frontend technologies that are just loosely coupled to the backend application. With modern client-centric JavaScript frameworks being used more and more, the coupling to the backend also decreases. The workflow and life cycle of developing frontends can vary from the backend application. Therefore, it can make sense to split the technology into several sub-projects or even several software projects. The topic, *Structuring for modern frontend technologies*, covers how to tackle these situations.

These situations, however, also fit the concept of mapping *artifacts* in the broader sense to project modules. A system test project is used and executed separately from the production code. Developing and building the frontend project could equally be differ from the backend part. There may be some other situations where it is advisable as well.

# Build systems for Java EE

The project modules are specified as modules of the build system. Whether we can follow the straightforward way of having a single project or multiple projects; for example, motivated by system tests, we will build and execute them as part of the build process.

A good build system needs to ship certain features. The main task of it is to compile the sources and package the binaries as artifacts. Required dependencies are also resolved and used for compilation or packaged, respectively. There are several scopes where dependencies are required, such as during compilation, testing, or runtime. Different scope definition specify whether dependencies are shipped with the artifact.

The project should be built in a reliable, reproducible way. Several builds with identical project contents and build configuration must produce the same results. This is important for implementing **Continuous Delivery** (**CD**) pipelines, which enable reproducible builds. That said the build system must be able to run on a **Continuous Integration** (**CI**) server, such as **Jenkins** or **TeamCity**. This requires the software to ship a command-line interface, especially for Unix-based systems. Chapter 6, *Application Development Workflows*, will show the motivations behind Continuous Delivery.

The build system will be used by software engineers working on various environments and operating systems, which should be supported as well. For JVM-based build systems this portability is usually given. It may be the case that projects have specific requirements such as native code that needs to be built on specific environments. For Java enterprise applications, however, this is usually not the case.

In general the build process should run as fast as possible. Booting up and configuring the build system should not require much time. The longer the build takes the higher the turnaround times and the slower the feedback engineers get from the build pipeline. In Chapter 4, *Lightweight Java EE*, we will cover more of this topic.

At the time of writing, Apache Maven is the most used build system well known to the majority of Java developers.

Maven is a Java-based build system configured by XML. It's projects are defined by a so-called **project object model** (**POM**). Maven makes use of a **convention over configuration** approach that minimizes the required configuration. The default configuration is well suited for Java applications.

Another build tool with high usage is Gradle. Gradle is a build tool that offers a Groovy-based **Domain-Specific Language** (**DSL**) to configure fully extensible and scriptable project builds. Since Groovy is a full programming language Gradle build scripts are naturally powerful and flexible.

Both Gradle and Maven include a sophisticated dependency management and are well suited to build Java-based projects. There are certainly still other build systems, such as SBT, however, Gradle and Maven are, by far, the most-used ones and will be covered in the following section.

## Apache Maven

Apache Maven is widely used in Java-based projects and known to the vast majority of enterprise developers. The wide-spread usage and the familiarity of this tool is certainly a benefit.

Maven is based on a **convention over configuration** approach which simplifies straightforward use cases. Maven's configuration, however, does not always provide flexibility. In fact, this inflexibility is sometimes a feature. Since it's cumbersome to change the default Maven project structure and build process, most of the Java enterprise projects come in a very similar and familiar way. New developers easily find their way through the project's build configuration.

The following snippet shows a typical example of a Maven project structure:

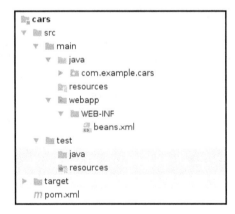

This will seem familiar to the majority of enterprise Java developers. This example web application is packaged as a WAR file.

One of the shortcomings of Apache Maven is its somewhat nontransparent way of defining used build plugins and dependencies thereof. Using the default build convention without explicitly specifying versions for plugins such as the **Maven Compiler Plugin** can result in unwanted changes of used versions. This violates the principle of repeatable builds.

Because of this, projects that require reproducibility often explicitly specify and override the plugin dependency versions in the POMs. By doing so, projects will be built using the same versions all the time, even if the default plugin versions change.

Super POM definitions are another common solution to specify exact plugin versions. Project POMs can inherit from parent projects and reduce boilerplate plugin definitions.

Developers can use the *effective POM* view that shows the resulting POM, after applying the default configuration and potential inheritance.

A typical issue with Maven POMs is that enterprise projects very often overuse the XML definitions. They prematurely introduce plugins or configuration that already would be covered by the build conventions. The following snippet shows the minimum POM requirements for a Java EE 8 project:

```xml
<project xmlns="http://maven.apache.org/POM/4.0.0"
         xmlns:xsi="http://www.w3.org/2001/XMLSchema-instance"
         xsi:schemaLocation="http://maven.apache.org/POM/4.0.0
         http://maven.apache.org/xsd/maven-4.0.0.xsd">
    <modelVersion>4.0.0</modelVersion>

    <groupId>com.example.cars</groupId>
    <artifactId>car-manufacture</artifactId>
    <version>1.0.1</version>
    <packaging>war</packaging>

    <dependencies>
        <dependency>
            <groupId>javax</groupId>
            <artifactId>javaee-api</artifactId>
            <version>8.0</version>
            <scope>provided</scope>
        </dependency>
    </dependencies>

    <build>
        <finalName>car-manufacture</finalName>
    </build>
```

```
        <properties>
            <maven.compiler.source>1.8</maven.compiler.source>
            <maven.compiler.target>1.8</maven.compiler.target>
            <failOnMissingWebXml>false</failOnMissingWebXml>
            <project.build.sourceEncoding>UTF-8</project.build.sourceEncoding>
        </properties>
    </project>
```

The *car manufacture* application is built into a WAR artifact. The `finalName` overrides the implied name of the WAR file, here resulting in `car-manufacture.war`.

The specified Java EE 8 API is the only production dependency that a straightforward enterprise solution requires. `Chapter 4`, *Lightweight Java EE* will deeply cover the topic of project dependencies and their impact.

The provided `properties` tag removes the need to explicitly configure the build plugins. Maven plugins per convention uses properties for configuration. Specifying these will reconfigure the used plugin without needing to explicitly declare the full definitions.

The properties cause the project to be built using Java SE 8, with all source files considered to be encoded as UTF-8. The WAR file doesn't need to ship a `web.xml` deployment descriptor; this is why we instruct Maven not to fail the build on a missing descriptor. In the past, the Servlet API required deployment descriptors in order to configure and map the application's Servlets. Since the advent of Servlet API version 3, `web.xml` descriptors are not necessarily required anymore; Servlets are configurable using annotations.

Maven defines its build process in several phases, such as *compile, test*, or *package*. Depending on the chosen phase, multiple steps will be executed. For example, triggering the *package* phase will compile the `main` as well as `test` sources, run the test cases, and package all classes and resources into the artifact.

The Maven build commands are triggered in the IDE or the `mvn` command line, for example, as `mvn package`. This command triggers the *package* phase, resulting in a packaged artifact. More details on phases and functionality of Apache Maven can be found under its official documentation.

# Gradle

At the time of writing, Gradle is less commonly used in Java enterprise projects than Apache Maven. This may be due to enterprise developers often being unfamiliar with dynamic JVM languages such as Groovy, which Gradle uses as its build script language. However, writing Gradle build files doesn't require deep knowledge of Groovy.

Gradle comes with quite a few benefits, most importantly its flexibility. Developers can leverage the full power of a programming language in order to define and potentially customize the project build.

Gradle will keep a daemon running in the background, that is being reused after the first build, to speed up subsequent build executions. It also keeps track of build inputs and outputs, whether changes have been made since the last build execution. This enables the system to cache steps and decrease the development build time.

However, depending on the complexity of the project and its used dependencies this optimization might not even be required. Chapter 4, *Lightweight Java EE* will cover the impact of project dependencies and zero-dependency applications.

The following snippet shows the build structure of a Gradle project:

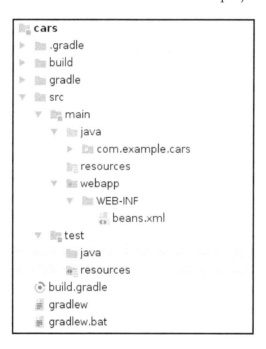

As you can see, the structure is quite similar to Maven projects, with the difference being that built binaries are per default placed into the build directory.

It's common for Gradle projects to include a wrapper script for environments that have no Gradle installations.

The following code demonstrates an example of a `build.script` file:

```
plugins {
    id 'war'
}

repositories {
    mavenCentral()
}

dependencies {
    providedCompile 'javax:javaee-api:8.0'
}
```

Gradle build tasks are triggered via the command line, using `gradle` or the provided wrapper scripts. Executing `gradle build`, for example, is the analog of `mvn package`, compiling the sources, executing tests and building the artifact.

There are certain benefits of having a fully-fledged programming language defining the build files. With the build scripts being treated as code, developers are encouraged to apply clean code principles for definitions that become too complex. Sophisticated build steps can, for example, be refactored into several, readable methods.

However, this power also brings the danger of over-engineering the build. As said, the inflexibility of Apache Maven can be considered a feature; the possibility of easily customizing build scripts eventually leads to build definitions that are very specific to the project. Compared to Maven, overly-customized builds can be an obstacle for developers who are unfamiliar with the project.

Experience shows that the vast majority of enterprise project builds are quite similar. This raises the question of whether the flexibility Gradle provides is required. Projects that don't have any special requirements, unlike for example product development, are sufficiently covered using Maven as build system.

The rest of this book will thus use Maven when a build system is required as an example. All code examples, however, are equally well suited to use Gradle.

# Structuring for modern frontend technologies

After shedding light on modern build systems for enterprise systems, let's have a look at how to integrate frontend technologies into the backend.

Traditionally, this was pretty straightforward. The frontend of web applications were, in most of the cases, server-side rendered HTML pages, powered by JSP or JSF. The HTML was crafted on the server on demand, that is, on request, and returned to the client. In order to realize that, the JSP or JSF pages, respectively, have to reside on the backend. Therefore, the whole enterprise application would be shipped and deployed as single artifact.

## Enter JavaScript frameworks

With new frontend technologies, basically sophisticated JavaScript frameworks, and especially single page applications, this premise has changed quite a bit. The web frontend frameworks became more and more client-centric and included much more business logic than in the past. On the server side this meant that the interaction between backend and frontend moved from fine grained methods to more coarse grained, business use case methods.

So, the more client-centric and powerful the JavaScript frameworks became, the more the communication between frontend and backend went from tightly coupled requests and responses to a more *API-like* usage, typically JSON via HTTP. This also meant that the server-side became more client-agnostic. For example, communicating solely via *RESTful-like*, JSON-format APIs enables native or mobile clients such as smartphones to use the same API like the frontend does.

We have seen this movement in a lot of enterprise projects. However, one could argue about the relevance of putting more and more logic into the client side or whether a hybrid solution of having some parts rendered on the server-side and some on the client-side is more appropriate. Without going too much into this topic, let us look at a few key points.

Preparation of data or content will be performed faster on the server-side. There are more capabilities and resources available than on the client. The server can also utilize features such as caching and use the advantage of *seeing* the whole picture.

Sophisticated frontend technologies often include a navigation logic that makes use of so-called *hashbang* pages. An example of a hashbang page URL is /car-manufacture/#!/cars/1234. These pages, for example, *car 1234*, do not reside on the server, but are only rendered on the client-side. The URL of that sub-page is determined after the hash-sign, which is not taken into account while requesting resources over HTTP. That means that the client requests a generic *entry page* that then does the whole navigation logic including rendering sub-pages. This clearly reduces the number of requests, but has the drawback that the server cannot support preparing or pre-rendering content; everything happens on the client-side. There have been big companies such as Twitter that originally pursued this approach but went away from it again, due to this reason. In particular, viewing these pages on mobile devices comes with certain challenges. With potential slow mobile connections and less computing power, rendering and executing sophisticated client-logic on these devices do take longer than displaying pre-rendered HTML.

Compared to statically typed, high-level languages such as Java, JavaScript frontends do have the issue that dynamically typed languages introduce more potential errors while programming that would have been prevented by a compiler. Because of this reason, we have seen more sophisticated frontend technologies such as TypeScript emerging, which introduced static types and higher language features that are processed into JavaScript again.

# Organizing modern frontends

However, no matter which specific frontend technology is chosen, enterprise projects do have more sophisticated frontends than in the past. This comes with new challenges of how to organize the daily development work. Typically the work cycles of the frontend and the backend will vary slightly. Some developers will typically see themselves more on the backend and others more on the frontend side. Even if the team solely consists of *full-stack* developers, some de-facto roles are likely to emerge over time.

Depending on the used technology it therefore makes sense to separate the frontend into a single project. As said before, as soon as some part of the software is shipped individually or has different life cycles than the rest, it makes sense to create a dedicated project module.

If the frontend technology can be deployed without any backend dependencies other than the HTTP usage, organizing the project is pretty straightforward. The project can be built and deployed on a web server individually and will use one or several backends from the client side. This project then only consists of static resources, such as HTML, JavaScript, or CSS files, which are transferred to the client and executed there. There will be no tight technical dependencies to the used backends, besides the HTTP API.

This aspect clearly has to be communicated well upfront during development, as well as documented on the backend side. Typically, the backend defines HTTP resources that serve required content in JSON format, which can optionally be filtered by query parameters if necessary. The reason behind the JSON format being popular is that JavaScript client code can use the response directly as JavaScript objects without any other transformation required.

If the frontend will be deployed together with the backend as a single artifact the project structure requires more coordination. The artifact contains both layers of technology and compiles and packages both at build time. During development this combination isn't necessarily helpful if the cycles of developing the frontend vary from the backend side. A programmer currently focusing on the frontend side probably doesn't want to build the backend part each and every time. The same is true with the backend technology waiting for potentially slow JavaScript compilation and packaging.

In these cases, it makes sense to split the project into several modules that can be built individually. What has proven itself well is to package the frontend module as an individual module and to introduce it as a dependency of the backend module, which then will package it altogether. By doing this, the frontend module clearly can be built individually, whereas a backend developer can rebuild the backend part as well by using their latest version of the frontend. Therefore, build times are reduced on both sides.

To realize this feature, the Servlet API can deliver static resources that are packed not only in the archive, but also in contained JAR files. Resources that reside under `META-INF/resources` of a JAR file that is contained in the WAR file, are delivered by the Servlet container, as well. The frontend project contains all its required frontend technology, framework and tools, and builds a separate JAR file.

This enables developers to separate the frontend from the backend project to adapt to different life cycles.

The rest of this book will focus on the backend technology and business use cases that are accessible via machine to machine communication such as web services.

# Enterprise project code structure

After seeing how we can organize our enterprise project structure, let's have a closer look at the detailed structure within a project. Assuming we have modeled an enterprise system that is reasonable in size and responsibility, we now map the concerns of the project into code structures.

Previously, we have discussed vertical versus horizontal module layers. This is precisely one of the aspects we need to look into when structuring the project.

# Situation in enterprise projects

The structure of typical enterprise projects has traditionally been a three-tier architecture. Three-tiers means three technically motivated layers, namely the *presentation*, *business*, and *data layer*. That being said, the project is organized horizontally, with three sub-modules, or packages, respectively.

The idea is to separate concerns from the data layer, from the business layer, and both of them from the presentation layers, as well. Functionality on a *lower* layer can therefore not have any dependencies on a *higher* layer, only the other way around. The business layer cannot use functionality of the presentation layer, only vice versa. The same is true for the data layer not depending on the business layer.

Each technically motivated layer or module has its own internal dependencies, that cannot be used from the outside as well. For example, only the *data layer* would be able to use the database, no direct invocations from the *business* layer would be possible.

Another motivation is to be able to swap implementation details without impacting other layers. If the database technology would be changed in favor of another, that would in theory not affect the other two layers, since the data layer encapsulates these details. The same is true if the presentation technology changes. In fact, even several *presentation* layers can be developed with all of them using the same *business* layer components, at least if the layers are organized as separate modules.

We have seen heated discussions, mostly from high-level architects, about the necessity of organizing and separating responsibilities by technical concerns. However, there are some drawbacks from this approach.

# Horizontal versus vertical layering

Clean code is all about code that aims to be understood by humans not machines. The same holds true for designing domains and organizing responsibilities. We want to find structures that easily tell the engineers what the project is all about.

The challenge with structuring by technical concerns at already high layers of abstractions is that the purpose and domain of the software gets obfuscated and hidden in lower layers of abstraction. When someone unfamiliar with the project looks at the code structure the first thing that they see are the three technical layers, although names and numbers might differ in some cases. This will at least look familiar to them, but it tells nothing about the actual domain.

Software engineers seek to understand domain modules, not necessarily technical layers.

For example, when touching the *accounts* functionality, developers regard everything related to the accounts domain, not all the database access classes at once. Other than that, developers hardly search for *all database access classes*, but for that single class which handles that logic of their current domain.

The same is true when changes have to be made to the system. Changes in functionality are more likely to affect all technical layers of a single or a few business domains, but hardly all classes of a single technical layer at once. For example, changing a field to the user account likely affects the user model, database accesses, business use cases, and even the presentation logic, but not necessarily all the other model classes as well.

To make the idea what aspects developers are interested in more clearer, let me give another example. Imagine a family organized their clothes in a single big wardrobe. They could cluster all pants from all family members in a single drawer, as well as separate drawers for all socks and all shirts, respectively. But the family members won't likely search for all pants at once when they try to dress. Rather than this, they're just interested in their individual clothes, be it pants, shirts, socks, or something else. Therefore, it would make sense for them to organize by several areas of the wardrobe first, one per family member and then structuring by *technical clothes* aspects second, ideally following a similar structure. The same can be seen for software responsibilities.

# Business-driven structure

Uncle Bob once wrote about *Screaming Architectures* that should aim to at first tell the engineer what the whole enterprise project is about. The idea was that when looking at blueprints of buildings and seeing the structure and the detailed interior you immediately can tell: *this is a house, this is a library, this is a train station*. The same should hold true for software systems. You should be able to look at the project structure and be able to say: *this is an accounting system, this is a book store inventory system, this is an order management system*. Is this the case for the most projects we have? Or, does looking at the highest level of modules and packages rather tell us: *this is a Spring application, this system has a presentation, business and data layer, this system uses a Hazelcast cache*?

The technical implementations are certainly important to us developers. But again, the first thing that we focus on is business concerns. Following this approach, these aspects should be reflected in the project and module structure as well.

Most importantly, this means our domain should be reflected in the application structure. Just by looking at the highest hierarchy of package names should give a good idea of what the software is trying to do. We therefore layer after business concerns first, implementation details second.

Blueprint plans for buildings will also first build up a picture what the building is about, how the rooms are separated, and where doors and windows are located. Then, as a secondary priority they may specify used materials, bricks, and types of concrete being used.

As an outlook for microservices consider the following: designing vertical modules enables the team to split up the application into a system of several applications much more easily. Looking at the module dependencies, for example through static code analysis, provides a picture of where the integration points between the systems would be. These integration points would emerge in some form of communication between the applications. In theory, we can then take that single module, plus minimal *plumbing*, and package it as a separate, self-sufficient application.

A point on names: by using the term *modules* we, by now, focus on business driven modules that are realized in Java packages and sub-packages, not build project modules. The term *modules* then serves more as a concept, less as a strict technical realization.

# Designing reasonable modules

More down to earth, how do we find reasonably sized and structured modules?

Putting business concerns first, a good start is to draw overviews of all the responsibilities and use cases of the application. This may be part of a brainstorming session, ideally together with business domain experts if that step hasn't been done before. What are the application's responsibilities? What business motivated use cases do we have? Which coherent functionality can be seen? The answers to these questions already give a good idea which modules are likely to be represented, without focusing on external systems, implementation details, or framework choices.

In this step we also already consider dependencies between these business concerns. Dependencies are helpful indicators of whether modules should be split up or, especially when circular dependencies are found, should be merged together. Constructing these overview diagrams, starting from a higher level and working the way down in several iterations will give a clearer image of what the business contents of the application are. Generally speaking, the identified modules should match well with the business aspects identified by the domain experts.

To give an example, an online shopping application could identify modules for *users, recommendation, articles, payment,* and *shipping.* These would be reflected as the base domain modules:

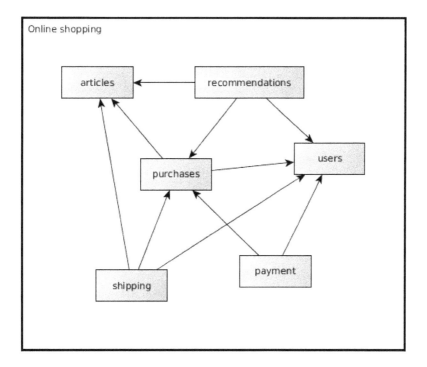

The identified modules represent the base Java packages in our application.

It makes sense to put some effort into these considerations. However, as always, any *definitive* structure or implementation, no matter whether on code or module level, should be able to be changed later on. New requirements might emerge or there might be a better understanding later on, once the developers start to deep dive into the domain. Iterative refactoring, no matter on which level, will improve the quality of the system.

Chapter 8, *Microservices and System Architecture*, will show similar motivations and methodologies when designing systems that comprise distributed applications. Particularly, the Domain-Driven Design approaches of bounded contexts and context maps will be discussed.

# Realizing package structures

Assuming we found appropriate base Java packages to start with. Now, how do you realize the inner package structure, that is, which sub-packages to use?

## Package contents

At first let's have a look at the contents of a vertically sliced module. Since it is modeled after business concerns, the module will include everything necessary to fulfill certain functionality.

First of all, the module includes technical entry points for use cases such as HTTP endpoints, presentation framework controllers, or JMS endpoints. These classes and methods usually make use of Java EE principles, such as inversion of control, to be called from the container as soon as some communication hits the application.

The functionalities that initiate the actual use cases are the next and equally important concern. They usually differ from the technical endpoints such that they don't contain any communication logic. The business use case boundaries are the entry point of our domain logic. They are implemented as managed beans, usually Stateless Sessions Beans, EJBs in other words, or CDI managed beans.

The boundaries initiate and implement the business logic. In cases where the logic of a use case consists of just a few steps the boundary can sufficiently contain the whole logic in the business method or private methods in the class definition. Then no other delegate is required. For the vast majority of use cases the boundary would delegate logic to corresponding services. These delegates have finer-grained responsibilities. Depending on the domain this includes implementing detailed business logic or accessing external systems such as databases. Following Domain-Driven Design language, these classes include services, transaction scripts, factories, and repositories.

The next type of objects are all classes that typically would be considered as *model* content, such as entities, value objects, and transfer objects. These classes represent the entities in the domain, but also can, and should, implement business logic. Examples are entity beans that are managed in the database, other POJOs, and enumerations.

In some cases the package might also contain cross-cutting concerns such as interceptors with business or technical responsibilities. All these types of components now have to be organized within a module.

# Horizontal package layering

If we were to organize the module contents, our first attempt probably would be to design the inner package structure by technical layering. Slicing up by business concerns first and technical ones second at least sounds reasonable.

In the *users* package this would mean to have sub-packages such as *controller*, *business* or *core*, *model*, *data* and *client*, respectively. By following this approach, we split up responsibilities inside the *users* package by their technical categories. In order to be consistent, all the other modules and packages in the project would have similar packages, depending on their contents. The idea is similar to a three-tier architecture, but inside of the domain modules.

One of the sub-packages would be considered to be the technical entry point, for instance *controller*. This package would contain the communication endpoints initiating the use case logic and serve as entry point outside of the application. The following shows the structure of a horizontally organized users package:

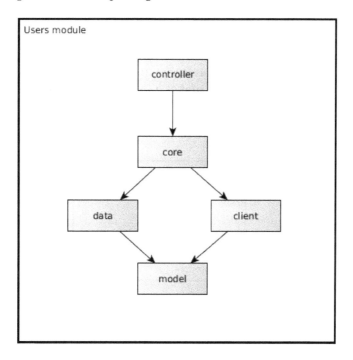

This structure is realized in Java packages as follows:

# Flat module package

An even simpler and more straightforward approach to organize module contents is to directly put all related classes into this module package in a flat hierarchy. For the `users` package this means to place all classes, including user related use case entry points, user database access code, potential external system functionality, and the user entity classes themselves, directly into this package.

Depending on the complexity of the modules this can be a clean and straightforward approach or it can become too unorganized over time. Especially entities, value objects, and transfer objects can reach a number of classes that, if put into a single package, drastically reduce clarity and overview. However, it makes a lot of sense to start with this approach and refactor later.

The following shows the package structure of an example `users` package:

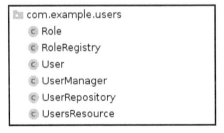

A benefit of this approach is that it's well supported by the Java language. By default Java classes and methods come with package-private visibility. This fact together with organizing all classes in one place leverages encapsulations and visibility practices. Components, that are desired to be accessible from outside of the package, get public visibility; all classes and methods that are only accessed from within this package define package-private visibility. The package can therefore encapsulate all internal concerns.

# Entity Control Boundary

Coping with the number of classes in the module package, there is another approach similar to technical layering, but with fewer and clearer defined packages. The idea is to structure due to what is a use case boundary of the module, which are subsequent business logic components, and which are entity classes.

This focuses on organizing module packages by their responsibilities, but with fewer technical details at the top package layer, compared to horizontal layering. The **boundary** package contains the use cases initiators, the boundaries, which are accessed from the outside of the system. These classes typically represent HTTP endpoints, message driven beans, frontend related controllers, or simply Enterprise Java Beans. They will implement the business driven use cases and optionally delegate to subsequent classes residing in the optional **control** package. The **entity** package contains all the *nouns* in the module, domain entities or transfer objects.

Ivar Jacobson has formed the term **Entity Control Boundary** for following way of organizing modules:

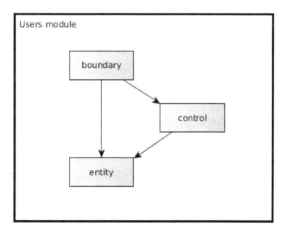

## Packages

Let's have a closer look at the boundary package. The idea was that all business use cases called from the frontend or outside of the system are initiated here. Invocations for creation, update, or deletion of users, first land in classes residing in this package. Depending on the complexity of the use cases, the boundary either completely handles the logic itself or delegates into the control before becoming too complex.

For a Java enterprise application, classes in the boundary package are implemented as managed beans. As mentioned before, typically EJBs are used here.

If the logic in the boundary becomes too complex and not manageable within a single class anymore, we refactor the logic into delegates that are used in the boundary. These delegates or *controls* are placed in the control package. They typically fulfill more detailed business logic or handle database or external system access by acting within the technical transaction that was initiated in the boundary.

This structure increases cohesion and reusability and honors the single responsibility principle. The structure of the business use case becomes more readable, once we introduce these abstraction layers. You can start by looking at the boundary as the entry point of the use case, and retrace every delegated step one after another.

In Domain-Driven Design language, the contents of the control package includes services, transaction scripts, factories and repositories. However, the existence of a control package for business use cases is optional.

At the heart of our domain we have all entities and value objects. These, together with transfer objects, build up the model of our domain module, the objects that a use case typically deals with. They are organized within the entity package, the last one of the Entity Control Boundary pattern.

Now, what about presentation-related components and cross-cutting concerns such as Interceptors or framework *plumbing* logic? Fortunately, in a modern Java EE project required framework plumbing is kept within limits as we will see in Chapter 3, *Implementing Modern Java Enterprise Applications*. The few things that are required, for example bootstrapping JAX-RS with the application activator class, are placed in the root package of our project or in a specific platform package. The same is true for cross-cutting concerns such as technically motivated interceptors that are not bound to a specific module, but the application as a whole. The number of these classes is typically not too high; if so, then a dedicated package makes sense. The danger of having such a platform package is that it naturally tempts developers to put other components in there as well. This place is just meant for the few platform specific classes; everything else should reside in its own business motivated module package.

The following is an example of the `users` module, using the Entity Control Boundary pattern:

## Package access

Not all accesses from every package of the Entity Control Boundary pattern are allowed or make sense, respectively. In general, the logic flow starts at the boundary, going down to the control and entity package. The boundary package therefore, has dependencies to both the control, if existent, and the entity package. Using boundaries of other modules are not allowed and won't make sense, since the boundary represents a business use case. Accessing another boundary would mean to invoke something that should be a separate, standalone use case. Therefore boundaries can only go *down* the hierarchy to controls.

However, dependencies and invocations from boundaries to controls of other modules are allowed and do make sense in some cases. Developers have to pay attention that the transaction scopes are still chosen correctly when accessing components from other modules. When accessing controls of other modules, it will also happen that they work with or return entities of that foreign module. This happens for more than trivial use cases and won't be an issue, as long as care is taken where the responsibilities are placed, and that the controls and entities are being used correctly.

Controls may access controls of other modules and their own and foreign entities. For the same reason as with boundaries, it makes no sense that a control invokes functionality of any boundary. This would be equivalent to starting new top-level business use cases within a running use case.

Entities are only allowed to depend on other entities. In some cases it will be necessary to have imports on controls, for example, if JPA entity listeners or JSON-B type converters exist that can implement sophisticated logic. These technically motivated cases are the exception where it should be allowed for simplicity to import these classes. Ideally, these entity *supporting* components, such as entity listeners or converters should reside directly in the entity package. Due to other dependencies and usage of delegates this premise cannot always be fulfilled, which should not lead to overly complex technical workarounds.

This also brings us to another more general topic.

# Don't over-enforce architecture

Whichever architectural pattern you choose, the main priority of the application should be the business domain. This is true for both finding reasonable, domain-motivated modules, but also how to structure the packages within a module, so that developers can work with it with least effort.

This is one important thing to note: developers should be able to work on the project without too complex or overly enforced structures and architectures. We have seen too many examples in the past that deliberately used technically driven layers or overly strict patterns, just to *match the book* and fulfill certain constraints. But these constraints are often self-motivated and don't fulfill any higher purpose. We should sensibly reconsider what is required and what just bloats the development processes. Search for the term *cargo cult programming* when you have the time, and you will find an interesting real-world story of following rules and rituals without questioning their purpose.

Therefore, don't over-complicate or over-enforce architecture. If there is a simple and straightforward way that fulfills what currently is required, just go for it. This is not only true for premature refactoring, but also for architectural design. If putting a few classes in a single, well-named package serves the purpose and clearly documents the reasoning, why not? If a business use case boundary class can already fulfill the whole, simple logic, why introduce empty delegates?

The trade-off of following an architectural pattern, even if not required in all places, is consistency versus simplicity. Having all packages, modules, and projects showing the same patterns and structure shows a picture familiar to developers. However, in Chapter 8, *Microservices and System Architecture* we will see that in greater detail, ultimately, consistency is a goal that isn't likely to be achieved within the whole organization, or even single projects. The benefits of crafting something simpler and eventually more flexible outweighs uniformity in many cases.

The same is true for overly trying to encapsulate the implementation using technical layers. It is definitely the case that modules as well as classes should encapsulate implementation details and provide clean and clear interfaces. However, these responsibilities can and should be contained in single, ideally self-sufficient packages or classes. Packaging the module's concerns by technical terms ultimately exposes the details to the rest of the module, for example, that a database or a client to an external system is being used. Organizing by domain motivation first, enables us to encapsulate functionality into single points of responsibility, transparent to the rest of the modules or application.

In order to prevent accidental misuse of a way of packaging, the easiest and most transparent way is to introduce static code analysis. Package imports in classes and whole packages can be scanned and analyzed to detect and prevent unwanted dependencies. This represents a security measurement, similar to test cases, to avoid careless mistakes. Static code analyses will typically run as an extended part of the build process on the Continuous Integration server, as they may take some time to build. In Chapter 6, *Application Development Workflows* we will cover this topic in more depth.

# Summary

Enterprise software should be built with the main priority to solve business problems, leading to business-driven applications and technology rather than to technology-driven solutions. The business use cases are what ultimately will generate revenue for the company.

If possible, enterprise applications should be developed in one build project per artifact, kept under version control. Splitting up a project into several, independent build modules that are in the end boiled down to a single artifact, doesn't add much value. For the coarse project structure it's advisable to structure the software modules vertically, not horizontally. This means to structure by business rather than technical concerns. Looking at the project structure should immediately tell developers what the project's domain and responsibilities are about.

An individual application module can, in the simplest way, be designed as a single, flat Java package. This is advisable if the number of classes per module is small. For more complex modules it makes sense to add another hierarchical layer using patterns such as Entity Control Boundary.

Software engineers should be reminded not to over-enforce software architecture. Well-thought-out design and bureaucratic organization certainly support developers a lot in crafting high quality software. Still, there is always a happy medium between reasonable design and over-engineering.

After seeing the course structure of enterprise projects and how to design modules, let's dive down one level to how to realize project modules. The following chapter will show you what it takes to implement enterprise applications with Java EE.

# 3
# Implementing Modern Java Enterprise Applications

Now after we saw what components are contained in projects and modules and how to find and construct reasonably sized modules and packages, let's get more down to earth and discuss the topic of Java EE. It certainly makes sense to think about the business concerns first and follow the practices of Domain-Driven Design to identify bounded context and modules with all the contents of our domain.

Let's see how to realize the identified business modules and use cases.

This chapter will cover:

- How to implement application use case boundaries
- What the Java EE core domain components are
- Design patterns and Domain-Driven Design with Java EE
- Application communication
- How to integrate persistence
- Technical cross-cutting concerns and asynchronous behavior
- Concepts and principles of Java EE
- How to achieve maintainable code

## Use case boundaries

Organizing packages after domain concerns leads us to an architectural structure, where the actual business, rather than technical details are reflected.

The business use cases handle all logic required to fulfill the business purpose, using all our module contents. They act as a starting point into the application's domain. The use cases are exposed and invoked via the system boundaries. The enterprise systems offers communication interfaces to the outside world, mostly via web services or web-based frontends, that invoke the business functionalities.

When starting a new project, it makes sense to start with the domain logic first, indifferent to system boundaries or any technical implementation details. This contains constructing all contents of the domain, designing types, dependencies and responsibilities, and prototyping these into code. As we will see in this chapter, the actual domain logic is implemented primarily in plain Java. The initial model can be self-sufficient and tested solely using code level tests. After a sufficiently matured domain model has been found, we target the remaining technical concerns that are outside of the domain module, such as accessing databases or external systems, as well as system endpoints.

In a Java EE application, a boundary is implemented using managed beans, that is, **Enterprise JavaBeans** (**EJB**) or **Contexts and Dependency Injection for Java** (**CDI**) managed beans. The topic *EJB and CDI - differenciation and integration* will show the differences and significance of these technologies.

Depending on the complexity of the individual use cases, we introduce *delegates* which are realized as CDI managed beans or EJBs, as well, depending on the requirements. These delegates reside in the control package. Entities are realized as POJOs, optionally annotated to integrate technical functionality such as specifying the database mapping or serialization.

# Core domain components of modern Java EE

Plain Java together with CDI and EJB form the core domain components of a modern Java EE application. Why is it called core domain? As mentioned, we want to pay attention to the actual business. There are aspects, components, and functionality that serve the business purpose at their core, whereas others just *support*, make the business domain accessible, or fulfill other technical requirements.

Java EE ships with many APIs that support realizing dozens of technical requirements. Most of them are technically motivated though. The biggest advantage of the Java EE platform, however, is that clean Java business logic can be implemented with minimal code impact of the technology. The APIs required for that are mainly CDI and EJB. Other APIs, that are required for technical motivations, such as JPA, JAX-RS, JSON-P, and many others, are introduced with a secondary priority.

Managed beans, no matter whether CDI or EJB, are implemented as annotated Java classes, without any technical super classes or interfaces required. In the past, this was called the no-interface view. Nowadays this is the default case. Extending classes obscure the picture on the domain and also come with other shortcomings when it comes to testability. A modern framework integrates itself as simply and as lean as possible.

# EJB and CDI - differentiation and integration

Now the question is, whether to use EJBs or CDI managed beans.

In general, EJBs ship more functionality that is already usable out of the box. CDI managed beans offer a somewhat lighter alternative. What are the main differences between these technologies and how does it affect the developer's work?

The first difference are the scopes. EJB session beans are either stateless, that is, active during the duration of the client request, stateful, that is, active during the lifespan of a client's HTTP session, or singletons. CDI managed beans come with similar scopes plus more possibilities, such as adding custom scopes and the default dependent scope which is active depending on the lifespan of its injection point. The topic *Scopes* will handle bean scopes more detailed.

Another difference between EJBs and CDI beans is that EJBs implicitly comprise certain cross-cutting concerns, such as monitoring, transactions, exception handling, and managing concurrency for singleton beans. For example, calling an EJB business method implicitly starts a technical transaction, which is active during the method execution and which integrates datasources or external systems.

Also, stateless EJBs are pooled after usage. This means that after a stateless session bean's business method has been invoked, the bean instance can and will be reused from the container. Due to this fact, EJBs perform a little better than CDI beans, which are instantiated every time their scope requires it.

Practically, the technical differences don't impact the developer's work too much. Besides using different annotations, both technologies can be used in the same look and feel. The direction of Java EE moves toward a more open choice of these two; for instance, since Java EE 8 it's possible to handle asynchronous events solely with CDI, not just EJB.

The integration of functionality that CDI provides is, however, one of the biggest features of the Java EE APIs. Just alone dependency injection, CDI producers, and events are effective means to tackle various situations.

The single most used CDI feature is dependency injection using the @Inject annotation. The injection is built in such a way that no matter which Java EE technology manages the beans, it *just works* for developers. You can mix and match CDI beans and EJBs with all scopes; the framework will take care of which beans are instantiated or used in which scope, respectively. This enables a flexible usage, such as cases when beans with a shorter scope are injected into longer scoped beans; for example, when a session scoped bean is injected into a singleton.

This feature supports the business domain in such a way that boundaries and controls can just inject required dependencies without worrying about instantiating or managing them.

The following code demonstrates how a boundary implemented as stateless session bean injects the required controls.

```java
import javax.ejb.Stateless;
import javax.inject.Inject;

@Stateless
public class CarManufacturer {

    @Inject
    CarFactory carFactory;

    @Inject
    CarStorage carStorage;

    public Car manufactureCar(Specification spec) {
        Car car = carFactory.createCar(spec);
        carStorage.store(car);
        return car;
    }
}
```

The CarManufacturer class represents a stateless EJB. The injected CarFactory and CarStorage beans are realized as dependent scoped CDI beans that will be instantiated and injected into the EJB. The Java EE platforms simplifies dependency resolution by enabling to use @Inject to inject any project-specific beans. This was not always the case; In the past, the @EJB annotation was used to inject EJBs. @Inject simplifies the usage within Java EE.

Attentive readers may have noticed the field-based injection with package-private Java scopes. Field-based injection has the least impact on the contents of a class - since a custom constructor can be avoided. Package-private visibility enables developers to set and inject dependencies in a test scope. We will cover this topic and potential alternatives in Chapter 7, *Testing*.

# CDI producers

CDI producers are another Java EE feature that is especially helpful to realize factories of all kinds of sorts. The producers, mostly realized as producer methods, provide the object that can be injected in other managed beans. This decouples creation and configuration logic from the usage. Producers are helpful when custom types other than managed bean types need to be injected.

The following shows the definition of a CDI producer method:

```
import javax.enterprise.inject.Produces;

public class CarFactoryProducer {

    @Produces
    public CarFactory exposeCarFactory() {
        CarFactory factory = new BMWCarFactory();
        // use custom logic
        return factory;
    }
}
```

The exposed `CarFactory` type can simply be injected using `@Inject`, as seen previously in the `CarManufacturer` example. CDI invokes the `exposeCarFactory()` method once a `CarFactory` instance is required and inserts the returned object into the injection point.

These techniques already cover most of the requirements for the core domain logic use cases.

# Emitting domain events

CDI provides an eventing feature for cases where business functionality needs to be decoupled even more. Beans can fire event objects, which act as payloads and which are handled in event observers. By emitting and handling CDI events, we decouple the main business logic from side aspects of handling the event. This idea particularly matches use cases, where the business domain already comprises the concept of events. By default, CDI events are handled in a synchronous way; interrupting the execution at the point where they are fired. CDI events can also be handled asynchronously or at specific points in the life cycle of the technical transaction.

The following code demonstrates how to define and fire CDI events as part of a business use case:

```java
import javax.enterprise.event.Event;

@Stateless
public class CarManufacturer {

    @Inject
    CarFactory carFactory;

    @Inject
    Event<CarCreated> carCreated;

    public Car manufactureCar(Specification spec) {
        Car car = carFactory.createCar(spec);
        carCreated.fire(new CarCreated(spec));
        return car;
    }
}
```

The `CarCreated` event is immutable and contains information that is relevant to the domain event, such as the car specification. The event is handled in the `CreatedCarListener` class, which resides in the control package:

```java
import javax.enterprise.event.Observes;

public class CreatedCarListener {

    public void onCarCreated(@Observes CarCreated event) {
        Specification spec = event.getSpecification();
        // handle event
    }
}
```

The listener is therefore decoupled from the main business logic. The CDI container will take care of connecting the event handling functionality and synchronously calling the `onCarCreated()` method.

The topic *Flow of execution,* shows how events can be fired and handled asynchronously or alternatively at specific points in the life cycle of the transaction.

CDI events are a way how to decouple the definition of domain events from handling them. The event handler logic can be changed or enhanced without touching the car manufacturer component.

# Scopes

Bean scopes are quite important for the cases when state is kept in the application for longer than the duration of a single request.

If the whole business process can be implemented in a stateless way, by just executing some logic and discarding all state afterwards, scope definitions are pretty straightforward. Stateless session beans with dependent scoped CDI beans already fulfill a lot of these cases.

The EJB singleton scope and the CDI application scope, respectively, are used quite frequently as well. Single instances of a bean type are a straightforward way to store or cache information that have a long lifespan. Besides all the sophisticated caching technology, a singleton containing simple collections or maps with managed concurrency is still the most simple way to design application-specific, volatile stores. Singletons also provide a single point of responsibility for functionality that for some reason needs to be accessed in a restricted way.

The last scope of both EJBs and CDI beans is the session scope, which is bound to the client's HTTP session. Beans of this scope will be active and reused with all their states as long as the user's session is active. However, storing session data in stateful beans introduces the challenge that clients need to reconnect to the same application server again. This is certainly possible but prevents designing stateless applications which are easier to manage. If the application becomes unavailable, all temporary session data is lost as well. In modern enterprise applications, state is typically kept in the database or in caches for optimization purposes. Therefore, session scoped beans aren't used too much anymore.

CDI managed beans come with more built-in scopes, namely the conversation scope or the default dependent scope. There are also possibilities for adding custom scopes for special requirements. However, experience shows that the built-in scopes are usually sufficient for the majority of enterprise applications. The CDI specification provides further information how to extend the platform and develop custom scopes.

As you have seen, we can already achieve a lot with these Java EE core components. Before looking into integration technologies, such as HTTP communication or database access, let's have a closer look into design patterns used in our core domain.

# Patterns in Java EE

A lot has been written about design patterns. The most prominent and always recited example is the well-known book *Design Patterns* by the *Gang of Four* (GoF). It describes common situations in software design that are solved using specific implementation patterns.

Whereas the design and motivation for specific patterns are still valid today, the actual implementation may have changed, especially in the enterprise area. Besides the well-known design patterns which are applicable for all kind of applications, there are also a lot of enterprise-related patterns that have emerged. In particular, a variety of J2EE-related enterprise patterns came up in the past. Since we are in the age of Java EE 8, not J2EE anymore, there are now easier ways to implement various patterns which tackle specific situations.

## Design patterns revisited

The design patterns described in the GoF book are categorized into creational, structural, and behavioral patterns. Each of the patterns describe a typical challenge in software and shows a way to tackle and solve those situations. They represent implementation blueprints and are not dependent on any specific technology. That is why the idea of each of these patterns can be realized without precisely matching the described implementation. In the modern world of Java SE 8 and EE 8, we have more language features available than was the case in the past. I want to show some of the Gang of Four design patterns, their motivations, and how they can be realized in Java EE.

## Singleton

The singleton pattern is a well-known pattern or, as some would argue, anti-pattern. Singletons have only one single instance per class within the whole application. The motivation for this pattern is the capability of storing states as well as being able to coordinate actions at a central place. Singletons definitely have their right to exist. If a certain state needs to be shared reliably among several consumers, a single point of entry is definitely the simplest solution.

However, there are some points to be aware of. Having a single point of responsibility also introduces concurrency that needs to be managed. Therefore, singletons need to be thread-safe. That said, we should keep in mind that singletons naturally don't scale, since there's only one instance. The more synchronization we introduce due to the contained data structure, the less our class will scale for concurrent access. However, depending on the use case, this might or might not be a issue.

The GoF book describes a static singleton instance that is managed in the singleton class. In Java EE the concept of singletons is directly built into EJBs with singleton session beans and CDIs with the application scope. These definitions will create one managed bean that is used in all clients.

The following demonstrates an example of a singleton EJB:

```
import javax.ejb.Singleton;

@Singleton
public class CarStorage {

    private final Map<String, Car> cars = new HashMap<>();

    public void store(Car car) {
        cars.put(car.getId(), car);
    }
}
```

There is some difference in whether we implement singletons using EJB singleton sessions beans or CDI application scoped beans.

By default, the container manages the concurrency of EJB singletons. This ensures that only one public business method is executed at a time. The behavior can be changed by providing the `@Lock` annotation which declares methods either as write-lock or read-lock, respectively, where the beans acts as a read-write lock. All EJB singleton business methods are implicitly write-locked. The following shows an example of using an EJB with container managed concurrency and lock annotations:

```
import javax.ejb.Lock;
import javax.ejb.LockType;

@Singleton
public class CarStorage {

    private final Map<String, Car> cars = new HashMap<>();

    @Lock
    public void store(Car car) {
```

```
            cars.put(car.getId(), car);
    }

    @Lock(LockType.READ)
    public Car retrieve(String id) {
        return cars.get(id);
    }
}
```

The concurrency can also switched off using bean managed concurrency. Then the bean will be called concurrently and the implementation itself has to ensure thread-safety. Using a thread-safe data structure, for example, doesn't require the EJB singleton to manage concurrent accesses. The business methods of the EJB instance will then be called in parallel, similarly to CDI application scoped beans:

```
import javax.ejb.ConcurrencyManagement;
import javax.ejb.ConcurrencyManagementType;

@Singleton
@ConcurrencyManagement(ConcurrencyManagementType.BEAN)
public class CarStorage {

    private final Map<String, Car> cars = new ConcurrentHashMap<>();

    public void store(Car car) {
        cars.put(car.getId(), car);
    }

    public Car retrieve(String id) {
        return cars.get(id);
    }
}
```

CDI application scoped beans don't restrict concurrent access and the implementation always has to deal with concurrency itself.

These solutions tackle situations where a singleton is required; for example, a state that needs to be shared in-memory in the whole application.

CDI application scoped beans or EJB singletons with bean managed concurrency and thread-safe data structures provide an application-wide, non-clustered in-memory cache that scale really well. If distribution is not required this is a simplest yet elegant solution.

Another widely used scenario for EJB singletons is the ability to invoke a single process at application startup. By declaring the `@Startup` annotation, the bean will be instantiated and prepared at application startup, invoking the `@PostConstruct` method. Startup processes can be defined for all EJBs, but using singletons we can realize processes that need to be set up exactly once.

# Abstract factory

The GoF abstract factory pattern aims to separate the creation of objects from their usage. Creating complex objects may involve knowledge about certain prerequisites, implementation details, or which implementation class to be used. Factories help us creating these objects without deep knowledge about the internals. Later in this chapter, we will talk about Domain-Driven Design factories, which are closely related to this pattern. The motivations are the same. Abstract factories aim toward having several implementations of an abstract type where the factory itself is also an abstract type. The users of the functionality develop against interfaces, whereas the concrete factory will produce and return the concrete instances.

There may be an abstract `GermanCarFactory` with concrete implementations as `BMWFactory` and `PorscheFactory`. Both car factories may produce some implementation of `GermanCar`, be it a `BMWCar` or `PorscheCar`, respectively. The client that just wants to have some German car won't care about which actual implementation class the factory will use.

In the Java EE world, we already have a powerful functionality that is in fact a factory framework, namely CDI. CDI provides tons of features to create and inject instances of certain types. Whereas the motivations and outcome are the same, the implementation differs in detail. In fact, there are many ways to realize abstract factories, depending on the use case. Let's have a look at a few of them.

A managed bean can inject instances that are concrete or abstract and even parameterized types. If we want to have only one instance in our current bean, we directly inject a `GermanCar`:

```
@Stateless
public class CarEnthusiast {

    @Inject
    GermanCar car;

    ...
}
```

Having multiple implementations of the `GermanCar` type would lead to a dependency resolving exception at this point since the container cannot know which actual car to inject. To resolve this issue, we can introduce qualifiers that explicitly ask for a specific type. We could use the available `@Named` qualifier with defined string values; however, doing so won't introduce typesafety. CDI gives us the possibility to specify our own typesafe qualifiers that will match our use case:

```
@BMW
public class BMWCar implements GermanCar {
    ...
}

@Porsche
public class PorscheCar implements GermanCar {
    ...
}
```

Qualifiers are custom runtime-retention annotations, themselves annotated with `@Qualifier` and typically `@Documented`:

```
import javax.inject.Qualifier;
import java.lang.annotation.Documented;
import java.lang.annotation.Retention;
import java.lang.annotation.RetentionPolicy;

@Qualifier
@Documented
@Retention(RetentionPolicy.RUNTIME)
public @interface BMW {
}
```

The qualifiers are specified at the injection point. They qualify the injected type and decouple the injection from the actual type being used:

```
@Stateless
public class CarEnthusiast {

    @Inject
    @BMW
    GermanCar car;

    ...
}
```

Obtaining an instance of `CarEnthusiast` will now create and inject a dependent-scoped `BMWCar`, since this type matches the injection point.

We could now even define a sub-type of a BMW car, that will be used without changing the injection point. This is realized by *specializing* the BMWCar type with a different implementation. The ElectricBMWCar type sub-classes BMWCar and specifies the @Specializes annotation:

```
import javax.enterprise.inject.Specializes;

@Specializes
public class ElectricBMWCar extends BMWCar {
    ...
}
```

Specialized beans inherit the types and qualifiers of their parent type and will be transparently used instead of the parent type. In this example, injecting a GermanCar with @BMW qualifier will provide you an instance of ElectricBMWCar.

However, to be closer to the design pattern described in the book, we could also define a car factory type used to create several cars as desired:

```
public interface GermanCarManufacturer {
    GermanCar manufactureCar();
}
```

This car factory is implemented with different specifics:

```
@BMW
public class BMWCarManufacturer implements GermanCarManufacturer {

    @Override
    public GermanCar manufactureCar() {
        return new BMWCar();
    }
}

@Porsche
public class PorscheCarManufacturer implements GermanCarManufacturer {

    @Override
    public GermanCar manufactureCar() {
        return new PorscheCar();
    }
}
```

Doing so, the client would now inject and use a manufacturer directly to create new German cars:

```
@Stateless
public class CarEnthusiast {

    @Inject
    @BMW
    GermanCarManufacturer carManufacturer;

    // create German cars
}
```

Injecting types that are explicitly defined and qualified, such as our two German cars, provides a lot of flexibility for implementations.

# Factory method

To understand the factory method, let's look into another pattern that has similar motivations, but which is realized differently. Factory methods define factories that are implemented as methods on specific types. There is no single class responsible for creating certain instances; rather, the creation becomes the responsibility of the factory method which is defined as part of a domain class.

For example, let's consider a car that uses its recorded trips to generate a driver's logbook. It perfectly makes sense to include a createDriverLog() method in the car type which returns a logbook value type, since the class itself can provide the logic in a self-sufficient manner. These solutions would be implemented purely in Java without any frameworks or annotations required:

```
public class Car {

    ...

    public LogBook createDriverLog() {
        // create logbook statement
    }
}
```

As we will see later in this chapter, Domain-Driven Design factories don't distinguish between abstract factories and factory methods. They are more directed toward the motivations of the domain. In some cases, it makes sense to encapsulate factories as methods together with other responsibilities of a class. In other cases, where creation logic is that particular, single points of responsibility in form of separate classes are more appropriate. Generally speaking, putting the creation logic into domain types is desirable since it may make use of other functionalities and properties of that domain class.

Let's have a look at CDI producers. Producers are defined as methods or fields that are used dynamically to look up and inject instances of certain types. We have full flexibility of what values a field contains or a method returns, respectively. We can equally specify qualifiers to ensure that the producers don't collide with other potentially produced types. The beans that defines the producer method can also contain further properties that is used in the producer:

```
import javax.enterprise.inject.Produces;

public class BMWCarManufacturer {

    ...

    @Produces
    @BMW
    public GermanCar manufactureCar() {
        // use properties
        ...
    }
}
```

This matches the idea of factory methods implemented as CDI producers.

The scope of the produced instances needs to be considered. As any other CDI managed bean, the producers are by default dependent scoped. The scope defines the life cycle of managed beans and how they are injected. It affects how often the producer method will be invoked. For the default scope, the method is invoked once per injected instance when the calling managed bean is instantiated. Every time the bean that injects the produced value is injected, the producer method will be called. If that bean has a longer lifetime, the producer method won't be invoked again for that duration.

Later in this chapter, we will see more sophisticated usages of CDI producers.

# Object pool

The object pool design pattern was designed for performance optimization. The motivation behind pools is to avoid to constantly create new instances of required objects and dependencies, by retaining them in a pool of objects for a longer period of time. A required instance is retrieved from this pool of objects and released after usage.

This concept is already built into Java EE containers in different forms. As mentioned earlier, stateless session beans are pooled. This is the reason why they perform exceptionally well. However, developers have to be aware of the fact that instances are being reused; instances must not retain any state after they have been used. The container keeps a pool of these instances.

Another example is the pooling of database connections. Database connections are rather expensive to initiate and it makes sense to keep a few of them alive for later use. Depending on the persistence implementation, these connections are reused once a new query is requested.

Threads are also pooled in enterprise applications. In a Java server environment, a client request typically results in a Java thread that handles the logic. After handling the request, the threads will be reused again. Thread pool configuration as well as having different pools is an important topic for further performance optimization. We will cover this topic in `Chapter 9`, *Monitoring, Performance, and Logging*.

Developers won't typically implement the object pool pattern themselves. The container already includes this pattern for instances, threads, and databases. The application developer implicitly uses these available features.

# Decorator

Another well-known design pattern is the decorator pattern. This pattern allows us to add behavior to an object without affecting other objects of that class. Quite often this behavior is composable with several subtypes.

A good example is food. Everybody has their own preferences in tastes and compositions. Let's take coffee as an example. We can drink just plain black coffee, with milk, with sugar, with both milk and sugar, or even with syrup, cream, or whatever will be popular in the future. And that's not taking into account the different ways of how to brew coffee.

The following shows a realization of the decorator pattern using plain Java.

We specify the following `Coffee` type which can be decorated using the sub-type `CoffeeGarnish`:

```java
public interface Coffee {

    double getCaffeine();
    double getCalories();
}

public class CoffeeGarnish implements Coffee {

    private final Coffee coffee;

    protected CoffeeGarnish(Coffee coffee) {
        this.coffee = coffee;
    }

    @Override
    public double getCaffeine() {
        return coffee.getCaffeine();
    }

    @Override
    public double getCalories() {
        return coffee.getCalories();
    }
}
```

The default coffee garnish just delegates to its parent coffee. There may be several implementations of a coffee:

```java
public class BlackCoffee implements Coffee {

    @Override
    public double getCaffeine() {
        return 100.0;
    }

    @Override
    public double getCalories() {
        return 0;
    }
}
```

Besides regular black coffee, we also specify some garnishes:

```
public class MilkCoffee extends CoffeeGarnish {

    protected MilkCoffee(Coffee coffee) {
        super(coffee);
    }

    @Override
    public double getCalories() {
        return super.getCalories() + 20.0;
    }
}

public class SugarCoffee extends CoffeeGarnish {

    protected SugarCoffee(Coffee coffee) {
        super(coffee);
    }

    @Override
    public double getCalories() {
        return super.getCalories() + 30.0;
    }
}

public class CreamCoffee extends CoffeeGarnish {

    protected CreamCoffee(Coffee coffee) {
        super(coffee);
    }

    @Override
    public double getCalories() {
        return super.getCalories() + 100.0;
    }
}
```

Using the coffee types, we can compose our desired coffee with its specific behavior:

```
Coffee coffee = new CreamCoffee(new SugarCoffee(new BlackCoffee()));
coffee.getCaffeine(); // 100.0
coffee.getCalories(); // 130.0
```

An example for the decorator pattern in the JDK is the InputStream class with the possibility to add specific behavior for files, byte arrays, and so on.

In Java EE, we again make use of CDI which ships with a decorator functionality. Decorators add specific behavior to a bean. Invocations on an injected bean call the decorator instead of the actual bean; the decorator adds specific behavior and delegates to the bean instance. The original bean type becomes a so-called delegate of the decorator:

```
public interface CoffeeMaker {
    void makeCoffee();
}

public class FilterCoffeeMaker implements CoffeeMaker {

    @Override
    public void makeCoffee() {
        // brew coffee
    }
}
```

The delegate type must be an interface. The CountingCoffeeMaker decorates the existing coffee maker functionality:

```
import javax.decorator.Decorator;
import javax.decorator.Delegate;
import javax.enterprise.inject.Any;

@Decorator
public class CountingCoffeeMaker implements CoffeeMaker {

    private static final int MAX_COFFEES = 3;
    private int count;

    @Inject
    @Any
    @Delegate
    CoffeeMaker coffeeMaker;

    @Override
    public void makeCoffee() {
        if (count >= MAX_COFFEES)
            throw new IllegalStateException("Reached maximum coffee
limit.");
        count++;

        coffeeMaker.makeCoffee();
    }
}
```

The decorator functionality is activated via the `beans.xml` descriptor.

```xml
<?xml version="1.0" encoding="UTF-8"?>
<beans xmlns="http://xmlns.jcp.org/xml/ns/javaee"
       xmlns:xsi="http://www.w3.org/2001/XMLSchema-instance"
       xsi:schemaLocation="http://xmlns.jcp.org/xml/ns/javaee
       http://xmlns.jcp.org/xml/ns/javaee/beans_1_1.xsd"
       bean-discovery-mode="all">
    <decorators>
        <class>com.example.coffee.CountingCoffeeMaker</class>
    </decorators>
</beans>
```

After activating the decorator, injected instances of the `CoffeeMaker` type use the decorated functionality instead. This happens without changing the original implementation:

```java
public class CoffeeConsumer {

    @Inject
    CoffeeMaker coffeeMaker;

    ...
}
```

Managed beans can have several decorators. If necessary, ordering can be specified on the decorators using the Java EE `@Priority` annotation.

This CDI functionality applies to managed beans. Depending on whether we want to add additional behavior to our domain model classes or the services involved, we will use the pattern either with plain Java, as described first, or by using CDI decorators.

# Facade

The facade design pattern is used to provide a clean and simple interface to certain functionalities. Encapsulation and abstraction layers are certainly among the most important principles for writing code. We introduce facades which encapsulate complex functionality or legacy components that are cumbersome to use, into simpler interfaces. A facade is therefore a prime example for abstraction.

Let's consider a rather complex setup in a coffee shop. There are grinders, coffee machines, scales, and various tools in use that all need to be configured accordingly:

```java
public class BaristaCoffeeShop {

    private BeanStore beanStore;
    private Grinder grinder;
    private EspressoMachine espressoMachine;
    private Scale scale;
    private Thermometer thermometer;
    private Hygrometer hygrometer;

    public GroundBeans grindBeans(Beans beans, double weight) { ... }

    public Beans fetchBeans(BeanType type) { ... }

    public double getTemperature() { ... }

    public double getHumidity() { ... }

    public Coffee makeEspresso(GroundBeans beans, Settings settings) { ...
}
}
```

One could certainly argue that this class already needs refactoring. However, legacy classes may not be changeable easily. We will introduce a barista that acts as a facade:

```java
@Stateless
public class Barista {

    @Inject
    BaristaCoffeeShop coffeeShop;

    public Coffee makeCoffee() {
        // check temperature & humidity
        // calculate amount of beans & machine settings
        // fetch & grind beans
        // operate espresso machine
    }
}
```

In the Java EE world, the most prominent example of facades are boundaries implemented with EJBs. They provide the facade to the business use cases that are part of our business domain. Besides that, facades can be implemented using all kinds of managed beans. Facades delegate and orchestrate complex logic appropriately. Well-chosen abstractions improve the software design and are an aim to strive for.

# Proxy

The proxy design pattern is probably the most obvious one that is included in Java EE. Injected bean references contain in almost all cases not a reference to the actual instance, but a proxy. Proxies are thin wrappers around instances that can add certain functionalities. The client doesn't even notice that it interacts with a proxy instead of the actual object.

Proxies enable the cross-cutting functionality which is required in an enterprise environment, such as interceptors, transactions, logging, or monitoring. They are also required to perform dependency injection in the first place.

Application developers typically don't use the proxy pattern directly. However, it is recommended to understand how the proxy pattern works in general and how it's used in the Java EE platform in particular.

# Observer

The observer design pattern describes how an object manages and notifies observers in case of change in the overall state. Observers register themselves at the subject and will be notified later on. The notification of observers can happen in a synchronous or asynchronous way.

As seen before, CDI includes an eventing functionality, which implements the observer pattern. Developers do not need to handle the registration and notification logic themselves; they just declare the loose coupling using annotation. As shown in the topic *Core domain components of modern Java EE*, the `Event<T>` type and `@Observes` annotations declare the event publishing and observation. In the topic *Flow of execution*, we will cover asynchronous CDI events.

# Strategy

The strategy design pattern is used to dynamically choose an implementation algorithm, a strategy, at runtime. The pattern is used, for example, to select different business algorithms depending on the circumstances.

We have several possibilities to make use of the strategy pattern, depending on the situation. We can define different implementations of an algorithm as separate classes. Java SE 8 includes the functionality of lambda methods and method references that can be used as a lightweight strategy implementation:

```java
import java.util.function.Function;

public class Greeter {

    private Function<String, String> strategy;

    String greet(String name) {
        return strategy.apply(name) + ", my name is Duke";
    }

    public static void main(String[] args) {
        Greeter greeter = new Greeter();

        Function<String, String> formalGreeting = name -> "Dear " + name;
        Function<String, String> informalGreeting = name -> "Hey " + name;

        greeter.strategy = formalGreeting;
        String greeting = greeter.greet("Java");

        System.out.println(greeting);
    }

}
```

The example shows that functional interfaces can be used to dynamically define strategies that are applied and chosen at runtime.

In a Java EE environment, we can again make use of CDI dependency injection. To showcase that CDI supports any Java type, we will use the same example with a strategy that is represented by a functional interface. The greeting strategy is represented by the Function type:

```java
public class Greeter {

    @Inject
    Function<String, String> greetingStrategy;
```

```
    public String greet(String name) {
        return greetingStrategy.apply(name);
    }
}
```

A CDI producer method dynamically selects the greeting strategy:

```
public class GreetingStrategyExposer {

    private Function<String, String> formalGreeting = name -> "Dear " +
name;
    private Function<String, String> informalGreeting = name -> "Hey " +
name;

    @Produces
    public Function<String, String> exposeStrategy() {
        // select a strategy
        ...
        return strategy;
    }
}
```

In order to complete the example, let's introduce specific classes for the algorithm implementations. CDI is able to inject all instances of a certain type that can dynamically be selected.

The GreetingStrategy type is selectable after daytime appropriateness:

```
public interface GreetingStrategy {
    boolean isAppropriate(LocalTime localTime);
    String greet(String name);
}


public class MorningGreetingStrategy implements GreetingStrategy {
    @Override
    public boolean isAppropriate(LocalTime localTime) {
        ...
    }

    @Override
    public String greet(String name) {
        return "Good morning, " + name;
    }
}

public class AfternoonGreetingStrategy implements GreetingStrategy { ... }
public class EveningGreetingStrategy implements GreetingStrategy { ... }
```

The CDI producer can inject all possible `GreetingStrategy` instances and select based on their specification:

```
public class GreetingStrategySelector {

    @Inject
    @Any
    Instance<GreetingStrategy> strategies;

    @Produces
    public Function<String, String> exposeStrategy() {
        for (GreetingStrategy strategy : strategies) {
            if (strategy.isAppropriate(LocalTime.now()))
                return strategy::greet;
        }
        throw new IllegalStateException("Couldn't find an appropriate
greeting");
    }
}
```

The `@Any` qualifier implicitly exists on any managed bean. Injection points with the `Instance` type and this qualifier inject all instances that match the corresponding type, here `GreetingStrategy`. The `Instance` type allows us to dynamically obtain and qualify instances of a certain type. It implements an iterator over all eligible types.

By providing custom selection logic, we chose an appropriate strategy that is then injected into the greeter.

CDI allows several ways to specify and choose different strategies. Depending on the situation, dependency injection can be used to separate the selection logic from the usage.

# Further patterns

Besides the mentioned patterns that are implemented with specific Java EE functionalities, there are other design patterns that still are implemented with pure Java, as described in the GoF book. The presented list is certainly not complete, but includes design patterns that are usually being used in enterprise projects.

There are some design patterns that are at the core of Java EE, such as the proxy pattern. Another example is the mediator pattern that encapsulates communication between a set of objects. For example, to design loosely coupled communication, we would not implement this pattern ourselves rather than use API functionality that implements it internally, such as CDI events.

There are many other patterns that aren't used much by the Java EE API, but would be implemented using plain Java. Depending on the actual case, CDI could be used to support the creation and instantiation of objects. Examples for these patterns are prototype, builder, adapter, bridge, composite, flyweight, chain of responsibility, state, and visitor.

Again if we look into the Enterprise API, we will find, for example, the builder pattern being heavily used in the JSON-P API. I refer to the *Design Patterns* book by the Gang of Four, for further usage and patterns.

# Domain-Driven Design

Now we have seen how the GoF design patterns are implemented in the age of Java EE. Besides that, I want to point out some patterns and concepts that are applied in our core domain before continuing to more purely technical concerns. The book *Domain-Driven Design* by Eric Evans, extensively describes these patterns and concepts that support constructing software models that match the actual business domain as accurately as possible. In particular, the importance of communicating with domain experts, sharing a common, *ubiquitous* domain language, deeply understanding the underlying domain model, and gradually refactoring it, is pointed out. Domain-Driven Design also introduces certain concepts in the software world, such as repositories, services, factories, or aggregates.

Now the question arises as to whether and how these concepts are realizable with Java Enterprise? Domain-Driven Design always aims to include important aspects of the application directly into the domain model rather than just *outside* as part of a service or transaction script. We will see how this fact plays well with EJBs or CDI managed beans.

## Services

The Domain-Driven Design language defines the concept of a service. Services are responsible for orchestrating various business logic processes. Typically, they are an entry point for use cases and create or manage objects of the domain model. Services hold the single business process steps together.

If you map this concept with the idea and contents of the Entity Control Boundary packaging, you will see that it fulfills the same purpose as boundaries or controls, respectively. In Java EE, these services would therefore be implemented as EJBs or CDI managed beans. Services that represent the entry point of a use case are implemented as boundaries; whereas services that orchestrate further business logic, access databases or external systems represent controls.

# Entities

Domain-Driven Design also defines so-called entities. As the name already suggests, an entity represents a business domain entity in essence. These entities are identifiable instances of a concept deeply contained in the specific domain. Users, articles, and cars are examples of such entities. It is important to the domain that the entities can be separately identified. It makes a difference whether user *John Doe* or user *John Smith* invoked some use case. This aspect distinguishes entities from value objects.

Entities, as well as other model objects, are implemented as plain Java classes. For the sole business domain to function, there is no framework support required. Ideally, entities already encapsulate certain business logic that is self-contained within the entity type. That means that we will not only model simple POJOs with properties plus getter and setter methods but also business relevant methods that operate on that entity. Integrating business logic directly at the core of the business entities increases cohesion, understanding, and embraces the single responsibility principle.

Typically, entities as well as other domain model types, are persisted in a database. Java EE does support object-relational mapping with JPA which is used to persist and retrieve objects and object hierarchies. In fact, the JPA annotation used to declare entity types is called `@Entity`. In a later sub-chapter, we will see in detail how JPA supports to persist domain model types with minimal disruption on the model classes.

# Value objects

Types of the business domain that do not form identifiable entities but only specific *values* are called value objects. Value objects are preferably immutable and therefore reusable, since the content can't change. Java enumerations are a good example of this. Any objects where identity doesn't matter will be realized as value objects. For example, for Java enumerations it doesn't matter which instance of `Status.ACCEPTED` is returned, here there is even only one enum instance which is used in all places. The same is true for a lot of types in the domain, such as addresses. As long as the value of the address pointing to *42 Wallaby Way, Sydney* remains the same, it doesn't matter which address instance we refer to.

Depending on whether the set of values is finite, value objects are either modeled as enumerations or POJOs, ideally immutable. Immutability represents the concept of value objects and reduces the probability of potential errors. Changing a mutable object that is shared by multiple locations can lead to unplanned side effects.

As value objects are not identified directly they also won't be persisted and managed directly in a database. They certainly can be persisted indirectly, as part of a graph of objects, referenced from an entity or aggregate. JPA supports managing persistence of objects that are not entities or aggregates.

# Aggregates

Aggregates represent a concept in the Domain-Driven Design language, which is sometimes confusing to developers. Aggregates are complex models that consist of several entities or value objects, respectively, which form a whole. For consistency reasons, this conglomerate of objects should be accessed and managed as a whole as well. Accessing methods of some contained objects directly could lead to inconsistencies and potential errors. The idea behind aggregates it to represent a root objects for all operations. A good example is a car consisting of four wheels, an engine, a chassis, and so on. Whenever some operation, such as *drive* is required, it will be invoked on the whole car, potentially involving several objects at once.

Aggregates are entities that also define the root of an object hierarchy. They are implemented as plain Java classes containing business domain functionality and holding reference onto entities and value objects, respectively.

Therefore, aggregates can be persisted using JPA as well. All persistence operations are invoked on the aggregate, the root object, and cascaded to its contained objects. JPA supports persistence of complex object hierarchies, as we will see in later sub-chapters.

# Repositories

Speaking of database access Domain-Driven Design defines repositories that will manage persistence and consistency of entities. The motivation behind repositories was to have a single point of responsibility that enables the domain model to be persistent with consistency in mind. Defining these functionalities should not clutter the domain model code with persistence implementation details. Therefore, Domain-Driven Design defines the concept of repositories which encapsulate these operations in a self-sufficient and consistent way.

The repositories are the entry point for persistence operations for a specific entity type. Since only instances of aggregates and entities need to be identified, only these types require repositories.

In Java EE and JPA, there is already a functionality that matches the idea of repositories well, JPA's `EntityManager`. The entity manager is used to persist, retrieve, and manage objects that are defined as entities or potential object hierarchies thereof. The fact that the JPA managed objects need to be identifiable entities perfectly fits the constraints set by the Domain-Driven Design idea of entities.

The entity manager is injected and used in managed beans. This matches the idea that services, either as boundaries or controls, are meant to orchestrate the business use case, here by invoking the entity manager to provide the persistence of the entities.

# Factories

The motivation behind Domain-Driven Design factories is that creating domain objects can require logic and constraints that are more complex than just calling a constructor. Creation of consistent domain objects may need to perform validations or complex processes. Therefore, we define the creation logic in specific methods or classes that encapsulate this logic from the rest of the domain.

This is the same motivation behind the abstract factory and factory method design patterns discussed earlier. Therefore, the same realization using CDI features hold true here as well. The CDI specification is in fact a factory functionality.

Domain object factories can also be implemented as methods being part of another domain model class such as an entity. These solutions would be implemented purely in Java without any frameworks or annotations required. The car driver's logbook functionality discussed in the factory method design pattern is a good example for a factory method being included in a domain entity. If the domain class itself can provide the logic in a self-sufficient manner it perfectly makes sense to include the factory logic there as well.

# Domain event

Domain events represent events that are relevant to the business domain. They usually emerge from business use cases and have specific domain semantics. Examples for domain events are `UserLoggedIn`, `ActiclePurchased`, or `CoffeeBrewFinished`.

Domain events are typically implemented as value objects containing the required information. In Java, we realize events as immutable POJOs. Events happened in the past and can't be changed later on, so it is highly recommended to make them immutable. As seen before, we can use the CDI events functionality to publish and observe events with loose coupling. In CDI, all Java types can be used to be published as events. The concept of domain events is therefore a business definition rather than a technical one.

Domain events are particularly important for event sourcing and event-driven architectures, which we will extensively discuss in Chapter 8, *Microservices and System Architecture*.

# External and cross-cutting concerns in enterprise applications

Now we have seen the concepts and implementations necessary to realize domain logic in our application. In theory it's already sufficient to implement standalone business logic; however, the use cases won't provide much value to the customer if they can't be accessed from outside of the system.

Therefore, let's have a look at technically motivated external and cross-cutting concerns. These are functionalities that are not at the core of the business domain, but that need to be fulfilled as well. Examples for technically motivated concerns are accessing external systems or databases, configuring the application, or caching.

## Communication with external systems

Communicating to the outside world is one of the most important technical aspects of an enterprise application. Without that communication, the application will hardly bring any value to the customer.

## How to choose communication technology

When enterprise systems require communication, the question of which communication protocols and technologies to use arises. There are many forms of synchronous and asynchronous communications to choose from. There are some considerations to make upfront.

Which communication technology is supported by the chosen languages and frameworks? Are there any existing systems that require a certain form of communication? Do the systems exchange information in a synchronous or asynchronous way? What solution is the team of engineers familiar with? Does the system reside in an environment where high performance is crucial?

Looking from a business perspective again, communication between systems is necessary and should not *get in the way* of implementing a business use case. That said, exchanging information should at first be implemented in a straightforward way, matching the specific domain, regardless of whether the communication is performed synchronously or asynchronously. These considerations have a big impact not only on the actual implementation, but also as to whether the whole use case matches the chosen solution. Therefore, this is one of the first questions to be asked, whether the communication happens in a synchronous or asynchronous way. Synchronous communication ensures consistency and ordering of the exchanged information. However, it also comes with less performance compared to asynchronous calls and will not scale infinitely. Asynchronous communication leads to looser coupling of the systems involved, increases the overall performance as well as overhead and enables scenarios where systems are not reliably available all the time. For reasons of simplicity enterprise applications typically use synchronous communication, and also in regard to consistency.

The chosen way of communication needs to be supported not only by the language and frameworks, but also the environments and tools being used. Does the environment and network setup make any constraints on the communication? In fact, this was one of the reasons why the SOAP protocol was widely chosen in the past; being able to be transmitted over network port 80, which was permitted by the majority of network configurations. Tool support, especially during development and for debugging purposes is another important aspect. This is the reason why HTTP in general is widely used.

In the Java world, arguably most of the communication solutions out there are supported, either natively, such as HTTP, or by third-party libraries. This is certainly not the case with other technologies. This was, for example, one of the issues with the SOAP protocol. Implementation of the SOAP protocol was effectively only seen in Java and .NET applications. Other technologies typically chose different forms of communication.

Performance of the communication technology is an issue to consider, not only in high performance environments. Exchanging information over the network always introduces a huge overhead compared to both inter- or intra-process communication. The question is how big that overhead is. This essentially regards the density of information and the performance of processing messages or payloads. Is the information exchanged in a binary or plain text format? Which format does the content type represent? Generally speaking, binary formats with high information density and low verbosity perform better and transmit less data sizes, but are also harder to debug and comprehend.

Another important aspect is the flexibility of the communication solution. The chosen technology should not constrain the exchange of information too much. Ideally, the protocol supports different ways of communicating; for example, both synchronous and asynchronous communication, binary formats, or Hypermedia. Since our application's main concerns is the business logic, the chosen technology can ideally adapt to the overall requirements.

In today's systems, the communication protocol with the greatest usage is HTTP. There are several reasons for this. HTTP is well supported by all kinds of language platforms, frameworks, and libraries. The variety of tool choices is extremely high and the protocol is well known to most software engineers. HTTP does not make many constraints on how it is used and can therefore be applied to all kinds of information exchange. It can be used to realize both synchronous or asynchronous communication, Hypermedia, or straightforward invocations of remote functionality, such as remote procedure calls. However, HTTP does encourage certain usage. We will discuss semantic HTTP, remote procedure calls and REST in the next topic.

There are communication protocols that are, not necessarily, but typically, built on top of HTTP. The most prominent example from the past was SOAP; a more recent example is gRPC. Both protocols implement a remote procedure call approach. Remote procedure calls represent a straightforward form of calling a function of another system over the wire. The function needs to be specified with input and output values. SOAP realized these remote procedure calls in the XML format whereas gRPC uses binary protocol buffers to serialize data structures.

Depending on what the business requirements are in terms of synchronous or asynchronous behavior of the communication, it is highly recommended to implement the behavior consistently. In general, you should avoid mixing synchronous or asynchronous behavior. Wrapping services that contain asynchronous logic in a synchronous way doesn't make sense. The caller will be blocked until the asynchronous process is completed and the whole functionality will not scale. On the contrary, it sometimes makes sense to use asynchronous communication in order to encapsulate long-running synchronous processes. This includes external systems which cannot be changed or legacy applications. The client component will connect to the system in a separate thread, allowing the calling thread to continue immediately. The client thread either blocks until the synchronous process has finished or makes use of polling. However, it is preferred to model the systems and the style of communication after what makes sense for the business requirements.

There are quite a few protocols and formats of communications to choose from, a lot of them are proprietary. It is advisable for engineers to be aware of the different concepts and ways of communicating in general. Communication technology changes but the principles of exchanging data are timeless. As of writing this book, HTTP is the most widespread communication protocol being used. This is arguably one of the most important technologies to implement, it is well-understood, and has a great tooling support.

# Synchronous HTTP communication

Most of today's synchronous communication within enterprise systems is realized via HTTP. Enterprise applications expose HTTP endpoints that are accessed by the clients. These endpoints are typically in the form of web services or web frontends as HTML over HTTP.

Web services can be designed and specified in various ways. In the simplest form, we just want to call a function of another system over the wire. That function needs to be specified with input and output values. These functions or **remote procedure calls** (**RPC**) are in this case realized over HTTP, typically using an XML format that specifies the parameter arguments. In the age of J2EE, these types of web services were pretty common. The most prominent example for this was the SOAP protocol which is implemented with the JAX-WS standard. However, the SOAP protocol and its XML format was quite cumbersome to use and not well supported by other languages other than Java and .NET.

In today's system, the REST architectural style with its concept and constraints is used far more often.

## Representational State Transfer

The ideas and constraints of **Representational State Transfer** (**REST**), as initiated by Roy T. Fielding, provide an architectural style of web services that in many ways suit the needs of enterprise applications better. The ideas lead to systems that are coupled more loosely with interfaces that are accessed from various clients in a uniform and straightforward way.

The REST constraint of a *uniform interface* requires the resources to be identified in requests using the URI in web-based systems. The resources represent our domain entities; for example, users or articles which are individually identified by URLs of the enterprise application. That said, the URLs no longer represent RPC methods, but actual domain entities. These representations are modified in a uniform way, in HTTP using the HTTP methods such as GET, POST, DELETE, PATCH, or PUT. The entities may be represented in different formats that are requested by the client, such as XML or JSON. If supported by the server, clients are free to choose whether they access the specific user in its XML or JSON representation.

Another aspect of the uniform interface constraint is to make use of Hypermedia as the engine of the application state. Hypermedia means linking resources that are related together using hyperlinks. REST resources that are transferred to the client can include links to other resources with semantic link relations. If some user includes information about their manager, that information can be serialized using a link to the resource of the second user, the manager.

The following shows an example for a book representation with Hypermedia links included in a JSON response:

```
{
    "name": "Java",
    "author": "Duke",
    "isbn": "123-2-34-456789-0",
    "_links": {
        "self": "https://api.example.com/books/12345",
        "author": "https://api.example.com/authors/2345",
        "related-books": "https://api.example.com/books/12345/related"
    }
}
```

In websites designed for humans, these links are one of the main aspects. In a Hypermedia API, these links are used by the REST clients to navigate through the API. The concept of discoverability decreases coupling and increases evolvability of the systems involved. If this concept is fully embraced, clients only need to know an entry point of the API and discover the available resources using semantic link relations, such as `related-books`. They will follow the known relations using the provided URLs.

In most REST APIs, it's not sufficient for clients to only follow links and fetch resource representation using the HTTP GET method. Information is exchanged using HTTP methods that change state such as POST or PUT and request bodies which contain the payload. Hypermedia supports these so-called actions as well, using Hypermedia controls. Actions describe not only the target URL, but also the HTTP method and required information to send.

The following demonstrates a more sophisticated Hypermedia example using the concept of actions. This example shows the Siren content type and is meant to give you an idea of potential contents of Hypermedia responses:

```
{
    "class": [ "book" ],
    "properties": {
        "isbn": "123-2-34-456789-0",
        "name": "Java",
        "author": "Duke",
        "availability": "IN_STOCK",
        "price": 29.99
    }
    "actions": [
        {
            "name": "add-to-cart",
            "title": "Add Book to cart",
            "method": "POST",
            "href": "http://api.example.com/shopping-cart",
            "type": "application/json",
            "fields": [
                { "name": "isbn", "type": "text" },
                { "name": "quantity", "type": "number" }
            ]
        }
    ],
    "links": [
        { "rel": [ "self" ], "href": "http://api.example.com/books/1234" }
    ]
}
```

This is one example of a content type that enables Hypermedia controls. At the time of writing this book, none of the hypermedia-enabled content type such as Siren, HAL, or JSON-LD has emerged as a standard or de facto standard yet. However, this Siren content type should sufficiently communicate the concepts of links and actions.

Using Hypermedia decouples the client from the server. First of all, the responsibility of URLs solely reside on the server side. Clients cannot make any assumption how the URLs are created; for example, that the book resource resides under `/books/1234`, which is constructed from the path `/books/` plus the book ID. We have seen many of these assumption that duplicate URL logic into the clients in real-world projects.

The next aspect that is decoupled is how state is changed on the server. For example, the instruction that clients need to POST a JSON content type to `/shopping-cart` with a certain JSON structure is no longer baked into the client, but retrieved dynamically. The client will only refer to the Hypermedia action using its relation or name, here `add-to-cart`, and the information provided in the action. By using this approach, the client only needs to know the business meaning of the *add-to-cart* action and the origin of the required ISBN and quantity field. This is certainly client logic. The field values could be retrieved from the resource representation itself or from a client process. For example, the quantity of books could be presented as a drop-down field in the UI.

Another potential of using Hypermedia is to decouple business logic from the client. By using links and actions to direct the client to available resources, the information contained in the available links and actions is used to implicitly tell clients which use cases are possible with the current state of the system. For example, assuming that only books which have a certain availability can be added to the shopping cart. Clients that implement this behavior, that is, only showing an *add-to-cart* button for these situations, need to be aware of this logic. The client functionality then will check whether the book availability meets the criteria, and so on. Technically, this business logic should reside on the server-side only. By dynamically providing links and actions to available resources, the server dictates which functionality is possible under the current state. The *add-to-cart* action would then only be included if the book can actually be added to the cart. The client logic therefore is simplified to checking whether links and actions with known relations or names, respectively, are included. Therefore, the client only displays an active *add-to-cart* button if the corresponding action is provided in the response.

Together with the advent of Java EE, the REST architectural style gained more and more attention. While most web services out there don't implement all of the constraints that the REST architectural style defines, especially Hypermedia, they are mostly considered as REST services.

For more information about REST constraints, I refer you to the dissertation of Roy T. Fielding's *Architectural Styles and the Design of Network-based Software Architectures.*

## Java API for RESTful web services

In Java EE, the **Java API for RESTful web services (JAX-RS)** is used to both define and access REST services. JAX-RS is widely used in the Java ecosystem, even by other enterprise technologies. Developers especially like the declarative development model that makes it easy to develop REST services in a productive way.

So-called JAX-RS resources specify REST resources which will be available under a certain URL. The JAX-RS resources are methods in a resource class that implement the business logic once the URL is accessed with a specific HTTP method. The following shows an example of a JAX-RS resource class for users:

```java
import javax.ws.rs.Path;
import javax.ws.rs.GET;
import javax.ws.rs.Produces;
import javax.ws.rs.core.MediaType;

@Path("users")
@Produces(MediaType.APPLICATION_JSON)
public class UsersResource {

    @Inject
    UserStore userStore;

    @GET
    public List<User> getUsers() {
        return userStore.getUsers();
    }
}
```

The getUsers() method is the JAX-RS resource method that will be invoked by the container once the HTTP call GET ... /users is performed by a client. The list of users is then returned to the client in the JSON format, that is, as a JSON array containing JSON objects for each of the users. That is specified via the @Produces annotation that will here implicitly use the **Java API for JSON Binding (JSON-B)** to map Java types to their corresponding JSON representation.

Here you can see the inversion of control principle at work. We don't have to wire up or register the URL ourselves, the declaration using the @Path annotation is sufficient. The same is true for mapping Java types into representations such as JSON. We specify in a declarative way which representation formats we want to provide. The rest is handled by the container. The JAX-RS implementation also takes care of the required HTTP communication. By returning an object, here the list of users, JAX-RS implicitly assumes the HTTP status code 200 OK, which is returned to the client together with our JSON representation.

In order to register JAX-RS resources to the container, the application can ship a sub-class of Application which bootstraps the JAX-RS runtime. Annotating this class with @ApplicationPath automatically registers the provided path as Servlet. The following shows a JAX-RS configuration class which is sufficient for the vast majority of use cases:

```java
import javax.ws.rs.ApplicationPath;
import javax.ws.rs.core.Application;

@ApplicationPath("resources")
public class JAXRSConfiguration extends Application {
    // no configuration required
}
```

JAX-RS, as well as the other standards in the Java EE umbrella, make use of the convention over configuration principle. The default behavior of this REST resource is plausibly sufficient for most of the use cases. If not, then the default behavior can always be overridden with custom logic. This is the reason why JAX-RS, among others, provides a productive programming model. The default cases are realizable very quickly with the option to enhance further.

Let's look at a more comprehensive example. Assuming we want to create a new user in the system that is provided by a client using our REST service. Following HTTP semantics, that action would be a POST request to the user's resource, since we are creating a new resource that may not be identified yet. The difference between the POST and the PUT method is that the latter is omnipotent, only changing the accessed resource with the provided representation, whereas POST will create new resources in the form of new URLs. This is the case here. We are creating a new user that will be identifiable with a new, generated URL. If the resource for the new user is created, the client should be directed toward that URL. For creating resources, this is typically realized with the `201 Created` status code, which indicates that a new resource has been created successfully, and the `Location` header, which contains the URL where the resource will be found.

In order to fulfill that requirement, we have to provide more information in our JAX-RS resource. The following demonstrates how this is accomplished in the `createUser()` method:

```
import javax.ws.rs.Consumes;
import javax.ws.rs.PathParam;
import javax.ws.rs.POST;
import javax.ws.rs.core.Context;
import javax.ws.rs.core.Response;
import javax.ws.rs.core.UriInfo;

@Path("users")
@Produces(MediaType.APPLICATION_JSON)
@Consumes(MediaType.APPLICATION_JSON)
public class UsersResource {

    @Inject
    UserStore userStore;

    @Context
    UriInfo uriInfo;

    @GET
    public List<User> getUsers() {
        return userStore.getUsers();
    }

    @GET
    @Path("{id}")
    public User getUser(@PathParam("id") long id) {
        return userStore.getUser(id);
    }

    @POST
```

```
public Response createUser(User user) {
    long id = userStore.create(user);

    URI userUri = uriInfo.getBaseUriBuilder()
            .path(UsersResource.class)
            .path(UsersResource.class, "getUser")
            .build(id);

    return Response.created(userUri).build();
}

}
```

We make use of the `UriInfo` feature included in JAX-RS, so that we don't need to repeat ourselves when constructing the new URL. That feature uses the path information which is already present in the annotations of our resource class. The `Response` method is used to specify the actual HTTP response using a builder pattern approach. JAX-RS notices that the return type of our method is now a response specification and will respond to the client appropriately. By this approach, we have full control and flexibility as to what the response to the client looks like.

As you can see, these methods are the entry point to our business use cases. We inject the `UserStore` boundary which in our case is implemented as EJB, providing the logic to return the list of users and creating new users, respectively.

JAX-RS provides a productive and straightforward way to expose business functionality with RESTful web services. Developers don't have to write any low-level HTTP *plumbing* if the default behavior is sufficient.

## Mapping HTTP content types

With the same mindset of giving developers as much productivity as possible, Java EE includes standards to transparently map POJOs to JSON or XML. The example you saw with JAX-RS implicitly used JSON-B to map our `User` types to JSON objects and arrays, respectively.

This again uses the principle of convention over configuration. If nothing is else specified JSON-B assumes to map the POJO properties directly as JSON object key-value pairs. The user's *id* was present in the JSON output as well.

The same holds true for the **Java Architecture for XML Binding (JAXB)** and its XML
binding, which was included in Java EE much earlier than JSON-B. Both standards support
a declarative configuration approach using annotations that are placed on the mapped Java
types. If we're about to change the JSON representation of the type, we annotate the
corresponding fields:

```
import javax.json.bind.annotation.JsonbProperty;
import javax.json.bind.annotation.JsonbTransient;

public class User {

    @JsonbTransient
    private long id;

    @JsonbProperty("username")
    private String name;

    ...
}
```

If we want to implement more sophisticated resource mapping, such as in the Hypermedia
book examples shown before, we can do so using the declarative mapping approach. For
instance, to map the links into the books resource, we can use a map containing links and
link relations:

```
public class Book {

    @JsonbTransient
    private long id;

    private String name;
    private String author;
    private String isbn;

    @JsonbProperty("_links")
    private Map<String, URI> links;

    ...
}
```

These links are set in the JAX-RS resource appropriately:

```
@Path("books")
@Produces(MediaType.APPLICATION_JSON)
public class BooksResource {

    @Inject
```

```
    BookStore bookStore;

    @Context
    UriInfo uriInfo;

    @GET
    public List<Book> getBooks() {
        List<Book> books = bookStore.getBooks();
        books.forEach(this::addLinks);
        return books;
    }

    @GET
    @Path("{id}")
    public Book getBook(@PathParam("id") long id) {
        Book book = bookStore.getBook(id);
        addLinks(book);
        return book;
    }

    private void addLinks(Book book) {
        URI selfUri = uriInfo.getBaseUriBuilder()
                .path(BooksResource.class)
                .path(BooksResource.class, "getBook")
                .build(book.getId());

        book.getLinks().put("self", selfUri);
        // other links
    }
}
```

The output of the list of books will look similar to the following:

```
[
    {
        "name": "Java",
        "author": "Duke",
        "isbn": "123-2-34-456789-0",
        "_links": {
            "self": "https://api.example.com/books/12345",
            "author": "https://api.example.com/authors/2345",
            "related-books": "https://api.example.com/books/12345/related"
        }
    },
    ...
]
```

Using this approach, we can now programmatically introduce links with relations that are used and being followed within the client. However, using a Hypermedia approach pretty quickly reaches the point where a declarative mapping introduces too much overhead on the model. The map of links and relations already is not part of the business domain, but a technical necessity and should therefore be questioned. We could introduce transfer object types that separate the technical mapping from the domain model. But this would certainly introduce a lot of duplication and clutter our project with a number of classes that serve no value to the business.

Another challenge to be faced is the flexibility that Hypermedia requires. Even for simpler examples that make use of Hypermedia controls, we want to specify and include links and actions depending on the current state of the system. It's in the nature of Hypermedia to control the flow of clients and direct them to certain resources. For example, a client response should only include the action to place an order if a book is in stock or certain credit is on their account. This requires the response mapping to be changeable on demand. Since a declarative mapping can't be changed easily at runtime, we would need a more flexible approach.

Since Java EE 7, there is the **Java API for JSON Processing (JSON-P)** standard which provides programmatic mapping of JSON structures in a builder pattern-like fashion. We can simply invoke the builder types `JsonObjectBuilder` or `JsonArrayBuilder` to create arbitrary complex structures:

```java
import javax.json.Json;
import javax.json.JsonObject;
...

JsonObject object = Json.createObjectBuilder()
    .add("hello", Json.createArrayBuilder()
        .add("hello")
        .build())
    .add("key", "value")
    .build();
```

The resulting JSON object looks as follows:

```json
{
    "hello": [
        "hello"
    ],
    "key": "value"
}
```

Especially in situations where we need a lot of flexibility such as in Hypermedia this approach is quite helpful. The JSON-P standard, as well as JSON-B or JAXB, seamlessly integrates with JAX-RS. JAX-RS resource methods that return JSON-P types, such as `JsonObject`, will automatically return the JSON content type together with the corresponding response. No further configuration is required. Let's have a look how the example containing resource links is implemented using JSON-P.

```java
import javax.json.JsonArray;
import javax.json.stream.JsonCollectors;

@Path("books")
public class BooksResource {

    @Inject
    BookStore bookStore;

    @Context
    UriInfo uriInfo;

    @GET
    public JsonArray getBooks() {
        return bookStore.getBooks().stream()
                .map(this::buildBookJson)
                .collect(JsonCollectors.toJsonArray());
    }

    @GET
    @Path("{id}")
    public JsonObject getBook(@PathParam("id") long id) {
        Book book = bookStore.getBook(id);
        return buildBookJson(book);
    }

    private JsonObject buildBookJson(Book book) {
        URI selfUri = uriInfo.getBaseUriBuilder()
                .path(BooksResource.class)
                .path(BooksResource.class, "getBook")
                .build(book.getId());

        URI authorUri = ...

        return Json.createObjectBuilder()
                .add("name", book.getName())
                .add("author", book.getName())
                .add("isbn", book.getName())
                .add("_links", Json.createObjectBuilder()
                        .add("self", selfUri.toString())
```

```
                    .add("author", authorUri.toString())))
            .build();
    }
}
```

The JSON-P objects are created dynamically using a builder pattern approach. We have full flexibility over the desired output. This approach of using JSON-P is also advisable if a communication needs a representation of an entity different to the current model. In the past, projects always introduced transfer objects or DTOs for this purpose. Here the JSON-P objects are in fact transfer objects. By using this approach, we eliminate the need for another class that also duplicates the majority of structures of the model entity.

However, there is also some duplication in this example. The property names of the resulting JSON objects are now provided by strings. To refactor that example a little bit, we would introduce a single point of responsibility, such as a managed bean responsible for creating the JSON-P objects from the model entities.

This bean, for example `EntityBuilder`, would be injected in this and other JAX-RS resource classes. Then the duplication is still existent, but encapsulated in that single point of responsibility and reused from multiple resource classes. The following code shows an example `EntityBuilder` for books and potentially other objects to be mapped to JSON.

```
public class EntityBuilder {

    public JsonObject buildForBook(Book book, URI selfUri) {
        return Json.createObjectBuilder()
                ...
    }
}
```

If the representation to some endpoint or external system differs from our model, we won't be able to fully avoid duplication without other downsides. By using this approach, we decouple the mapping logic from the model and have full flexibility. The mapping of the POJO properties happens in the builder pattern invocations. Compared to introducing separate transfer object classes and mapping them in another functionality, this results in less obfuscation and ultimately less code.

Let's take up on the Hypermedia example using the *add-to-cart* Siren actions again. This example gave an idea of the potential content of Hypermedia responses. For responses like these, the output needs to be dynamic and flexible, depending on the application's state. Now we can imagine the flexibility and strength of a programmatic mapping approach such as JSON-P. This output is not really feasible using declarative POJO mapping, which would introduce a quite complex graph of objects. In Java EE, it is advisable to either use JSON-P in a single responsibility or a third-party dependency for the desired content type.

For mapping Java objects into JSON or XML payloads, JAXB, JSON-B, and JSON-P offers seamless integration into other Java EE standards, such as JAX-RS. Besides the integration into JAX-RS that we just saw we can also integrate CDI injection; this interoperability holds true as for all modern Java EE standards.

JSON-B type adapters enable to map custom Java types that are unknown to JSON-B. They transform custom Java types into known and mappable types. A typical example is serializing references to objects as identifiers:

```
import javax.json.bind.annotation.JsonbTypeAdapter;

public class Employee {

    @JsonbTransient
    private long id;
    private String name;
    private String email;

    @JsonbTypeAdapter(value = OrganizationTypeAdapter.class)
    private Organization organization;

    ...
}
```

The type adapter specified on the `organization` field is used to represent the reference as the organization's ID. To resolve that reference, we need to look up valid organizations. This functionality can be simply injected into the JSON-B type adapter:

```
import javax.json.bind.adapter.JsonbAdapter;

public class OrganizationTypeAdapter implements JsonbAdapter<Organization,
String> {

    @Inject
    OrganizationStore organizationStore;

    @Override
    public String adaptToJson(Organization organization) {
        return String.valueOf(organization.getId());
    }

    @Override
    public Organization adaptFromJson(String string) {
        long id = Long.parseLong(string);
        Organization organization = organizationStore.getOrganization(id);

        if (organization == null)
```

```
            throw new IllegalArgumentException("Could not find organization
    for ID " + string);

        return organization;
    }
}
```

This example already shows the benefit of having several standards that work well with each other. Developers can simply use and integrate the functionalities without spending time on configuration and *plumbing*.

## Validating requests

JAX-RS offers an integration of HTTP endpoints into our system. This includes mapping of requests and responses into Java types of our application. However, the client requests need to be validated in order to prevent misuse of the system.

The **Bean Validation** standard provides validation of all kind of sorts. The idea is to declare validation constraints, such as *this field must not be null*, *this integer must not be negative* or *this salary raise must align with the company policies*, to Java types and properties. The standard already ships the typically required technically motivated constraints. Custom constraints, especially those that are motivated by the business functionality and validation, can be added as well. This becomes interesting not only from a technical, but a domain perspective. Validation logic that is motivated by the domain can be implemented using this standard.

The validation is activated by annotating method parameters, return types, or properties with @Valid. Whereas validation can be applied in many points in the application, it is particularly important to endpoints. Annotating a JAX-RS resource method parameter with @Valid will validate the request body or parameter, respectively. If the validation fails, JAX-RS automatically responds to the HTTP request with a status code indicating a client error.

The following demonstrates the integration of a user validation:

```
import javax.validation.Valid;
import javax.validation.constraints.NotNull;

@Path("users")
@Produces(MediaType.APPLICATION_JSON)
@Consumes(MediaType.APPLICATION_JSON)
public class UsersResource {

    ...
```

```
        @POST
        public Response createUser(@Valid @NotNull User user) {
            ...
        }
    }
```

The user type is annotated with validation constraints:

```
    import javax.validation.constraints.Email;
    import javax.validation.constraints.NotBlank;

    public class User {

        @JsonbTransient
        private long id;

        @NotBlank
        private String name;

        @Email
        private String email;

        ...
    }
```

The annotations placed on the JAX-RS method tell the implementation to validate the request body as soon as a client request arrives. The request body must be available, not `null`, and valid following the configuration of the user type. The user's name property is constrained to not be blank; that is, it should not be `null` or not just containing whitespace, respectively. The user's email property has to comply with a valid email address format. These constraints are enforced when validating a user object.

Internally, a `Validator` included in Bean Validation validates the objects. The validator will throw `ConstraintViolationExceptions` if the validation fails. This validator functionality can also be obtained by dependency injection and called programmatically. JAX-RS automatically calls the validator and sends an appropriate response to the client if the validation fails.

This example would fail on illegal HTTP POST invocations to the `/users/` resource, such as providing user representations without a name. This results in `400 Bad Request` status codes, the JAX-RS default behavior for failed client validations.

If the clients need more information about why a request was declined, the default behavior can be extended. The violation exceptions which are thrown by the validator can be mapped to HTTP responses with the JAX-RS exception mapper functionality. Exception mappers handle exceptions that are thrown from JAX-RS resource methods to appropriate client responses. The following demonstrates an example of such an `ExceptionMapper` for `ConstraintViolationExceptions`:

```java
import javax.validation.ConstraintViolationException;
import javax.ws.rs.ext.ExceptionMapper;
import javax.ws.rs.ext.Provider;

@Provider
public class ValidationExceptionMapper implements
ExceptionMapper<ConstraintViolationException> {

    @Override
    public Response toResponse(ConstraintViolationException exception) {
        Response.ResponseBuilder builder =
Response.status(Response.Status.BAD_REQUEST);

        exception.getConstraintViolations()
                .forEach(v -> {
                    builder.header("Error-Description", ...);
                });
        return builder.build();
    }
}
```

Exception mappers are providers for the JAX-RS runtime. Providers are either configured programmatically in the JAX-RS base application class or, as shown here, in a declarative way using the `@Provider` annotation. The JAX-RS runtime will scan the classes for providers and apply them automatically.

The exception mapper is registered for the given exception type and sub-types. All the constraint violation exceptions thrown by a JAX-RS resource method here are mapped to a client response including a basic description of which fields caused the validation to fail. The violation messages are a functionality of Bean Validation providing human readable, global messages.

If the built-in validation constraints are not sufficient for the validation, custom validation constraints can be used. This is especially required for validation rules that are specific to the domain. For example, usernames could need more sophisticated validation based on the current state of the system. In this example, the usernames must not be taken when creating new users. Other constraints on the format or allowed characters could be set as well, obviously:

```
public class User {

    @JsonbTransient
    private long id;

    @NotBlank
    @UserNameNotTaken
    private String name;

    @Email
    private String email;
    ...
}
```

The `@UserNameNotTaken` annotation is a custom validation constraint defined by our application. Validation constraints delegate to a constraint validator, the actual class that performs the validation. Constraint validators have access to the annotated object, such as the class or field in this case. The custom functionality checks whether the provided object is valid. The validation method can use the `ConstraintValidatorContext` to control custom violations including messages and further information.

The following shows the custom constraint definition:

```
import javax.validation.Constraint;
import javax.validation.Payload;

@Constraint(validatedBy = UserNameNotTakenValidator.class)
@Documented
@Retention(RUNTIME)
@Target({METHOD, FIELD, ANNOTATION_TYPE, CONSTRUCTOR, PARAMETER, TYPE_USE})
public @interface UserNameNotTaken {

    String message() default "";

    Class<?>[] groups() default {};
    Class<? extends Payload>[] payload() default {};
}
```

Our constraint is validated by the `UserNameNotTakenValidator` class:

```
import javax.validation.ConstraintValidator;
import javax.validation.ConstraintValidatorContext;

public class UserNameNotTakenValidator implements
ConstraintValidator<UserNameNotTaken, String> {

    @Inject
    UserStore userStore;

    public void initialize(UserNameNotTaken constraint) {
        // nothing to do
    }

    public boolean isValid(String string, ConstraintValidatorContext
context) {
        return !userStore.isNameTaken(string);
    }
}
```

As with other standards, constraint validators can use dependency injection to use managed beans. This is very often required for custom validation logic that makes calls to controls. In this example, the validator injects the `UserStore`. Once again, we can reuse different standards within the Java EE umbrella.

Custom validation constraints are very often motivated by the business domain. It can make sense to encapsulate complex, composed validation logic into such custom constraints. When applied, this approach also leverages the single responsibility principle, separating the validation logic into a single validator rather than spreading them in atomic constraints.

Bean Validation offers more complex functionality for scenarios where different ways of validation are required for the same types. Therefore, the concept of groups is used to group certain constraints together into groups which can possibly be validated individually. For more information on this, I refer the reader to the Bean Validation specification.

As shown previously, HTTP JSON payloads can also be mapped in JAX-RS using the JSON-P standard. This is also true for HTTP request bodies. The request bodies parameters can be provided as JSON-P types containing JSON structures that are read dynamically. As well as for response bodies, it makes sense to represent request bodies using JSON-P types if the object structure differs from the model types or needs more flexibility, respectively. For this scenario, validation of the provided objects is even more important, since the JSON-P structures can be arbitrary. To rely on certain JSON properties being existent on the request object, these objects are validated using a custom validation constraint.

Since JSON-P objects are built programmatically and there are no pre-defined types, programmers have no way of annotating fields in the same way as for Java types. Therefore, custom validation constraints are used on the request body parameters that are bound to a custom validator. The custom constraints define the structure of a valid JSON object for the specific request bodies. The following code shows the integration of a validated JSON-P type in a JAX-RS resource method:

```
@Path("users")
@Produces(MediaType.APPLICATION_JSON)
@Consumes(MediaType.APPLICATION_JSON)
public class UsersResource {

    ...

    @POST
    public Response createUser(@Valid @ValidUser JsonObject json) {

        User user = readUser(json);
        long id = userStore.create(user);
        ...
    }

    private User readUser(JsonObject object) {
        ...
    }
}
```

The custom validation constraint `ValidUser` references the used constraint validator. Since the structure of the provided JSON-P objects is arbitrary, the validator has to check for the presence and type of properties:

```
@Constraint(validatedBy = ValidUserValidator.class)
@Documented
@Retention(RUNTIME)
@Target({METHOD, FIELD, ANNOTATION_TYPE, CONSTRUCTOR, PARAMETER, TYPE_USE})
public @interface ValidUser {
```

```
    String message() default "";

    Class<?>[] groups() default {};

    Class<? extends Payload>[] payload() default {};
}
```

The custom constraint validator is applicable on JSON-P types, as well:

```
public class ValidUserValidator implements ConstraintValidator<ValidUser,
JsonObject> {

    public void initialize(ValidUser constraint) {
        // nothing to do
    }

    public boolean isValid(JsonObject json, ConstraintValidatorContext
context) {
        ...
    }
}
```

After the provided JSON-P object has been validated, the defined properties can safely be extracted. This example showcases how the flexible, programmatic types are integrated and validated in JAX-RS methods. The resource class extracts the request body into a domain entity type and uses the boundary to invoke the business use case.

## Mapping errors

As we have seen in the last examples, JAX-RS provides the ability to map exceptions to custom responses. This is a helpful functionality to implement transparent custom error handling without impacting the production code workflow.

A common issue when dealing with EJBs is that any thrown exception will be wrapped in an EJBException when accessed by any non-EJB context; for example, a request scoped JAX-RS resource. This makes exception handling quite cumbersome, as the EJBException would have to be unwrapped to inspect the cause.

By annotating custom exception types with @ApplicationException, the cause will not be wrapped:

```
import javax.ejb.ApplicationException;

@ApplicationException
public class GreetingException extends RuntimeException {
```

```
        public GreetingException(String message) {
            super(message);
        }
    }
```

Calling an EJB that throws the `GreetingException` will not result in a wrapped `EJBException` and produce the exception type directly. The application can then define a JAX-RS exception mapper for the actual `GreetingException` type, similar to the one mapping constraint violations.

Specifying `@ApplicationException(rollback = true)` will furthermore cause the container to roll back an active transaction when the exception occurs.

## Accessing external systems

We have now seen how our business domain is accessed from the outside via HTTP.

In order to perform the business logic, the majority of enterprise applications need to access other external systems as well. External systems don't include databases that are owned by our application. Usually external systems are external to the application's domain. They reside in another bounded context.

In order to access external HTTP services, we integrate a client component into our project, usually as a separate control. This control class encapsulates the functionality required to communicate with the external system. It is advisable to carefully construct the interface and not to mix domain concerns with communication implementation details. These details include potential payload mappings, the communication protocol, HTTP information if HTTP is being used, and any other aspect not relevant to the core domain.

JAX-RS ships with a sophisticated client feature that accesses HTTP services in a productive way. It provides the same type mapping functionalities as it does for resource classes. The following code represents a control that accesses an external system to order coffee beans:

```
import javax.annotation.PostConstruct;
import javax.annotation.PreDestroy;
import javax.enterprise.context.ApplicationScoped;
import javax.ws.rs.client.*;
import java.util.concurrent.TimeUnit;

@ApplicationScoped
public class CoffeePurchaser {

    private Client client;
    private WebTarget target;
```

```
        @PostConstruct
        private void initClient() {
            client = ClientBuilder.newClient();
            target =
    client.target("http://coffee.example.com/beans/purchases/");
        }

        public OrderId purchaseBeans(BeanType type) {
            // construct purchase payload from type
            Purchase purchase = ...

            BeanOrder beanOrder = target
                    .request(MediaType.APPLICATION_JSON_TYPE)
                    .post(Entity.json(purchase))
                    .readEntity(BeanOrder.class);

            return beanOrder.getId();
        }

        @PreDestroy
        public void closeClient() {
            client.close();
        }
    }
```

The JAX-RS client is built and configured by the client builder and uses web targets to access URLs. These targets can be modified using a URI builder functionality, similar to the one in the JAX-RS resources. Targets are used to build new invocations that represent the actual HTTP invocations. The invocations can be configured in regard to HTTP information, such as content types, headers, as well as specifics of mapped Java types.

In this example, the target that points to the external URL builds a new request for the JSON content type with a HTTP POST method. The returned JSON structure is expected to be mappable to a `BeanOrder` object. The client performs further logic to extract the necessary information.

The client instance will be closed properly on container shutdown in the @PreDestroy-method to prevent resource leaks.

## Stability when consuming HTTP

This example, however, lacks some aspects in regard to resilience. Calling this client control without further consideration could lead to unwanted behavior.

The client request blocks until the HTTP invocation either returned successfully or the connection timed-out. The HTTP connection timeout configuration depends on the JAX-RS implementation, which is set to infinite blocking in some technologies. For resilient clients, this is obviously not acceptable. A connection could wait forever, blocking the thread and, in a worst-case scenario, could block the whole application if all available threads are stuck at that location, waiting for their individual HTTP connection to finish. To prevent this scenario, we configure the client to use custom connection timeouts.

The timeout values depend on the application, especially the network configuration to the external system. It varies what are reasonable values for HTTP timeouts. To get sensible timeout values, it is advisable to gather statistics about the latency to the external system. For systems where load and network latency vary a lot, for example e-commerce systems with selective high utilization during certain seasons, the nature of variations should be considered.

The HTTP connect timeout is the maximum time allowed until a connection has been established. Its value should be small. The HTTP read timeout specifies how long to wait to read data. Its value depends on the nature of the external service being consumed. Following the gathered statistics, a good starting point for configuring the read timeout is to calculate the mean response times plus three times the standard deviation. We will cover the topic of performance and service backpressure in Chapter 9, *Monitoring, Performance, and Logging*.

The following shows how to configure both the HTTP connect and read timeout:

```
@ApplicationScoped
public class CoffeePurchaser {

    ...

    @PostConstruct
    private void initClient() {
        client = ClientBuilder.newBuilder()
                .connectTimeout(100, TimeUnit.MILLISECONDS)
                .readTimeout(2, TimeUnit.SECONDS)
                .build();
        target =
client.target("http://coffee.example.com/beans/purchases/");
    }

    ...
}
```

Client invocations can result in potential errors. The external service could respond with an unexpected status code, an unexpected response, or no response at all.This needs to be considered when implementing client components.

The `readResponse()` client call expects the response to be of the HTTP status code `SUCCESSFUL` family and the response body to be mappable into the given Java type from the requested content type. If something goes wrong, a `RuntimeException` is thrown. Runtime exceptions enable engineers to write code without obfuscating try-catch blocks, but also require them to be aware of the potential errors.

The client method could catch the runtime exceptions in order to prevent them from being thrown to the calling domain service. There is also another, leaner possibility using interceptors. Interceptors provide cross-cutting functionalities that are applied without being tightly coupled to the decorated functionality. For example, this client method should intentionally return `null` when the external system could not deliver a reasonable response.

The following demonstrates an interceptor that intercepts method invocations and applies this behavior on occurred exceptions. This interceptor is integrated by annotating the method of the `CoffeePurchaser` control:

```
import javax.interceptor.AroundInvoke;
import javax.interceptor.Interceptor;
import javax.interceptor.InvocationContext;

@Interceptor
public class FailureToNullInterceptor {

    @AroundInvoke
    public Object aroundInvoke(InvocationContext context) {
        try {
            return context.proceed();
        } catch (Exception e) {
            ...
            return null;
        }
    }
}
```

The `purchaseBean()` method is annotated with `@Interceptors(FailureToNullInterceptor.class)`. This activates the cross-cutting concerns for that method.

In regard to resilience, the client functionality could include further logic. If several systems are available, the client can retry failed invocations on a different system. Then, only as a last resort, the invocation would fail without a result.

In the topic, *Cross-cutting concerns*, we will see how to implement further cross-cutting concerns.

## Accessing Hypermedia REST services

HTTP web services that apply REST constraints, especially in regard to Hypermedia, need more sophisticated logic on the client side. Services direct clients to corresponding resources that need to be accessed in certain ways. Hypermedia decouples services and enables API features such as evolvability and discovery, but also require more dynamic and logic on the client side.

The Siren content type example earlier gives an impression of how service responses direct REST clients to available subsequent calls. Assume the client retrieves the response of an order and wants to follow the add-to-cart action:

```
{
    ... example as shown before
    ... properties of book resource
    "actions": [
        {
            "name": "add-to-cart",
            "title": "Add Book to cart",
            "method": "POST",
            "href": "http://api.example.com/shopping-cart",
            "type": "application/json",
            "fields": [
                { "name": "isbn", "type": "text" },
                { "name": "quantity", "type": "number" }
            ]
        }
    ],
    "links": ...
}
```

The client is only coupled to the knowledge of what business meaning the *add-to-cart* action has and how to provide the field value information for ISBN and quantity. This is certainly client domain logic that needs to be implemented. The information on how the subsequent resource, the shopping cart, is accessed, using which HTTP method, and what content type is now dynamic and not baked into the client.

In order to add a book to the shopping cart, the client will first access the book's resource. The *add-to-cart* use case is called subsequently, extracting the information of the specified Hypermedia action. The information for the required fields needs to be provided by the invocation. The client then accesses the second resource, using the information provided both by the REST service and the invocation by the control:

```java
public class BookClient {

    @Inject
    EntityMapper entityMapper;

    public Book retrieveBook(URI uri) {
        Entity book = retrieveEntity(uri);
        return entityMapper.decodeBook(uri, book.getProperties());
    }

    public void addToCart(Book book, int quantity) {
        Entity bookEntity = retrieveEntity(book.getUri());

        JsonObjectBuilder properties = Json.createObjectBuilder();
        properties.add("quantity", quantity);

        Entity entity = entityMapper.encodeBook(book);
        entity.getProperties().forEach(properties::add);

        performAction(bookEntity, "add-to-cart", properties.build());
    }

    private Entity retrieveEntity(URI uri) {
        ...
    }

    private void performAction(Entity entity, String actionName,
            JsonObject properties) {
        ...
    }
}
```

The Entity type encapsulates information of the Hypermedia entity types. The EntityMapper is responsible for mapping the content type into domain models and vice versa. In this example, all the required fields for the action result from the properties of the resource plus the provided quantity parameter. To enable a certain dynamic, all entity properties are added into a map and are provided to the performAction() method. Depending on the action specified by the server, the required fields are extracted from this map. If more fields are required, the client logic obviously has to change.

It certainly makes sense to encapsulate logic for accessing Hypermedia services as well as mapping domain models to a content types into separate delegates. Functionality for accessing REST services could also sensibly be replaced by a library.

You might notice how the URI has now leaked into the public interface of the client class. This was not accidental, but required to identify resources over several use case calls. That said, the URIs move into the business domain as general identifier of resources. Since the logic of how URLs are created from technical IDs reside on the client side, the whole URL of an entity resource becomes the *identifier*. However, when designing client controls, engineers should take care of the public interface. In particular, no information about the communication to the external system should leak into the domain. Using Hypermedia supports this approach well. All the required transport information is retrieved and used dynamically. The navigation logic that follows Hypermedia responses resides in the client control.

This example aims to give the reader an idea how a client uses Hypermedia REST services.

# Asynchronous communication and messaging

Asynchronous communication leads to looser coupling of the systems. It generally increases the overall responsiveness as well as overhead and enables scenarios where systems are not reliably available all the time. There exist many forms of how to design asynchronous communication, on a conceptual or technical level. Asynchronous communication doesn't imply that there can't be synchronous calls on a technical level. The business process can be built in an asynchronous way that models one or several synchronous invocations that are not performed or handled immediately. For example, an API can offer synchronous methods to create long-running processes that are frequently polled for updates later on.

On a technical level, asynchronous communication is usually designed in a message-oriented way implemented using message queues or the publish-subscribe pattern. Applications only directly communicate with a message queue or a broker, respectively, and messages are not directly passed to a specific receiver.

Let's have a look at the various ways to accomplish asynchronous communication.

## Asynchronous HTTP communication

The request response model of HTTP communication usually involves synchronous communication. A client requests a resource at a server and blocks until the response has been transmitted. Asynchronous communication using HTTP is therefore typically archived on a conceptual basis. The synchronous HTTP invocations can trigger long-running business processes. The external system can then either notify the caller by another mechanism later on or offer functionality for polling for updates.

For example, a sophisticated user management system offers methods to create users. Assume users need to be registered and legitimized in external systems as part of a longer-running, asynchronous business process. The application would then offer an HTTP functionality, such as `POST /users/`, which starts the process to create new users. However, invoking that use case does not guarantee that the user will be created and registered successfully. The response of that HTTP endpoint would only acknowledge the attempt to create a new user; for example, by the `202 Accepted` status code. This indicates that the request has been accepted, but has not necessarily been processed completely. The `Location` header field could be used to direct to the resource where the client can poll for updates on the partly-finished user.

On a technical level, HTTP does not only support synchronous invocations. In Sub-chapter *Server-sent events*, we will have a look at server-sent events as an example of a HTTP standard using asynchronous message-oriented communication.

## Message-oriented communication

Message-oriented communication exchanges information in asynchronously sent messages, usually implemented using message queues or the publish-subscribe pattern. It offers the advantage of decoupling systems since applications only directly communicate with the message queue or the broker, respectively. The decoupling not only affects dependencies on systems and used technology, but also the nature of communication by decoupling business processes by the asynchronous messages.

Message queues are queues where messages are sent to that are consumed later by one consumer at a time. In enterprise systems, message queues are typically realized in a **message-oriented middleware** (**MOM**). We have seen these MOM solutions quite regularly in the past with message queue systems such as ActiveMQ, RabbitMQ, or WebSphere MQ.

The publish-subscribe pattern describes consumers that subscribe to a topic and receive messages that are published to the topic. The subscribers register for the topic and receives messages that are sent by the publisher. This concept scales well for a bigger number of peers involved. Message-oriented middleware typically can be used to take advantages of both message queuing and publish-subscribe approaches.

However, as well as for asynchronous communication in general, message-oriented solutions also have certain shortcomings. The reliable delivery of messages is a first aspect to be aware of is. Producers send the messages in an asynchronous, *fire and forget* fashion. Engineers have to be aware of the defined and supported semantics of message delivery, whether a message will be received *at most once*, *at least once,* or *exactly once*. Choosing technology that supports certain delivery semantics, especially *exactly once* semantics, will have an impact on scalability and throughput. In Chapter 8, *Microservices and System Architecture* we will cover that topic in detail when discussing event-driven applications.

For Java EE applications, the **Java Message Service** (**JMS**) API can be used to integrate message-oriented middleware solutions. The JMS API supports solutions for both message queuing and publish-subscribe approaches. It only defines interfaces and is implemented with the actual message-oriented middleware solutions.

However, the JMS API does not have a high developer acceptance and, at the time of writing, is arguably not used that much in current systems. Compared to other standards, the programming model is not that straightforward and productive. Another trend in message-oriented communication is that instead of traditional MOM solutions, more lightweight solutions are gaining popularity. As of today, a lot of these message-oriented solutions are integrated using proprietary APIs. An example of such a solution is Apache Kafka, which utilizes both message queuing and the publish-subscribe model. Chapter 8, *Microservices and System Architecture* shows the integration of Apache Kafka as an example of a MOM solution into Java EE applications.

## Server-sent events

**Server-sent events** (**SSE**) is an example of an asynchronous, HTTP-based, publish-subscribe technology. It offers an easy-to-use one-way streaming communication protocol. Clients can register for a topic by requesting a HTTP resource that leaves an open connection. The server sends messages to connected clients over these active HTTP connections. Clients cannot directly communicate back, but can only open and close connections to the streaming endpoint. This lightweight solution fits use cases with broadcast updates, such as social media updates, stock prices, or news feeds.

The server pushes UTF-8 text-based data as content type `text/event-stream` to clients who previously registered for the topics. The following shows the format of the events:

```
data: This is a message

event: namedmessage
data: This message has an event name

id: 10
```

```
data: This message has an id which will be sent as
  'last event ID' if the client reconnects
```

The fact that server-sent events are based on HTTP makes them easy to integrate in existing networks or developer tools. SSE natively support event IDs and reconnects. Clients that reconnect to a streaming endpoint provide the last received event ID to continue subscribing where they left off.

JAX-RS supports server-sent events on both the server-side and client-side. SSE streaming endpoints are defined using JAX-RS resources as follows:

```java
import javax.ws.rs.DefaultValue;
import javax.ws.rs.HeaderParam;
import javax.ws.rs.InternalServerErrorException;
import javax.ws.rs.core.HttpHeaders;
import javax.ws.rs.sse.*;

@Path("events-examples")
@Singleton
public class EventsResource {

    @Context
    Sse sse;

    private SseBroadcaster sseBroadcaster;
    private int lastEventId;
    private List<String> messages = new ArrayList<>();

    @PostConstruct
    public void initSse() {
        sseBroadcaster = sse.newBroadcaster();

        sseBroadcaster.onError((o, e) -> {
            ...
        });
    }

    @GET
    @Lock(READ)
    @Produces(MediaType.SERVER_SENT_EVENTS)
    public void itemEvents(@HeaderParam(HttpHeaders.LAST_EVENT_ID_HEADER)
                           @DefaultValue("-1") int lastEventId,
                           @Context SseEventSink eventSink) {

        if (lastEventId >= 0)
            replayLastMessages(lastEventId, eventSink);

        sseBroadcaster.register(eventSink);
```

```
    }

    private void replayLastMessages(int lastEventId, SseEventSink
eventSink) {
        try {
            for (int i = lastEventId; i < messages.size(); i++) {
                eventSink.send(createEvent(messages.get(i), i + 1));
            }
        } catch (Exception e) {
            throw new InternalServerErrorException("Could not replay
messages ", e);
        }
    }

    private OutboundSseEvent createEvent(String message, int id) {
        return
sse.newEventBuilder().id(String.valueOf(id)).data(message).build();
    }

    @Lock(WRITE)
    public void onEvent(@Observes DomainEvent domainEvent) {
        String message = domainEvent.getContents();
        messages.add(message);

        OutboundSseEvent event = createEvent(message, ++lastEventId);

        sseBroadcaster.broadcast(event);
    }
}
```

The text/event-stream content type is used for Server-sent events. The registered SseEventSink instructs JAX-RS to keep the client connection open for future events sent through the broadcaster. The SSE standard defines that the Last-Event-ID header controls where the event stream will continue. In this example, the server will resend the messages that have been published while clients were disconnected.

The itemEvents() method implements the streaming registration and immediately resends missing events to that client if required. After the output is registered the client, together will all other active clients, will receive future messages that are created using Sse.

The asynchronous integration into our enterprise application happens via the observed DomainEvent. Every time a CDI event of this type is fired somewhere in the application, active SSE clients will receive a message.

JAX-RS also supports the ability to consume SSE. `SseEventSource` offers a functionality to open a connection to an SSE endpoint. It registers an event listener that is called as soon as a message arrives:

```
import java.util.function.Consumer;

public class SseClient {

    private final WebTarget target =
ClientBuilder.newClient().target("...");
    private SseEventSource eventSource;

    public void connect(Consumer<String> dataConsumer) {
        eventSource = SseEventSource.target(target).build();

        eventSource.register(
                item -> dataConsumer.accept(item.readData()),
                Throwable::printStackTrace,
                () -> System.out.println("completed"));

        eventSource.open();
    }

    public void disconnect() {
        if (eventSource != null)
            eventSource.close();
    }
}
```

After the `SseEventSource` successfully opens the connection, the current thread continues. The listener, in this case, `dataConsumer#accept`, will be called as soon as events arrive. `SseEventSource` will handle all required handling defined by the SSE standard. This includes, for example, reconnecting after connection loss and sending a `Last-Event-ID` header.

Clients also have the possibility for more sophisticated solutions with manually controlling headers and reconnects. Therefore the `SseEventInput` type is requested with the `text/event-stream` content type from a conventional web target. For more information, please refer to the JAX-RS specification.

Server-sent events offer an easy-to-use one-way streaming solution over HTTP that integrates itself well into the Java EE technology.

# WebSocket

Server-sent events compete with the more powerful **WebSocket** technology which supports bi-directional communication. WebSocket which has been standardized by the IETF is another example for message-oriented, publish-subscribe communication. It was intended to be used in browser-based applications, but can be used for any client-server exchange of messages. WebSocket usually uses the same ports as the HTTP endpoints, but with its own TCP-based protocol.

WebSocket is supported in Java EE as part of the **Java API for WebSocket**. It includes server, and client-side support.

The programming model for server-side endpoint definitions again matches the overall Java EE picture. Endpoints can be defined using a programmatic or declarative, annotation-driven approach. The latter defines annotations that are added on endpoint classes, similar to the programming model of JAX-RS resources:

```java
import javax.websocket.*;
import javax.websocket.server.ServerEndpoint;

@ServerEndpoint(value = "/chat", decoders = ChatMessageDecoder.class,
encoders = ChatMessageEncoder.class)
public class ChatServer {

    @Inject
    ChatHandler chatHandler;

    @OnOpen
    public void openSession(Session session) {
        ...
    }

    @OnMessage
    public void onMessage(ChatMessage message, Session session) {
        chatHandler.store(message);
    }

    @OnClose
    public void closeSession(Session session) {
        ...
    }
}
```

The annotated methods of the server endpoint class will be called on initiated sessions, arriving messages and closing connections, respectively. The sessions represent the conversation between two endpoints.

WebSocket endpoints can define decoders and encoders, respectively, in order to map custom Java types to binary or plain text data and vice versa. This example specifies a custom type for chat messages which is mapped using custom decoders and encoders. Similar to JAX-RS, WebSocket ships with default serialization capabilities for usual serializable Java types such as strings. The following code demonstrates an encoder for our custom domain type:

```java
import javax.websocket.EncodeException;
import javax.websocket.Encoder;
import javax.websocket.EndpointConfig;

public class ChatMessageEncoder implements Encoder.Binary<ChatMessage> {

    @Override
    public ByteBuffer encode(ChatMessage object) throws EncodeException {
        ...
    }

    ...
}
```

These types correspond to the `MessageBodyWriter` and `MessageBodyReader` types in the JAX-RS standard. The following shows the corresponding message decoder:

```java
import javax.websocket.DecodeException;
import javax.websocket.Decoder;
import javax.websocket.EndpointConfig;

public class ChatMessageDecoder implements Decoder.Binary<ChatMessage> {

    @Override
    public ChatMessage decode(ByteBuffer bytes) throws DecodeException {
        ...
    }

    ...
}
```

Client endpoints are defined similarly to server endpoints. The difference is that only WebSocket servers listen to new connection on a path.

The client functionality of the WebSocket API can not only be used in an enterprise environment, but also in Java SE applications. The same is true for JAX-RS on the client-side. Implementing a WebSocket client endpoint is left as an exercise to the reader.

WebSocket, as well as server-sent events, offers well-integrated, message-oriented technologies. What applications choose to use, of course, highly depends on the business requirements, existing environments, and the nature of the communication.

# Connecting enterprise technology

Some external enterprise systems that need to be integrated from an application don't offer standard interfaces or Java APIs. Legacy systems as well as other systems being used within the organization may fall under this category. The **Java EE Connector Architecture (JCA)** API can integrate these so-called **Enterprise Information Systems (EIS)** into Java EE applications. Examples of EISs include transaction processing systems, messaging systems, or proprietary databases.

JCA resource adapters are deployable EE components that integrate information systems into the application. They include contracts such as connections, transactions, security, or life cycle management. The information system can be integrated better into the application compared to other connection technologies. Resource adapters are packaged as **Resource Adapter Archives (RAR)** and can be accessed within the application using the functionality of the `javax.resource` package and its sub-packages. Some EIS vendors provide resource adapters for their systems. For developing and deploying resource adapters, refer to the JCA specification.

JCA offers a variety of integration possibilities for external information systems. However, the standard is not widely used and has not a high acceptance by enterprise engineers. Developing resource adapters is quite cumbersome, the JCA API is not well known among developers, and companies usually choose to integrate systems in other ways. In fact, it should be considered whether the effort of writing resource adapters is preferred over integrating information systems using other integration technology. Other solutions include integration frameworks such as Apache Camel or Mule ESB.

# Database systems

The majority of enterprise applications use database systems as their persistence. Databases are at the core of the enterprise system, containing the application's data. As of today, data is already one the most important commodities. Companies spend a lot of time and effort gathering, securing, and using data.

There are several ways in which a state is represented in enterprise systems; however, relational databases are still the most popular. The concepts and usages are well understood and well integrated in enterprise technology.

# Integrating RDBMS systems

The **Java Persistence API (JPA)** is used to integrate relational database systems into enterprise applications. Compared to outdated approaches of the J2EE era, JPA integrates well with domain models built after the concepts of Domain-Driven Design. Persisting entities does not introduce much overhead and does not set many constraints on the model. This enables constructing the domain model first, focusing on business aspects, and integrating the persistence layer afterwards.

Persistence is integrated into the domain as a necessary part of handling the business use case. Depending on the complexity of use cases, the persistence functionality is invoked either in dedicated controls or directly in the boundary. Domain-Driven Design defines the concept of repositories which, as mentioned before, matches the responsibilities of JPA's entity manager well. The entity manager is used to obtain, manage, and persist entities and to perform queries. Its interface was abstracted with the intention to be used in a general way.

In the J2EE era, the **data access object (DAO)** pattern was used heavily. The motivation behind this pattern was to abstract and encapsulate functionality to access data. This includes the type of the accessed storage system, such as RDBMSs, object-oriented databases, LDAP systems, or files. Whereas the reasoning certainly makes sense, following the pattern in times of Java EE is not required for the majority of use cases.

Most enterprise applications use relational databases that support both SQL and JDBC. JPA already abstracts RDBMS systems so that engineers usually don't deal with vendor specifics. Changing the nature of the used storage system to something other than a RDBMS will impact the application's code anyway. Mapping domain entity types into storage does not require the use of transfer objects anymore, since JPA integrates well into domain models. Directly mapping domain entity types is a productive approach to integrate persistence without much overhead. For straightforward use cases, such as persisting and retrieving entities, a DAO approach is therefore not required. However, for complex database queries involved, it does make sense to encapsulate that functionality into separate controls. These repositories then contain the whole persistence for the specific entity types. It is advisable though to start with a straightforward approach and only refactor the persistence into a single point of responsibility if the complexity increases.

Boundaries or controls, respectively, obtain an entity manager to manage the persistence of entities. The following shows how to integrate an entity manager into a boundary:

```
import javax.persistence.EntityManager;
import javax.persistence.PersistenceContext;

@Stateless
public class PersonAdministration {
```

```
        @PersistenceContext
        EntityManager entityManager;

        public void createPerson(Person person) {
            entityManager.persist(person);
        }

        public void updateAddress(long personId, Address newAddress) {
            Person person = entityManager.find(Person.class, personId);

            if (person == null)
                throw new IllegalArgumentException("Could not find person with
ID " + personId);

            person.setAddress(newAddress);
        }
    }
```

The `persist()` operation on creating new persons makes the person a managed entity. It will be added into the database once the transaction commits and can be obtained later using its assigned ID. The `updateAddress()` method showcases this. A person entity is retrieved using its ID into a managed entity. All changes in the entity; for example, changing its address will be synchronized into the database at transaction commit time.

## Mapping domain models

As mentioned before, entities, aggregates, and value objects are integrated with JPA without introducing many constraints on the model. Entities as well as aggregates, are represented as JPA entities:

```
import javax.persistence.*;

@Entity
@Table(name = "persons")
public class Person {

    @Id
    @GeneratedValue
    private long id;

    @Basic(optional = false)
    private String name;

    @Embedded
    private Address address;
```

```
    ...
}

@Embeddable
public class Address {

    @Basic(optional = false)
    private String streetName;

    @Basic(optional = false)
    private String postalCode;

    @Basic(optional = false)
    private String city;


    ...
}
```

The person type is an entity. It needs to be identifiable using an ID that will be the primary key in the `persons` table. Every property is mapped into the database in a certain way, depending on the nature of the type and relation. The person's name is a simple text-based column.

The address is a value object that is not identifiable. From a domain perspective, it does not matter *which* address we refer to, as long as the values match. Therefore the address is not an entity and thus is not mapped into JPA as such. Value objects can be implemented via JPA embeddable types. The properties of these types will be mapped to additional columns in the table of the entity that refers to them. Since the person entity includes a specific address value, the address properties will be part of the persons table.

Root aggregates that consist of several entities can be realized by configuring the relations to be mapped in appropriate database columns and tables, respectively. For example, a car consists of an engine, one or more seats, a chassis, and many other parts. Some of them are entities that potentially can be identified and accessed as individual objects. The car manufacturer can identify the whole car or just the engine and repair or replace it accordingly. The database mapping can be placed on top of this existing domain model as well.

The following code snippets show the car domain entity, including JPA mapping:

```
import javax.persistence.CascadeType;
import javax.persistence.OneToMany;
import javax.persistence.OneToOne;

@Entity
@Table(name = "cars")
```

```
public class Car {

    @Id
    @GeneratedValue
    private long id;

    @OneToOne(optional = false, cascade = CascadeType.ALL)
    private Engine engine;

    @OneToMany(cascade = CascadeType.ALL)
    private Set<Seat> seats = new HashSet<>();

    ...
}
```

The seats are included in a collection. The `HashSet` is instantiated for new `Car` instances; Java collections that are `null` should be avoided.

The engine represents another entity in our domain:

```
import javax.persistence.EnumType;
import javax.persistence.Enumerated;

@Entity
@Table(name = "engines")
public class Engine {

    @Id
    @GeneratedValue
    private long id;

    @Basic(optional = false)
    @Enumerated(EnumType.STRING)
    private EngineType type;

    private double ccm;

    ...
}
```

The car seats represent entities as well, identifiable by their ID:

```
@Entity
@Table(name = "seats")
public class Seat {

    @Id
    @GeneratedValue
```

```
    private long id;

    @Basic(optional = false)
    @Enumerated(EnumType.STRING)
    private SeatMaterial material;

    @Basic(optional = false)
    @Enumerated(EnumType.STRING)
    private SeatShape shape;

    ...
}
```

All entities, referenced from other entities or standalone, need to be managed in the persistence context. If the engine of a car is replaced by a new entity, this needs to be persisted separately as well. The persist operations are either called explicitly on the individual entities or cascaded from object hierarchies. The cascades are specified on the entity relations. The following code shows the two approaches of persisting a new car engine from a service:

```
public void replaceEngine(long carIdentifier, Engine engine) {
    Car car = entityManager.find(Car.class, carIdentifier);
    car.replaceEngine(engine);

    // car is already managed, engine needs to be persisted
    entityManager.persist(engine);
}
```

After loading the car from its identifier, it is a managed entity. The engine still needs to be persisted. The first approach persists the engine explicitly in the service.

The second approach cascades a merge operation, that also handles new entities, from the car aggregate:

```
public void replaceEngine(long carIdentifier, Engine engine) {
    Car car = entityManager.find(Car.class, carIdentifier);
    car.replaceEngine(engine);

    // merge operation is applied on the car and all cascading relations
    entityManager.merge(car);
}
```

It is highly advisable to apply the latter approach. Aggregate roots are responsible to maintain an integer and consistent state of the overall state. The integrity is achieved more reliably when all operations are initiated and cascaded from the root entity.

## Integrating database systems

An entity manager manages persistent entities within a persistence context. It uses a single persistence unit that corresponds to a database instance. Persistence units include all managed entities, entity managers, and mapping configurations. If only one database instance is accessed then the entity manager can be obtained directly, as shown in the previous example. The persistence context annotation then refers to the sole persistence unit.

Persistence units are specified in the `persistence.xml` descriptor file, which resides under the `META-INF` directory. This is one of the few cases in modern Java EE where XML-based configuration is used. The persistence descriptor defines the persistence unit and optional configuration. The datasource is referenced only by its JNDI name in order to separate the configuration for accessing the database instance from the application. The actual configuration of the datasource is specified in the application server. If the application server contains only one application that uses a single database, developers can use the application server's default datasource. In that case, the datasource name can be omitted.

The following snippet shows an example `persistence.xml` file showing a single persistence unit using the default datasource:

```
<?xml version="1.0" encoding="UTF-8"?>
<persistence version="2.2"
xmlns="http://xmlns.jcp.org/xml/ns/persistence"
        xmlns:xsi="http://www.w3.org/2001/XMLSchema-instance"
        xsi:schemaLocation="http://xmlns.jcp.org/xml/ns/persistence
        http://xmlns.jcp.org/xml/ns/persistence/persistence_2_2.xsd">
    <persistence-unit name="vehicle" transaction-type="JTA">
    </persistence-unit>
</persistence>
```

This example is already sufficient for a majority of enterprise applications.

The next snippet demonstrates a `persistence.xml` file containing several persistence unit definitions for multiple datasources:

```
<?xml version="1.0" encoding="UTF-8"?>
<persistence version="2.2" xmlns="http://xmlns.jcp.org/xml/ns/persistence"
        xmlns:xsi="http://www.w3.org/2001/XMLSchema-instance"
        xsi:schemaLocation="http://xmlns.jcp.org/xml/ns/persistence
        http://xmlns.jcp.org/xml/ns/persistence/persistence_2_2.xsd">

    <persistence-unit name="vehicle" transaction-type="JTA">
        <jta-data-source>jdbc/VehicleDB</jta-data-source>
    </persistence-unit>
    <persistence-unit name="order" transaction-type="JTA">
```

```
        <jta-data-source>jdbc/OrderDB</jta-data-source>
    </persistence-unit>
</persistence>
```

Injecting entity managers need to reference the desired persistence unit by its name. Entity managers always correspond to a single persistence context that uses a single persistence unit. The following `CarManagement` definition shows the previous example in an environment of several persistence units:

```
@Stateless
public class CarManagement {

    @PersistenceContext(unitName = "vehicle")
    EntityManager entityManager;

    public void replaceEngine(long carIdentifier, Engine engine) {
        Car car = entityManager.find(Car.class, carIdentifier);
        car.replaceEngine(engine);

        // merge operation is applied on the car and all cascading
relations
        entityManager.merge(car);
    }
}
```

Optionally, injection of specific entity managers can be simplified by using CDI producer fields. By explicitly emitting entity managers using custom qualifiers, injection can be implemented in a typesafe way:

```
public class EntityManagerExposer {

    @Produces
    @VehicleDB
    @PersistenceContext(unitName = "vehicle")
    private EntityManager vehicleEntityManager;

    @Produces
    @OrderDB
    @PersistenceContext(unitName = "order")
    private EntityManager orderEntityManager;

}
```

The emitted entity managers can be injected, now using `@Inject` and the typesafe qualifier:

```
public class CarManagement {

    @Inject
    @VehicleDB
    EntityManager entityManager;

    ...
}
```

This approach can simplify usage in environments where different entity managers are injected in many locations.

There are also other possible approaches to map domain models to databases. Database mapping can also be defined in XML files. However, past approaches in J2EE, have shown that declarative configuration using annotations allows a more productive usage. Annotating domain models also provides a better overview.

## Transactions

Persistence operations need to be performed in a transaction context. Managed entities that are modified are synchronized into the datasource at transaction commit time. Therefore, a transaction spans the modifying action, and typically the whole business use case.

If the boundary is implemented as EJB, a transaction is active during the business method execution by default. This matches the typical scenarios for JPA persistence being involved in the application.

The same behavior is realized with CDI managed beans that annotate their methods with `@Transactional`. Transactional boundaries specify a specific behavior once the business method is entered. By default, this behavior defines that a transaction is REQUIRED; that is, a transaction is either created or reused if the calling context is already executed within an active transaction.

REQUIRES_NEW behavior will always start a new transaction that is executed individually and resumes a potential previous transaction once the method and the new transaction has completed. This is useful for longer-running business processes that handle a great amount of data that can be processed in several, individual transactions.

Other transaction behavior is possible as well, such as enforcing an already active transaction or not supporting transactions at all. This is configured by annotating business methods with `@Transactional`. EJBs implicitly define REQUIRED transactions.

RDBMS systems integrate well into Java EE applications. Following convention over configuration, the typical use cases are implemented in a productive way.

## Relational databases versus NoSQL

In the past years, a lot has happened in database technology, especially with regard to distribution. Traditional relational databases are, however, still the most used choice as of today. Their most significant characteristics are the table-based data schemas and the transactional behavior.

**NoSQL** (**non SQL** or **not only SQL**) database systems provide data in other forms than relational tables. These forms include document stores, key-value stores, column-oriented stores, and graph databases. Most of them compromise consistency in favor of availability, scalability, and network partition tolerance. The idea behind NoSQL not making use of full support of relational table structures, **ACID** transactions (**Atomicity, Consistency, Isolation, Durability**), and foreign keys as well as table joins, was to support horizontal scalability. This goes back to the well-known CAP theorem. The **CAP** theorem (**Consistency, Availability, Partition tolerance**) claims that it is impossible for distributed datastores to guarantee at most two of the three specified constraints. Since distributed networks do not operate reliably (partition tolerance), systems can basically choose whether they want to guarantee consistency or horizontal scalability. Most NoSQL databases choose scalability over consistency. This fact needs to be considered when choosing a datastore technology.

The reason behind NoSQL systems lays in the shortcomings of relational databases. The biggest issue is that relational databases supporting ACID don't scale well horizontally. Database systems are at the core of the enterprise system, usually accessed by multiple application servers. Data that needs to be updated consistently needs to be synchronized in a central place. This synchronization happens in the technical transaction of the business use case. Database systems that are replicated and should both retain consistency would need to maintain distributed transactions in-between themselves. However, distributed transactions do not scale and arguably do not reliably work in every solution.

Still, relational database systems scale well enough for the majority of enterprise applications. If horizontal scalability becomes an issue so that a centralized database is not an option anymore, one solution is to split up persistence using approaches such as event-driven architectures. We will cover that topic in detail in Chapter 8, *Microservices and System Architecture*.

NoSQL databases also have some shortcomings, especially with regard to transactional behavior. It highly depends on the business requirements of the application as to whether data needs to be persistent in a transactional approach. Experience shows that in almost all enterprise systems at least some parts of persistence demand reliability; that is, transactions. However, sometimes there are different categories of data. Whereas certain domain models are more crucial and require transactional handling, other data may be recalculated or regenerated; for example, statistics, recommendations, or cached data. For the latter type of data, NoSQL datastores may be a good choice.

At the time of writing, no NoSQL system has emerged as a standard or de facto standard yet. Many of them also vary widely in their concepts and usages. There is also no standard targeting NoSQL included in Java EE 8.

Therefore, accessing NoSQL systems is usually realized using the Java APIs provided by the vendors. These make use of lower level standards such as JDBC or their proprietary APIs.

# Cross-cutting concerns

Enterprise applications require some technically motivated cross-cutting concerns. Examples of these are transactions, logging, caching, resilience, monitoring, security, and other non-functional requirements. Even for systems that solely target business, use cases need some amount of *technical plumbing*.

We just saw in the handling of transactions, an example of a non-functional cross-cutting concern. Java EE doesn't require much time and effort spent by engineers to integrate transactional behavior. The same is true for other cross-cutting concerns.

Java EE interceptors is a prime example for cross-cutting concerns. Following the concept of aspect-oriented programming, the implementation of the cross-cutting concern is separated from the decorated functionality. Methods of managed beans can be decorated to define interceptors, which interrupt the execution and perform the desired task. Interceptors have full control over the execution of the intercepted method including returned values and thrown exceptions. To match the idea of other APIs, interceptors are integrated in a lightweight fashion, not setting many constraints on the decorated functionality.

The previous example of transparently handling errors in a HTTP client class showed the usage of an interceptor. Business methods also can be decorated using custom interceptor bindings. The following demonstrates a business motivated process tracking aspect realized via custom annotations:

```
@Stateless
public class CarManufacturer {

    ...

    @Tracked(ProcessTracker.Category.MANUFACTURER)
    public Car manufactureCar(Specification spec) {
        ...
    }
}
```

The `Tracked` annotation defines a so-called interceptor binding. The annotation parameter represents a non-binding value that configures the interceptor:

```
import javax.enterprise.util.Nonbinding;
import javax.interceptor.InterceptorBinding;

@InterceptorBinding
@Inherited
@Documented
@Target({TYPE, METHOD})
@Retention(RUNTIME)
public @interface Tracked {

    @Nonbinding
    ProcessTracker.Category value();
}
```

The interceptor is activated via the binding annotation:

```
import javax.annotation.Priority;

@Tracked(ProcessTracker.Category.UNUSED)
@Interceptor
@Priority(Interceptor.Priority.APPLICATION)
public class TrackingInterceptor {

    @Inject
    ProcessTracker processTracker;

    @AroundInvoke
    public Object aroundInvoke(InvocationContext context) throws Exception
    {
```

```
        Tracked tracked = resolveAnnotation(context);

        if (tracked != null) {
            ProcessTracker.Category category = tracked.value();
            processTracker.track(category);
        }

        return context.proceed();
    }

    private Tracked resolveAnnotation(InvocationContext context) {
        Function<AnnotatedElement, Tracked> extractor = c ->
c.getAnnotation(Tracked.class);
        Method method = context.getMethod();

        Tracked tracked = extractor.apply(method);
        return tracked != null ? tracked :
extractor.apply(method.getDeclaringClass());
    }
}
```

By default, interceptors bound via interceptor bindings are not enabled. An interceptor must either be explicitly enabled via specifying a priority via @Priority, like demonstrated in this example. Another possibility is to activate it in the beans.xml descriptor.

```
<?xml version="1.0" encoding="UTF-8"?>
<beans xmlns="http://xmlns.jcp.org/xml/ns/javaee"
       xmlns:xsi="http://www.w3.org/2001/XMLSchema-instance"
       xsi:schemaLocation="http://xmlns.jcp.org/xml/ns/javaee
       http://xmlns.jcp.org/xml/ns/javaee/beans_1_1.xsd"
       bean-discovery-mode="all">
    <interceptors>
        <class>com.example.cars.processes.TrackingInterceptor</class>
    </interceptors>
</beans>
```

Interceptors can use reflection to retrieve potential annotation parameters, such as the process tracking category in the example. Interceptor bindings can be placed either on method or class level.

Interceptors decorate behavior on methods without tightly coupling them. They especially make sense for scenarios where the cross-cutting aspects need to be added to a lot of functionality.

Interceptors are similar to CDI decorators. Both concepts decorate managed beans with custom behavior that is encapsulated in a different place. The difference is that decorators are meant to be used for decorating business logic, which is also mostly specific to the decorated bean. Interceptors, however, are mostly used for technical concerns. They offer a broader usage, making it possible to annotate all kind of beans. Both concepts are a helpful functionality to realize cross-cutting aspects.

# Configuring applications

Application behavior that cannot be hardcoded but needs to be defined dynamically is realized via configuration. It depends on the application and the nature of the dynamic behavior how the configuration is implemented.

What aspects need to be configurable? Is it sufficient to define configuration files that are already part of the shipped artifact? Does the packaged application need to be configurable from the outside? Is there a requirement for changing behavior during runtime?

Configuration that does not need to change after the application has been built can easily be implemented in the project itself, that is, in the source code. Assuming we require more flexibility.

In a Java environment, the arguably most straightforward way is to provide property files that contain key-value pairs of configuration values. The configured values need to be retrieved in order to be used in the code. It certainly is possible to write Java components that programmatically provide property values. In a Java EE environment, dependency injection will be used to retrieve such components. At the time of writing, no Java EE standard supports out-of-the-box configuration yet. However, using CDI features provide this functionality in a few lines of code. The following shows a possible solution, that enables to inject configuration values identified by keys:

```
@Stateless
public class CarManufacturer {

    @Inject
    @Config("car.default.color")
    String defaultColor;

    public Car manufactureCar(Specification spec) {
        // use defaultColor
    }
}
```

In order to unambiguously inject configuration values, for example, provided as strings, qualifier such as @Config are required. This custom qualifier is defined in our application. The goal is to inject values identified by the provided key:

```
@Qualifier
@Documented
@Retention(RUNTIME)
public @interface Config {

    @Nonbinding
    String value();
}
```

A CDI producer is responsible for retrieving and providing specific configuration values:

```
import javax.enterprise.inject.spi.InjectionPoint;
import java.io.*;
import java.util.Properties;

@ApplicationScoped
public class ConfigurationExposer {

    private final Properties properties = new Properties();

    @PostConstruct
    private void initProperties() {
        try (InputStream inputStream = ConfigurationExposer.class
                .getResourceAsStream("/application.properties")) {
            properties.load(inputStream);
        } catch (IOException e) {
            throw new IllegalStateException("Could not init configuration",
e);
        }
    }

    @Produces
    @Config("")
    public String exposeConfig(InjectionPoint injectionPoint) {
        Config config =
injectionPoint.getAnnotated().getAnnotation(Config.class);
        if (config != null)
            return properties.getProperty(config.value());
        return null;
    }
}
```

The reference key in the `@Config` annotation is a non-binding attribute since all injected values are handled by our CDI producer method. The `InjectionPoint` provided by CDI contains information about the location where the dependency injection is specified. The producer retrieves the annotation with the actual configuration key and uses it to look up the configured property. The properties file `application.properties` is expected to reside in the classpath. This approach comprises configuration values that need to be available at runtime. Since the properties map is initiated once, the values will not change after they have been loaded. The configuration exposer bean is application-scoped to only load the required values into the properties map once.

If a scenario requires changing the configuration at runtime, the producer method would have to reload the configuration file. The scope of the producer method defines the life cycle of the configured value, how often the method will be called.

This example implements configuration using plain Java EE. There are some third-party CDI extensions available that provide similar, as well as more sophisticated, functionality. At the time of writing, an often used example for such a solution is Apache Deltaspike.

Besides the enterprise technology, an important aspect to consider, as well, is the environment in which the container runs; especially, as container technologies set certain constraint on the runtime environment. `Chapter 5`, *Container and Cloud Environments with Java EE* covers the topic of modern environments and their impact on the Java EE runtime, including how to design dynamic configuration.

The power of CDI producers lays in their flexibility. Any source of configuration can easily be attached to expose configured values.

# Caching

Caching is a technically motivated cross-cutting concern that becomes interesting once applications face issues in performance, such as slow external systems, expensive and cachable calculations, or huge amount of data. In general, caching aims to lower response times by storing data that is costly to retrieve in a potentially faster cache. A typical example is to hold responses of external systems or databases in memory.

Before implementing caching, a question that needs to be asked is whether a cache is required or even possible. Some data doesn't qualify for being cached, such as data that needs to be calculated on demand. If the situation and data is potentially eligible for caching, it depends on the situation if another solution other than caching is possible. Caching introduces duplication and the possibility of receiving outdated information and, generally speaking, for the majority of enterprise applications, should be avoided. For example, if database operations are too slow, it is advisable to consider whether other means, such as indexing, can help.

It depends a lot on the situation and what caching solutions are required. In general, caching directly in memory in the application already solves a lot of scenarios.

The most straightforward way of caching information is in a single place in the application. Singleton beans perfectly fit this scenario. A data structure that naturally fits the purpose of a cache is a Java `Map` type.

The `CarStorage` code snippet presented earlier, represents a singleton EJB with bean-managed concurrency containing a thread-safe map to store data. This storage is injected and used in other managed beans:

```
@Singleton
@ConcurrencyManagement(ConcurrencyManagementType.BEAN)
public class CarStorage {

    private final Map<String, Car> cars = new ConcurrentHashMap<>();

    public void store(Car car) {
        cars.put(car.getId(), car);
    }

    public Car retrieve(String id) {
        return cars.get(id);
    }
}
```

If more flexibility is required, for example pre-loading cache contents from a file, the bean can control the life cycle using post-construct and pre-destroy methods. To guarantee functionality to be executed during application startup time, the EJB is annotated using `@Startup`:

```
@Singleton
@Startup
@ConcurrencyManagement(ConcurrencyManagementType.BEAN)
public class CarStorage {
```

```
    ...

    @PostConstruct
    private void loadStorage() {
        // load contents from file
    }

    @PreDestroy
    private void writeStorage() {
        // write contents to file
    }
}
```

Interceptor can be used for adding cache in a transparent way, without needing to programmatically inject and use a cache. The interceptor interrupts the execution before a business method is being called and will return cached values instead. The most prominent example for this is the `CacheResult` functionality of the **Java Temporary Caching API** (**JCache**). JCache is a standard that is targeted for Java EE but, as of writing this book, not included in the umbrella specification. For applications that add the JCache functionality, the eligible business methods are annotated with `@CacheResult` and transparently being served by a specific cache.

JCache, in general, provides sophisticated caching capabilities for scenarios where simple Java EE solutions are not sufficient. This includes distributed caching provided by JCache implementations. As of today, caching solutions typically being used are **Hazelcast**, **Infinispan**, or **Ehcache**. This is especially the case when several caches need to be integrated with specific concerns, such as cache eviction. JCache, and its implementations, provide powerful solutions.

# Flow of execution

Business processes that run in enterprise applications describe certain flows of process executions. For use cases that are triggered, this either includes a synchronous request-response approach or asynchronous handling of the triggered process.

Use case invocations run in a separate thread, one thread per request or invocation, respectively. The threads are created by the container and pooled for reuse once the invocation has been handled successfully. By default, the business processes defined in the application classes, as well as cross-cutting concerns, such as transactions, run sequentially.

# Synchronous execution

For a typical use case triggered by a HTTP request and involving a database query this works as follows. The request thread handles the request that goes into the boundary; for example, a JAX-RS `UsersResource`, by the inversion of control principle, the JAX-RS resource method is called by the container. The resource injects and uses a `UserManagement` EJB, which is also invoked indirectly by the container. All operations executed by the proxies happen in synchronous terms. The EJB will use an entity manager to store a new `User` entity and as soon as the business method that initiated the currently active transaction returns, the container will try to commit the transaction to the database. Depending on the transaction result, the boundary resource method resumes and constructs the client response. All this happens synchronously while the client call blocks and waits for the response.

Synchronous execution includes the handling of synchronous CDI events. Events decouple firing domain events from handling them; however, the event handling is performed synchronously. There are several kinds of transactional observer methods. By specifying the transaction phase, the event will be handled at transaction commit time, either before completion, after completion, only after a failed transaction, or after a successful transaction, respectively. By default, or when no transaction is active, CDI events are handled immediately when they are fired. This enables engineers to implement sophisticated solutions; for example, involving events that happen only after entities have been added to the database successfully. Again, in all cases, this handling is executed synchronously.

# Asynchronous execution

Whereas the synchronous flow of execution fulfills a lot of business use cases, other scenarios need asynchronous behavior. The Java EE environment sets a few constraints to the application in regard to threading. The container manages and pools resources and threads. External concurrency utilities outside of the container are not aware of these threads. Therefore, the application's code is not supposed to start and manage own threads, but to use Java EE functionality to do so. There are several APIs that natively support asynchronicity.

# Asynchronous EJB methods

A straightforward way to invoke asynchronous behavior is to annotate an EJB business method, or the EJB class, with `@Asynchronous`. Invocations to these methods immediately return, optionally with a `Future` response type. They are executed in a separate, container-managed thread. This usage works well for simple scenarios but is limited to EJBs:

```java
import javax.ejb.Asynchronous;

@Asynchronous
@Stateless
public class Calculator {

    public void calculatePi(long decimalPlaces) {
        // this may run for a long time
    }
}
```

# Managed Executor Service

For asynchronous execution in CDI managed beans or by using Java SE concurrency utilities, Java EE includes container-managed versions of `ExecutorService` and `ScheduledExecutorService` functionality. These are used to execute asynchronous tasks in container-managed threads. Instances of `ManagedExecutorService` and `ManagedScheduledExecutorService` are injected into the application's code. These instances can be used to execute their own runnable logic; however, they shine when combined together with Java SE concurrency utilities such as completable futures. The following shows the creation of completable futures using container-managed threads:

```java
import javax.annotation.Resource;
import javax.enterprise.concurrent.ManagedExecutorService;
import java.util.Random;
import java.util.concurrent.CompletableFuture;

@Stateless
public class Calculator {

    @Resource
    ManagedExecutorService mes;

    public CompletableFuture<Double> calculateRandomPi(int
maxDecimalPlaces) {
        return CompletableFuture.supplyAsync(() -> new
Random().nextInt(maxDecimalPlaces) + 1, mes)
                .thenApply(this::calculatePi);
```

```
    }

    private double calculatePi(long decimalPlaces) {
        ...
    }
}
```

The calculator bean returns a value of type *completable future of double* that may still be calculated while the calling context resumes. The future can be asked whether the calculation has finished. It can also be combined into subsequent executions. No matter where new threads are required in an enterprise application, Java EE functionality should be used to manage them.

## Asynchronous CDI events

CDI events can also be handled in an asynchronous way. The same holds true that the container will provide a thread for executing the event handling. To define asynchronous event handlers, the method is annotated with @ObservesAsync and the event is fired using the fireAsync() method. The next code snippets demonstrate asynchronous CDI events:

```
@Stateless
public class CarManufacturer {

    @Inject
    CarFactory carFactory;

    @Inject
    Event<CarCreated> carCreated;

    public Car manufactureCar(Specification spec) {
        Car car = carFactory.createCar(spec);
        carCreated.fireAsync(new CarCreated(spec));
        return car;
    }
}
```

The event handler is called in an own, container-managed thread:

```
import javax.enterprise.event.ObservesAsync;

public class CreatedCarListener {

    public void onCarCreated(@ObservesAsync CarCreated event) {
        // handle event asynchronously
    }
}
```

For backwards compatibility reasons, synchronous CDI events can also be handled in an EJB asynchronous method. Therefore, the events and handlers are defined in a synchronous way, but the handler method is an EJB business method annotated with `@Asynchronous`. Before asynchronous events were added to the CDI standard in Java EE 8, this was the only way to provide this feature. To avoid confusion, this implementation should be avoided in Java EE 8 and newer.

# Scopes in asynchronicity

Since the container cannot make any assumption on how long asynchronous tasks may run, usage of scopes is limited. Request-scoped or session-scoped beans that were available as the asynchronous task started are not guaranteed to be active during the whole execution; the request and session may have ended a long time ago. Threads that are running asynchronous tasks, for example, provided by a managed executor service or asynchronous events, can therefore not access the request-scoped or session-scoped bean instances that were active during the originating invocation. This also includes accessing references to injected instances, for example, in lambda methods that are part of the originating synchronous execution.

This has to be taken into account when modeling asynchronous tasks. All invocation-specific information needs to be provided at task start time. An asynchronous task can, however, have its own instances of scoped beans.

# Timed execution

Business use cases cannot only be invoked from the outside, for example, by a HTTP request, but also emerge from the inside of the application, by a job that runs at a defined time.

In the Unix world, cron jobs are a well-known functionality to trigger periodic jobs. EJBs provide similar possibilities using EJB timers. Timers invoke business methods based on a recurring pattern or after a specific time. The following shows the definition of a scheduled timer that times out every 10 minutes:

```
import javax.ejb.Schedule;
import javax.ejb.Startup;

@Singleton
@Startup
public class PeriodicJob {

    @Schedule(minute = "*/10", hour = "*", persistent = false)
```

```
        public void executeJob() {
            // this is executed every 10 minutes
        }
    }
```

All EJBs, singleton, stateful, or stateless beans can define timers. However, in the majority of use cases it makes sense to define timers on singleton beans. The timeout is invoked on all active beans and it usually is desired to invoke the scheduled job reliably; that is, on a singleton bean. For the same reason this example defines the EJB to be active during application startup. This guarantees that the timer is executed from the beginning.

Timers can be defined as persistent, which extends their lifetime beyond the JVM life cycle. The container is responsible for keeping timers persistent, usually in a database. Persistent timers that would have been executed while an application is unavailable are triggered at startup. This also enables the possibility to share timers across multiple instances. Persistent timers together with corresponding server configuration are a straightforward solution for business processes that need to be executed exactly once across multiple servers.

The timers that are automatically created using the `@Schedule` annotation are specified using Unix-like cron expressions. For more flexibility, EJB timers are defined programmatically using the container-provided timer service that creates `Timers` and `@Timeout` callback methods.

Periodic or delayed jobs can also be defined outside EJB beans using the container-managed scheduled executor service. A `ManagedScheduledExecutorService` instance that executes tasks after a specified delay or periodically is injectable into managed beans. Executing these tasks will happen using container-managed threads:

```
    @ApplicationScoped
    public class Periodic {

        @Resource
        ManagedScheduledExecutorService mses;

        public void startAsyncJobs() {
            mses.schedule(this::execute, 10, TimeUnit.SECONDS);
            mses.scheduleAtFixedRate(this::execute, 60, 10, TimeUnit.SECONDS);
        }

        private void execute() {
            ...
        }
    }
```

Invoking `startAsyncJobs()` will cause `execute()` to run in a managed thread, 10 seconds after the invocation and continuously, every 10 seconds, after an initial minute has passed.

# Asynchronous and reactive JAX-RS

JAX-RS supports asynchronous behavior to not unnecessarily block request threads on the server-side. Even if an HTTP connection is currently waiting for a response, the request thread could potentially handle other requests while the long-running process on the server is handled. Request threads are pooled by the container and this pool only has a certain size. In order to not unnecessarily occupy a request thread, JAX-RS asynchronous resource methods submit tasks that are executed while the request thread returns and is free to be reused again. The HTTP connection is being resumed and responded after the asynchronous task has been finished or when a timeout occurs. The following code shows an asynchronous JAX-RS resource method:

```
@Path("users")
@Consumes(MediaType.APPLICATION_JSON)
public class UsersResource {

    @Resource
    ManagedExecutorService mes;

    ...

    @POST
    public CompletionStage<Response> createUserAsync(User user) {
        return CompletableFuture.supplyAsync(() -> createUser(user), mes);
    }

    private Response createUser(User user) {
        userStore.create(user);

        return Response.accepted().build();
    }
}
```

For the request thread not to be occupied for too long, the JAX-RS method needs to return fast. This is due to the resource method being called from the container using inversion of control. The completion stage's result will be used to resume the client connection once processing has finished.

Returning completion stages is a fairly recent approach in the JAX-RS API. If a timeout declaration, together with more flexibility on the asynchronous response, is required, the `AsyncResponse` type can be injected into the method. The following code snippet demonstrates this approach.

```java
import javax.ws.rs.container.AsyncResponse;
import javax.ws.rs.container.Suspended;

@Path("users")
@Consumes(MediaType.APPLICATION_JSON)
public class UsersResource {

    @Resource
    ManagedExecutorService mes;

    ...

    @POST
    public void createUserAsync(User user, @Suspended AsyncResponse
response) {

        response.setTimeout(5, TimeUnit.SECONDS);
        response.setTimeoutHandler(r ->
r.resume(Response.status(Response.Status.SERVICE_UNAVAILABLE).build()));

        mes.execute(() -> response.resume(createUser(user)));
    }
}
```

Using custom timeouts, the client request will not wait infinitely, only until either the result is completed or the invocation timed out. The calculation, however, will continue since it's executed asynchronously.

For JAX-RS resources being implemented as EJBs, `@Asynchronous` business methods can be used to omit the asynchronous invocation using an executor service.

The JAX-RS client also supports asynchronous behavior. Depending on the requirements, it makes sense to not block during HTTP invocations. A previous example showed how to set timeouts on client requests. For long running and especially parallel external system calls, asynchronous and *reactive* behavior provides benefits.

Imagine several backends that provide weather information. The client component accesses all of them and provides the average weather forecast. Accessing the systems ideally happens in parallel.

```java
import java.util.stream.Collectors;

@ApplicationScoped
public class WeatherForecast {

    private Client client;
    private List<WebTarget> targets;

    @Resource
    ManagedExecutorService mes;

    @PostConstruct
    private void initClient() {
        client = ClientBuilder.newClient();
        targets = ...
    }

    public Forecast getAverageForecast() {
        return invokeTargetsAsync()
                .stream()
                .map(CompletableFuture::join)
                .reduce(this::calculateAverage)
                .orElseThrow(() -> new IllegalStateException("No weather
service available"));
    }

    private List<CompletableFuture<Forecast>> invokeTargetsAsync() {
        return targets.stream()
                .map(t -> CompletableFuture.supplyAsync(() -> t
                        .request(MediaType.APPLICATION_JSON_TYPE)
                        .get(Forecast.class), mes))
                .collect(Collectors.toList());
    }

    private Forecast calculateAverage(Forecast first, Forecast second) {
        ...
    }

    @PreDestroy
    public void closeClient() {
        client.close();
    }
}
```

The `invokeTargetsAsync()` method invokes the available targets asynchronously, using the managed executor service. The `CompletableFuture` handles are returned and used to calculate the average results. Calling the `join()` method will block until the invocation has finished and will deliver the individual results.

By invoking the available targets asynchronously, they call and wait for the potentially slow resource in parallel. Waiting for the weather service resources then only takes as long as the slowest response, not the sum of all responses.

The latest version of JAX-RS natively supports completion stages, which reduces boilerplate code in the applications. Similar to using completable futures, the invocation immediately returns a completion stage instance for further usage. The following demonstrates reactive JAX-RS client functionality using the `rx()` invocation:

```
public Forecast getAverageForecast() {
    return invokeTargetsAsync()
            .stream()
            .reduce((l, r) -> l.thenCombine(r, this::calculateAverage))
            .map(s -> s.toCompletableFuture().join())
            .orElseThrow(() -> new IllegalStateException("No weather
service available"));
}

private List<CompletionStage<Forecast>> invokeTargetsAsync() {
    return targets.stream()
            .map(t -> t
                    .request(MediaType.APPLICATION_JSON_TYPE)
                    .rx()
                    .get(Forecast.class))
            .collect(Collectors.toList());
}
```

The preceding example doesn't require to lookup the managed executor service. The JAX-RS client will manage this internally.

Before the `rx()` method was introduced, the client contained an explicit `async()` invocation that behaves similarly, but only returns `Futures`. The reactive client approach usually fits the need in projects better.

As seen before, we are using the container-managed executor service since we're in a Java EE environment.

# Concepts and design principles of modern Java EE

The Java EE API is built around conventions and design principles that are present throughout the whole set of standards. Software engineers will find familiar API patterns and approaches while developing applications. Java EE aims to maintain consistent API usage.

For applications that focus on business use cases first, the most important principle of the technology is *not getting in the way*. As mentioned earlier, engineers should be able to focus on solving business problems, not spending the majority of their time dealing with technology or framework concerns. Ideally, the domain logic is implemented using plain Java and *enhanced* with annotations and aspects that enable enterprise environments without affecting or obfuscating the domain code. This implies that the technology doesn't need much engineer attention by enforcing overly complex constraints. In the past, J2EE required many of these overly-complex solutions. Managed beans as well as persistent beans needed to implement interfaces or extend base classes. This obfuscates the domain logic and complicates testability.

In the age of Java EE, the domain logic is implemented in plain Java classes annotated with annotations that tell the container runtime how to apply the enterprise concerns. Clean code practices often suggest writing code for delectability, not reusability. Java EE supports this approach. If for some reason the technology needs to be replaced and the domain logic extracted, this is possible by simply removing the corresponding annotations.

As we will see in `Chapter 7`, *Testing* the programming approach highly supports testability, since for the developers, the majority of Java EE specifics are not more than annotations.

A design principle that is existent throughout the whole API is **inversion of control** (**IoC**), in other words, *don't call us, we'll call you*. We see this especially in application boundaries such as JAX-RS resources. The resource methods are defined by annotation Java methods that are later invoked by the container in the correct context. The same holds true for dependency injection that needs to resolve producers or include cross-cutting concerns such as interceptors. Application developers can focus on implementing the logic and defining relationships and leave the actual plumbing to the container. Another, not that obvious example, is declaring the mapping of Java objects to JSON and back via JSON-B annotations. The objects are mapped implicitly in a declarative approach, not necessarily in an explicit, programmatic way.

Another principle that enables engineers to use the technology in a productive way is **convention over configuration**. By default, Java EE defines specific behavior that matches the majority of use cases. If that is not sufficient or doesn't match the requirements, behavior can be overridden, often at several levels.

There are countless examples of convention over configuration. JAX-RS resource methods mapping Java functionality into HTTP responses is one such method. If JAX-RS's default behavior regarding responses is not adequate, the `Response` return type can be used. Another example is the specification of managed beans that is usually realized using annotations. To override this behavior, the `beans.xml` XML descriptor can be used. The welcoming aspect for developers is that in a modern Java EE world, enterprise applications are developed in a pragmatic and highly productive way that does not usually require at lot of XML usage like in the past.

In terms of developer productivity, another important design principle of Java EE is that the platform requires the container to integrate the different standards. As soon as containers support a specific set of APIs, which is the case if the whole Java EE API is supported, it is also required that implementations of the APIs enable straightforward integration of other APIs. A good example is that JAX-RS resources are able to use JSON-B mapping and Bean Validation without explicit configuration other than annotations. In previous examples, we saw how functionalities that are defined in separate standards can be used together without additional effort required. This is also one of the biggest advantages of the Java EE platform. The umbrella specification ensures that the specific standards play well together. Developers can rely on certain features and implementation being provided by the application server.

# Preserving maintainable code with high quality

Developers generally agree that code quality is a goal to strive for. Yet not all technology supports this ambition equally well.

As mentioned from the start, the business logic should be the main focus of applications. If changes in the business logic or new knowledge after working in the domain emerge, the domain model, as well as the source code, needs to be refactored. Iterative refactoring is a necessity to achieve and maintain high quality of the modeled domain as well as the source code in general. Domain-Driven Design describes this effort of deepening the understanding of the business knowledge.

A lot has been written on refactoring at the code level. After the business logic has initially been represented into the code and verified by tests, developers should spend some time and effort to rethink and improve the first attempt. This includes identifier names, methods, and classes. Especially, **naming**, **layers of abstractions** and **single points of responsibility** are important aspects.

Following the reasoning of Domain-Driven Design, the business domain should fit its code representations as much as possible. This includes, especially, the language of the domain; that is, how developers and business experts talk about certain features. The goal of the whole team is to find a uniform, *ubiquitous language* that is used and well represented not only in discussions and presentation slides, but also in the code. Refinement of business knowledge will happen in an iterative approach. As well as refactoring at the code level, this approach implies that an initial model won't perfectly match all the requirements from the beginning.

Therefore, the technology being used should support changes in the model and code. Too many restrictions become hard to change later on.

For application development in general, but especially for refactoring, it is crucial to have a sufficient coverage of automated software tests. As soon as the code is changed, regression tests ensure that no business functionality has accidentally been damaged. Sufficient test cases thus support refactoring attempts, giving engineers clarity as to whether functionality still works as expected after it has been touched. The technology should ideally support testability by not constraining code structures. Chapter 7, *Testing* will cover that topic in detail.

In order to achieve *refactorability*, loose coupling is favored over tight coupling. All functionality that explicitly invokes or requires other components needs to be touched if either of those change. Java EE supports loose coupling in several aspects; for example, dependency injection, eventing, or cross-cutting concerns, such as interceptors. All of these simplify code changes.

There are some tools and methods that measure the quality. Especially, static code analysis can gather information about complexity, coupling, relationships of classes and packages, and implementation in general. These means can help engineers to identify potential issues and provide an overall picture of the software project. Chapter 6, *Application Development Workflows* covers how to verify code quality in an automated way.

In general, it is advisable to refactor and improve the code quality constantly. Software projects are often driven to implement new functionality that generates revenue instead of improving existing functionality. The issue with that is that refactoring and improving quality is often seen to not provide any benefit from the business perspective. This is, of course, not true. In order to achieve a steady velocity and to integrate new features with satisfying quality, it is absolutely necessary to reconsider existing features. Ideally periodical refactor cycles are already built into the project schedule. Experience shows that project managers are often not aware of this issue. However, it is a responsibility of the software engineer team to address the relevance of quality.

# Summary

Engineers are advised to focus on the domain and business logic first, by starting from the use case boundaries and stepping down the abstraction layers. Java EE core domain components, namely EJBs, CDI, CDI producers and events, are used to implement the plain business logic. Other Java EE APIs are mainly used to support the business logic in technical necessities. As we have seen, Java EE implements and encourages numerous software design patterns as well as the approaches of Domain-Driven Design in modern ways.

We have seen how to choose and implement communication, in both synchronous and asynchronous ways. The communication technology depends on the business requirements. Especially HTTP is widely used and well-supported in Java EE via JAX-RS. REST is a prime example of an communication protocol architectural style that supports to loosely couple system.

Java EE ships with functionality that implements and enables technical cross-cutting concerns such as managed persistence, configuration, or caching. Especially the use of CDI realizes various technically-motivated use cases. Required asynchronous behavior can be implemented in different ways. Applications should not manage own threading or concurrency management, rather than use Java EE features. Container-managed executor services, asynchronous CDI events, or EJB timers are examples that should be used instead.

The concepts and principles of the Java EE platform support developing enterprise applications with focusing on business logic. Especially the lean integration of different standards, inversion of control, convention over configuration, and the principle of *not getting in the way*, support this aspect. Engineers should aim to maintain high code quality, not only by code level refactoring, but also by refining the business logic and the *ubiquitous language* the teams share. Refining code quality as well as suitability of the domain model happens in iterative steps.

Therefore, technology should support changes in model and code and not putting too many restrictions onto solutions. Java EE supports this by minimizing the framework impact on the business code and by enabling to loosely couple functionality. Teams should be aware of refactoring together with automated testing being a necessity of high quality software.

The following chapter will cover what other aspects make the Java EE a modern and suitable platform for developing enterprise applications. We will see what deployment approaches are advisable and how to lay the foundation for productive development workflows.

# 4
# Lightweight Java EE

Lightweight Java EE. Is that even possible? In the past, J2EE applications and especially application servers have been considered a heavyweight and cumbersome technology. And up to some degree deservedly so. APIs were quite unwieldy to use. There was a lot of XML configuration required, which eventually led to the use of **XDoclet**, a tool used to generate XML based on meta information put into JavaDoc comments. Application servers were also cumbersome to work with, especially with regard to startup and deployment times.

However, since the name change to Java EE and especially since version 6, these assumptions are not true anymore. Annotations were introduced, which originally emerged from the XDoclet-motivated JavaDoc tags. And a lot has happened to improve the productivity and developer experience.

This chapter will cover the following topics:

- What makes a technology lightweight
- Why Java EE standards help reducing work
- How to choose project dependencies and archive formats
- The benefits of zero-dependency enterprise applications
- Modern Java EE application servers
- The *one application per application server* approach

# Lightweight enterprise technology

What makes a technology *lightweight*? And how lightweight, productive and relevant is Java EE in the age of containers and cloud?

One of the most important aspects of a lightweight technology is the productivity and effectiveness it enables. The time the development team spends is precious and expensive and the less time spent on overhead the better. This includes developing glue code, building projects, writing and executing tests, and deploying software, on both local and remote environments. Ideally, engineers can spend as much time as possible on implementing revenue-generating business functionality.

A technology should therefore not add much overhead on top of the business use cases. Technical cross-cutting concerns are certainly necessary but should be kept to a minimum. In the previous chapter, we have seen how Java EE enables developers to implement business use cases in a productive way. Project artifact builds and deployments should in the same way aim to minimize the required time and effort.

This and the following chapter will show how Java EE supports crafting productive development workflows.

# Why Java EE standards?

One of the principles of Java EE is to provide a productive enterprise API. As seen in the *Concepts and design principles of modern Java EE* section in the previous chapter, one of the biggest advantages is the ability to integrate different standards without developer-side configuration required. The Java EE umbrella requires the different standards to work well together. The enterprise container has to meet this requirement. The software engineers only develop against the APIs and let the application server do the *hard integration work*.

Following the convention over configuration approach, using different, integrated standards that are part of the umbrella specification doesn't require initial configuration. As seen in various examples previously, the technologies that have emerged from different standards within Java EE work well with each other. We have seen examples such as using JSON-B to automatically map objects to JSON in JAX-RS resources; integrating Bean Validation into JAX-RS and therefore HTTP responses by introducing a single annotation; injecting managed beans into instances defined by other standards, such as Bean Validation validators or JSON-B type adapters; or managing technical transactions that span JPA database operations in EJBs.

What is the alternative to using an umbrella standard that embraces various reusable technologies? Well, to introduce vendor-specific frameworks with third-party dependencies that need to be wired together with manual developer work involved. One of the biggest advantages of the Java EE API is having the whole variety of technology right at the developer's fingertips; providing productive integration and saving developers time for focusing on business use cases.

# Convention over configuration

Pursuing the idea of convention over configuration, further, enterprise applications can be developed without any initial configuration required. The APIs provide default behavior that matches the majority of use cases. Engineer are only required to put extra effort in if that behavior is not sufficient.

This implies that in today's world, enterprise projects can be set up with minimal configuration involved. The days of extensive XML configuration are over. Especially, applications that don't ship web frontend technology can keep XML files to a minimum.

Let's start with a simple example of an application that offers REST endpoints, and accesses databases and external systems. REST endpoints are integrated by JAX-RS that internally uses servlets to handle requests. Servlets traditionally are configured using the `web.xml` deployment descriptor file residing under `WEB-INF`. However, JAX-RS ships a shortcut by sub-classing `Application`, annotated with `@ApplicationPath`, as shown in the previous chapter. This registers a JAX-RS application servlet for the provided path. At startup time, the project will be scanned for JAX-RS related classes such as resources or providers. After the application has been started, the REST endpoints are available to handle requests even without a provided `web.xml` file.

Managed beans are traditionally configured using a `beans.xml` configuration file. In web archive applications this file also resides under `WEB-INF`. Nowadays, it is primarily used to specify the bean discovery mode, that is, which CDI beans are considered per default. It's advisable to configure the `bean-discovery-mode` of `all`, not just `annotated` beans. The `beans.xml` file can override CDI bean composition of all sorts, such as interceptors, alternatives, decorators, and so on. As the CDI specification states, for the simplest example it's sufficient for this file to be empty.

The JPA persistence units are configured using the `persistence.xml` file under `META-INF`. As previously shown, it comprises the datasource definitions that are used in the the application. Mapping JPA entities to database tables is configured via annotations in domain model classes. This approach keeps the concerns in a single place and minimizes XML usage.

For the majority of enterprise applications that don't include a web frontend, this amount of configuration is already sufficient. Frontend technologies such as JSF are usually configured via `web.xml` and `faces-config.xml` or if required, via additional, implementation-specific files.

In the past, vendor-specific configuration files, such as `jboss-web.xml` or `glassfish-web.xml`, were quite common. In a modern Java EE world, the majority of applications don't require these workarounds anymore. In order to allow portability, it is highly advisable to implement features using standard APIs first and only if this is not possible within reasonable effort to go with vendor-specific features. Experience with legacy projects showed that this approach leads to better manageable situations. Unlike vendor-specific features, Java EE standards are guaranteed to continue to work in the future.

At application startup, the container scans the available classes for annotations and known types. Managed beans, resources, entities, extensions, and cross-cutting concerns are discovered and configured appropriately. This mechanism is a great benefit for developers. They don't need to explicitly specify required classes in configuration files but can rely on the server's discovery; inversion of control at its best.

# Dependency management of Java EE projects

The dependency management of an enterprise project targets the dependencies that are added on top of the JDK. This includes dependencies that are required during compilation, tests, and at runtime. In a Java enterprise project, the Java EE API is required with *provided* dependency scope. Since the APIs are available on the application server, they don't have to be included in the packaged archive. The provided Java EE API therefore doesn't have an implication on the package size.

Real-world enterprise projects usually include more dependencies than this. Typical examples for third-party dependencies include logging frameworks such as **Slf4j**, **Log4j**, or **Logback**, JSON mapping frameworks such as **Jackson**, or general purpose libraries such as **Apache Commons**. There are several issues with these dependencies.

First of all, third-party dependencies are usually not provided, thus increasing the size of the artifact. This doesn't sound that harmful, but has some implications that we'll see later. The more dependencies are added to the resulting artifact, the longer the build will take. Build systems need to copy potentially big dependencies into the artifact each and every time the project is built. As we will see in Chapter 6, *Application Development Workflows*, project builds need to be as fast as possible. Every dependency added to the package increases the turnaround time.

Potential collisions of dependencies and their versions represent an even bigger challenge. This includes both packaged dependencies and transitive dependencies as well as libraries that already exist on the application server. For example, logging frameworks are often already present in the container's classpath, potentially in a different version. Different versions being used introduce potential issues with the aggregate of libraries being there. Experience shows that implicit dependencies that are added transitively represent the biggest challenge in this regard.

Aside from technical reasons, there are some other aspects to consider before lightheadedly introducing dependencies to a software project. Dependency licenses, for example, can become an issue when developing a software product that is shipped to customers. It's not only required that the company is permitted to use certain dependencies, but also that involved licenses are compatible to each other, when shipped in a software package. The simplest way to meet licensing criteria is to avoid dependencies, at least, if they serve no business purpose. Engineers should make similar consideration in regard to security, especially for software being developed for sectors with high demands in security.

I was once involved in a *firefighter* job responsible for updating versions of used frameworks in an enterprise project. The project included a lot of build dependencies. With all its included third-party dependencies, the project runtime eventually contained *all* known logging frameworks. The same was true for JSON mapping frameworks, which introduced a lot of version conflicts and runtime dependency mismatches. This was before the advent of JSON-B and JSON-P. We spent most of the time configuring the project build, untangling and excluding the transitive dependencies from the project artifact. This is a typical issue when using third-party libraries. The price for saving project code is to spend time and effort configuring the project build and potentially untangling dependencies, especially if they introduce a lot of transitive functionality.

By managing build dependencies, engineers focus on aspects that are insignificant to the business use cases. The question to be asked is whether it pays off to save some lines of code, when at the same time we introduce dependencies. Experience shows that the trade-off of duplication versus lightweightness, such as in dependency-free projects, is too often in favor of avoiding duplication. A prime example for this are projects that introduce the whole Apache Commons library to use a functionality that could have been realized with a few lines of code.

Whereas it's good practice to not reinvent the wheel by developing own versions of functionality that could be reused, the consequences also have to be considered. Experience shows that introduced dependencies are quite often neglected and only utilized marginally. Most of them serve little business value.

When engineers inspect code quality, for example using code analysis tools, what also should be considered is the ratio of dependencies and project code that target business use cases versus *plumbing*. There is a straightforward method that can be applied for dependencies. Before a third-party dependency is introduced, consider a few questions. Does adding the functionality add value to the business? How much project code does it save? How big is the impact on the resulting artifact?

For example, imagine part of the use case of the car manufacture application is to communicate with specific factory software using a proprietary Java API. Obviously, the communication is crucial to fulfill the business purpose and it makes a lot of sense to include this dependency in the project. On the contrary, adding a different logging framework hardly improves the application's business value. Furthermore, Chapter 9, *Monitoring, Performance, and Logging* will discuss the issues with traditional logging.

However, in order not to unnecessarily increase the build size, crucial dependencies can be installed on the application server and be declared as provided in the project's build.

In the first chapter, we saw the difficulties with shared business dependencies such as shared models. Ideally, applications are as self-sufficient as possible. Chapter 8, *Microservices and System Architecture* will deep-dive into self-contained systems and the motivation for architectures that share nothing.

In regard to technical dependencies, however, the Java EE API already includes the technology that the majority of enterprise applications need. Ideally, engineers develop zero-dependency Java EE applications that are packaged as thin deployment artifacts containing the application-relevant classes only. If some use cases require third-party dependencies, they can be installed in the container. The goal is to have a light footprint of deployment artifacts.

For production code, this means that only provided dependencies are included, ideally, only the Java EE API. Test dependencies, however, are a different story; software tests require some additional technology. Chapter 7, *Testing* covers the required dependencies for the test scope.

# Lightweight way of packaging applications

The approach of zero-dependency applications simplifies many project build concerns. There is no need to manage third-party dependencies with regard to versions or collisions since there aren't any included.

What other aspects does this approach simplify? Project builds, no matter whether Gradle or Maven are being used, always show the best performance when nothing needs to be added to the artifact. The resulting size of the packages directly impacts the build time. In the case of zero-dependency applications, only the compiled classes are included, that is, only the actual business logic. Therefore, the resulting build times are as minimal as they will get. All build time is spent on compiling the project's classes, running the test cases, and packaging the classes into a thin deployment artifact. Building this approach should happen in seconds. Yes, seconds. As a general rule, every project build that takes more than 10 seconds should be reconsidered.

This rule, of course, puts certain pressure on project builds. It naturally requires to avoid including any larger dependency or implementation; these should be provided by the application server. Test run times are usually another aspect that prevents fast builds. `Chapter 7`, *Testing*, will shed light on how to develop tests in an effective way.

Fast builds are one benefit of crafting zero-dependency applications. Another implication is fast artifact transmission. Built artifacts, such as WAR or JAR files, are usually kept in an artifact repository for later use, for example, **Sonatype Nexus** or **JFrog Artifactory**. Transmitting these artifacts over the wire greatly speeds up if only a few kilobytes of data are involved. This applies to all sorts of artifact deployment. No matter where the built archives are shipped to, smaller footprints always pay off especially when workflows are executed often, as it is the case for Continuous Delivery.

The goal of reconsidering practices and stripping everything which does not provide value also targets the way of packaging applications. Traditionally, enterprise applications have been shipped as EAR files. The structure of these included a web archive, a WAR file, and one or more enterprise JARs. Enterprise JAR archives contained the business logic, usually implemented in EJBs. The web archive contained the web services and frontend technology communicating with the business logic using local or remote EJBs. However, this separation is not necessary, as all components are shipped on a single server instance.

Packaging several technical concerns in several sub-archives is not required anymore. All business logic as well as web services and cross-cutting concerns are packaged into a single WAR file. This greatly simplifies the project setup as well as the build process. Applications don't have to be zipped in multiple hierarchies just to be unzipped on a single server instance again. WAR files containing the required business code deployed in a container is the best implementation of thin artifacts. Because of this reason, deploying thin WAR files is faster than the corresponding EAR files.

The following demonstrates the contents of a thin web application artifact with typical components:

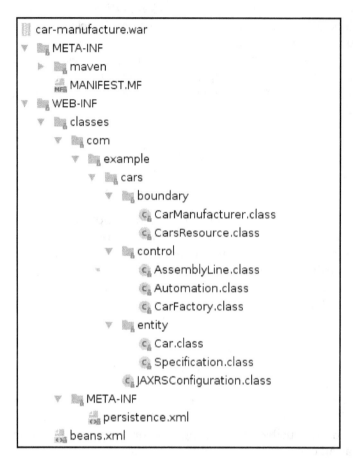

The deployment artifact only contains classes that are required to implement the business use case, no technology-specific implementation, and only minimal configuration. Especially, there are no library JAR files included.

The architecture of the Java EE platform encourages lightweight artifacts. This is due to the platform separating the API from the implementations. Developers only program against the API; the application server implements the API. This makes it possible to ship only the business logic, which includes certain aspects in lightweight artifacts. Besides the obvious benefits of avoiding dependency collisions and building vendor-independent solutions, this approach also enables fast deployments. The less content the artifacts include, the less unpacking needs to be done on the container side. Therefore, it's highly advisable to package enterprise applications into a single WAR file.

In the last year, we have seen more and more interest in shipping enterprise applications as *fat* JARs, that is, shipping the application together with the implementation. The approaches of fat deployment artifacts have usually been used in enterprise frameworks such as the Spring Framework. The motivation behind these approaches is that the versions of the required dependencies and frameworks are explicitly specified and shipped together with the business logic. Fat deployment artifacts can be created as fat WARs, which are deployed on a servlet container, or fat JARs started as standalone, executable JARs. A Java EE application packaged as fat JAR therefore ships the enterprise container together with the application in an executable JAR. However, as stated before, the build, shipping, and deployment times increase greatly if third-party dependencies are added to the artifact.

Experience shows that explicitly shipping the enterprise implementation together with the application is in most cases not technically but business-politically motivated. Operational environments within companies that are inflexible regarding application server and Java installations, especially regarding version upgrades, in some cases force developers to find workarounds. Enterprise applications that are built using newer technology cannot be deployed on older, existing server installations. Sometimes, the business-politically easier solution is to ignore the existing installations altogether and to directly execute the standalone JAR, which only requires a certain Java version. However, whereas these solutions are certainly justified, the technically more reasonable solutions would be to package applications into thin deployment artifacts. Interestingly, as we will see in the next chapter, shipping software in Linux containers holds the advantages of both approaches.

There is another interesting approach that enables to ship the whole application as an executable package and to keep fast workflows of thin deployments. Several application server vendors provide the solution to ship a custom application container as executable JAR that deploys the thin application as additional argument at startup time. By doing so, the whole package of both artifacts includes the business logic as well as the implementation and is started as a standalone application. The application is still separated from its runtime and packaged as thin artifact, as a so-called *hollow* JAR or WAR file. This approach especially makes sense if the addressed flexibility is required without the use of Linux containers.

As a conclusion, it is highly advisable to build thin deployment artifacts, ideally thin WAR files. If this approach does not work for business-political reasons, hollow JARs can provide a reasonable workaround. However, as we will see in the next chapter, container technologies such as Docker don't require to make use of executable JAR approaches and provide the same benefits.

# Java EE application servers

What else makes an enterprise technology lightweight besides the productiveness of the API? What about the runtime, the enterprise container?

Developers often complained about J2EE application servers being too slow, too cumbersome, and unwieldy to use. Installation sizes and memory consumption were quite high. Typically, a lot of applications ran on a server instance in parallel with being redeployed individually. This approach sometimes introduced additional challenges, such as classloader hierarchy issues.

Modern application servers are far from this negative image. Most of them have been heavily optimized for startup and deployment time. Especially, server-internal module approaches such as **Open Service Gateway Initiative** (**OSGi**) tackled the necessity of supporting the full Java EE API by loading required modules on demand and greatly speeding up operations. In terms of resource usage, application servers also greatly improved compared to the past. A modern container consumes less memory than a running browser instance on a desktop computer. For example, an **Apache TomEE** instance starts up in one second, consumes less than 40 megabytes on disk and less than 30 megabytes of memory.

The performance overhead of managed beans is equally negligible. In fact, compared to CDI managed beans and other frameworks such as Spring Framework, stateless EJBs show the best results. This is due to the fact that stateless session beans are pooled and reused after their business methods have been invoked.

Besides that, application servers manage pools of connections and threads and they enable engineers to gather statistics and performance insights out of the box. The container is responsible for providing monitoring for these aspects. DevOps engineers have the possibility to directly use this data without introducing custom metrics.

Besides these aspects, the application servers also manage the bean instances and life cycles, resources, and database transactions, as we have seen in the previous chapter.

This is the point of having an application container. It does the required work to run an enterprise application in production; the software engineers are responsible for dealing with the business logic. The container provides and manages the required resources and is forced by the standards to provide insights into deployed applications. Due to the vendors that put a lot of effort into optimizing the required technologies, the resource overhead can be kept low.

Application servers' installation sizes are still somewhat bigger than other enterprise frameworks. As of writing this book, vendors are striving to provide smaller, on-demand runtimes tailored for the application's needs. The **MicroProfile** initiative includes several application server vendors that define additional enterprise profiles complementary to the Java EE umbrella. These profiles are assembled from Java EE standards as well. This is a very interesting approach for developers since it doesn't require any change on the application side. The runtime, that is, the set of standards included, will be fitted to what the application needs in order to fulfill its business logic.

# One application per application server

Traditionally, with big installation sizes and long startup times, application servers have been used to deploy several, if not dozens of, enterprise applications. A server instance was shared among several teams, sometimes a whole company. This comes with certain inflexibility, similar to shared application models. Teams cannot simply choose newer JDK or server versions, or restart or reconfigure the application server without coordinating with other teams. This naturally inhibits fast and productive processes, and complicates Continuous Delivery.

In terms of team working methods, and project and application life cycles, the easiest approach therefore is to deploy an application on a dedicated application server. The DevOps team has full control over its version, configuration, and life cycle. This approach simplifies processes and avoids potential issues such as collisions with other teams and used technology. Issues with hierarchical classloading that deploying several applications could introduce are avoided as well.

An application server certainly represents quite a construct for just a single application. However, as we have seen previously, the installation sizes of application servers have already decreased compared to the past. Apart from that, developers should care more about the sizes of the deployment artifacts, since these are the moving parts of the development workflow. In a Continuous Delivery approach, the application is potentially built and packaged many times a day. The longer the time spent on the project build and transmitting artifacts, the longer the turnaround times. This affects each and every build and can add up to a lot of overhead during a day. The application server is not installed and shipped that often. Therefore, it is advisable to deploy an application to a single, dedicated Java EE server:

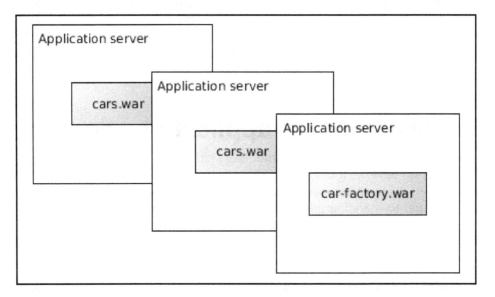

In the next chapter, we will see how container technologies such as Docker support this approach. Shipping the application, including the whole stack down to the operating system as a container, encourages the approach of one application per application server.

# Summary

The seamless integration of multiple Java EE standards with the convention over configuration approach minimizes the amount of boilerplate work developers have to do. The configuration of modern enterprise applications is thus kept to a minimum. Especially the default conventions, which work for the majority of enterprise applications and the possibility of overriding configuration only if required, increases the developer's productivity.

Enterprise applications should minimize their dependencies ideally to only the provided Java EE API. The third-party dependencies should only be added if they are a business necessity and not a technical one.

Java EE applications should be packaged as thin WAR files, following a zero-dependency approach. This has a positive impact on the time spend to build as well as to publish the application.

Modern Java EE applications are far from the negative image of heavyweight J2EE runtimes. They start up and deploy fast and try to reduce the memory impact. Whereas application servers might not be the most lightweight runtime out there, they ship with enough benefits for enterprise applications such as integrating technology or managing life cycles, connections, transactions, or threads, that would have to be implemented otherwise.

In order to simplify application life cycles and deployments it's advisable to deploy one application per application server. This gets rid of a few potential challenges and perfectly fits into a modern world of container technologies. The next chapter will show you this modern world in the age of cloud platforms, what container technologies are about and how Java EE fits into this picture.

# 5
# Container and Cloud Environments with Java EE

The last years have shown a lot of interest in container as well as cloud technology. The vast majority of companies building software is at least considering migrating environments to these modern approaches. In all of my recent projects these technologies have been a point of discussion. Especially, introducing container orchestration technologies greatly affects the way how applications are run.

What are the benefits of container technologies? And why should companies care about the cloud? It seems a lot of these concerns are used as buzzwords, as a *silver bullet* approach. This chapter will examine the motivations behind these technologies. We will also see if and how the Java EE platform is ready for this new world.

This chapter will cover:

- How infrastructure as code supports operations
- Container technologies and orchestration
- Why especially Java EE fits these technologies
- Cloud platforms and their motivations
- 12-factor, cloud native enterprise applications

# Motivations and goals

What are the motivations behind containers, container orchestration, and cloud environments? Why do we see such momentum in this area?

Traditionally, enterprise application deployment worked something like the following. Application developers implemented some business logic and built the application into a packaged artifact. This artifact was deployed manually on an application server that was managed manually as well. During deployment or reconfiguration of the server, the application usually faced a downtime.

Naturally, this approach is a rather high-risk process. Human, manual tasks are error-prone and are not guaranteed to be executed in the same manner each and every time. Humans are rather bad at executing automated, repetitive work. Processes such as installing application servers, operating systems and servers in general, require precise documentation, especially for future reproducibility.

In the past, tasks for operation teams typically were ordered using a ticket system and performed manually. By doing so, installation and configuration of servers held the risk of transforming the system into a non-reproducible state. Setting up a new environment identical to the current one required a lot of manual investigation.

Operational tasks need to be automated and reproducible. Installing a new server, operating system or runtime should always execute in exactly the same manner. Automated processes not only speed up the execution but introduce transparency, revealing which precise steps have been executed. Reinstalling environments should produce exactly the same runtime including all configuration and setup as before.

This also includes deployment and configuration of the application. Instead of manually building and shipping applications, Continuous Integration servers are in charge of building software in an automated, reliable, and reproducible way. CI servers act as *golden source of truth* for software builds. The artifacts produced there are deployed on all involved environments. A software artifact is built once, on the Continuous Integration server, and then verified in integration and end-to-end tests, until it ends up in production. The same application binary that is deployed to production is therefore reliably tested upfront.

Another very important aspect is to be explicit in the software versions that are being used. This includes all used software dependencies, from the application server and Java runtime, down to the operating system and its binaries. Rebuilding or reinstalling software should result in exactly the same state each and every time. Software dependencies are a complex subject which comes with a lot of possibilities for potentials errors. Applications are tested to work properly on specific environments with specific configurations and dependencies. In order to guarantee that the application will work as expected, it is shipped in exactly that configuration that has been verified before.

This aspect also implies that test and staging environments which are used to verify the application's behavior should be as similar to production as possible. In theory this constraint sounds reasonable. From experience the used environments vary quite a lot from production in terms of software versions being used, network configuration, databases, external systems, number of server instances, and so on. In order to test applications properly these differences should be erased as much as possible. In section *Containers* we will see how container technology supports us here.

# Infrastructure as code

A logical conclusion to enable reproducible environments is to make use of **infrastructure as code** (**IaC**). The idea is that all required steps, configuration, and versions are explicitly defined as code. These code definitions are directly used to configure the infrastructure. Infrastructure as code can be implemented in a procedural form, such as scripts, or in a declarative way. The latter approach specifies the desired target state and is executed using additional tooling. No matter which approach is preferred, the point is that the whole environment is specified as code, being executed in an automated, reliable, and reproducible way, always producing the same results.

In any way, the approach implies that the manual steps are kept to a minimum. The easiest form of infrastructure as code are shell scripts. The scripts should be executed from soup to nuts without human involvement. The same holds true for all IaC solutions.

Naturally the responsibility of installing and configuring environments moves from an operations team more toward developers. Since the development team sets certain requirements on the required runtime it makes sense for all engineering teams to work together. This is the idea behind the DevOps movement. In the past the mindset and method of operating too often was that application developers implemented software and literally passed the software and responsibilities toward operations - without further involvement on their side. Potential errors in production primarily concerned the operations team. This unfortunate process not only leads to tensions between engineering teams but ultimately lower quality. However, the overall goal should be to deliver high quality software that fulfills a purpose.

This goal requires the accountability of application developers. By defining all required infrastructure, configuration, and software as code, all engineering teams naturally move together. DevOps aims toward accountability of the software team as a whole. Infrastructure as code is a prerequisite which increases reproducibility, automation, and ultimately software quality.

In the topic *Containers* and *Container orchestration frameworks*, we will see how the presented technologies implement IaC.

# Stability and production readiness

The practices of Continuous Delivery include what needs to be done in order to increase the quality and value of the software. This includes the stability of the application. Reconfiguring and redeploying software does not have to result in any downtime. New features and bugfixes do not have to be shipped exclusively during maintenance windows. Ideally the enterprise software can continuously improve and move forward.

A *zero downtime* approach involves a certain effort. In order to avoid an application being unavailable, at least one other instance of the software needs to be present at a time. A load balancer or proxy server upfront needs to direct the traffic to an available instance. *Blue-green* deployments make use this technique:

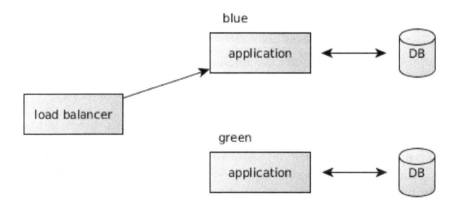

The application instances including their databases are replicated and proxied by a load balancer. The involved applications typically represent different software versions. Switching the traffic from the *blue* to the *green* path and vice versa instantly changes the version, without any downtime. Other forms of blue-green deployments can include scenarios of multiple application instances that are all configured to use the same database instance.

This approach obviously does not have to be realized using some shiny new technology. We have seen blue-green deployments that enable zero-downtime in the past using home-grown solutions. However, modern technologies support these techniques increasing stability, quality, and production-readiness out of the box without much engineering effort required.

# Containers

The last years have shown a lot of interest in **Linux container** technology. Technically this approach is not that new. Linux operating systems such as **Solaris** supported containers a long time ago. However, **Docker** made a the breakthrough in this technology by providing features to build, manage and ship containers in a uniform way.

What is the difference between containers and **virtual machines** (**VMs**) and what makes containers that interesting?

Virtual machines act like a computer in a computer. They allow the runtime to be easily managed from the outside such as creating, starting, stopping, and distributing machines in a fast and ideally automated way. If new servers need to be setup, a blueprint, an image, of the required type can be deployed without installing software from scratch every time. Snapshots of running environments can be taken to easily backup the current state.

In many ways containers behave like virtual machines. They are separated from the host as well as other containers, run in their own network with their own file system and potentially own resources. The difference is that virtual machines run on a hardware abstraction layer, emulating a computer including operating system, whereas containers run directly in the host's kernel. Unlike other kernel processes, containers are separated from the rest of the system using operating system functionality. They manage their own file system. Therefore, containers behave like separate machines but with native performance without the overhead of an abstraction layer. The performance of virtual machines is naturally decreased by their abstraction. Whereas virtual machines provide full flexibility in choosing operating systems, containers will always run in the same kernel and therefore in the same version as the host operating system. Containers therefore do not ship their own Linux kernel and can be minimized to their required binaries.

Container technologies such as Docker provide functionality to build, run, and distribute containers in a uniform way. Docker defines building container images as IaC which again enables automation, reliability, and reprocibility. Dockerfiles define all the steps that are required to install the application including its dependencies, for example, an application container and the Java runtime. Each step in the Dockerfile corresponds to a command that is executed at image build time. Once a container is started from an image it should contain everything which is required to fulfill its task.

Containers usually contain a single Unix process which represents a running service, for example an application server, a web server, or a database. If an enterprise system consists of several running servers, they run in individual containers.

One of the biggest advantages of Docker containers is that they make use of a **copy-on-write** file system. Every build step, as well as every running container later on, operates on a layered file system, which does not change its layers but only adds new layers on top. Built images therefore comprise multiple layers.

Containers that are created from images are always started with the same initial state. Running containers potentially modify files as new, temporary layers in the file system, which are discarded as soon as the containers are stopped. By default, Docker containers are therefore stateless runtime environments. This encourages the idea of reproducibility. Every persistent behavior needs to be defined explicitly.

The multiple layers are beneficial when rebuilding and redistributing images. Docker caches intermediate layers and only rebuilds and retransmits what has been changed.

For example, an image build may consist of multiple steps. System binaries are added first, then the Java runtime, an application server, and finally our application. When changes are made to the application and a new build is required, only the last step is re-executed; the previous steps are cached. The same is true for transmitting images over the wire. Only the layers that have been changed and that are not yet existent on the target registry, are actually retransmitted.

The following illustrates the layers of a Docker image and their individual distribution:

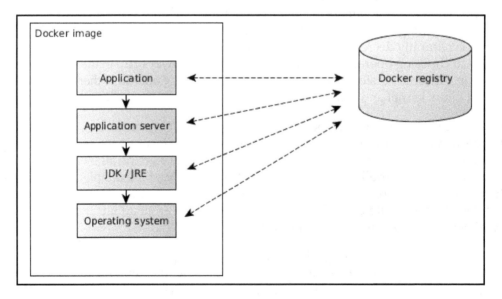

Docker images are either built from scratch, that is from an empty starting point, or built upon an existing base image. There are tons of base images available, for all major Linux distributions containing package managers, for typical environment stacks as well as for Java-based images. Base images are a way to build upon a common ground and provide basic functionality for all resulting images. For example, it makes sense to use a base image including a Java runtime installation. If this image needs to be updated, for example, to fix security issues, all dependent images can be rebuilt and receive the new contents by updating the base image version. As said before, software builds need to be repeatable. Therefore we always need to specify explicit versions for software artifacts such as images.

Containers that are started from previously built Docker images need access to these images. They are distributed using Docker registries such as the publicly available DockerHub or company-internal registries to distribute own images. Locally built images are pushed to these registries and retrieved on the environments that will start new containers later on.

# Java EE in the container

As it turns out the approach of a layered file system matches Java EE's approach of separating the application from the runtime. Thin deployment artifacts only contain the actual business logic, the part which changes and which is rebuilt each and every time. These artifacts are deployed onto an enterprise container which does not change that often. Docker container images are built step-by-step, layer-by-layer. Building an enterprise application image includes an operating system base image, a Java runtime, an application server and finally the application. If only the application layer changes, only this step will have to be re-executed and retransmitted - all the other layers are touched only once and then cached.

Thin deployment artifacts leverage the advantages of layers since only a matter of kilobytes has to be rebuilt and redistributed, respectively. Therefore, zero-dependency applications is the advisable way of using containers.

As seen in the previous chapter, it makes sense to deploy one application per application server. Containers execute a single process which in this case is the application server containing the application. The application server therefore needs to run on a dedicated container that is included in the container as well. Both the application server and the application are added at image build time. Potential configuration, for example regarding datasources, pooling, or server modules, is also made during build time, usually by adding custom configuration files. Since the container is owned by the single application these components are configured without affecting anything else.

Once a container is started from the image it should already contain everything that is required to fulfill its job. The application as well as all required configuration must already be present. Therefore, applications are not deployed on a previously running container anymore but added during the image build time, to be present at container runtime. This is usually achieved by placing the deployment artifact into the container's auto-deployment directory. As soon as the configured application server starts, the application is deployed.

The container image is built only once and then executed on all the environments. Following the idea of reproducible artifacts before, the same artifacts that run in production have to be tested upfront. Therefore the same Docker image that has been verified will be published to production.

But what if applications are configured differently in various environments? What if different external systems or databases need to be communicated with? In order to not interfere with several environments, at least the used database instances will differ. Applications shipped in containers are started from the same image but sometimes still need some variations.

Docker offers the possibility of changing several aspects of running containers. This includes networking, adding volumes, that is, injecting files and directories that reside on the Docker host, or adding Unix environment variables. The environment differences are added by the container orchestration from outside of the container. The images are only built once for a specific version, used and potentially modified in different environments. This brings the big advantage that these configuration differences are not modeled into the application rather than managed from the outside. The same is true for networking and connecting applications and external systems, which we will see in the coming sections.

Linux containers, by the way, solve the business-politically motivated issue of shipping the application together with the implementation in a single package for the reason of flexibility. Since containers include the runtime and all dependencies required, including the Java runtime, the infrastructure only has to provide a Docker runtime. All used technology including the versions are the responsibility of the development team.

The following code snippet shows the definition of a `Dockerfile` building an enterprise application `hello-cloud` onto a **WildFly** base image.

```
FROM jboss/wildfly:10.0.0.Final

COPY target/hello-cloud.war /opt/jboss/wildfly/standalone/deployments/
```

The `Dockerfile` specifies the `jboss/wildfly` base image in a specific version which already contains a Java 8 runtime and the WildFly application server. It resides in the application's project directory, pointing to the `hello-cloud.war` archive which was previously built by a Maven build. The WAR file is copied to WildFly's auto-deployment directory and will be available at that location at container runtime. The `jboss/wildfly` base image already specifies a run command, how to run the application server, which is inherited by the Dockerfile. Therefore it doesn't have to specify a command as well. After a Docker build the resulting image will contain everything from the `jboss/wildfly` base image including the *hello-cloud* application. This matches the same approach of installing a WildFly application server from scratch and adding the WAR file to the auto-deployment directory. When distributing the built image, only the added layer including the thin WAR file needs to be transmitted.

The deployment model of the Java EE platform fits the container world. Separating the application for the enterprise container leverage the use of copy-on-write file systems, minimizing the time spent on builds, distribution, or deployments.

# Container orchestration frameworks

Let's go up one abstraction layer from containers. Containers include everything required to run specific services as stateless, self-contained artifacts. However, the containers need to be orchestrated to run in the correct network, being able to communicate with other services and being started with the correct configuration, if required. The straightforward approach is to develop home-grown scripts that run the required containers. However, in order to realize a more flexible solution that also enables production-readiness such as zero-downtime, the use of container orchestration frameworks is advisable.

Container orchestration frameworks such as **Kubernetes**, **DC/OS** or **Docker Compose** are not only responsible to run containers, but to orchestrate, connect and configure them appropriately. The same motivations and principles apply that are true for container technologies as well: automation, reproducibility and IaC. Software engineers define the desired target state as code and let the orchestration tool reliably setup the environments as required.

Before going into a specific orchestration solution, let's have a closer look at the rough concepts.

Orchestration frameworks enable us to connect multiple containers together. This usually involves service lookup using logic names via DNS. If multiple physical hosts are used, the framework resolves IP addresses over these nodes. Ideally an application running in a container just connects to an external system using a logical service name that is resolved by the container orchestration. For example, a car manufacturing application using the *vehicle* database connects using the `vehicle-db` hostname. This hostname is then resolved via DNS, depending on the environment which the application runs in. Connecting via logical names reduces the required configuration in the application code, since the configured connection is always the same. The orchestration just connects the desired instance.

This is true for all offered systems. Applications, databases, and other servers are abstracted to logical service names which are accessed and resolved during runtime.

Configuring containers depending on their environment is another aspect that orchestration frameworks solve. In general it's advisable to reduce the required configuration in applications. However, there are cases where some configuration effort is required. It is the framework's responsibility to provide container configuration by dynamically injecting files or environment variables depending on the circumstances.

The production-readiness features that some of the container orchestration frameworks offer represent one of their biggest advantages. Ongoing development of an application triggers new project builds and result in new container image versions. The running containers need to be replaced by containers that are started from these new versions. In order to avoid downtime the container orchestration swaps the running containers using a zero-downtime deployment approach.

In the same way, container orchestration makes it possible to increase the workload by scaling up the number of container instances. In the past, certain applications ran on multiple instances simultaneously. If the number of instances needed to be increased, more application servers had to be provisioned. In a container world the same goal is achieved by simply starting more of the stateless application containers. The developers increase the configured number of container replicas; the orchestration framework implements this change by starting more container instances.

In order to run containers in production some orchestration aspects have to be considered. Experience shows that some companies tend to build their own solutions rather than using de facto standard technology. However, container orchestration frameworks already solve these issues well and it is highly advisable to at least consider them.

# Realizing container orchestration

We've now seen which challenges container orchestration framework tackle. This section will show you the core concepts of **Kubernetes**, a solution originally developed by Google to run their workloads. At the time of writing this book Kubernetes has a enormous momentum and is also the basis for other orchestration solutions such as **OpenShift** by RedHat. I chose this solution because of its popularity but also because I believe that it does the job of orchestration very well. However, the important point is less about comprehending the chosen technology rather than the motivations and concepts behind it.

Kubernetes runs and manages Linux containers in a cluster of nodes. The Kubernetes master node orchestrates the worker nodes which do the actual work, that is, to run the containers. The software engineers control the cluster using the API provided by the master node, via a web-based GUI or command-line tool.

The running cluster consists of so-called resources of a specific type. The core resource types of Kubernetes are **pods**, **deployments**, and **services**. A pod is an atomic workload unit, running one or more Linux container. This means the application runs in a pod.

The pods can be started and managed as standalone, single resources. However, it makes a lot of sense to not directly specify separate pods but to define a deployment, which encapsulates and manages running pods. Deployments enable the functionality that provide production-readiness such as upscaling and downscaling of pods or rolling updates. They are responsible for reliably running our applications in the specified versions.

A system defines services in order to connect to running applications from outside of the cluster or within other containers. The services provide the logical abstraction described in the last section that embraces a set of pods. All pods that run a specific application are abstracted by a single service which directs the traffic onto active pods. The combination of services routing to active pods and deployments managing the rolling update of versions enables zero-downtime deployments. Applications are always accessed using services which direct to corresponding pods.

All core resources are unique within a Kubernetes **namespace**. Namespaces encapsulate aggregates of resources and can be used to model different environments. For example, services that point to external systems outside of the cluster can be configured differently in different namespaces. The applications that use the external systems always use the same logical service name which are directed to different endpoints.

Kubernetes supports resources definition as IaC using JSON or YAML files. The YAML format is a human-readable data serialization format, a superset of JSON. It became the de facto standard within Kubernetes.

The following code snippet shows the definition of a service of the `hello-cloud` application:

```
---
kind: Service
apiVersion: v1
metadata:
  name: hello-cloud
spec:
  selector:
    app: hello-cloud
  ports:
    - port: 8080
---
```

The example specifies a service which directs traffic on port 8080 toward `hello-cloud` pods that are defined by the deployment.

The following shows the `hello-cloud` deployment:

```
---
kind: Deployment
apiVersion: apps/v1beta1
metadata:
  name: hello-cloud
spec:
  replicas: 1
  template:
    metadata:
      labels:
        app: hello-cloud
    spec:
      containers:
      - name: hello-cloud
        image: docker.example.com/hello-cloud:1
        imagePullPolicy: IfNotPresent
        livenessProbe:
          httpGet:
            path: /
            port: 8080
        readinessProbe:
          httpGet:
            path: /hello-cloud/resources/hello
            port: 8080
      restartPolicy: Always
---
```

The deployment specifies one pod from the given template with the provided Docker image. As soon as the deployment is created Kubernetes tries to satisfy the pod specifications by starting a container from the image and testing the container's health using the specified probes.

The container image `docker.example.com/hello-cloud:1` includes the enterprise application which was built and distributed to a Docker registry earlier.

All these resource definitions are applied to the Kubernetes cluster by either using the web-based GUI or the CLI.

After creating both the deployment and the service, the *hello-cloud* application is accessible from within the cluster via the service. To be accessed from the outside of the cluster a route needs to be defined, for example using an **ingress**. Ingress resources route traffic to services using specific rules. The following shows an example ingress resource that makes the `hello-cloud` service available:

```
---
kind: Ingress
apiVersion: extensions/v1beta1
metadata:
  name: hello-cloud
spec:
  rules:
  - host: hello.example.com
    http:
      paths:
      - path: /
        backend:
          serviceName: hello-cloud
          servicePort: 8080
---
```

These resources now specify the whole application, which is deployed onto a Kubernetes cluster, accessible from the outside and abstracted in a logical service inside of the cluster. If other applications need to communicate with the application, they can do so via the Kubernetes-internal, resolvable `hello-cloud` DNS hostname and port `8080`.

The following diagram shows an example setup of the *hello-cloud* application with a replica of three pods that runs in a Kubernetes cluster of two nodes:

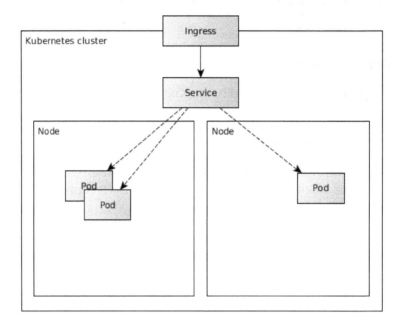

Besides service lookup using logical names, some applications still need additional configuration. Therefore Kubernetes as well as other orchestration technology has the possibility of inserting files and environment variables into the container dynamically at runtime. The concept of **config maps**, key-value-based configuration is used for this. The contents of config maps can be made available as files, dynamically mounted into a container. The following defines an example config map, specifying the contents of a properties file:

```
---
kind: ConfigMap
apiVersion: v1
metadata:
  name: hello-cloud-config
data:
  application.properties: |
    hello.greeting=Hello from Kubernetes
    hello.name=Java EE
---
```

The config map is being used to mount the contents as files into containers. The config map's keys will be used as file names, mounted into a directory, with the value representing the file contents. The pod definitions specify the usage of config maps mounted as volumes. The following shows the previous deployment definition of the *hello-cloud* application, using `hello-cloud-config` in a mounted volume:

```
---
kind: Deployment
apiVersion: apps/v1beta1
metadata:
  name: hello-cloud
spec:
  replicas: 1
  template:
    metadata:
      labels:
        app: hello-cloud
    spec:
      containers:
      - name: hello-cloud
        image: docker.example.com/hello-cloud:1
        imagePullPolicy: IfNotPresent
        volumeMounts:
        - name: config-volume
          mountPath: /opt/config
        livenessProbe:
          httpGet:
            path: /
            port: 8080
        readinessProbe:
          httpGet:
            path: /hello-cloud/resources/hello
            port: 8080
      volumes:
      - name: config-volume
        configMap:
          name: hello-cloud-config
      restartPolicy: Always
---
```

The deployment defines a volume which references to the `hello-cloud-config` config map. The volume is mounted to the path `/opt/config` resulting in all key-value pairs of the config map being inserted as files in this directory. With the config map demonstrated previously this would result in a `application.properties` file containing the entries for keys `hello.greeting` and `hello.name`. The application expects that at runtime the file resides under this location.

Separate environments will specify different contents of the config maps, depending on the desired configuration values. Configuring applications using dynamic files is one approach. It is also possible to inject and override specific environment variables. The following code snippet demonstrates this example as well. This approach is advisable when the number of configuration values is limited:

```
# similar to previous example
# ...
        image: docker.example.com/hello-cloud:1
        imagePullPolicy: IfNotPresent
        env:
        - name: GREETING_HELLO_NAME
          valueFrom:
            configMapRef:
              name: hello-cloud-config
              key: hello.name
          livenessProbe:
# ...
```

Applications need to configure credentials, used for example to authorize against external systems or as database accesses. These credentials are ideally configured in a different place than uncritical configuration values. Besides config maps, Kubernetes therefore also includes the concept of **secrets**. These are similar to config maps, also representing key-value pairs, but obfuscated for humans as Base64-encoded data. Secrets and their contents are typically not serialized as infrastructure as code since the credentials should not have unrestricted access.

A common practice is to make credentials accessible in containers using environment variables. The following code snippet shows how to include a value configured in secret `hello-cloud-secret` into the *hello-cloud* application:

```
# similar to previous example
# ...
        image: docker.example.com/hello-cloud:1
        imagePullPolicy: IfNotPresent
        env:
        - name: TOP_SECRET
          valueFrom:
            secretKeyRef:
              name: hello-cloud-secret
              key: topsecret
          livenessProbe:
# ...
```

The environment variable `TOP_SECRET` is created from referencing the `topsecret` key in secret `hello-cloud-secret`. This environment variable is available at container runtime and can be used from the running process.

Some applications packaged in containers cannot solely run as stateless applications. Databases are a typical example of this. Since containers are discarded after their processes have exited, the contents of their file system are also gone. Services such as databases need persistent state though. To solve this issue Kubernetes includes **persistent volumes**. As the name suggests these volumes are available beyond the life cycle of the pods. Persistent volumes dynamically make files and directories available which are used within the pod and retain after it has exited.

Persistent volumes are backed by network attached storage or cloud storage offerings, depending on the cluster installation. They make it possible to run storage services such as databases in container orchestration clusters as well. However, as a general advise, persistent state in containers should be avoided.

The YAML IaC definitions are kept under version control in the application repository. The next chapter covers how to apply the file contents to a Kubernetes cluster as part of a Continuous Delivery pipeline.

# Java EE in orchestrated containers

The orchestration framework orchestrates and integrates enterprise applications in clustered environments. It takes a lot of work off the used application technology. Container orchestration also vastly simplifies how to configure applications and how to connect to external services. This section will showcase this.

## Connecting external services

Client controls require URLs to connect against in order to integrate external services. The URLs traditionally have been configured in files, which potentially differed in various environments. In an orchestrated environment the application can resolve external services using a logical name, via DNS. The following code snippet shows how to connect against the *cloud processor* application:

```
@ApplicationScoped
public class HelloCloudProcessor {

    private Client client;
    private WebTarget target;
```

```
    @PostConstruct
    private void initClient() {
        client = ClientBuilder...
        target = client.target("http://cloud-
processor:8080/processor/resources/hello");
    }

    public String processGreeting() {
        ...
    }
}
```

The same holds true for other URLs, for example datasources definitions. The application server configuration can simply point to the name of the database service and use it to resolve the corresponding instance at runtime.

# Configuring orchestrated applications

Resolving services by logical names already eliminates a lot of configuration in the application. Since the same container image is being used in all environments, potentially different configuration needs to be inserted from the orchestration environment. As shown in the previous example, Kubernetes config maps tackle this situation. The *hello-cloud* application expects that at runtime a properties file will reside under `/opt/config/application.properties`. The project code will therefore access this location. The following demonstrates the integration of the properties file using a CDI producer:

```
public class HelloGreeter {

    @Inject
    @Config("hello.greeting")
    String greeting;

    @Inject
    @Config("hello.name")
    String greetingName;

    public String processGreeting() {
        return greeting + ", " + greetingName;
    }
}
```

The CDI producer is defined similarly to the configuration example shown previously:

```
@ApplicationScoped
public class ConfigurationExposer {

    private final Properties properties = new Properties();

    @PostConstruct
    private void initProperties() {
        try (InputStream inputStream =
                new FileInputStream("/opt/config/application.properties"))
{

            properties.load(inputStream);
        } catch (IOException e) {
            throw new IllegalStateException("Could not init configuration",
e);
        }
    }

    @Produces
    @Config("")
    public String exposeConfig(InjectionPoint injectionPoint) {
        Config config =
injectionPoint.getAnnotated().getAnnotation(Config.class);
        if (config != null)
            return properties.getProperty(config.value());
        return null;
    }
}
```

The definition of the @Config qualifier is similar to the previous example in Chapter 3, *Implementing Modern Java Enterprise Applications*. The application loads the contents of the properties file into the properties map and produces the configured values using CDI. All managed beans can inject these values which emerge from the Kubernetes config map.

In order to realize secret configuration values, Kubernetes includes the concept of secrets as previously shown. A common practice is to make the contents of the secrets accessible in containers using environment variables.

Java applications use the System.getenv() method to access environment variables. This functionality is used for both secrets and config map values, respectively.

The demonstrated approaches and examples enable an enterprise application to be deployed, managed, and configured in a container orchestration cluster. They are sufficient for the majority of use cases.

# 12-factor applications and Java EE

As of writing this book, **12-factor** applications has emerged as a way of developing **Software as a Service (SaaS)** applications. The 12-factor application approach define 12 software development principles. The motivations behind these principles aim to minimize time and effort, avoid software erosion, and embrace Continuous Delivery and cloud platforms.

In other words the 12-factors aim to to implement enterprise applications in a modern way. Some of the principles sound obvious to most engineers, while others seem to contradict the common practice of building enterprise applications.

The list of the 12-factors includes:

- I. Have one codebase tracked in revision control, many deploys
- II. Explicitly declare and isolate dependencies
- III. Store config in the environment
- IV. Treat backing services as attached resources
- V. Strictly separate build and run stages
- VI. Execute the app as one or more stateless processes
- VII. Export services via port binding
- VIII. Scale out via the process model
- IX. Maximize robustness with fast startup and graceful shutdown
- X. Keep development, staging, and production as similar as possible
- XI. Treat logs as event streams
- XII. Run admin/management tasks as one-off processes

The following explains the motivations of each principle and its realization with Java EE.

# Have one codebase tracked in revision control, many deploys

This principle sounds pretty obvious to software engineers, declaring that a software code should be kept under version control, a single repository, even for multiple *deploys*. Deploys relate to software instances, running on specific environments. Therefore the codebase of a single application is tracked in a single repository, not several codebases per application or vice versa, containing all specifications for potentially different environments.

This principle leverages developer productivity since all information is found under one repository. It is indifferent to the chosen technology and therefore supported by Java EE applications, as well.

The repository should contain all source files that are required to build and run the enterprise application. Besides Java sources and configuration files, this includes infrastructure as code.

# Explicitly declare and isolate dependencies

Software dependencies and their versions that are required in order to run the application must be specified explicitly. This includes not only dependencies which the application is programmed against, for example third-party APIs, but also implicit dependencies on the Java runtime or operating system, respectively. Explicitly specifying the required versions leads to far less compatibility issues in production. A composition of software versions is sufficiently tested during the development workflow. Dependency versions that differ when rebuilding binaries introduce potential issues. It is therefore advisable to explicitly declare all software versions to reduce probability of error and enable reproducibility.

Container technology simplifies this principle by explicitly specifying all software installation steps. Versions of used base images should be explicitly declared, so that image rebuilds result in the same result. The Docker `latest` tag should therefore be avoided in favor of definite versions. All software installations specified in Dockerfiles should point to explicit versions as well. Docker rebuilds, with or without cache, should produce the same outcome.

Java applications specify their dependencies using build systems. The first chapter already covered what is necessary to enable reproducible builds using both Maven and Gradle. In Java EE applications these dependencies are ideally minimized to the Java EE API.

Whenever possible, it's advisable to specify explicit dependency versions, not just *latest* ones. Only software using explicit versions can be tested reliably.

Isolating dependencies is a necessity for distributed development throughout the software team. Software artifacts should be accessible via well-defined processes, for example artifact repositories. Dependencies, which are added during the software build, no matter whether Java runtime installations, Java artifacts, or operating system components, need to be distributed from a central place. Repositories such as **Maven Central**, **DockerHub** or company-internal repositories enable this approach.

# Store config in the environment

Application configuration, that differ for separate environments, such as databases, external systems, or credentials, need to be existent at runtime. This configuration should not be reflected in the source code but dynamically modifiable from outside of the application. This implies that configuration is retrieved via files, environment variables or other external concerns.

Container technology and orchestration frameworks support these approaches as previously shown. Configuration for different environments, such as *test*, *staging*, and *production* is stored in Kubernetes config maps and dynamically used in pods in volumes or environment variables.

The 12-factor principles state that an application "[...] stores config in environment variables". Environment variables are a straightforward way of inserting specific variations that is supported by all kinds of technology. However, if configuring the application involves a lot of individual configuration values, engineers may consider to use configuration files contained in container volumes, instead.

# Treat backing services as attached resources

Databases and external systems that are accessed in the application are called *resources*. It should make no difference to the system where an external service or database is part of the application. The *resources* should be attached to the application in a loosely coupled way. External systems and databases should be able to be replaced by new instances without affecting the application.

Applications abstract the accessed external system, first of all in the communication technology being used. Communication via HTTP or JDBC, for example, abstracts the implementations and enables systems to be replaced by others. By doing so, applications are only coupled to their contract: the communication protocol and defined schemas. JPA, JAX-RS, and JSON-B are examples that support this approach.

Container orchestration frameworks take this approach even further and abstract services into logic names. As shown previously applications can use service names as hostnames, resolved by DNS.

In general, application developers should loosely couple systems together, ideally only depending on protocols and schemas. At a code level backing services are abstracted into own components, such as individual controls with clean interfaces. This minimizes changes if attached resources change.

# Strictly separate build and run stages

This principle advises to separate the application build, the deployment, and the run processes. This is a well-known approach to Java enterprise developers. Application binaries are built, deployed, and run in separate steps. Software or configuration changes happen in the source code or in the deployment step, respectively, and not directly in production. The deployment step brings application binaries and potential configuration together. Well-defined change and release management processes keep the integrity of the enterprise software.

For the vast majority of software projects, it is common practice to separate these steps and orchestrate stages in a Continuous Integration server. This is necessary to ensure reliability and reproducibility. Chapter 6, *Application Development Workflows* covers this topic in depth.

# Execute the app as one or more stateless processes

Ideally, applications run as stateless processes where every use case is executed self-sufficiently, without affecting other running processes. Potential state is either stored in an attached resource such as a database or discarded. Session state that lives longer than a single request is therefore a violation of this principle. The challenge with traditional user session state is that it only resides in a local application instance and not accessible from other instances. The need for so-called *sticky sessions* on load balancers is an indicator for not having a stateless application.

A lot of modern technology supports this approach. Docker containers with their copy-on-write file system are an example. Stopped containers will be discarded and therefore all of their state is gone as well. Stateless EJBs are based on a similar motivation. However, instances of stateless session beans are pooled and reused, therefore developers need to ensure that no state retains after the business use case invocations.

Enterprise applications should be able to be restarted from scratch without affecting their behavior. This also implies that applications share no state except via well-defined attached resources.

# Export services via port binding

Web applications are traditionally deployed to a certain software stack. Java enterprise applications for examples are deployed to an enterprise or Servlet container whereas server-side scripting languages such as PHP run on top of a web server. The applications therefore depend on their immediate runtime.

This 12-factor principle advise to develop self-sufficient applications that expose their functionality via network ports. Since web-based enterprise applications will communicate via the network, binding services to ports is the way of least coupling.

Java EE applications that run in a container support this approach, only exporting a port which is used to communicate with the application. Containers only depend on the Linux kernel, the application runtime is therefore transparent. Container orchestration frameworks leverage this idea, connecting services to pods via logical names and ports, as shown in a previous example. Java EE supports the use of containers and therefore this principle as well.

# Scale out via the process model

Modern applications as well as their environments should enable scalability when the workload on them increases. Applications ideally are able to scale out horizontally, rather than just vertically. The difference is that scaling horizontally aims to adds more individual, self-contained nodes to the software whereas scaling vertically increases the resources on single nodes or processes. However, scaling vertically is limited, since resources on physical nodes cannot be increased infinitely.

12-factor applications describe the procedure of adding concurrency to the software with adding more self-contained, *shared-nothing* processes. Workloads should be distributable within several physical hosts, by increasing the number of processes. The processes represent the request or worker threads who handle the system's workload.

This approach shows the necessity of implementing stateless application in a shared-nothing manner. Containers that run stateless Java enterprise applications enable the system to scale out. Kubernetes managed scalability in deployments via managing the number of replicas.

The bottleneck of enterprise applications, however, is typically not the application instances rather than central databases. `Chapter 8`, *Microservices and System Architecture* and `Chapter 9`, *Monitoring, Performance, and Logging* cover the topics of scalability in distributed systems as well as performance in Java EE projects in general.

# Maximize robustness with fast startup and graceful shutdown

`Chapter 4`, *Lightweight Java EE* already showed the necessity of fast turnarounds. This principle of 12-factor applications requires technology that enables velocity and elasticity. In order to rapidly scale up, the software should startup in a matter of seconds, making it possible to tackle a growing workload.

Application shutdowns should gracefully finish in-flight requests and properly close all open connections and resources. Especially requests and transactions that are executed while the shutdown signal occurs should be finished properly not to maliciously abort client use cases. In a Unix process approach shutdown signals are sent as `SIGTERM` signals. Linux containers are stopped in the same way, giving the container process a chance to shutdown properly. When building container images, developers should pay attention that the process handles Unix signals properly, resulting in a graceful shutdown of the application server when it receives a `SIGTERM` signal.

Java EE supports both fast startups and graceful shutdowns. As shown previously, modern application servers start up and deploy applications in a matter of seconds.

Since the application servers manage beans, resources, pooling, and threading, they take care of closing the resources properly at JVM shutdown. The developers don't need to take care of this aspect themselves. Beans that manage custom resources or handles that need to be closed, use pre-destroy methods to implemented proper closing. The following shows a client control using a JAX-RS client handle which is closed on server shutdown:

```
@ApplicationScoped
public class CoffeePurchaser {

    private Client client;

    ...

    @PreDestroy
    public void closeClient() {
        client.close();
    }
}
```

The platform guarantees that the pre-destroy methods of all managed beans are called once the application server shuts down.

# Keep development, staging, and production as similar as possible

This 12-factor principle aims to minimize differences between environments.

Enterprise applications traditionally have quite some differences between the environments of the development process. There are development environments, maybe several of them, such as local workstations or dedicated server environments and finally there is the production environment. These environments differ in regard of time when software artifacts in certain versions and configuration are deployed during the development process. The longer the time span of simultaneously having different versions in the set of environments the greater this difference becomes.

There is also a difference in teams and people. Traditionally software developers maintain their own development environment while an operations team takes care of production. This introduces potential gaps in communication, processes, and used technology.

The technical difference between environments contains the biggest risk. Development or test environments that use different tools, technology, external services and configuration than production introduce the risk that these differences will lead to errors. Software is tested automatically on these environments before going to production. Every difference from production that is not tested can and eventually will introduce bugs that could have been prevented. The same is true for exchanging tools, backend services, or used stacks for lightweight alternatives in development or local environments.

It is therefore advisable to keep the environments as similar as possible. Especially, container technologies and orchestration frameworks highly support this approach. As we saw previously, differences in configuration, services, and technology are minimized or at least explicitly defined via the environment. Ideally, software landscapes are identical on development, test environments, staging, and production. If that is not possible, service abstractions as well as environment-managed configuration support to manage the differences.

The difference in time and people is tackled by usage of Continuous Delivery, not just from a technical but also organizational point of view. The overall time to production should be as small as possible, enabling fast delivery of features and bug fixes. Implementing Continuous Delivery naturally moves teams and responsibilities together. The DevOps movement describes how all engineers are responsible for the overall software. This leads to a culture where all teams closely work together or merge into single teams of software engineers.

# Treat logs as event streams

Enterprise applications traditionally write logs to log files on disk. Some engineers argue that this information is one of the most important insights into the application. The software project usually includes configuration of the contents and format of these logfiles. However, storing log data in log files is first of all just an output format, usually having a single log event per line.

This principle of 12-factor applications argues that logging should be treated as a stream of log events, that are emitted by the application. Applications should, however, not concern themselves with routing and storing the log file into specific output formats. Instead they log to the process' standard output. The standard out is captured and processed by the runtime environment.

This approach is uncommon to most enterprise developers with all logging frameworks, output formats and tools being around. However, environments where a lot of services run in parallel need to capture and process log events externally anyway. Solutions such as **Elasticsearch**, **Logstash**, and **Kibana** have proven themselves well to process and comprehend complex situations with log events from several sources. Storing log events in log files not necessarily supports these approaches.

Logging to the application's standard out not only simplifies development, since routing and storing is not a responsibility of the application anymore. It also reduces the need for external dependencies, such as logging frameworks. Zero-dependency applications support this approach. The environment such as a container orchestration framework takes care of capturing and routing the event stream. In Chapter 9, *Monitoring, Performance, and Logging*, we will cover the topic of logging, its necessity and shortcomings.

# Run admin/management tasks as one-off processes

This principle describes that administrative or management tasks should be executed as separate short-lived processes. The technology ideally supports command execution in a shell that operates on the running environment.

Although containers encapsulate Unix processes, they provide additional functionality to execute single commands or to open a remote shell into the container. Engineers can therefore execute the management and administration scripts provided by the Java EE application server. Still, in Java EE applications, the number of required administration and management tasks are limited. A Container runs the application server process, which auto-deploys the application; no further application life cycle management is required.

Administrative tasks are usually required for debugging and troubleshooting purposes. Therefore containers and container orchestration frameworks offer possibilities to open remote shells into the containers or execute one-time commands. Apart from that, the Chapter 9, *Monitoring, Performance, and Logging* will show you what is necessary to gather further monitoring information about enterprise applications.

The motivations of the 12-factors are to develop stateless, scalable enterprise applications that embrace Continuous Delivery and modern environment platforms, optimize time and effort spent in development and try to avoid software erosion. 12-factor application have a clean contract with their underlying system and ideally declarative infrastructure definitions.

# Cloud, Cloud native, and their benefits

As of writing this book, there is a lot of interest in cloud platforms. We currently see big companies moving their IT infrastructure into cloud offerings. But what benefits does *the cloud* have to offer?.

First of all, we have to be aware that modern environments do not necessarily have to run on top of a cloud platform. All the benefits of container technology and container orchestration frameworks can equally be achieved using company-internal infrastructure. On premise installations of platforms such as Kubernetes or OpenShift at first provide the same advantages for software teams. In fact, one of the biggest benefits of container runtimes is to abstract the environment where the containers are running. Why are cloud platforms interesting for companies then?

As mentioned in the beginning of this book, the software world is moving faster than ever. The key for companies to keep pace with the trends in their business is to embrace agility and velocity in terms of moving fast. The time to market of new products and features thereof need to be as short as possible. Moving in iterative steps, adapting to customers' needs and continuously improving software meets this demand. In order to realize this goal, IT infrastructure, as well as all other aspects of software engineering, needs to be fast and flexible. New environments should be setup via automated, reliable and reproducible processes. The same principles for continuous software delivery apply to server environments. Cloud platforms offer this possibility.

Companies that want to embrace agility and to adapt to their customers' demands need to ask themselves the question: *How long does it take to provision new environments?* This is the prerequisite of being able to adapt quickly. Provisioning whole new environments should be a matter of minutes, should not require overly complex processes and ideally no human intervention. As said before it is definitely possible to realize such approaches on premises. Cloud offerings, however, offer these benefits out of the box with sufficient, scalable resources. **Infrastructure as a Service** (**IaaS**) or **Platform as a Service** (**PaaS**) offerings take a lot of work off the hands of companies, enabling them to focus on building their products.

Still, big companies are often skeptical when it comes to cloud services, especially in terms of data security. Interestingly, experience of projects shows that when comparing infrastructure environments down to earth, cloud platforms run by sophisticated enterprises offer more secure environments than most on premises. Cloud platform providers put a lot of time and effort into building proper solutions. Especially combining cloud platform offerings with orchestration solutions, such as Docker Compose, Kubernetes, or OpenShift hold a lot of potential.

Interestingly, one of the main arguments of companies to move their IT into the cloud is because of economic reasons. From experience, a lot of companies want to save costs by using cloud platforms. In fact, when taking the whole process of migrating and transforming environments, teams, technology, and most of all know-how, into account, on premises solutions are usually still cheaper. However, the main advantage of cloud offerings is flexibility and the ability to move fast. If an IT company maintains a well-orchestrated landscape, including automation, reliable and reproducible processes, it is advisable to keep, and continuously improve, this approach. That said, the question about modern environments is less about whether to use cloud platforms than about processes, team mindsets, and reasonable technology.

# Cloud native

Besides the interest in cloud technology there is a lot of interest in the term **cloud native** which describes applications that, besides following the 12-factors, have a strong relationship to cloud platforms. Cloud native and 12-factor applications are not synonymous; rather than cloud native includes the 12-factors, among other things.

Cloud native applications are designed to run on cloud PaaS offerings with all their benefits and challenges, embrace container technology and elastic scalability. They are built with the claim to provide modern, scalable, stateless and resilient applications, manageable within modern orchestration environments. Unlike the term *native* suggests, applications that follow this approach do not necessarily have to be built as *green-field* projects that support cloud technology from day one.

Important aspects for cloud native applications beyond the 12-factors are monitoring and application health concerns, which can be summarized as telemetry. Telemetry for enterprise applications include responsiveness, monitoring, domain-specific insights, health checks, and debugging. As we have seen previously, container orchestration supports us at least with the last two concerns: health checks and debugging. Running applications are probed whether they are still alive and healthy. Debugging and troubleshooting is possible by evaluating the log event streams, connecting into the running containers or executing processes.

Application monitoring need to be exposed by the running container. This requires a bit more effort from software developers. Domain-specific metrics need to be defined by the business experts first. It depends which metrics are interesting to business departments and will be exposed by the application. Technical metrics are gathered from the running application as well. Chapter 9, *Monitoring, Performance, and Logging* covers the topic of monitoring in regard to modern environments.

Another aspect that the 12-factors don't include are APIs and security thereof. SaaS applications communicate via exposed APIs that have to be made known to other teams of developers. The nature and structure of web services needs to be documented and agreed upon during development. This is especially the case when HTTP APIs don't implement Hypermedia. The applications need to know the nature and structure of exchanged information - ideally as early as possible in the development process. This also covers authentication and authorization. Application developers should be aware of security mechanisms they need to address before communicating to other services. In general it is not advisable to only think of security aspects after development. Chapter 10, *Security* covers this topic concerning cloud environments and integration into Java EE applications.

In order to build an umbrella for all technologies that embrace cloud platforms, the **Cloud Native Computing Foundation** was formed by several software vendors. It is part of the Linux Foundation, representing an foundation for cloud native Open Source Software. It contains technology that orchestrates, manages, monitors, traces or in some other way supports containerized **microservices** running in modern environments. As of writing this book, examples for technology projects being part of the Cloud Native Computing Foundation are **Kubernetes**, **Prometheus**, **OpenTracing**, or **containerd**.

# Summary

Operational tasks need to be automated. Setting up application environments should always produce the same outcome, including installations, network, and configuration. Container technologies as well as infrastructure as code support this by defining, automating and distributing software installations and configuration. They fulfill the necessity of rebuilding software and systems in a fast and reproducible way.

Infrastructure as code definitions specify the required infrastructure together with all dependencies as part of the application code, kept under version control. This approach supports the ideas behind the DevOps movement. The responsibilities of not only defining the application but also its runtime with all requirements move different teams together. It should be a responsibility of all engineers to deliver quality software that serves a business purpose.

Container technologies such as Docker provides functionality to build, manage, and ship containers in a uniform way. Docker's copy-on-write layered file system enables us to minimize build and publishing times by only re-executing steps that have changed. Java EE zero-dependency applications encourage the use of container technology by separating the application logic from its implementation. The changing layer therefore only contains business code.

Container orchestration frameworks such as Kubernetes manage containers in their life cycle, network, and external configuration. They are responsible to lookup services, provide production readiness such as zero-downtime deployments and scale up and down application instances. Container orchestration supports infrastructure as code definitions, that contain the configuration of the whole runtime environment required by the application.

The 12-factor and cloud native approaches aim to develop modern enterprise applications with minimal time and effort, avoiding software erosion, and supporting Continuous Delivery and cloud platforms. The 12-factor principles target software dependencies, configuration, dependent services, runtime environments, logging and administration processes. Similarly, cloud native applications aim to build enterprise software that works well on cloud platforms, supporting monitoring, resilience, application health, and security. Since these approaches are not bound to a specific technology, they are realizable using Java EE. We have seen the motivations why to follow these principles.

The following chapter will show you how to build productive application development workflows, that are based on container technologies.

# 6
# Application Development Workflows

kIn the previous chapter, we saw the necessity for software companies to move fast. This has an impact on the infrastructure and runtime environments and on the way teams of engineers are working together. The motivations behind modern environments are scalability, flexibility and minimizing time and effort.

Development workflows are even more important than the infrastructure alone. The whole process of writing source code until the running application is in production should be specified in a reasonable and productive way. Again, moving fast in a fast-moving world implies that these processes run automated and reliably with as little human intervention as possible.

This chapter will cover the following topics:

- The motivations and necessity of Continuous Delivery
- The contents of a productive pipeline
- How to automate all steps involved
- How to sustainably ensure and improve software quality
- The required team culture and habits

# Motivation and goals of productive development workflows

Moving fast in terms of development workflows aims to enable fast feedback by fast turnarounds. In order to increase productivity, developers who work on the application's behavior need to verify the implemented features and bug fixes in a timely manner. This includes the time spent on builds, software tests, and deployments.

The key to productive workflows is automation. Software engineers should spend as much time as possible on designing, implementing, and discussing business logic and as little as possible on cross-cutting concerns and repetitive tasks. Computers are designed for quickly and reliably performing deterministic, straightforward tasks. Humans, however, are better at designing, thinking, and brainstorming creative and complex tasks. Simple, straightforward processes that don't require a lot of decision-making should therefore be performed by software.

Build systems are a good start. They automate compiling, resolving dependencies, and packaging of software projects. Continuous Integration servers take this approach further. They orchestrate the whole development workflow from building artifacts to automated testing and deployments. Continuous Integration servers are the *golden source of truth* of software delivery. They continuously integrate the work of all developers in a central place, making sure the project is in a shippable state.

Continuous Delivery continues the approach of Continuous Integration by automatically shipping the built software to certain environments on each build. Since software changes have to be verified properly before they go to production, applications are first deployed to test and staging environments. All deployment actions have to make sure the environment is prepared and configured and rolled out properly. Automated and manual end-to-end tests make sure the software works as expected. Deployment to production is then done in a *half-automated* way by triggering the automated deployment manually.

The difference between Continuous Delivery and Continuous Deployment is that the latter automatically deploys each committed software version to production, if the quality requirements are met, of course.

All these approaches minimize the developer intervention required, minimize turnaround times, and improve productivity.

Ideally, the Continuous Delivery approach supports not only rollouts but also reliable rollbacks. Software versions, although verified before, sometimes need to be rolled back for some reason. In such a situation, there is either the way of rolling forward, for example, by committing a new version that will undo the recent changes, or by rolling back to the working state.

As mentioned earlier, software should be built in a reliable way. All versions of used technology, such as build dependencies or application servers, are specified explicitly. Rebuilt applications and containers produce the same result. In the same way, pipeline steps of development workflows should result in the same outcome. It is crucial that the same application artifact that has been verified in test environments is deployed to production later on. Later in this chapter, we cover how to achieve reproducible, repeatable, and independent builds.

In terms of reliability, automated processes are an important aspect as well. Especially, deployments that are executed by software rather than human intervention are far less prone to error. All necessary pipeline steps are well defined and implicitly verified each and every time they are executed. This builds confidence into the automated processes, ultimately more than executing processes manually.

Verification and testing are important prerequisites of Continuous Delivery. Experience shows that the vast majority of software tests can be executed in an automated way. The next chapter will cover this topic in depth. Besides testing, quality assurance also covers the software quality of the project in regard to architecture and code quality.

Continuous Delivery workflows include all steps necessary in order to build, test, ship, and deploy software in a productive and automated way. Let's see how to build effective workflows.

# Realizing development workflows

Continuous Delivery pipelines consist of several pipeline build steps that are executed in sequence or in parallel, respectively. All the steps are executed as part of a single build. Builds are usually triggered by committing or rather pushing code changes into version control.

The following examines the aspects of a Continuous Delivery pipeline. These general steps are indifferent to the used technology.

The following diagram shows a high-level overview of a simplified Continuous Delivery pipeline. The steps are executed in a Continuous Integration server and use external repositories such as version control, artifact, and container repositories:

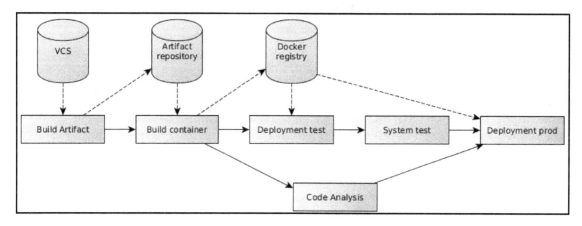

# Version control everything

Developers agree that source code should be kept under version control. Distributed version controls such as Git have been widely accepted as state-of-the-art tools. However, as mentioned earlier, besides application source code, there are more assets to track.

The motivation behind infrastructure as code is to keep all artifacts needed to ship the application in one central place. All changes made to the application, configuration, or environment are represented as code and checked in to the repository. Infrastructure as code leverages reproduciblity and automation. Taking this approach further also includes the definition of Continuous Delivery pipelines as code. The *Pipeline as code* section will cover this approach with the widely used Jenkins server as an example.

As we have seen in the previous chapter, the first principle of 12-factor applications is in fact to keep all files and artifacts needed to build and run the application in one repository.

The first step of the Continuous Delivery pipeline is to check out a specific commit from the version control repository. Teams that use distributed version control systems need to synchronize the desired state to a centralized repository. The Continuous Integration server takes the state of a specific commit in history to start the build process.

The reason behind taking a specific commit version rather than just the latest state is to enable reproducibility. Rebuilding the same build version can only reliably result in the same outcome if the build is based on a specific commit. This is only possible if the build originated from checking-in to version control with a particular commit. Check-in actions usually trigger builds from the corresponding commit version.

Checking out the state of the repository provides all sources and files necessary. The next step is to build the software artifacts.

# Building binaries

As we have seen in the first chapter, the term binaries includes all executable artifacts that run the enterprise application. The project repository only contains source code and files and artifacts required by the infrastructure. The binaries are built by the Continuous Integration server.

A step in the pipeline is responsible for building these binaries and making them accessible in a reliable way.

## Java artifacts

In Java EE, binaries first of all include the packaged enterprise application in form of an archive. Following the approach of zero-dependency applications results in building and packaging the project into a thin WAR file, containing only the application's business logic. This build action includes to resolve required dependencies, compile Java sources, and package the binary classes and other files into the archive. The WAR files are the first produced artifact within the build pipeline.

The application artifacts are built using build systems such as Maven or Gradle, which are installed and executed on the CI server. Usually, the project build already executes basic code level tests. Tests that are executed on code level without requiring a container runtime can verify the behavior of classes and components early in the pipeline. The Continuous Delivery approach of failing fast and breaking the build as early as possible minimizes turnaround times.

If required, build systems can publish the artifacts onto an artifact repository. Artifact repositories, such as **Sonatype Nexus** or **JFrog Artifactory**, save the built artifact versions for later retrieval. However, if the application is shipped in Linux containers, the artifact doesn't necessarily have to be deployed onto a repository.

As shown in `Chapter 2`, *Designing and Structuring Java Enterprise Applications*, a Java project is built using Maven via the command `mvn package`. The package phase compiles all Java production sources, compiles and executes the test sources, and packages the application in our case, to a WAR file. The CI server executes a build system command similar to this to build the artifact in its local workspace directory. The artifact can be deployed to an artifact repository, for example, using the `mvn deploy` command, to be used in subsequent steps; or it will be taken directly from the workspace directory.

# Artifact versions

As mentioned earlier, the build systems need to produce artifacts in a reliable way. This requires that Java artifacts are built and archived with a distinct version, which is identifiable later on. Software tests verify specific versions of enterprise applications. Later deployments need to refer the identical versions in later build steps as well. Being able to identify and refer to distinct artifact versions is necessary. This is true for all binaries.

One of the 12-factor principles is to explicitly declare dependencies, not only for dependencies being used but also in regard to their versions. As mentioned earlier, the same holds true for container builds. Specified Docker base images as well as installed software should be explicitly, uniquely identified by their versions.

It is quite common, however, to specify Java builds as *snapshot* versions, for example, `0.1-SNAPSHOT`. A snapshot, as opposed to a release version, represents a software state which is currently being developed. Dependency resolution always attempts to include the latest snapshot when several snapshot versions are existent, comparable to the Docker `latest` tag. The workflow behind snapshots is to release the snapshot version to a uniquely numbered version, once the level of development is sufficient.

However, snapshot versioning contradicts the idea of Continuous Delivery. In CD pipelines every commit is a potential candidate for production deployment. Snapshot versions are naturally not meant to be deployed on production. This implies that the workflow would need to change the snapshot to a release version, once the software version has been sufficiently verified. However, once built, Java artifacts are not meant to be changed. The same artifact that has been verified should be used for deployment. Therefore, snapshot versions do not fit Continuous Delivery pipelines.

Following the widely adopted approach of **semantic versioning**, application developers need to take care of their versions in regard to backward-compatibility. A semantic versioning describes software versions such as 1.1.0, 1.0.0-beta, or 1.0.1+b102. In order to represent versions that are both eligible for Continuous Delivery and provide semantic versioning metadata, properly numbered versions with unique build metadata are a good solution. An example is 1.0.1+b102, for *major* version 1, *minor* version 0, *patch* version 1, and build number 102. The part after the plus sign represents the optional build metadata. Even if the semantic version was not changed in between a number of builds, the produced artifacts are still identifiable. The artifacts can be published to an artifact repository and retrieved via these version numbers later on.

This versioning approach targets enterprise application projects rather than products. Products which have multiple shipped and supported versions at a time, require to have more complex versioning workflows.

At the time of writing, there isn't a de facto standard for versioning containers yet. Some companies follow a semantic versioning approach whereas others exclusively use CI server build numbers or commit hashes. All of these approaches are valid, as long as container images aren't rebuilt or distributed using the same tag twice. A single build must result in a distinct container image version.

# Building containers

Container images also represent binaries, since they contain the running application, including runtime and operating system binaries. In order to build container images, base images and all artifacts that are added at build time need to be present. If they don't already exist on the build environment, base images are retrieved implicitly.

For each build step defined in the Dockerfile, an image layer is added on top of the previous layer. Last but not least, the application that was built just before is added to the container image build. As shown previously, Java EE application containers consist of an installed and configured application server that auto-deploys the web archive at runtime.

This image build is orchestrated by the CI server as part of the pipeline. One solution is to have the Docker runtime installed, in the same way as the Maven build system. The pipeline step then simply invokes an image build similar to `docker build -t docker.example.com/hello-cloud:1 .` in the job workspace directory. The Docker image build, for example, takes the WAR file under Maven's `target` directory and adds it into the container.

The built image is tagged with an image name and unique tag, depending on the build number or some other unique information. Docker image names imply the registry they will be pushed to. An image identifier such as `docker.example.com/hello-cloud:1` will implicitly be transmitted from and to the host `docker.example.com`. The pipeline pushes the image to the Docker registry in most cases, a company-specific registry.

Depending on the company's workflow, Docker images can be re-tagged as part of the pipeline as well. For example, special tags such as the `latest` tag can refer to the actual *latest* built versions and so on. This is accomplished by explicitly re-tagging the image, so that two identifiers point to the same image. Unlike Java archives, Docker images can be re-tagged without changing their contents. The second tag needs to be pushed to the repository, as well. However, the rest of this chapter will show you that it's not required to refer to images using *latest* versions, such as the Docker `latest` tag. In fact, similar to snapshot versioning it's advisable to avoid *latest* versions. Being explicit in all artifact versions is less prone to error.

Some engineers argue that running Docker builds inside the CI server may not be the best idea if the CI server itself runs as a Docker container. Docker image builds start temporarily running containers. It is certainly possible to either run containers in a container or connect the runtime to another Docker host, without opening the whole platform to potential security concerns. However, some companies choose to build the images outside of the CI server instead. For example, OpenShift, a PaaS built on top of Kubernetes, provides build functionality that comprises a CI server as well as image builds. It is therefore possible to orchestrate image builds from the CI server which are then built in the OpenShift platform. This provides an alternative to building container images directly on the CI server.

# Quality assurance

The Java artifact build already performs some basic quality assurance. It executes included code level tests, such as unit tests. A reasonable pipeline consists of several test scopes and scenarios, all with slightly different strengths and weaknesses. The included unit tests operate at code level and can be executed without any further running environment. They aim to verify the behavior of the individual classes and components and provide fast feedback in case of test failures. We will see in the next chapter that unit tests need to run self-sufficiently and fast.

Test results are usually recorded from the CI server for visibility and monitoring reasons. Making the outcome of the pipeline steps visible is an important aspect of Continuous Delivery. The CI server can track the number of passed unit tests and show trends over time.

There are build system plugins available that track the code coverage of the executed tests. The coverage shows which parts of the code base have been executed during the test runs. Generally speaking, a greater code coverage is desirable. However, a high percentage of coverage alone tells nothing about the quality of tests and coverage of test assertions. The test results, together with their coverage, are just one of a few quality characteristics.

Source code can already provide a lot of information about the software's quality. So-called **static code analysis** performs certain quality checks on the static source code files of the project without executing them. This analysis gathers information about code statements, class and method sizes, dependencies between classes and packages, and complexity of methods. Static code analysis can already find potential errors in the source code, such as resources that are not properly closed.

**SonarQube** is one of the most well-known code quality tools. It provides information about the quality of software projects by correlating the results of different analysis methods, such as static code analysis or test coverage. The merged information is used to provide helpful quality metrics for software engineers and architects. For example, which methods are complex but at the same time sufficiently tested? Which components and classes are the biggest in size and complexity and therefore candidates to be refactored? Which packages have cyclic dependencies and likely contain components that should be merged together? How does the test coverage evolve over time? How many code analysis warnings and errors are there and how does this number evolve over time?

It's advisable to follow some basic guidelines regarding static code analysis. Some metrics just give insights in terms of rough ideas about the software quality. Test coverage is such an example. A project with high coverage does not necessarily imply well-tested software; the assertion statements could be impractical or insufficient. However, the trend of test coverage does give an idea about the quality, for example, whether software tests are added for new and existing functionality and bug fixes.

There are also metrics that should be strictly followed. Code analysis warnings and errors are one of these. Warnings and errors tell engineers about code style and quality violations. They are indicators about issues that need to be fixed.

First of all, there should be no such things as compilation or analysis warnings. Either the build passes the quality checks sufficiently, a *green traffic light*; or the quality is not sufficient for deployment, a *red traffic light*. There is nothing reasonable in between. Software teams need to clarify which issues are plausible and to be resolved and which aren't. Warnings that indicate minor issues in the project therefore are treated as errors; if there is a good reason to resolve them, then the engineers have to, otherwise the build should fail. If the detected error or warning represents a *false positive*, it won't be resolved; instead, it has to be ignored by the process. In that case, the build is successful.

Following this approach enables a **zero-warning policy**. Project builds and analyses that contain a lot of errors and warnings all the time, even if they are not critical, introduce certain issues. The existing warnings and errors obfuscate the quality view of the project. Engineers won't be able to tell on the first look whether the hundreds of issues are actually issues or not. Besides that, having a lot of issues already demotivates engineers to fix newly introduced warnings at all. For example, imagine a house that is in a terrible condition, with damaged walls and broken windows. Nobody would care if another window gets broken or not. But a recently broken window of an otherwise pristine house that has been taken good care of urges the person in charge to take action. The same is true for software quality checks. If there are hundreds of warnings already, nobody cares about that last commit's newly introduced violation. Therefore, the number of project quality violation should be zero. Errors in builds or code analyses should break the pipeline build. Either the project code needs to be fixed or the quality rules need to be adjusted for the issue to be resolved.

Code quality tools such as SonarQube are integrated in a build pipeline step. Since the quality analysis operates on static input only, the step can easily be parallelized to the next pipeline steps. If the quality gate does not accept the result, the build will fail and the engineers need resolve the issue before continuing development. This is an important aspect to integrate quality into the pipeline. The analysis should not only give insights but also actively prevent the execution to force action.

# Deployment

After the binaries have been built and after, or during, the software quality is being verified, the enterprise application will be deployed. There are usually several environments for testing purposes, depending on the project circumstances, such as test or staging and, of course, production. As mentioned earlier, these environments should be as similar as possible. This vastly simplifies the deployment process orchestrated by the CI server.

The process of deploying the application generally takes the binaries in the version that has just been built and deploys them onto the environment. Depending on what the infrastructure looks like, this can take place using plain scripts or more sophisticated technology. The principle should be the same, the binaries as well as the configuration are made available to the environment in an automated and reliable way. Preparation steps that are potentially required by the application or the environment will be executed in this step as well.

Modern environments such as container orchestration frameworks support infrastructure as code. Infrastructure configuration is captured in files in the project's repository and applied to all environments at deployment time. Potential differences, such as Kubernetes config maps contents, are represented as different manifestations in the repository as well.

Using IaC as well as containers provides even more reliability than home-grown shell scripts. The application should always be rolled out in an idempotent way, independent of which state the environment was in. Since container images contain the whole stack, the outcome is the same as if the software was installed from scratch. Required environment configuration is applied from IaC files as well.

New container image versions can be deployed by orchestration frameworks in many ways. There are certain commands that explicitly set Docker images used in Kubernetes deployments. However, in order to fulfill the requirement of reliability and reproducibility, it makes sense to only edit the infrastructure as code files and apply them on the cluster. This ensures that the configuration files stay the single source of truth. The CI server can edit the image definitions in the IaC files and commit the changes to the VCS repository.

As seen in the previous chapter, Docker images are specified in Kubernetes deployment definitions:

```
# deployment definition similar to previous chapter
# ...
   spec:
     containers:
     - name: hello-cloud
       image: docker.example.com/hello-cloud:1
       imagePullPolicy: IfNotPresent
       livenessProbe:
# ...
```

These image definitions are updated within the CI server process and applied to the Kubernetes cluster. The CI server executes Kubernetes commands via the `kubectl` CLI. This is the standard way to communicate with Kubernetes clusters. `kubectl apply -f <file>` applies the infrastructure as code contents of a file or directory containing YAML or JSON definitions. The pipeline step executes a command similar to this, providing the updated Kubernetes files which were updated in the project repository.

Following this approach enables that infrastructure as code files both contain the current state of the environments as well as changes made by engineers. All updates are rolled out by applying the Kubernetes files in the corresponding version to the cluster. The cluster aims to satisfy the new desired state, containing the new image version, and will therefore perform a rolling update. After triggering this the update, the CI server validates whether the deployment has been executed successfully. Kubernetes rollout actions can be followed by commands similar to `kubectl rollout status <deployment>`, which waits until the deployment is either rolled out successfully, or failed.

This procedure is executed on all environments. If single deployment definitions are used for several environments, the image tag definition only has to be updated once, of course.

To give a more concrete example, the following shows a potential configuration file structure of a Maven project:

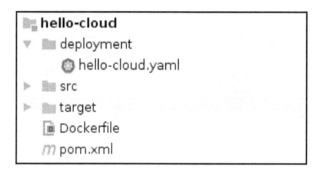

The `hello-cloud.yaml` file contains multiple Kubernetes resource definitions. This is possible by separating each YAML object definitions with a three-dashed line (`---`). It's equally doable to provide separate files for each resource type, such as `deployment.yaml`, `service.yaml`, and so on. Kubernetes can handle both approaches. The `kind` type definitions in the YAML objects indicate the type of the resource.

The previous chapter showed how container orchestration frameworks enable zero-downtime deployments out of the box. Applying new image versions to the environments orchestrated by the CI server also accomplishes this goal. The environments will therefore be able to serve traffic with at least one active application at a time. This approach is especially important for production environments.

# Configuration

Ideally, infrastructure as code covers all aspects required to define the whole environment, including runtimes, networking, and configuration. Using container technologies and container orchestration greatly supports and simplifies this approach. As mentioned earlier, confidential content such as credentials should not be put under version control. This should be configured manually on the environment by an administrator.

Configuration that differs in several environments can be represented using multiple files in the project repository. For example, it makes sense to include subfolders for each environment. The following image shows an example:

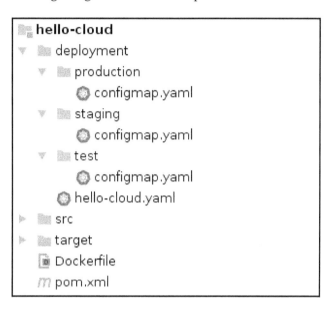

The contents of the `configmap.yaml` file include the specific config map contents as well as potentially different namespace definitions. As mentioned in the previous chapter, Kubernetes namespaces are a way to differentiate environments. The following code shows an example of a specific production config map:

```
---
kind: ConfigMap
apiVersion: v1
metadata:
  name: hello-cloud-config
  namespace: production
data:
  application.properties: |
    hello.greeting=Hello production
    hello.name=Java EE
---
```

# Credentials

Due to security reasons, secret content such as credentials is typically not included in the project repository. An administrator usually configures them manually on the specific environments. Similar to other Kubernetes resources, secrets are bound to a specific namespace.

If a project requires multiple secrets, for example, specific credentials for various external systems, manually configuring them can become cumbersome and difficult to keep track of. Configured secrets have to be documented and tracked in a secure form, external to the project repository.

Another approach is to store encrypted credentials that can be decrypted using a single master key in the repository. The repository can therefore safely contain the configured credentials, in encrypted form, and still be safe from disclosing the secrets. The running application will use the dynamically provided master key to decrypt the configured credentials. This approach provides security as well as manageability.

Let's look at a potential solution. Encrypted configuration values can safely be stored in Kubernetes config maps, since the decrypted values will only be visible to the container process. The project can define the encrypted credentials together with other configuration values in the config maps definitions as code. An administrator adds a secret to each environment, containing the master key which was used to symmetrically encrypt the credentials. This master key is provided to the running container, for example, using environment variables as seen earlier. The running application uses this single environment variable to decrypt all encrypted credential values.

Depending on the used technology and algorithm, one solution is to use the Java EE application to decrypt the credentials directly when loading properties files. To provide a secure solution using recent encryption algorithms, the **Java Cryptographic Extensions (JCE)** should be installed in the runtime. Another approach is to decrypt the values before the application is being deployed.

# Data migration

Applications that use a database to store their state are bound to a specific database schema. Changes in the schema usually require the application model to change and vice versa. With an application being actively developed and a domain model being continuously refined and refactored, the model will eventually require the database schema to change. New model classes or properties thereof which are added need to be persisted in the database as well. Classes and properties that are refactored or removed should be migrated in the database also, so that the schema doesn't diverge.

However, data migrations are more difficult than code changes. Stateless applications can simply be replaced by new versions thereof, containing the new functionality. A database that contains the application's state, however, needs to carefully migrate the state when the schema changes.

This happens in migration scripts. Relational databases support altering their tables while keeping the data intact. These scripts are executed before the new version of the software is deployed, making sure the database schema matches the application.

There is an important aspect to keep in mind when deploying applications using a zero-downtime approach. Rolling updates will leave at least one active instance running in the environment at a time. This results in having both the old and the new software version active for a short period of time. The orchestration should take care that the applications are gracefully started and shut down, respectively, letting in-flight requests finish their work. Applications that connect to a central database instance will result in several versions of the application simultaneously accessing the database. This requires the application to support so-called **N-1 compatibility**. The current application version needs to function with the same database schema version plus and minus one version, respectively.

To support N-1 compatibility, the rolling update approach needs to both deploy a new application version and to updates the database schema, making sure the versions do not differ more than one version. This implies that, the corresponding database migrations are executed just before the application deployment takes place. The database schema, as well as the application, therefore evolves in small migration steps, not in jumps.

This approach, however, is not trivial and involves certain planning and caution. Especially, application version rollbacks require particular attention.

# Adding database structures

Adding tables or table columns to a database schema is comparatively straightforward. The new table or column does not collide with older application versions, since they are unknown to them.

New tables that resulted from new domain entities can simply be added to the schema, resulting in version *N+1*.

New table columns that define certain constraints, such as *not null* or *unique*, need to take care of the current state of the table. The old application version can still write to the table; it will ignore the new column. Therefore, constraints can not necessarily be satisfied. New columns first need to be *nullable* and without further constraints. The new application version has to deal with empty values in that column, presumably `null` values, which originate from the old application version.

Only the next version (*N+2*) will then, after the current deployment has been completed, contain the correct constraints. This means that adding a column that defines constraints needs at least two separate deployments. The first deployment adds the column and enhances the application's model in a `null`-safe way. The second deployment makes sure all contained values fulfill the column constraints, adds the constraints, and removes the `null`-safe behavior. These steps are, of course, only required, if the column target state defines constraints.

Rollbacks to the old versions work in a similar way. Rolling back to the intermediate deployment (*N+2* to *N+1*) requires the constraints to be removed again.

Rolling back to the original state (*N+0*) would remove the whole column. However, data migrations should not remove data that is not transferred somewhere else. Rolling back to the state without the column could also simply leave the column untouched so as not to lose data. The question the business experts have to answer is: What happens with the data that was added in the meantime? Intentionally not deleting this data could be a reasonable approach. However, when the column is added again, the rollout script needs to take already existing columns into consideration.

# Changing database structures

Changing existing database tables or columns is more complex. Whether columns are renamed or changed in type or constraint, the transitions have to be executed in several steps. Directly renaming or changing columns would lead to incompatibilities with the deployed application instances; changes require intermediate columns.

Let's examine this approach using an example. Assume the car entity has a property *color*, which must be set, represented in the database column `color`. Assuming it will be refactored to the name *chassis color* or `chassis_color` in the database column.

Similar to the previous approach, the change is executed in several deployments. The first deployment adds a nullable column `chassis_color`. The application code is enhanced to use the new model property. Since the older application version doesn't know about the property yet, it is not reliably written from all places during the first deployment. Therefore, the first code version still reads the color from the old, `color` column, but writes values to both the old and new column.

The migration script on the next deployment updates the missing column values by overwriting the `chassis_color` column with the `color` column contents. By doing this, it is ensured that the new column is populated consistently. The not null constraint is added to the new column as well. The application code version will then only read from the new, but still write to both, because of the short period when the older version is still active.

The next deployment step removes the not null constraint from the `color` column. The application code of this version doesn't use the old column anymore, and both reads and writes to `chassis_color`.

The next and final deployment then drops the `color` column. Now all data has been gradually transferred to the new `chassis_color` column. The application code doesn't include the old model property anymore.

Changing column types or foreign key constraints require similar steps. The only way to gradually migrate databases with zero-downtime is to migrate in small steps, using intermediate columns and properties. It is advisable to perform several commits that only contain these changes to both the migration scripts and application code.

Similar to the previous approach, rollback migrations have to be executed in reverse, for both the database scripts and code changes.

# Removing database structures

Removing tables or columns is more straightforward than changing them. Once certain properties of the domain model are not required anymore, their usages can be removed from the application.

The first deployment changes the application code to stop reading from the database column but still to write to it. This is required to ensure that the old version can still read values other than `null`.

The next deployment will remove a potential not null constraint from the database column. The application code stops writing to column. In this step, occurrences of the model property can already be removed from the code base.

The final deployment step will drop the column. As mentioned before, it highly depends on the business use case whether column data should actually be dropped. Rollback scripts would need to recreate removed columns, which implies that the previous data is gone.

# Implementing migration

As we have seen, data migrations have to be executed in several steps. Rollout as well as rollback scripts are executed right before the deployment. This implies that the application supports N-1 compatibility as well as that only one deployment is being executed at a time.

The migration process requires to perform several software releases, each of them consistent in application code and schema migration scripts. Engineers need to plan their commits accordingly. It's advisable to perform the full schema migration in a timely manner, to keep the database schema clean and to ensure that ongoing migrations aren't simply forgotten about.

It's in the nature of the corresponding model refactoring, whether existing data needs to be kept or can be discarded. Generally speaking, it is advisable to not throw away data. This means not to drop structures containing data that doesn't exist somewhere else.

As we have seen in the examples, the migrations will be applied in graceful steps; especially in regard to database constraints, such as *not null* or referential integrity constraints. Migration scripts should be resilient. For example, the migration should not fail when trying to create already existing columns. They could already exist from previous rollbacks. In general, it makes sense to think through and test different rollout and rollback scenarios upfront.

Engineers need to keep the update time in mind when updating table contents. Updating huge tables at once will take a non-negligible amount of time in which the data is potentially locked. This needs to be considered upfront; ideally, by testing the scripts in a separate database. For huge amount of data involved, the update steps can be executed in shards, for example, by partitioning the data by their IDs.

All rollout and rollback migration scripts should reside in the project repository. The database schema comprises a schema version that corresponds to the numbered migration scripts. This version is stored in the database as metadata together with the current schema state. Before every deployment, the database schema is migrated to its desired version. Right after that, the application with a corresponding version is deployed, making sure that the versions don't differ by more than one.

In a container orchestration framework this means that the database migration needs to be performed right before the new application version is deployed via rolling updates. Since there can be many replicas of pods, this process has to be idempotent. Executing the migration of a database schema to the same version twice, has to result in the same outcome. Kubernetes pods can define so-called **init containers** which execute *one-shot* processes before the actual containers start. Init containers run mutually exclusive. They have to exit successfully before the actual pod container process can be started.

The following code snippet shows an example of `initContainer`:

```
# ...
    spec:
      containers:
      - name: hello-cloud
        image: .../hello-cloud:1
      initContainers:
      - name: migrate-vehicle-db
        image: postgres
        command: ['/migrate.sh', '$VERSION']
# ...
```

The preceding example implies that the init container image contains the correct tooling to connect to the database instance as well as all recent migration scripts. In order to make this possible, this image is built as part of the pipeline, as well, including all migration scripts from the repository.

There are, however, many solutions to migrate database schemas. The important aspect here is that the idempotent migration needs to be executed upfront, while no second deployment action is being rolled out. The migration scripts of the corresponding versions would be executed in ascending or descending order, depending on whether the database schema version is upgraded or rolled back, until the version matches. After the scripts have been executed, the metadata version is updated in the database, as well.

The correlation between code and database versions can be tracked in the project repository. For example, the most recent rollout script contained in a commit version corresponds to the required database schema. The *Build metadata* section covers the topic of required metadata and where to store it in more depth.

Since the chosen migration solution highly depends on the project's technology, there is no *silver bullet* approach that can be shown here. The following example gives one possible solution on migration file structure and execution in *pseudo code*. It shows migration files for the example of changing the `color` column to `chassis_color` discussed earlier:

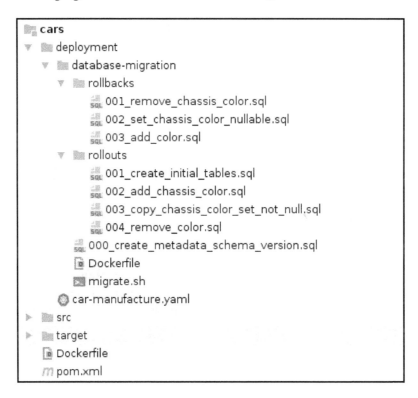

The preceding example shows the rollout and rollback scripts that migrate the database schema version to the desired state. Rollout script `004_remove_color.sql` transposes the schema version to version 4 by removing the `color` column of the example shown earlier. The corresponding rollback script `003_add_color.sql` rolls back the schema to version 3, where the `color` column still existed; in other words, version 3 contains the `color` column whereas version 4 doesn't, with these two migration files being able to roll back and forth.

The following shows the pseudo code of the script that performs the migrations. The desired version to migrate to is provided as an argument when invoking the script:

```
current_version = select the current schema version stored in the database

if current_version == desired_version
    exit, nothing to do

if current_version < desired_version
    folder = /rollouts/
    script_sequence = range from current_version + 1 to desired_version

if current_version > desired_version
    folder = /rollbacks/
    script_sequence = range from current_version - 1 to desired_version

for i in script_sequence
    execute script in folder/i_*.sql
    update schema version to i
```

This migration script is executed in the init container before the actual deployment.

# Testing

Verifying the output of the pipeline steps is one of the most important aspects in Continuous Delivery. It increases the software quality by detecting potential errors before going live. Proper verification creates reliability in the processes. By writing software tests in general and regression tests in particular, developers become confident in changing and refactoring functionality. Ultimately, software tests enable us to automate development processes.

Building binaries already executes code level tests. Other tests contained in the project may be executed in separate pipeline steps, depending whether they operate at code level or a running container. End-to-end tests, especially, require a running environment.

After the application has been deployed on test environments, end-to-end tests can be executed there. Usually, a project contains several layers of tests, with separate responsibilities, running in separate steps. There can be a great variety of tests, depending on the project and used technology. The approach is always to execute pipeline steps and sufficiently verify the outcome. By doing so, the risk of breaking new or existing functionality and introducing potential errors is minimized. Especially, container orchestration frameworks with their *production-ready* nature support companies in the goal to ship scalable, highly available enterprise applications with high quality. Chapter 7, *Testing*, covers all different manifestations of testing, including its execution in Continuous Delivery pipelines.

Failing tests will immediately cause the pipeline to stop and will prevent the corresponding binary from being used further. This is an important aspect to enable fast feedback and also to enforce software quality in the process. Engineers should absolutely avoid to bypass steps of the normal process and other *quick fixes*. They contradict the idea of continuous improvement and building quality into the Continuous Delivery process and ultimately lead to errors. If a test or quality gate fails, the build has to break and either the application's code or the verification has to change.

Failing tests should not only break the build but also provide insights into why the step failed and record the result. This is part of the build's metadata.

# Build metadata

Build metadata records all information that is gathered during the execution of the build. Especially, the specific versions of all assets should be tracked for further reference.

Builds that run from the beginning to the end don't necessarily need further information. The steps are executed in one run until either the build breaks or finishes successfully. If, however, specific steps or artifacts are required to be referenced or re-executed, further information is required.

Artifact versions are the prime example for this necessity. A WAR file and its contents corresponds to a specific version in the VCS commit history. In order to track the originating commit from a deployed application, this information needs to be tracked somewhere. The same is true for container image versions. In order to identify the origin and contents of a container, the versions need to be traceable. Database schema versions are another example. A database schema version matches a specific application version, including the previous and the next version, by following N-1 compatibility. A deployment that migrates the database schema needs to know the schema version to migrate to for the desired application version.

Build metadata is especially required when the process enables rolling out specific application versions. In general, Continuous Delivery deployments roll forward to the current repository version. However, especially with database schemas and migrations involved, the possibility of rolling the environments to an arbitrary state is a huge benefit. The process in theory works like this: *take this specific application version and perform everything required in order to run it on this specific environment*, no matter whether the rollout is moving forward or backward.

In order to improve traceability and reproducibility, it is advisable to track quality information about the build as well. This includes, for example, results of automated tests, manual tests, or code quality analyses. The deployment steps then are able to verify the existence of specific metadata before deploying.

There are many solutions possible for representing metadata. Some artifact repositories such as JFrog Artifactory provide the possibility of linking built artifacts with custom metadata.

Another approach is to use the CI server to track this information. This sounds like a good fit to store metadata for a build; however, depending on how the CI server is operated and set up, it is not necessarily advisable to use it to store persistent data. Old builds can be discarded and lose information.

In general, the number of *points of truth*, for example, to store artifacts and information, should be kept low and explicitly defined. Using artifact repositories for metadata therefore certainly makes sense.

Another, more custom solution, is to use company VCS repositories to track certain information. The big benefit of using, for example, Git to store metadata is that it provides full flexibility of the data and structure being persisted. CI servers already contain functionality to access VCS repositories, therefore no vendor-specific tooling is required. Repositories can store all kind of information that are persisted as files, such as recorded test result.

The metadata repository, however implemented, is accessed at various points in the pipeline, for example, when performing deployments.

# Going to production

The last step in the Continuous Delivery pipeline is deploying to production. This deployment is either triggered manually or, when sufficient verification and automated tests are implemented, automatically. The vast majority of companies use a manually triggered deployment. But even if the pipeline does not go *all the way* from the beginning, Continuous Delivery provides great benefits by automating all steps necessary.

The pipeline then only has two kick-off spots: the initial commit to the repository that triggers the execution, and the final deployment to production after all steps have been verified, manually and automatically.

In a container orchestration environment, deploying to production, that is, either deploying to a separate namespace or a separate cluster, happens in the same way as deploying to test environments. Since the infrastructure as code definitions are similar or ideally identical to the ones executed before, this technology lowers the risk of environment mismatches to production.

# Branching models

Software development processes can make use of different branching models. Software branches emerge from the same origin and differ in the state of development to make it possible to develop on multiple development stages in parallel.

Especially feature branches are a popular approach. Feature branching creates a separate branch which is used to develop a certain software feature. The branch is merged into the *master* branch or *trunk* after the feature is finished. The master branch and other branches remain untouched while the feature is being developed.

Another branching model is to use release branches. Release branches contain single software releases of a specific version. The idea is to have a dedicated point for a released version where bug fixes and features can be added. All changes made to the master branch that apply for the specific release as well are also made in the release branch.

However, branching models like these contradict the idea of Continuous Delivery. Feature branches, for example, postpone the integration of features into the master branch. The longer the integration of new functionality is delayed, the bigger the possibility for potential merge conflicts. Feature branches are therefore only advisable in Continuous Delivery pipelines if they are short-lived and integrated into master in a timely manner.

Release versions and working upon these releases in parallel contradicts the idea of continuously shipping versions as well. Features that are implemented are ideally shipped to production as soon as possible.

This is at least the case for enterprise projects. The continuous life cycle implies that every commit is a potential candidate for production deployment. It makes sense to integrate and apply the work on the master branch, making it possible to integrate and deploy features as early as possible, verified by automated tests. The branching model of Continuous Delivery and Continuous Deployment, respectively, therefore is quite straightforward. Changes are directly applied to the master branch, built, verified, and deployed by the build pipeline.

It's usually not required to manually tag releases. Every commit in the Continuous Delivery pipeline implicitly qualifies for being released and deployed to production, unless the automated verification identifies errors.

The following figure shows the concept of a Continuous Deployment branching model:

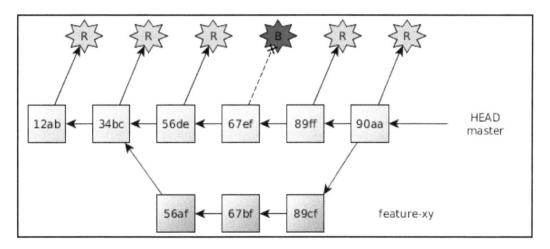

Individual features branches are kept short-lived and are merged back to *master* in a timely manner. The releases are implicitly created on successful builds. Broken builds won't result in a deployment to production.

Products, as well as libraries, however, may advisably have different branching models. With multiple supported *major* and *minor* versions, and their potential bug fixes, it makes sense to implement branches for separate release versions. The release version branches, such as v1.0.2 can then be used to continue support for bug fixes, for example, into v1.0.3, while the major development continues on a newer version, such as v2.2.0.

# Technology

When designing Continuous Delivery pipelines, the question remains, which technology to use. This includes not only the CI server itself, but all the tools used within the development workflow such as version control, artifact repositories, build systems, and runtime technologies.

What technology is being used depends on the actual requirements and not least of what the team is familiar with. The following examples will make use of Jenkins, Git, Maven, Docker, and Kubernetes. As of writing this book these are widely-used technologies. However, for engineers it's more important to comprehend the underlying principles and motivations. The technology is quite interchangeable.

No matter what tools are selected, it's advisable to use the tools for what they are meant for. Experience shows that tools are quite often being misused for tasks that would better be executed using different technology. A prime example for this is the build system, for example Maven. Projects often define build processes that have more responsibilities than just building the artifacts.

It makes sense not to mix responsibilities of building containers or deploying software into the artifact build. These concerns are preferably realized directly by the Continuous Integration server. Bringing these steps into the build process unnecessarily couples the build technology to the environment.

It's therefore advisable to use the tools for what they were intended to do, in a straightforward way. For example, Docker containers are advisably built via the corresponding Docker binaries rather than build system plugins. Required abstraction layers are rather added in pipeline as code definitions, as demonstrated in the following examples.

# Pipeline-as-code

We previously saw the benefits of representing configuration as code, primarily infrastructure as code files. The same motivations led to pipeline as code definitions, configuration that specifies the CI server pipeline steps.

In the past, many CI servers such as Jenkins required to be configured manually. CI server jobs had to be laboriously *clicked together* to build up pipelines. Especially, rebuilding pipelines for new applications or feature branches thereof required cumbersome manual work.

Pipeline as code definitions specify the Continuous Delivery pipeline as part of the software project. The CI server builds up and executes the pipeline appropriately, following the script. This vastly simplifies defining and reusing project build pipelines.

There are a lot of CI servers that support pipeline definitions as code. The most important aspect is that engineers understand the motivations and benefits behind this technology. The following shows examples for Jenkins, a widely used CI server in the Java ecosystem.

Users of Jenkins can craft pipelines in a `Jenkinsfile`, which is defined using a Groovy DSL. Groovy is an optionally typed, dynamic JVM language, that suits well for DSL and scripts. Gradle build scripts use a Groovy DSL, as well.

The following examples show the steps of a very simple pipeline of a Java enterprise project. The examples are meant to give a rough understanding of the executed process. For full information on Jenkinsfiles, their syntax and semantics, refer to the documentation.

The following shows an example `Jenkinsfile`, containing a basic pipeline definition.

```
node {
    prepare()

    stage('build') {
        build()
    }

    parallel failFast: false,
            'integration-test': {
                stage('integration-test') {
                    integrationTest()
                }
            },
            'analysis': {
                stage('analysis') {
                    analysis()
                }
            }

    stage('system-test') {
        systemTest()
    }

    stage('performance-test') {
        performanceTest()
    }

    stage('deploy') {
        deployProduction()
```

```
        }
    }

    // method definitions
```

The `stage` definitions refer to steps in the Jenkins pipeline. Since the Groovy script offers a full-fledged programming language, it is possible and advisable to apply clean code practices that produce readable code. Therefore, the contents of the specific steps are refactored to separate methods, all in the same layer of abstraction.

The `prepare()` step, for example, encapsulates several executions to fulfill build prerequisites, such as checking out the build repository. The following code shows its method definition:

```
def prepare() {
    deleteCachedDirs()
    checkoutGitRepos()
    prepareMetaInfo()
}
```

The build stage also encapsulates several sub-steps, from executing the Maven build, recording metadata and test results, to building the Docker images. The following code shows its method definition:

```
def build() {
    buildMaven()
    testReports()
    publishArtifact()
    addBuildMetaInfo()

    buildPushDocker(dockerImage, 'cars')
    buildPushDocker(databaseMigrationDockerImage,
'cars/deployment/database-migration')
    addDockerMetaInfo()
}
```

These examples provide insight into how to define and encapsulate specific behavior into steps. Providing detailed Jenkinsfile examples is beyond the scope of this book. I will show you the rough steps necessary to give an idea of what logical executions are required, and how to define them in these pipeline scripts in a readable, productive way. The actual implementations, however, heavily depend on the project.

Jenkins pipeline definitions provide the possibility to include so-called pipeline libraries. These are predefined libraries that contain often-used functionality to simplify usage and reduce duplication beyond several projects. It is advisable to outsource certain functionality, especially in regard to environment specifics, into company-specific library definitions.

The following example shows the deployment of the *car manufacture* application to a Kubernetes environment. The `deploy()` method would be called from within the build pipeline when deploying a specific image and database schema version to a Kubernetes namespace:

```
def deploy(String namespace, String dockerImage, String databaseVersion) {
    echo "deploying $dockerImage to Kubernetes $namespace"

    updateDeploymentImages(dockerImage, namespace, databaseVersion)
    applyDeployment(namespace)
    watchRollout(namespace)
}

def updateDeploymentImages(String dockerImage, String namespace, String
databaseVersion) {
    updateImage(dockerImage, 'cars/deployment/$namespace/*.yaml')
    updateDatabaseVersion(databaseVersion
'cars/deployment/$namespace/*.yaml')

    dir('cars') {
        commitPush("[jenkins] updated $namespace image to $dockerImage" +
            " and database version $databaseVersion")
    }
}

def applyDeployment(namespace) {
    sh "kubectl apply --namespace=$namespace -f car-
manufacture/deployment/$namespace/"
}

def watchRollout(namespace) {
    sh "kubectl rollout status --namespace=$namespace deployments car-
manufacture"
}
```

This example updates and commits the Kubernetes YAML definitions in the VCS repository. The execution applies the infrastructure as code to the Kubernetes namespace and waits for the deployment to finish.

These examples aim to give the reader an idea of how to integrate Continuous Delivery pipelines as pipeline as code definitions with a container orchestration framework such as Kubernetes. As mentioned earlier, it is also possible to make use of pipeline libraries to encapsulate often-used `kubectl` shell commands. Dynamic languages such as Groovy allow engineers to develop pipeline scripts in a readable way, treating them with the same effort as other code.

# Workflows with Java EE

The demonstrated examples cover general Java build piplines which are, of course, applicable to Java EE as well. In fact, using Java Enterprise highly supports productive development pipelines. Fast builds and therefore fast developer feedback is crucial to effective Continuous Delivery workflows.

Zero-dependency applications, especially when packaged in containers, leverage these principles as we have seen in `Chapter 4`, *Lightweight Java EE*. The enterprise application in the packaged artifact or the container layer, respectively, only contains the business logic that was developed against the API. The application container provides the implementation.

The Continuous Delivery pipeline benefits from zero-dependency applications, since the involved build and distribution steps only require short execution and transmission times, respectively. Artifact builds as well as container builds run as fast as they can get, with only copying what's absolutely necessary. In the same way, publishing and deploying artifacts, as well as container layers, only contain the required business concerns, to minimize transmission time. This leads to fast turnaround and fast feedback.

Having effective pipelines is crucial to implementing a Continuous Delivery culture in the development team. Engineers are motivated to check in early and often, since the pipeline runs fast, provides fast feedback, and increases the confidence that the software quality is met.

As mentioned earlier, build times should not take more than a few seconds. Build pipeline executions, including end-to-end tests, should not take more than a few minutes, ideally even faster.

Putting effort into making builds and pipelines run faster should be a goal of the engineering team. During a workday, developers often build and check in the project. Every check-in results in a Continuous Delivery build that is a potential candidate for production deployment. If this overall process takes just, for example, 1 minute longer, all developers in the team wait 1 minute longer, every time they build the software. One can imagine that this delay adds up to a big number over time. Developers are tempted to check in less often if they have to wait for their result.

Improving the stability and performance of the pipeline, therefore, is a long-term investment in the team's productivity. Tests and steps that provide quick, helpful feedback by breaking the build faster in case of errors should run as early as possible. If some end-to-end tests run inevitably longer in time, due to the nature of the project and the tests, they can be defined in separate downstream pipelines steps, to not delay feedback of earlier verification. Steps that can run in parallel, such as static code analyses, should do so, to speed up the overall execution. Using the modern approaches of Java EE development greatly supports crafting productive build pipelines.

Still, technology is only one aspect of effective Continuous Delivery. Introducing Continuous Delivery has an even bigger impact on the development team's culture. Let's have a closer look into this.

# Continuous Delivery culture and team habits

Effective Continuous Delivery depends on a healthy team culture. If the team does not live by the principles and recommendations Continuous Delivery makes, the best technology doesn't help much. Pipelines that implement automated deployments have little value if there aren't sufficient software tests verifying the deployed software. The most eager CI server can't help much if developers seldom check in their changes, making integration hard and cumbersome. Full test coverage and code quality checks have no value if the team doesn't react to failing tests or, in the worst case, set the test execution to ignore.

# Responsibility

Continuous Delivery starts with being responsible for the software. As mentioned earlier, for the DevOps movement, it is not sufficient for developers to just build their software and let other teams deal with potential errors. The development team that creates and owns the application knows about its responsibilities, used technologies, and troubleshooting in case of potential errors.

Imagine a small startup that has only a single developer who responsible for the application. This person obviously has to deal with all technical issues, such as development, builds, deployment, and troubleshooting the application. He or she will have the best knowledge about the application's internals and will be able to fix potential issues effectively. Obviously, this single point of responsibility approach is the opposite of scalability and only works for tiny teams.

In bigger companies, there are more applications, more developers, and more teams with different responsibilities. The challenge with splitting and shifting responsibilities is to transfer knowledge. The knowledge is ideally spread within a team of engineers who closely work on the same software. Like in small startups, the mantra for developing applications should be: *you build it, you run it*. For a single team, this is only possible with the support of central, well-defined and automated processes. Implementing Continuous Delivery pipelines implement these processes to reliably ship software.

Managing and refining these processes becomes the responsibility of the whole team of engineers and is no longer an *ops problem*. All developers are equally responsible for building and shipping working software that provides value to the business. This certainly involves some duties, or team habits.

# Check in early and often

Continuous Delivery has to be lived by the whole team. Developers who work on features or bug fixes should check in into the master branch early and often. This is crucial to enable Continuous Integration. The more time passes before changes are merged into the master branch, the harder the merging and integration of features becomes. Adding complex functionality in a big bang contradicts the idea of *continuous* evolution of software. Functionality that should not be visible to users yet can be excluded by feature toggles.

Checking in often encourages developers to write sufficient, automated software tests from the beginning. This is certainly an effort to make during development but will always pay off in the long run. While developing a feature, engineers are aware of its functionality and boundaries. It's far less effort to include not only unit tests but sophisticated end-to-end tests from the beginning then it is after the feature has been written.

Especially for less-experienced developers it's important to mention that committing early, premature versions of features is nothing to be embarrassed about, but part of the development process. Code which hasn't been refactored yet and doesn't look perfect, but fulfills the requirements and provides business value, can be cleaned up in a second run. It's far more helpful to commit code early in the process than refraining from committing until the very last minute.

# Immediately fixing issues

Immediately solving build errors is another important team habit to develop. Tests that fail should not be ignored or postponed but fixed as soon as possible. Builds that fail often and are not taken good care of decrease the productivity of all team members. A failing test that makes the project unable to be built, for example, prevents other developers from integrating and verifying their features. Still, failing builds due to test failures or quality violations is a sign that the validation works and is, obviously, much better than false negatives, that is, mistakenly green builds. It is, however, important to fix project builds as soon as they fail. Developers should execute basic and fast verifications, such as building the Java project and executing code level tests, on their local machines before pushing to the central repository. They should take care not to misuse the pipeline to find careless mistakes which unnecessarily disturb other team members.

As mentioned earlier, compiler or code analysis warnings should be treated as errors that break the build. This introduces a zero-warning policy that urges engineers to either fix the issue or adjust the validation. Build, compilation, or code style warnings are therefore also errors that break the build and need to be fixed as soon as possible.

The team member whose commit caused the build to break should ideally be the first to look into the root cause. It is, however, a responsibility of the whole team to keep the pipeline in a healthy state. This goes back to the whole team being responsible for the whole project. There should not be exclusive *code ownership*, that is, parts of the projects which are exclusively known to a single team member. It will always be the case that developers who wrote specific functionality have better knowledge about it. Still, in all cases, the team should be able to work on all areas of the project and fix potential issues.

# Visibility

The visibility that Continuous Delivery enables is another important aspect. The whole development process, including commits, builds, verifications, and deployments, can be tracked and comprehended in a single place. What visibility aspects are important in a Continuous Delivery pipeline?

First of all, it needs to be represented whether the software is in a shippable state. This includes the build's health in terms of compilation, tests, and code analyses. A dashboard or so-called **extreme feedback** device, such as physical green and red LEDs, provide a quick overview about it.

A reasonable build visibility ideally does not overload with information if the build is green but provides clear and direct insight in case of failing builds. This again follows the principle that there are no such things as warnings in the build; it either passes successfully and there is nothing else to do or it breaks and requires action. Dashboards or other devices that provide this *green or red* information already provide helpful insights. These visibility instruments should be accessible to all team members to embrace collaboration.

However, in order not to disrupt the day-to-day development too much, it makes sense to notify persons in charge, whose commits caused the build to break, first. They likely have further knowledge how to fix the build again without disturbing the work of their teammates if not necessary. CI servers provide functionality to send emails, use chat communication, or other forms of notification. This both increases the quality of the software as well as the developer's productivity.

The information that is gathered during builds can be used to measure the quality of the software project. This first of all includes build and test results and code quality metrics, such as test coverage. This information can be displayed over time to provide insights and trends about the software quality.

Other very interesting metadata concerns the build pipeline itself. How long does a build usually take? How many builds are there in a day? How often does the build fail? What is the most common failure cause? How long does it take a failing build to be fixed again (*time to recover*)? The answers to these questions provide helpful insights about the quality of the Continuous Delivery process.

The gathered information serves as good starting points to improve the process further. Visibility of Continuous Delivery not only illuminates the current project status but can also draw the engineers' attention to certain hotspots. The overall goal is to continuously improve the software.

# Improve continuously

The whole mindset of Continuous Delivery aims to delivery software with consistent quality. Automated processes encourage the usage of quality verifications.

Good software quality, of course, does not come for free. Sufficient test cases as well as code quality analyses require a certain time and effort. Automation and continuously improving the quality, however, will, after an initial threshold, pay off in the long run, and eventually lead to better software.

New features as well as found bugs need to be verified sufficiently during development in order to ensure that functionality works as expected. By automating the tests and keeping them as regression, developers can be sure that no new bugs can disrupt the functionality in the future. The same is true for code quality analyses. Once the analysis is set up with appropriate rules and the found errors are eradicated, it ensures that no new violations can find their way into the software. If new false positive violations emerge, the rules are adjusted and will prevent new false positives in the future.

Introducing new test scenarios, such as end-to-end tests, also highly supports this approach. Regression tests decrease the risk of newly introduced bugs more and more. Again, automation is the key. As we will see in `Chapter 7`, *Testing*, human intervention is helpful for defining reasonable test scenarios. However, it is crucial to the software quality that these test are then automated made part of the pipeline. By doing so, the quality is improved more and more over time.

This, of course, requires the engineers to put a certain priority into quality improvements. Improving software quality, as well as refactoring, doesn't provide any immediate benefits for the business. These efforts will, instead, pay off in the long run - by still being able to produce new features with a constant velocity or changing existing behavior with certainty that nothing else breaks.

# Summary

Productive development workflows require fast turnaround times as well as fast feedback. Automating repetitive tasks minimizes the times spent on build, tests and deployments. Zero-dependency Java EE applications supports fast feedback by minimizing build, publish, and deployment times.

It's important to define which category of errors will break the build. Developers should be aware that a build is either broken, due to legitimate errors, or passed, without anything to complain about. Warnings that have no effect on the build outcome have little value.

Data migration is another important topic to consider. Deploying stateless applications is comparably easy; what needs to be taken into account are the database schemas that need to match the application code. Rolling updates together with migration scripts, that rollout modifications in small changes, enable applications to be deployed with zero-downtime. Applications therefore need to support N-1 compatibility.

Continuous Delivery depends on a healthy team culture. It's not sufficient to implement just the technical necessities; all software engineers need to embrace the principles. Potential build issues, test results, software quality, and deployment statuses should be visible to the whole software team.

Continuous Delivery processes support to continuously improve the software. Verification steps that are added, such as automated software tests, run every time the application is built, enabling regression tests and avoiding specific bugs to happen twice. This of course requires developers to put effort into the quality improvement. The effort put into Continuous Delivery will pay off in the long run.

The following chapter stays in the field of software quality and will cover testing enterprise applications.

# 7
# Testing

As we have seen in the previous chapter, Continuous Delivery pipelines allow developers to ship software with constant velocity and quality. In order to meet this quality, automated software tests are required. Engineers that work on features want to be sure that everything works as expected. This is even more the case when the software project advances, changes, and potentially breaks existing behavior. Developers need to be sure that no unwanted side-effects are introduced.

Ideally, the software tests contained in a build pipeline are sufficient, without further manual verification, to deploy to production.

This chapter will cover the following topics:

- The requirements of software tests
- Different test levels and scopes
- Unit, component, integration, system, and performance tests
- How to run test scenarios locally
- How to craft maintainable tests
- Required test technology

## The necessity of tests

Tests are necessary to be able to rely on that a certain functionality behaves in a certain way later in production. In all kinds of manufacturing businesses, tests are a natural part of the process. A car has countless parts that need to be tested independently as well as interdependently. Nobody wants to drive a car which has its first test run on a real street with the actual customer.

Tests simulate production behavior and verify components in a safe environment. Manufactured parts that break during test runs are something positive; they have just pointed out potential errors and nothing more than time and materials is lost. Parts that break in production can cause more harm.

The same is true for software tests. Test failures are something positive, at worst they used up some time and effort, at best they prevent potential bugs from going to production.

As seen previously, tests need to run with the least required human interaction possible. Humans are good at thinking about reasonable test cases and crafting creative test scenarios. Computers, however, are better at executing them. Verifying complex tests is something computers also do well, after they have been given clear verification instructions. With software growing more complex over time, the effort of manually verifying behavior gets bigger and bigger and more prone to error over time. Computers perform better and more reliably at repetitive tasks.

Reliable automated software tests are a prerequisite of moving fast. Automated tests can be executed many times, verifying the whole application. Builds run many times a day, execute all tests every time - even if only minor changes were introduced - and enable verified versions to go to production. This would not be feasible with tests executed by humans.

Automated tests increase the reliability of and confidence in the Continuous Delivery process. For Continuous Deployment, that is, going directly to production, sufficient, automated test scenarios are absolutely required. When all commits are potential candidates for production deployment, all software behavior must be adequately verified upfront. Without this automated verification, Continuous Deployment wouldn't be possible.

# Requirements of well-crafted tests

Today's software world has agreed that tests are crucial to working software. But what makes a good software test? What software components do we have to test? And, more importantly, how can we develop well-crafted tests?

In general, tests should fulfill the following requirements:

- Predictability
- Isolation
- Reliability

- Fast execution
- Automation
- Maintainability

The following describes these requirements.

# Predictability

First of all, software tests have to be stable, predictable, and reproducible. The same project circumstances must predictably produce the same test case outcomes, that is, passing or failing. Tests that sometimes pass and sometimes fail are not helpful at all. They either distract developers by providing false positive results or suppress actual bugs with false negative outcomes.

Circumstances that need to be taken into account are, among others, the current time, time zones, locales, randomly generated data, and concurrent execution of other tests that could interfere. The test scenarios should be predictably and explicitly set up, so that these circumstances have no influence on the outcome. If the tested functionality is in fact influenced by these factors, this is a sign that there is a need for additional test scenarios, considering different configurations.

# Isolation

The requirement of predictability also relates to isolation. Test cases have to run self-sufficiently, without affecting other tests. Changing and maintaining test cases should also have no impact on other test scenarios.

Besides leveraging predictability and maintainability, isolating tests also has an impact on the reproducibility of errors. Complex test scenarios may contain a lot of concerns and responsibilities that can make it hard to find the root causes of failing tests. Isolated tests with smaller scope, however, limit the possibilities of causes and enable developers to find bugs faster.

The several test scopes an enterprise project usually has, which we will see later in this chapter, also come with several test isolation layers. Tests with a small scope, such as unit tests, run more isolated than, for example, end-to-end tests. It certainly makes sense to write test cases in different scopes, which implies different test isolation layers.

# Reliability

Ideally, software tests of a project reliably test all functionality. The mantra should be that software that passes the tests is ready for production usage. This is of course a goal to strive for, for example by continuous improvement.

Using Continuous Delivery and especially Continuous Deployment requires a reliable and sufficient test harness. The software tests are the ultimate quality barrier before production deployment.

Reliable tests that pass should not require any further interaction. Therefore, they should not output verbose logs if the overall execution was successful. While a detailed explanation of what happened during execution is very helpful in failing tests, it becomes distracting in passing runs.

# Fast execution

As said before, tests are required to execute quickly. Fast running tests are a necessity for development pipelines providing fast feedback. Especially with the number of tests growing over time by applying continuous improvement, the only way to keep the pipeline effective is to keep test execution time low.

Typically, test execution spends the most time in starting up the test technology. Integration tests in particular, which use an embedded container, consume a lot of startup time. The time spent performing the actual test is in most cases not such a big issue.

Tests that consume a lot of time contradict the idea of continuous improvement of quality. The more test cases and scenarios that are added to the project, the longer the overall test execution and the slower is the feedback. Especially with the challenges of a fast-moving world, software tests need to perform as fast as possible. The rest of this chapter will show you how we can achieve this goal, particularly in regard to end-to-end test scenarios.

# Automation

Automation is a prerequisite for fast feedback. Continuous Delivery pipeline steps should run with the least human intervention as possible. The same is true for test scenarios. Executing software tests and validating their results should run completely and reliably without human interaction.

The test cases define the functionality's expected behavior and validate the outcome against it. The test will then reliably pass without additional notice or fail with a detailed explanation. Passing tests should not require any further human interaction.

A scenarios with huge or complex test data in particular represent a certain challenge in automating test cases. In order to deal with this issue, engineers should craft test cases in a maintainable way.

# Maintainability

Developing test cases is one thing. Keeping efficient test cases with good coverage when functionality changes is another thing. The challenge with having poorly-crafted test scenarios is that as soon as production functionality changes, the tests need to change as well, requiring a lot of time and effort.

Crafting test cases requires the same attention and effort as production code. Experience shows that without this effort put in, tests contain a lot of duplication and multiple responsibilities. In the same way as for production code, test code requires refactoring.

It should be possible to change or extend test scenarios without much effort required. In particular the test data that changes needs to be represented effectively.

Maintainable tests are a prerequisite for enterprise projects that have proper test coverage and yet are flexible for changes in their business logic. Being able to adapt in a fast-moving world requires adjustable test scenarios as well.

# What to test

Before we go into the topic of how to craft effective, fast, reliable, automated, and maintainable test cases, let's have a look at what assets to test. There are tests on a code layer as well as end-to-end tests. Code layer tests are based on the project's source code and are usually executed during development and build time, whereas end-to-end tests, of all kinds, operate on a running application.

Depending on the test scopes, which we will get to know in the next section, there are different layers of tests, whether tests operate on classes, multiple components, enterprise applications, or whole environments. In all cases the test object needs to be isolated from external concerns. The nature of tests is that they verify certain behavior under specific conditions. The environment surrounding the test object, such as the test cases as well as used components, have to interact with the test object accordingly. The test case will therefore control the test object. This not only includes tests at code level, but also end-to-end tests with external systems being simulated and mocked away.

Most importantly, software tests should verify business behavior. The specified use cases all have to perform certain logic that has to be tested before production deployment. Software tests should therefore verify that the application fulfills the business requirements. Special and corner cases need to be covered as well as negative tests.

For example, testing authentication functionality not only needs to verify that a user can log in with the correct credentials, but also that they can not log in using wrong the credentials. A corner case of this example would be to verify that the authentication component notifies a user whose password is about to expire as soon as he logs in successfully.

Besides business behavior, technical aspects and cross-cutting components also need to be tested. Accessed databases and external systems and the form of the communication is required to be verified on both ends in order to guarantee a working team. These concerns are best tested in end-to-end tests.

In all cases the test object should not be modified during the test, but work in the way as it will in production. This is crucial for crafting reliable tests that will not alter their behavior later on. For code level tests, this only requires that the contents of all involved components are the same. For end-to-end tests, this includes the whole enterprise application as well as the installation and configuration of the application's runtime.

# Definition of test scopes

There are several test scopes and responsibilities to consider. The following will introduce the different scopes the rest of this chapter will cover.

Certain namings, such as *integation tests*, are used ambiguously in various enterprise projects. This sub-chapter defines consistent test scope names that are used for the rest of this book.

# Unit tests

Unit tests verify the behavior of individual units of an application. A unit test usually represents a single class, in some cases a few interdependent classes.

Unit tests operate on code level. They are usually executed in the IDE during development as well as part of the build process before the application is packaged. Unit tests have the shortest execution time of all test scopes. They only execute limited functionality that can be instantiated easily on code level. Potential dependencies of the units are simulated using mocks or dummy classes.

# Component tests

Component tests verify the behavior of a coherent component. They span more than just an individual unit, but still operate on code level. Component tests aim to integrate several components together, which verify the interdependent behavior without setting up container environments.

The scope of component tests is to provide more integration than unit tests without running the application in potentially slow, simulated environments. Similar to unit tests, they use mocking functionality to delimit and simulate test boundaries. An embedded or remote enterprise container is not required.

# Integration tests

There is a lot of disagreement as to what integration tests represent and how they are designed. The aimed integration can happen on various levels.

I will use the term as it is quite widely used in the Java ecosystem and as it is represented in the Maven conventions. Integration tests run on code level, providing integration of several units and components, and usually run some more-or-less complex testing framework. This is the main distinction from component tests here.

Integration tests have a similar scope as component tests also integrate several units; however, the focus is on the integration. This integration is more technology than business related. For example, managed beans can make use of CDI injection to acquire certain dependencies using qualifiers or CDI producers. Developers need to verify whether the CDI *plumbing* has been done properly, that is, the correct annotations have been used, without necessarily deploying the application to a server.

Testing frameworks start up an embedded runtime that will build up several components and run code level tests against them.

Component tests, however, solely focus on the business logic and are limited to simple dependencies that are easily resolvable without sophisticated containers. In general, component tests are preferable for testing business use cases since they contain less moving parts and will run faster.

# System tests

The term system tests is sometimes also used ambiguously. In this context, the term covers all test cases that run the application or the system as a whole, verifying use cases in an end-to-end manner. Sometimes the terms acceptance or integration tests are used respectively. However, this book consistently uses the term system tests to refer to end-to-end tests.

System tests are quite important to verify that a deployed application works as expected, including both business logic and technical concerns. Whereas the majority of business logic should already be covered by unit and component tests, system tests verify that the overall behavior, including all external systems, is met. This includes how functionality is integrated and interacts within the system landscape.

For an application to provide value, it is not sufficient to only include business logic, but also how that logic is accessed. This needs to be verified in an end-to-end manner.

Since this book is targeted for backend applications, UI level tests are not considered here; this includes UI end-to-end tests as well as UI reactiveness tests. Developers typically develop UI tests using test technology such as **Arquillian Graphene**. The system test approaches described in this chapter are applicable to UI level tests as well.

# Performance tests

Performance tests verify the non-functional aspect of how a system performs in terms of responsiveness and correct behavior under certain workloads.

It needs to be ensured that an application can provide business value, not only under laboratory conditions but also in production. In production the load on the system can vary heavily, depending on the nature of the application and its use cases. Applications that are publicly available also run the risk of becoming the target of denial of service attacks.

Performance tests are a helpful tool to detect potential performance issues that are caused by the application. This includes, for example, resource leaks, misconfiguration, deadlock situations, or missing timeouts. Putting the application under simulated workload will bring these issues to light.

However, as we will see in `Chapter 9`, *Monitoring, Performance, and Logging*, performance tests aren't necessarily helpful to predict production responsiveness or tune an application's performance. They should be used as a barrier against obvious mistakes, providing fast feedback.

For the rest of this book, I will use the term performance tests to describe performance as well as load or stress tests that put the application under performance load.

# Stress tests

Similar to performance tests, stress tests aim to put the system under a certain stress to verify correct behavior in abnormal situations. Whereas performance tests mainly target the application's performance in terms of responsibility and stability, stress tests can cover all aspects and attempts that try to bring the system down.

This includes invalid calls, neglecting communication contracts, or random, unexpected events from the environment. This list of tests is non-exhaustive here and beyond the scope of this book.

However, to give a few examples, stress test may verify against misuse of HTTP connections, such as SYN flooding, DDoS attacks in general, unexpected shutdowns of infrastructure, or further, so-called fuzz or monkey testing.

Creating a sophisticated test harness containing a lot of stress tests would practically be beyond the scope of most projects. However, for enterprise projects it makes sense to include a few reasonable stress tests that match the used environment.

# Implementing tests

After the motivations, requirements, and different scopes, let's have a closer look at how to craft test cases in Java Enterprise projects.

# Unit tests

Unit tests verify the behavior of individual units of an application. In a Java EE application, this usually regards single entity, boundary, and control classes.

In order to unit test a single class, no exhaustive test case should be required. Ideally, instantiating the test object and setting up minimum dependencies should be sufficient to be able to invoke and verify its business functionality.

Modern Java EE supports this approach. Java EE components, such as EJBs as well as CDI managed beans are testable in a straightforward way by simply instantiating the classes. As we saw previously, modern enterprise components represent plain Java objects, including annotations, without extending or implementing technically motivated superclasses or interfaces, so-called no-interface views.

This allows tests to instantiate EJB or CDI classes and to wire them up as required. Used delegates such as injected controls that are irrelevant to the test case are mocked away. By doing so, we define the boundaries of the test case, what should be tested, and what is not relevant. Mocked delegates enable to verify the test object interaction.

A mock object simulates behavior of an actual instance of its type. Calling methods on mocks usually only returns dummy or mock values. Test objects are not aware that they communicate with a mock object. The behavior of mocks, as well as the verification of invoked methods, is controlled within the test scenario.

# Implementation

Let's start with a unit test of a Java EE core component. The `CarManufacturer` boundary executes certain business logic and invokes a `CarFactory` delegate control:

```
@Stateless
public class CarManufacturer {
    @Inject
    CarFactory carFactory;

    @PersistenceContext
    EntityManager entityManager;

    public Car manufactureCar(Specification spec) {
        Car car = carFactory.createCar(spec);
        entityManager.merge(car);
        return car;
    }
}
```

Since the EJB boundary is a plain Java class, it can be instantiated and set up in a unit test. The most commonly used Java unit test technology is **JUnit** together with **Mockito** for mocking. The following code snippet shows the car manufacturer test case, instantiating the boundary test object and using Mockito to mock away used delegates:

```java
import org.junit.Before;
import org.junit.Test;
import static org.assertj.core.api.Assertions.assertThat;
import static org.mockito.ArgumentMatchers.any;
import static org.mockito.Mockito.*;

public class CarManufacturerTest {

    private CarManufacturer testObject;

    @Before
    public void setUp() {
        testObject = new CarManufacturer();
        testObject.carFactory = mock(CarFactory.class);
        testObject.entityManager = mock(EntityManager.class);
    }

    @Test
    public void test() {
        Specification spec = ...
        Car car = ...

        when(testObject.entityManager.merge(any())).then(a ->
a.getArgument(0));
        when(testObject.carFactory.createCar(any())).thenReturn(car);

        assertThat(testObject.manufactureCar(spec)).isEqualTo(car);

        verify(testObject.carFactory).createCar(spec);
        verify(testObject.entityManager).merge(car);
    }
}
```

The JUnit framework instantiates the CarManufacturerTest test class once during the test execution.

The `@Before` method, `setUp()` here, is executed every time before a `@Test` method runs. Similarly, methods annotated with `@After` run after every test run. The `@BeforeClass` and `@AfterClass` methods, however, are only executed once per test class, before and after the execution, respectively.

Mockito methods, such as `mock()`, `when()`, or `verify()` are used to create, set up, and verify mocking behavior, respectively. Mock objects are instructed to behave in a certain way. After the test execution, they can verify whether certain functionality has been called on them.

This is an admittedly easy example, but it contains the essence of unit testing core components. No further custom test runner, neither an embedded container is required to verify the boundary's behavior. As opposed to custom runners, the JUnit framework can run unit tests at a very high rate. Hundreds of examples like these will be executed on modern hardware in no time. The startup time is short and the rest is just Java code execution, with a tiny overhead from the testing framework.

Some readers may have noticed the package-private visibility on the `CarManufacturer` class. This is due to providing better testability in order to be able to set the delegate on instantiated classes. Test classes that reside in the same package as the boundary are able to modify its dependencies. However, engineers might argue that this violates the encapsulation of the boundary. Theoretically they're right, but no caller will be able to modify the references once the components run in an enterprise container. The referenced object is not the actual delegate, but a proxy thereof, hence the CDI implementation can prevent misuse. It certainly is possible to inject the mock object using reflection or by using constructor-based injection. However, field-based injection together with directly setting the dependencies in the test cases provides better readability with the same production behavior. As of today, many enterprise projects have agreed upon using field dependency injection with package-private visibility.

Another discussion is whether to use custom JUnit runners such as `MockitoJUnitRunner` together with custom mocking annotations or a plain setup approach, as shown previously. The following code snippet shows a more dense example using a custom runner:

```
import org.junit.runner.RunWith;
import org.mockito.InjectMocks;
import org.mockito.Mock;
import org.mockito.junit.MockitoJUnitRunner;

@RunWith(MockitoJUnitRunner.class)
public class CarManufacturerTest {

    @InjectMocks
    private CarManufacturer testObject;
```

```
@Mock
private CarFactory carFactory;

@Mock
private EntityManager entityManager;

@Test
public void test() {
    ...
    when(carFactory.createCar(any())).thenReturn(car);
    ...
    verify(carFactory).createCar(spec);
}
}
```

Using the custom Mockito runner allows developers to configure tests with less code as well as to define injections with private visibility in the service class. Using a plain approach, as shown previously, provides more flexibility for complex mock scenarios. However, which method to use in order to run and define Mockito mocks is indeed a question of taste.

Parameterized tests is an additional JUnit functionality to define test cases that are similar in the scenario, but differ in input and output data. The `manufactureCar()` method could be tested with a variety of input data, resulting in a slightly different outcome. Parameterized test cases enable to develop these scenarios more productively. The following code snippet shows an example of such test cases:

```
import org.junit.runners.Parameterized;

@RunWith(Parameterized.class)
public class CarManufacturerMassTest {

    private CarManufacturer testObject;

    @Parameterized.Parameter(0)
    public Color chassisColor;

    @Parameterized.Parameter(1)
    public EngineType engineType;

    @Before
    public void setUp() {
        testObject = new CarManufacturer();
        testObject.carFactory = mock(CarFactory.class);
        ...
    }
```

```
@Test
public void test() {
    // chassisColor & engineType
    ...
}

@Parameterized.Parameters(name = "chassis: {0}, engine type: {1}")
public static Collection<Object[]> testData() {
    return Arrays.asList(
            new Object[]{Color.RED, EngineType.DIESEL, ...},
            new Object[]{Color.BLACK, EngineType.DIESEL, ...}
    );
}
```

Parameterized test classes are instantiated and executed following the data in the `@Parameters` test data method. Each element in the returned collection results in a separate test execution. The test class populates its parameter properties and continues the text execution as usual. The test data contains test input parameters as well as expected values.

The benefit of this parameterized approach is that it enables developers to add new test cases by simply adding another line within the `testData()` method. The preceding example shows the combination of a parameterized unit test using mocks. That combination is only possible using a plain Mockito approach, as described previously, instead of using `MockitoJUnitRunner`.

# Technology

These examples use JUnit 4 which, at the time of writing, is the most used unit testing framework version. Mockito is used to mock objects and it provides sufficient flexibility for the majority of use cases. In order to assert conditions, these examples use **AssertJ** as the test matching library. It provides functionality to verify the state of objects using productive method-chaining invocations.

These technologies serve as examples for the required test aspects. The point here, however, is not to dictate certain functionalities rather it is to showcase specific, reasonable choices for these test requirements. Other technology that provides similar functionality and benefits is equally advisable.

A typical example of another widely-used technology is Hamcrest matchers as a test matching library or the less frequently used **TestNG** unit test framework.

By the time you're reading this, JUnit version 5 will have emerged, which provides some additional functionalities, especially regarding to dynamic tests. Dynamic tests have similar motivations as parameterized tests, by programmatically and dynamically defining test cases.

# Component tests

Component tests verify the behavior of a coherent component. They provide more integration than unit tests without running the application in simulated environments.

## Motivation

The behavior of coherent functionality represented by several interdependent classes needs to be verified in order to test the integration thereof. Component tests should run as fast as unit tests by still isolating functionality, that is, testing coherent units. Therefore they aim to provide fast feedback by integrating yet more logic than just unit tests. Component tests verify business use cases, from the boundary down to involved controls.

Code level component tests are possible since the vast majority of managed beans use quite straightforward delegates. The injected types are in most cases directly resolvable without interfaces or qualifiers and could practically be instantiated and injected, even without embedded containers. This enables component tests to be implemented using the same testing frameworks as unit tests. Required delegates and mocks are set up as part of the test case. The test scenario we want to show starts from the beginning of a business use case down to injected controls.

The following examples will examine how to implement component tests with some basic code quality practices, that help writing maintainable tests.

## Implementation

Imagine the whole manufacture car use case shown in the previous example in the *Unit tests* section, needs to be tested. A car is created, using a delegate `CarFactory`, and then is persisted into the database. Testing the persistence layer is out of this test scope, therefore the entity manager will be mocked away.

The following code snippet shows the component test to the manufacture car use case:

```
public class ManufactureCarTest {

    private CarManufacturer carManufacturer;
```

```
    @Before
    public void setUp() {
        carManufacturer = new CarManufacturer();
        carManufacturer.carFactory = new CarFactory();
        carManufacturer.entityManager = mock(EntityManager.class);
    }

    @Test
    public void test() {
        when(carManufacturer.entityManager.merge(any())).then(a ->
a.getArgument(0));

        Specification spec = ...
        Car expected = ...

assertThat(carManufacturer.manufactureCar(spec)).isEqualTo(expected);
        verify(carManufacturer.entityManager).merge(any(Car.class));
    }
}
```

The preceding example is quite similar to the previous ones, with the exception that
CarFactory is instantiated, using the actual business logic. The mocks, which represent the
boundaries of the test case, verify correct behavior.

However, while this approach works for straightforward use cases, it is somewhat naive in
regard to more sophisticated real-world scenarios. The boundaries of the test case are as
seen in the test class, for the CarFactory delegate to be self-sufficient and not inject further
controls. Of course, all interdependent units that are part of a component test can define
delegates. Depending on the nature of the test and the use case, these nested delegates also
need to be instantiated or mocked away.

This will eventually lead to a lot of effort required in setting up the test case. We could
make use of test framework functionality such as Mockito annotations here. Doing so, the
test case injects all classes that are involved in the test case. Developers specify which of
them will be instantiated or mocked away, respectively. Mockito provides functionality to
resolve references, which is sufficient for the majority of use cases.

The following code snippet shows a component test of a similar scenario, this time using a
CarFactory delegate that has an AssemblyLine and Automation as nested dependencies.
These are mocked away in the test case:

```
    @RunWith(MockitoJUnitRunner.class)
    public class ManufactureCarTest {

        @InjectMocks
        private CarManufacturer carManufacturer;
```

```
@InjectMocks
private CarFactory carFactory;

@Mock
private EntityManager entityManager;

@Mock
private AssemblyLine assemblyLine;

@Mock
private Automation automation;

@Before
public void setUp() {
    carManufacturer.carFactory = carFactory;

    // setup required mock behavior such as ...
    when(assemblyLine.assemble()).thenReturn(...);
}

@Test
public void test() {
    Specification spec = ...
    Car expected = ...

assertThat(carManufacturer.manufactureCar(spec)).isEqualTo(expected);
    verify(carManufacturer.entityManager).merge(any(Car.class));
}
}
```

The `@InjectMocks` functionality of Mockito attempts to resolve object references with mock objects injected as `@Mock` in the test case. The references are set using reflection. If boundaries or controls define new delegates, they need to be defined at least as a `@Mock` object in the test cases to prevent `NullPointerException`. However, this approach only partially improves the situation since it leads to a lot of dependencies being defined in the test class.

An enterprise project with a growing number of component tests introduces a lot of verbosity and duplication if it follows only this approach.

To make the test code less verbose and restrict this duplication, we could introduce a test superclass for a specific use case scenario. That superclass would contain all @Mock and @InjectMock definitions, setting up required dependencies, delegates, and mocks. However, such test superclasses also contain a lot of implicit logic, which delegates are defined and being used somewhere in the extended test cases. This approach leads to test cases that are tightly coupled to commonly used superclasses, eventually leading to implicitly coupling the test cases.

## Delegating test components

It is more advisable to use delegation rather than extension.

Mocking and verification logic that depends on the used components is delegated to separate test objects. The delegates thus encapsulate and manage this logic individually.

The following code snippet shows the test case using components that define the car manufacture and car factory dependencies:

```java
public class ManufactureCarTest {

    private CarManufacturerComponent carManufacturer;
    private CarFactoryComponent carFactory;

    @Before
    public void setUp() {
        carFactory = new CarFactoryComponent();
        carManufacturer = new CarManufacturerComponent(carFactory);
    }

    @Test
    public void test() {
        Specification spec = ...
        Car expected = ...

        assertThat(carManufacturer.manufactureCar(spec)).isEqualTo(expected);

        carManufacturer.verifyManufacture(expected);
        carFactory.verifyCarCreation(spec);
    }
}
```

The Component test dependencies specify the declared dependencies and mocks including the setup and verification behavior for our test cases. The idea is to define components that are reusable within multiple component tests, wiring up similar logic.

The following code snippet shows the definition of CarManufacturerComponent:

```
public class CarManufacturerComponent extends CarManufacturer {

    public CarManufacturerComponent(CarFactoryComponent
carFactoryComponent) {
        entityManager = mock(EntityManager.class);
        carFactory = carFactoryComponent;
    }

    public void verifyManufacture(Car car) {
        verify(entityManager).merge(car);
    }
}
```

The class resides in the same package as the CarManufacturer class, but under the test sources. It can subclass the boundary to add mocking and verification logic. In this example, it is dependent on the CarFactory component, that also provides additional test logic:

```
public class CarFactoryComponent extends CarFactory {

    public CarFactoryComponent() {
        automation = mock(Automation.class);
        assemblyLine = mock(AssemblyLine.class);
        when(automation.isAutomated()).thenReturn(true);
    }

    public void verifyCarCreation(Specification spec) {
        verify(assemblyLine).assemble(spec);
        verify(automation).isAutomated();
    }
}
```

These components serve as reusable test objects that wire up certain dependencies and configure mocking behavior, accordingly. They can be reused within multiple component tests and enhanced without affecting usages.

These examples aim to give an idea of what is possible in order to write maintainable tests. For components being reused, more refactoring approaches should be considered, for example, using a builder-pattern like configuration to satisfy different situations. The *Maintaining test data and scenarios* section in this chapter contains more about how to write maintainable test code.

The benefit of component tests is that they run as fast as unit tests and yet verify more complex integration logic. The complex logic is tackled by delegation and encapsulation, increasing maintainability. The code and overhead required to setup is limited.

It makes sense to verify coherent business logic using component tests. Use case invocations are tested on a business level with technical low-level aspects being mocked away.

# Technology

These examples again demonstrate plain JUnit and Mockito test approaches. With some code quality practices, it's certainly possible to write maintainable, dense test cases with limited configuration overhead.

Component tests implemented as shown previously are a practical approach to wire up components that use straightforward dependency injection. If the production code makes use of CDI producers and qualifiers, the injection logic of the test components will change accordingly.

Component tests aim to verify the business use case behavior of coherent units. They usually don't verify the technical wiring. It's advisable to use integration tests in order to verify whether CDI injection was used correctly, for example, in terms of custom qualifiers, producers, or scopes.

However, there are test technologies that provide dependency injection into test cases. Examples for these are **CDI-Unit** or the more sophisticated **Aquillian Testing Framework**. Test cases using these frameworks run in containers, either embedded or even remotely, and are able to further verify the integration of components.

Sophisticated test frameworks certainly provide test cases that are closer to the enterprise application, but also come with the challenge of slow application startups. The containers are usually executed and configured in every test case, typically taking a few hundred milliseconds or more. This does not sound that much but quickly adds up as more tests arrive.

For component tests that aim to solely verify business behavior, faster, and lightweight approaches like the one presented, are therefore preferable. With their fast nature, component tests as well as unit tests are per default executed during the project build. They should be the default way how to verify application business logic.

The following shows code level integration tests that make use of simulated containers.

# Integration tests

Component tests verify coherent business logic in isolated and fast tests. Sophisticated Java EE integration behavior, such as injection, custom qualifiers, CDI events, or scopes are not covered by these tests.

Integration tests aim to verify the technical collaboration of components within the enterprise system. This covers concerns such as configuration of Java EE core components, communication with external systems, or persistence. Are the Java EE components annotated correctly? Does the JSON-B mapping produce the desired JSON format? Is the JPA ORM mapping defined properly?

The idea behind code level integration tests is to provide faster feedback by verifying correct integration without the need to build and deploy the application to a test environment.

# Embedded containers

Since unit test technology is not aware of Java EE specifics, integration tests need more sophisticated test functionality in the form of containers. There are several technologies available that start up an embedded container and make parts of the application available.

An example for this is CDI-Unit. It provides functionality to run test cases in a CDI container, further enabling developers to enhance and modify its configuration. CDI-Unit scans the dependencies of tested objects and configures them accordingly. Required mocks and test specific behavior are defined in a declarative approach. A managed bean such as the car manufacturer boundary is set up within the test case, with all required dependencies and mocks.

This approach detects configuration errors, such as missing CDI annotations. The following code snippet shows a car manufacture test, similar to the component test before, that instantiates the boundary:

```
import org.jglue.cdiunit.CdiRunner;

@RunWith(CdiRunner.class)
public class ManufactureCarIT {

    @Inject
    CarManufacturer carManufacturer;

    @Mock
    EntityManager entityManager;
```

```
    @Before
    public void setUp() {
        carManufacturer.entityManager = entityManager;
    }

    @Test
    public void test() {
        Specification spec = ...
        Car expected = ...

assertThat(carManufacturer.manufactureCar(spec)).isEqualTo(expected);
        verify(entityManager).merge(expected);
    }
}
```

The custom JUnit runner detects beans injected into the test case and resolves them accordingly. Since CDI-Unit only supports the CDI standard and not the full Java EE API, the test explicitly mocks and sets the entity manager. All other used controls, such as the car factory, automation, and assembly line, are instantiated and injected, accordingly.

CDI-Unit tests can be enhanced to serve more sophisticated scenarios. It's possible to produce beans that are being used within the test scope.

However, this technology certainly has its limits. CDI-Unit is helpful to quickly verify configuration and collaboration of managed beans.

Another, more sophisticated technology for testing applications is Arquillian. Arquillian bundles integration test cases into deployable archives, manages enterprise containers, either embedded or remotely, and deploys, executes, and verifies the test archives. It makes it possible to enhance test cases with custom test behavior depending on the scenario.

The advantage of Arquillian is that it supports containers with full Java EE support. This enables integration tests to operate in more production-near scenarios.

The following code snippet shows a simple example of deploying the car manufacturer boundary to an embedded enterprise container managed by Arquillian:

```
import org.jboss.arquillian.container.test.api.Deployment;
import org.jboss.arquillian.junit.Arquillian;
import org.jboss.shrinkwrap.api.ShrinkWrap;
import org.jboss.shrinkwrap.api.asset.EmptyAsset;
import org.jboss.shrinkwrap.api.spec.WebArchive;

@RunWith(Arquillian.class)
public class ManufactureCarIT {

    @Inject
```

```
    CarManufacturer carManufacturer;

    @Deployment
    public static WebArchive createDeployment() {
        return ShrinkWrap.create(WebArchive.class)
                .addClasses(CarManufacturer.class)
                // ... add other required dependencies
                .addAsWebInfResource(EmptyAsset.INSTANCE, "beans.xml");
    }

    @Test
    public void test() {
        Specification spec = ...
        Car expected = ...

assertThat(carManufacturer.manufactureCar(spec)).isEqualTo(expected);
    }
}
```

This test case will create a dynamic web archive that ships the boundary and required delegates and deploys it into an embedded container. The test itself can inject and call methods on the specific components.

The container does not necessarily have to run in an embedded way, it can also be a managed or remote container. Containers that run for longer than just the test execution avoid the container startup time and execute tests much more quickly.

Executing these integration tests will take a comparatively long time, but operate closer to production environments. Misconfigured managed beans will be detected during development before the application is shipped. The flexibility and customization of Arquillian, by including custom bean definitions that reside in the test scope, enables pragmatic test scenarios.

However, this example only slightly touches the functionality of embedded container tests. Test frameworks such as Arquillian can be used for validating the integration of container configuration, communication, persistence, and UI. In the rest of this chapter, we will see some shortcomings of integration tests that operate on simulated or embedded environments.

# Embedded databases

Mapping persistence of domain entities is usually defined using JPA annotations. Validating this mapping before an actual server deployment prevents careless mistakes and saves time.

In order to verify a correct database mapping, a database is required. Besides using deployed environment database instances, embedded databases provide similar verification with fast feedback. Embedded container tests running on frameworks such as Arquillian can be used to access this functionality. However, for basic verification it's not necessary for the application to run inside a container.

JPA ships with the possibility to run standalone, in any Java SE environment. We can make use of this and write test cases that wire up the JPA configuration and connect against an embedded or local database.

Imagine a car part that is manufactured and assembled in the car manufacture. The car part domain entity is mapped with JPA as follows:

```
@Entity
@Table(name = "car_parts")
public class CarPart {

    @Id
    @GeneratedValue
    private long id;

    @Basic(optional = false)
    private String order;

    @Enumerated(STRING)
    @Basic(optional = false)
    private PartType type;

    ...
}
```

In order to verify correct persistence, a test entity bean should at least be persisted and reloaded from the database. The following code snippet shows an integration test that sets up a standalone JPA persistence:

```
import javax.persistence.EntityTransaction;
import javax.persistence.Persistence;

public class CarPartIT {

    private EntityManager entityManager;
    private EntityTransaction transaction;

    @Before
    public void setUp() {
        entityManager =
Persistence.createEntityManagerFactory("it").createEntityManager();
```

```
        transaction = entityManager.getTransaction();
    }

    @Test
    public void test() {
        transaction.begin();

        CarPart part = new CarPart();
        part.setOrder("123");
        part.setType(PartType.CHASSIS);
        entityManager.merge(part);

        transaction.commit();
    }
}
```

Since the persistence runs standalone, there is no container taking care of handling transactions. The test case does this programmatically, as well as setting up the entity manager, using the persistence unit `it`. The persistence unit is configured in test scope `persistence.xml`. For this test purpose it's sufficient to configure a resource local transactional unit:

```
<?xml version="1.0" encoding="UTF-8"?>
<persistence version="2.2" xmlns="http://xmlns.jcp.org/xml/ns/persistence"
        xmlns:xsi="http://www.w3.org/2001/XMLSchema-instance"
        xsi:schemaLocation="http://xmlns.jcp.org/xml/ns/persistence
        http://xmlns.jcp.org/xml/ns/persistence/persistence_2_2.xsd">

    <persistence-unit name="it" transaction-type="RESOURCE_LOCAL">
        <class>com.example.cars.entity.CarPart</class>

        <exclude-unlisted-classes>true</exclude-unlisted-classes>
        <properties>
            <property name="javax.persistence.jdbc.url"
value="jdbc:derby:./it;create=true"/>
            <property name="javax.persistence.jdbc.driver"
value="org.apache.derby.jdbc.EmbeddedDriver"/>
            <property name="javax.persistence.schema-
generation.database.action" value="drop-and-create"/>
        </properties>
    </persistence-unit>
</persistence>
```

The involved entity classes such as `CarPart` have to be specified explicitly, since there is no container that takes care of annotation scanning. The JDBC configuration points to an embedded database, in this case **Apache Derby**.

The enterprise project does not include the Java EE implementation, only the API. Therefore, an JPA implementation, such as **EclipseLink**, is added as a test dependency, together with the Derby database.

This integration test provides faster feedback for configuration mismatches and careless mistakes by validating the persistence mapping locally. For example, the shown test case would fail because the `order` property of the `CarPart` type isn't able to be mapped, since `order` is a reserved SQL keyword. The solution to this is to change the column mapping, for example, by renaming the column with `@Column(name = "part_order")`.

This is a typical example of mistakes developers make while configuring the persistence. Preventing these errors, that otherwise won't be detected before deployment time, provides faster feedback and saves time and effort.

Of course, this approach will not find all database related integration mismatches. There is no container being used and persistence errors, for example, related to concurrent transactions, won't be found before fully-fledged system tests are executed. Still, it provides a helpful first verification in the pipeline.

# Running integration tests

Attentive readers may have noticed the naming convention of integration tests ending with `IT` for integration test. This naming emerged from a Maven naming convention, excluding test classes, that don't match the `Test` naming pattern, in the *test* phase. Classes ending with `IT` will be run by a different life cycle plugin.

This approach supports developers in crafting effective development pipelines, since code level integration tests shouldn't necessarily run in the first build step depending on the time they take. With the example of Maven, the **Failsafe Plugin** runs integration tests, using the command `mvn failsafe:integration-test failsafe:verify`, after the project has been built.

The IDE, of course, supports both running `Test` named tests as well as other naming conventions.

Gradle doesn't take this naming structure into account. In order to achieve the same goal, Gradle projects would use multiple sets of test sources that are executed separately.

# Code level integration tests versus system tests

Code level tests, such as unit, component, or integration tests, provide fast feedback during development. They enable developers to verify whether the business logic works as expected for isolated components and the overall configuration is sane.

## Shortcomings of integration tests

However, in order to verify the application's production behavior, these tests are not sufficient. There will be differences in technology, configuration, or runtime that eventually lead to gaps in the test cases. Examples are enterprise containers with different versions, mismatches in the bean configuration once the whole application is deployed, different database implementations, or differences in JSON serialization.

Ultimately, the application runs in production. It makes a lot of sense to verify the behavior in environments that are equivalent to production.

Certainly, it is advisable to craft several test scopes to both have tests with isolated scope and faster feedback as well as integrational tests. The shortcoming of code level integration tests is that they often take a great amount of time.

In my projects in the past, integration tests running containers such as Arquillian, usually were responsible for the vast majority of the build time, resulting in build with 10 minutes and more. This greatly slows down the Continuous Delivery pipeline, resulting in slow feedback and fewer builds. An attempt to solve this shortcoming is to use remote or managed containers in Arquillian tests. They will run with a longer life cycle than the test run and eliminate the startup times.

Code level integration tests are a helpful way to quickly verify application configuration, what cannot be tested using unit or component tests. They are not ideal for testing business logic.

Integration tests that deploy the whole application on simulated environments, such as embedded containers, provide certain value, but are not sufficient to verify production behavior since they are not equivalent to production. No matter whether on code level or simulated environments, integration tests tend to slow down the overall pipeline.

# Shortcomings of system tests

System tests which test an application that is deployed to a production-like environment in an end-to-end fashion provide the most representative verification. Since they run in a later step in the Continuous Delivery pipeline, they provide slower feedback. Test cases, such as verifying the JSON mappings of an HTTP endpoint, will take longer before they provide feedback to engineers.

Tackling and maintaining complex test scenarios is an aspect that takes quite some time and effort. Enterprise applications require definition and maintenance of test data and configuration, especially when many external systems are involved. For example, an end-to-end test that verifies creating a car in the car manufacture application requires external concerns such as the assembly line to be set up as well as test data. Managing these scenarios involves a certain effort.

End-to-end tests attempt to use external systems and databases similarly to production. This introduces the challenge to handle unavailable or erroneous environments. External systems or databases that are unavailable cause the tests to fail; however, the application is not responsible for this test failure. This scenario violates the requirement of predictability, that tests should not depend on external factors that provide false positives. Therefore, it's advisable that system tests mock away external systems that are not part of the application under test. Doing this enables to construct predictable end-to-end tests. The Sub-chapter *System tests* covers how to implement this approach.

# Conclusion

Code level unit and component tests verify isolated, specific business logic. They provide immediate feedback and prevent careless mistakes. Component tests, in particular, cover the integration of business related software units.

The delimitation of component tests is that they run without a simulated container, setting up the test cases in a programmatic fashion. Integration tests rely on inversion of control, similar to application containers that wire up components with less developer effort involved. However, crafting maintainable test cases using a programmatic approach with unit test technology ultimately leads to more effective tests. We will see in the *Maintaining test data and scenarios* section in this chapter, what methods support us in crafting productive test cases.

Integration tests verify the technical integration as well as configuration of application components. Their feedback is certainly faster than deploying the application as part of the pipeline. However, integration tests do not provide sufficient verification compared to production.

They are a good fit to provide a first basic barrier against common errors and careless mistakes. Since starting up integration tests usually takes quite some time, it makes a lot of sense to run a limited number of them. Ideally test frameworks such as Arquillian deploy to managed or remote containers that keep running beyond a single test case.

System tests verify the application's behavior in the most production-like fashion. They provide the ultimate feedback, whether the whole enterprise application works as expected, including business as well as technical aspects. In order to construct predictable test scenarios, it's important to consider external concerns, such as databases and external systems.

Crafting test cases, especially complex test scenarios, takes a lot of time and effort. The question is where does it make the most sense to spend this effort on? In order to test business logic, and especially coherent components, it's advisable to use component tests. Integration tests don't provide ultimate verification, but still take certain time and effort. It makes sense to use a few of them for fast integration feedback, but not to test business logic. Developers may also find ways to reuse created scenarios in several test scopes, for example both integration tests and system tests.

The overall goal should be to minimize the time and effort spent to craft and maintain test cases, to minimize the overall pipeline execution time and to maximize the application verification coverage.

# System tests

System tests run against a deployed enterprise application. The application contains the same code, configuration, and runtime as in production. The test cases use external communication, such as HTTP, to initiate use cases. They verify that the overall outcome, such as HTTP responses, database state, or communication with external systems, matches the expectations of the application.

System tests answer the question what to test with: the application that runs in the same way as in production, excluding external concerns, accessed using its regular interfaces. External concerns will be simulated, ensuring predictable tests and enabling verification of the communication. It depends on the scenario whether a used database is seen as part of the application and used similarly, or mocked away as well.

# Managing test scenarios

System test scenarios can easily get quite complex, involving several concerns and obfuscating the actual use case that is to be tested.

In order to manage the complexity of scenarios it makes sense to first craft the procedure of the test case without writing actual code. Defining the required steps in comments, or even on paper first, provides a good overview of what the test scenario is about. Implementing the actual test case afterwards with regard to reasonable abstraction layers will result in more maintainable test cases, with potentially reusable functionality. We will cover this approach in an example later in this sub-chapter.

It's important to take test data into consideration. The more responsibilities a scenario holds, the more complex it will be to define and maintain the test data. It makes sense to put some effort into test data functionality that is being used commonly in the test cases. Depending on the nature of the application and its domain, it may even make sense to define a specific engineer role for this. Providing reusable functionality that is usable effectively can provide some relief; however, it may still be necessary to at least define and document common test data and scenarios.

Ultimately it doesn't help to ignore the complexity of test data. If the application domain does include sophisticated scenarios, ignoring this situation by leaving out certain test cases or postponing test scenarios until production doesn't improve the application's quality.

In order to craft predictable isolated test cases, the scenario should run as stateless and self-sufficient as possible. Test cases should have a starting point similar to production and not rely on a certain state of the system. They should consider other potential tests and usages running simultaneously.

For example, creating a new car should not make assumptions about the number of existing cars. The test case should not verify that the list of all cars is empty before the creation or that it only contains the created car afterwards. It rather verifies that the created car is part of the list at all.

For the same reason it should be avoided that system tests have an impact on the environment life cycle. In situations that involve external systems, it's necessary to control the behavior of the mocked systems. If possible, these cases should be limited in order to enable to execute other scenarios concurrently.

# Simulating external concerns

System test scenarios use external systems in the same way as in production. However, similar to mock objects in unit and component tests, system tests simulate and mock away external systems. In this way, potential issues that the application isn't responsible for are eliminated. System tests run in dedicated environments, for example, provided by container orchestration frameworks. The test object is the sole application, deployed, executed and configured in the same way as in production.

Simulated external systems are configured to provide the expected behavior once accessed by the application. Similar to a mock object, they verify correct communication depending on the use case.

For the majority of use cases, used databases would not be mocked away. The test scenario can manage and populate database contents as part of the test life cycle, if required. If the database system contains a lot of concerns external to the application, for example containing a lot of database code or representing a search engine, it may make sense to mock and simulate this behavior.

Container orchestration strongly supports these efforts by abstracting systems as services. Pod images can be replaced by other implementations without affecting the tested application. The mocked services can be accessed and configured from within the running system test, defining behavior and external test data.

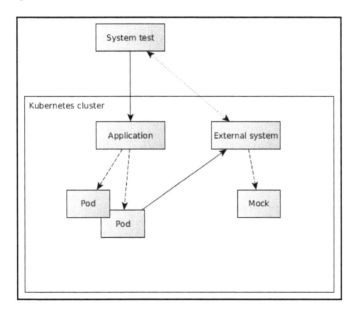

The dotted line illustrates the control and verification of the mocked system as part of the test scenario. The running application will use the external service as usual, with the difference that this service is in fact, backed by a mock.

# Designing system tests

System tests run as a step within the Continuous Delivery pipeline. They connect against a running application on a test environment, invoke business use cases, and verify the overall outcome.

System test cases usually don't impact the application's life cycle. The application is deployed upfront as part of the CD pipeline. If required, the system tests control the state and behavior of external mocks and contents of databases.

Generally speaking, it makes sense to develop system tests as separate build projects without any code dependency to the project. Since system tests access the application from the outside there should be no implications on how the system is being used. System tests are developed against the application's endpoint contracts. Similarly, the system tests should not use classes or functionality that is part of the application, such as using the application's JSON mapping classes. Defining technology and system access from the outside as separate build projects prevents unwanted side effects caused by existing functionality. The system test project can reside besides the application project in the same repository.

The following example will construct a system test from a top-down approach, defining test scenarios and appropriate abstraction layers.

The business use cases of the car manufacture application are accessed via HTTP. They involve external systems and database accesses. In order to verify the creation of a car, the system test will connect against the running application, as a real-world use case would.

In order to manage the test scenario, the case is crafted using logical steps with comments as placeholders first, and then implemented in several abstraction layers:

```
public class CarCreationTest {

    @Test
    public void testCarCreation() {

        // verify car 1234 is not included in list of cars

        // create car
        //    with ID 1234,
        //    diesel engine
```

```
//    and red color

// verify car 1234 has
//    diesel engine
//    and red color

// verify car 1234 is included in list of cars

// verify assembly line instruction for car 1234
        }
    }
```

These comments represent the logical steps that are executed and verified when testing creation of a car. They are related to the business rather than the technical implementation.

We realize these comments in private methods, or better, own delegates. The delegates encapsulate technical concerns, as well as potential life cycle behavior:

We define `CarManufacturer` and `AssemblyLine` delegates that abstract the access and behavior of the applications and delegates. They are defined as part of the system test and have no relation to or knowledge of the managed beans with the same name in the application code. The system test project code is defined independently. It could also be implemented using a different technology, only depending on the communication interface of the application.

The following code snippet shows the integration of the delegates. The car creation system test only contains business logic relevant to implementation, with the delegates realizing the actual invocations. This leverages readable as well as maintainable test cases. Similar system tests will reuse the delegate functionality:

```
import javax.ws.rs.core.GenericType;

public class CarCreationTest {

    private CarManufacturer carManufacturer;
    private AssemblyLine assemblyLine;

    @Before
    public void setUp() {
        carManufacturer = new CarManufacturer();
        assemblyLine = new AssemblyLine();

        carManufacturer.verifyRunning();
        assemblyLine.initBehavior();
    }
```

```
@Test
public void testCarCreation() {
    String id = "X123A345";
    EngineType engine = EngineType.DIESEL;
    Color color = Color.RED;

    verifyCarNotExistent(id);

    String carId = carManufacturer.createCar(id, engine, color);
    assertThat(carId).isEqualTo(id);

    verifyCar(id, engine, color);

    verifyCarExistent(id);

    assemblyLine.verifyInstructions(id);
}

private void verifyCarExistent(String id) {
    List<Car> cars = carManufacturer.getCarList();
    if (cars.stream().noneMatch(c -> c.getId().equals(id)))
        fail("Car with ID '" + id + "' not existent");
}

private void verifyCarNotExistent(String id) {
    List<Car> cars = carManufacturer.getCarList();
    if (cars.stream().anyMatch(c -> c.getId().equals(id)))
        fail("Car with ID '" + id + "' existed before");
}

private void verifyCar(String carId, EngineType engine, Color color) {
    Car car = carManufacturer.getCar(carId);
    assertThat(car.getEngine()).isEqualTo(engine);
    assertThat(car.getColor()).isEqualTo(color);
}
}
```

This serves as a basic example for an application system test. The delegates such as
CarManufacturer handle the lower-level communication and validation:

```
public class CarManufacturer {

    private static final int STARTUP_TIMEOUT = 30;
    private static final String CARS_URI =
"http://test.car-manufacture.example.com/" +
            "car-manufacture/resources/cars";

    private WebTarget carsTarget;
```

```
    private Client client;

    public CarManufacturer() {
        client = ClientBuilder.newClient();
        carsTarget = client.target(URI.create(CARS_URI));
    }

    public void verifyRunning() {
        long timeout = System.currentTimeMillis() + STARTUP_TIMEOUT * 1000;

        while (!isSuccessful(carsTarget.request().head())) {
            // waiting until STARTUP_TIMEOUT, then fail
            ...
        }
    }

    private boolean isSuccessful(Response response) {
        return response.getStatusInfo().getFamily() ==
Response.Status.Family.SUCCESSFUL;
    }

    public Car getCar(String carId) {
        Response response =
carsTarget.path(carId).request(APPLICATION_JSON_TYPE).get();
        assertStatus(response, Response.Status.OK);
        return response.readEntity(Car.class);
    }

    public List<Car> getCarList() {
        Response response =
carsTarget.request(APPLICATION_JSON_TYPE).get();
        assertStatus(response, Response.Status.OK);
        return response.readEntity(new GenericType<List<Car>>() {
        });
    }

    public String createCar(String id, EngineType engine, Color color) {
        JsonObject json = Json.createObjectBuilder()
                .add("identifier", id)
                .add("engine-type", engine.name())
                .add("color", color.name());

        Response response = carsTarget.request()
                .post(Entity.json(json));

        assertStatus(response, Response.Status.CREATED);

        return extractId(response.getLocation());
```

```
    }

    private void assertStatus(Response response, Response.Status
    expectedStatus) {
    assertThat(response.getStatus()).isEqualTo(expectedStatus.getStatusCode());
    }

    ...
}
```

The test delegate is configured against the car manufacture test environment. This configuration could be made configurable, for example, by a Java system property or environment variable in order to make the test reusable against several environments.

If the delegate needs to hook up into the test case life cycle, it can be defined as a JUnit 4 rule or JUnit 5 extension model.

This example connects against a running car manufacture application via HTTP. It can create and read cars, mapping and verifying the responses. The reader may have noted how the delegate encapsulates communication internals, such as HTTP URLs, status codes, or JSON mapping. Its public interface only comprises classes that are relevant to the business domain of the test scenario, such as Car or EngineType. The domain entity types used in system tests don't have to match the ones defined in the application. For reasons of simplicity, system tests can use different, simpler types that are sufficient for the given scenario.

## Deploying and controlling external mocks

We just saw how to connect a system test against a running enterprise application. But how can we control and manipulate the external system that is used inside the application's use case?

An external system can be mocked away using mock server technology such as **WireMock**. WireMock runs as a standalone web server, which is configured to answer specific requests accordingly. It acts like a code level test mock object, that stubs and verifies behavior.

The benefit of using container orchestration frameworks for system tests is that services can be easily replaced by mock servers. The external system's infrastructure as code configuration for the system test environment can contain a WireMock Docker image, which is executed instead of the actual system.

The following code snippet shows an example Kubernetes configuration for the assembly line system, using a WireMock Docker image in the running pods:

```
---
kind: Service
apiVersion: v1
metadata:
  name: assembly-line
  namespace: systemtest
spec:
  selector:
    app: assembly-line
  ports:
    - port: 8080
---
kind: Deployment
apiVersion: apps/v1beta1
metadata:
  name: assembly-line
  namespace: systemtest
spec:
  replicas: 1
  template:
    metadata:
      labels:
        app: assembly-line
    spec:
      containers:
      - name: assembly-line
        image: docker.example.com/wiremock:2.6
      restartPolicy: Always
---
```

The system test connects against this service, using an administration URL to set up and modify the mock server's behavior.

The following code snippet shows an implementation of the `AssemblyLine` test delegate, using the WireMock API to control the service:

```
import static
com.github.tomakehurst.wiremock.client.ResponseDefinitionBuilder.okForJson;
import static com.github.tomakehurst.wiremock.client.WireMock.*;
import static java.util.Collections.singletonMap;

public class AssemblyLine {

    public void initBehavior() {
        configureFor("http://test.assembly.example.com", 80);
```

```
        resetAllRequests();

        stubFor(get(urlPathMatching("/assembly-line/processes/[0-9A-Z]+"))
                .willReturn(okForJson(singletonMap("status",
"IN_PROGRESS")))));

        stubFor(post(urlPathMatching("/assembly-line/processes"))
                .willReturn(status(202)));
    }

    public void verifyInstructions(String id) {
        verify(postRequestedFor(urlEqualTo("/assembly-line/processes/" +
id))
                .withRequestBody(carProcessBody()));
    }

    ...
}
```

The initial behavior instructs the WireMock instance to answer HTTP requests appropriately. The behavior can also be modified during the test case, if more complex processes and conversations have to be represented.

If a more sophisticated test scenario involves asynchronous communication such as long-running processes, the test cases can use polling to wait for verifications.

The defined car manufacturer and assembly line delegates can be reused within multiple test scenarios. Some cases might require to run system tests mutually exclusively.

In the *Maintaining test data and scenarios* section, we will see what further methods and approaches support developers in writing maintainable test cases.

# Performance tests

Performance tests verify the non-functional requirement of how a system performs in terms of responsiveness. They don't verify business logic, they verify the application's technology, implementation, and configuration.

In production systems the load on the systems can vary heavily. This is especially true for applications that are publicly available.

# Motivation

Similar to tests that verify business behavior, it can be helpful to test upfront whether an application, or component thereof, is likely to meet their performance expectations in production. The motivation is to prevent major performance drops, potentially caused by introduced errors.

It's important to consider the application logic when constructing performance test scenarios. Some invocations perform more expensive processes than others. Generally it makes sense to construct performance tests after realistic production scenarios, in regard to the frequency and nature of requests.

For example, the ratio of guests browsing an online shop to customers actually performing purchase transactions should somehow reflect the real world.

However, it also makes sense to construct tests that excessively perform expensive invocations, to detect potential issues that emerge when the system is under stress.

In Chapter 9, *Monitoring, Performance, and Logging,* we will see why performance tests on environments other than production are a poor tool to explore the application's limits and potential bottlenecks. Instead of putting great effort into crafting sophisticated performance test scenarios, it makes more sense to invest into technical insights into production systems.

Still, we will see a few techniques of how to craft simple load tests that put a simulated application under pressure to find evident issues.

A reasonable attempt is to simulate usual load, ramp up the number of concurrent users, and explore at which point the application becomes unresponsive. If the responsiveness breaks sooner than from an earlier test run, this could indicate an issue.

# Key performance indicators

Key performance indicators give information about the application's responsiveness during normal behavior as well as under simulated workload. There are several indicators that can be gathered that directly affect the user, such as the response time or the error rate. These gauges represent the system's state and will provide insights about its behavior under performance tests. The indicated values will change depending on the number of concurrent users as well as the test scenario.

A first interesting insight is the application's response time - the time it takes to respond to a client's request including all transmissions. It directly affects the quality of the offered service. If the response time falls below a certain threshold, timeouts may occur that cancel and fail the request. The latency time is the time it takes until the server receives the first byte of the request. It mainly depends on the network setup.

During performance tests, it's especially interesting to see how the response time and latency time change compared to their average. When increasing the load on an application, at some point the application will become unresponsive. This unresponsiveness can originate from all kinds of reasons. For example, available connections or threads may be consumed, timeouts can occur, or database optimistic locking may fail. The request error rate represents the ratio of failed requests.

The number of concurrent users or load size in a specific interval of time affects the performance metrics of the application and needs to be considered in the test results. A higher number of users will put the system under more stress, depending on the nature of the request. This number is related to the number of concurrent transactions, technical transactions in this case, that indicate how many transactions the application can handle at a time.

The CPU and memory utilization provide insights about the application's resources. Whereas the values don't necessarily say much about the application's health, they represent the trend of resource consumption during load simulation.

Similarly, the overall throughput indicates the total amount of data that the server transmits to the connected users at any point in time.

The key performance indicators provide insights about the application's responsiveness. They help gather experience and especially trends during development. This experience can be used to verify future application versions. Especially after making changes in technology, implementation, or configuration, performance tests can indicate a potential performance impact.

# Developing performance tests

It makes sense to design performance test scenarios that are close to the real world. Performance test technology should support scenarios that not only ramp up a big amount of users, but simulate user behavior. Typical behavior could be, for example, a user visits the home page, logs in, follows a link to an article, adds the article to their shopping cart, and performs the purchase.

There are several performance test technologies available. At the time of writing, the arguably most used ones are **Gatling** and **Apache JMeter**.

Apache JMeter executes test scenarios that put applications under load and generates reports from the test execution. It uses XML-based configuration, supports multiple or custom communication protocols and can be used to replay recorded load test scenarios. Apache JMeter defines test plans that contain compositions of so-called samplers and logic controllers. They are used to define test scenarios that simulate user behavior. JMeter is distributed, using a master/slave architecture and can be used to generate load from several directions. It ships a graphical UI which is is used to edit the test plan configuration. Command-line tools execute the tests locally or on a Continuous Integration server.

Gatling provides a similar performance test solution, but it defines test scenarios programmatically written in Scala. It therefore provides a lot of flexibility in defining test scenarios, behavior of virtual users, and how the test progresses. Gatling can also record and reuse user behavior. Since the tests are defined programmatically, there are a lot of flexible solutions possible, such as dynamically feeding cases from external sources. The so-called checks and assertions are used to verify whether a single test request or the whole test case was successful.

Unlike JMeter, Gatling runs on a single host, not distributed.

The following code snippet shows the definition of a simple Gatling simulation in Scala:

```scala
import io.gatling.core.Predef._
import io.gatling.core.structure.ScenarioBuilder
import io.gatling.http.Predef._
import io.gatling.http.protocol.HttpProtocolBuilder
import scala.concurrent.duration._

class CarCreationSimulation extends Simulation {

  val httpConf: HttpProtocolBuilder = http
.baseURL("http://test.car-manufacture.example.com/car-manufacture/resources")
    .acceptHeader("*/*")

  val scn: ScenarioBuilder = scenario("create_car")
    .exec(http("request_1")
      .get("/cars"))
    .exec(http("request_1")
      .post("/cars")
      .body(StringBody("""{"id": "X123A234", "color": "RED", "engine": "DIESEL"}""")).asJSON
      .check(header("Location").saveAs("locationHeader")))
    .exec(http("request_1")
```

```
        .get("${locationHeader}"))

  pause(1 second)

  setUp(
    scn.inject(rampUsersPerSec(10).to(20).during(10 seconds))
  ).protocols(httpConf)
    .constantPauses

}
```

The `create_car` scenario involves three client requests, which retrieve all cars, create a car, and follow the created resource. The scenarios configure multiple virtual users. The number of users starts at `10` and is ramped up to `20` users within `10` seconds runtime.

The simulation is triggered via the command line and executed against a running environment. Gatling provides test results in HTML files. The following code snippet shows the Gatling HTML output of the test example run:

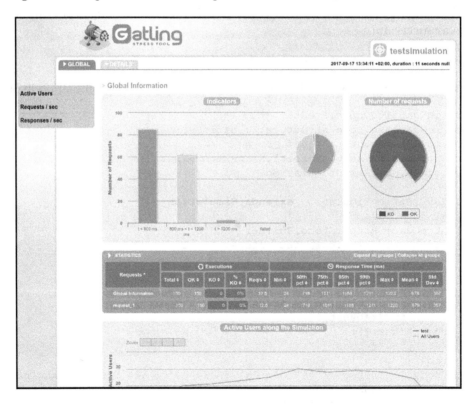

This example gives an idea of what is possible with Gatling tests.

Since performance tests should reflect somewhat realistic user scenarios, it makes sense to reuse existing system test scenarios for performance tests. Besides programmatically defining user behavior, pre-recorded test runs can be used to feed in data from external sources such as web server log files.

## Insights

The point in executing performance tests is less a *green* or *red* outcome than the insights gathered from the runs. The test reports and the application's behavior are collected during the test runs. These collections enable us to gain experience and discover trends in performance.

While the performance tests can be executed standalone, they ideally run continuously as part of a Continuous Delivery pipeline. It's already helpful to gain these insights without needing to affect the outcome of the pipeline step. After some metrics have been gathered, engineers can consider defining a performance run as failed if the measured performance indicated a major drop from the usual expectations.

This matches the idea of continuous improvement or in this case avoiding responsiveness deterioration.

# Running tests locally

The previous chapter covered development workflows and Continuous Delivery pipelines. It's crucial for modern enterprise applications to define an effective pipeline. However, while the CI server takes care of all build, test, and deploy steps, software engineers are still required to build and test on their local environments.

Continuous Delivery pipelines with proper tests sufficiently verify that enterprise applications work as expected. However, the shortcoming with only relying on the pipeline is that engineers receive feedback later and only after they have pushed their changes to the central repository. Whereas this is the idea behind Continuous Integration, developers still want certainty in their changes before committing them.

Committing changes that contain careless mistakes disturbs other team members by unnecessarily breaking the build. Errors that are easy to detect can be prevented by verifying the commit locally. This is certainly doable in code level tests, such as unit, component, and integration tests, which run on local environments as well. Performing code level tests before committing prevents the majority of mistakes.

When developing technical or cross-cutting concerns, such as interceptors or JAX-RS JSON mapping, engineers also want feedback before committing the changes to the pipeline. As mentioned before, system tests against actually running applications provide the most realistic verification.

For local environments, developers could write sophisticated integration tests, running on embedded containers, to receive faster feedback. However, as we saw previously, this requires quite some time and effort and still does not reliably cover all situations.

Using container technologies enables engineers to run the same software images on multiple environments, including locally. There are Docker installations available for the major operating systems. Local machines can run Docker containers in the same way as in production, setting up custom configuration or wiring up their own networks, if required.

This enables us to run fully-fledged system tests on local environments as well. Whereas this step doesn't necessarily have to be performed during development, it's helpful for developers that want to verify integrational behavior.

Developers can perform build and test steps locally, similar to the Continuous Delivery pipeline. Running steps via the command line greatly facilitates this approach. Docker `run` commands enable us to dynamically configure volumes, networks, or environment variables based on the local host.

In order to automate the process, the separate build, deploy, and test commands are combined into shell scripts.

The following code snippet shows one example of a Bash script that performs several steps. Bash scripts can be run on Windows as well, via Unix-console emulators:

```bash
#!/bin/bash
set -e
cd hello-cloud/

# build
mvn package
docker build -t hello-cloud .

# deploy
docker run -d \
  --name hello-cloud-st \
  -p 8080:8080 \
  -v
$(pwd)/config/local/application.properties:/opt/config/application.properti
es \
  hello-cloud
```

```
# system tests
cd ../hello-cloud-st/
mvn test

# stopping environment
docker stop hello-cloud-st
```

The *hello-cloud* application is contained in the `hello-cloud/` subfolder and built with Maven and Docker. The Docker `run` command configures a custom properties file. This is similar to the orchestration configuration example shown in `Chapter 5`, *Container and Cloud Environments with Java EE*.

The `hello-cloud-st/` directory contains system tests that connect against a running application. In order to direct the system test to the local environment, the *hosts* configuration of the local machine can be adapted. The Maven test run executes the system tests.

This approach enables developers to verify behavior in fully-fledged system tests that are executed in the Continuous Delivery pipelines as well as locally, if required.

If the system test scenario requires several external systems, they are equally run as Docker containers, similar to the test environment. Applications that run in container orchestration environments use logical service names to resolve external systems. The same is possible for natively running Docker containers, that are part of custom Docker networks. Docker resolves container names in containers running in the same network.

This approach is used to run all kinds of services locally and is especially useful to run mock servers.

The following snippet shows an example of the idea of running a local test environment:

```
#!/bin/bash
# previous steps omitted

docker run -d \
  --name assembly-line \
  -p 8181:8080 \
  docker.example.com/wiremock:2.6

docker run -d \
  --name car-manufacture-st \
  -p 8080:8080 \
  car-manufacture

# ...
```

Similar to the system test example, the WireMock server will be configured as part of the test case. The local environment needs to ensure that hostnames point to the corresponding localhost containers.

For more complex setups, it makes sense to run the services in a container orchestration cluster as well. There are local installation options for Kubernetes or OpenShift available. The container orchestration abstracts cluster nodes. It therefore makes no difference for infrastructure as code definitions, whether a cluster runs locally, as a single node, in a server environment on-premises, or in the cloud.

This enables engineers to use the very same definitions that are used in the test environments. Running a local Kubernetes installation simplifies the shell scripts to a few `kubectl` commands.

If installing Kubernetes or OpenShift locally is too oversized, orchestration alternatives such as Docker Compose can be used as lightweight alternatives. Docker Compose also defines multi-container environments and their configuration in infrastructure as code files - executable by a single command. It provides similar benefits as Kubernetes. Arquillian Cube is another sophisticated way of orchestrating and running Docker containers.

Automating steps locally via scripts, highly increases the developer's productivity. Running system tests on local machines benefits engineers by providing faster feedback with less disruption.

# Maintaining test data and scenarios

Test cases verify that the application will behave as expected when deployed to production. The tests also ensure that the expectations are still met when new features are developed.

However, it's not sufficient to define test scenarios and test data only once. Business logic will evolve and change over time and test cases need to adapt.

# Importance of maintainable tests

Both for writing and managing test cases, it's crucial to create maintainable test code. Over time the number of test cases will increase. In order to stay productive during development, some time and effort needs to be spent on the test code quality.

For production code, every engineer agrees that code quality is an important requirement. Since tests are not part of the application that is running in production they are often treated differently. Experience shows that developers rarely invest time and effort in test code quality. However, the quality of test cases has a huge impact on the developer's productivity.

There are some signs that indicate poorly written tests.

# Signs of lack of test quality

Generally speaking, development time that is overly spent in test code rather than in production code can be a sign of poorly designed or crafted tests. A feature that is being implemented or changed will cause some tests to fail. How fast can the test code adapt? How many occurrences of test data or functionality are there that need to be changed? How easy is it to add test cases to the existing code base?

Failing tests that are being `@Ignored` for more than a very short period of time are also an indicator of a potential flaw in test quality. If the test case is logically still relevant, it needs to be stabilized and fixed. If it becomes obsolete, it should be deleted. However, tests should never be deleted in order to save time and effort that would be necessary to fix them when the test scenarios would logically still be relevant.

Copy and pasting test code should also be an alarming signal. This practice is sadly quite common in enterprise projects, especially when test scenarios slightly differ in their behavior. Copy and pasting violates the **don't repeat yourself** (**DRY**) principle and introduces a lot of duplication which makes future changes expensive.

# Test code quality

While production code quality is important for keeping a constant development velocity, test code quality is so as well. Tests, however, are mostly not treated in the same way. Experience shows that enterprise projects rarely invest time and effort into refactoring tests.

In general the same practices for high code quality apply for test code as they do for live code. Certain principles are especially important for tests.

First of all, the DRY principle certainly has its importance. On code level this means to avoid repeating definitions, test procedures, and code duplication that contains just minor differences.

For test data, the same principle applies. Experience shows that multiple test case scenarios that use similar test data tempt developers to use copy and pasting. However, doing so will lead to an unmaintainable code base, once changes in the test data have to be made.

The same is true for assertions and mock verifications. Assert statements and verifications that are applied one by one directly in the test method, similarly lead to duplication and challenges with maintenance.

Typically the biggest issue in test code quality is missing abstraction layers. Test cases too often contain different aspects and responsibilities. They mix business with technical concerns.

Let me give an example of a poorly written system test in pseudo code:

```
@Test
public void testCarCreation() {
    id = "X123A345"
    engine = EngineType.DIESEL
    color = Color.RED

    // verify car X123A345 not existent
    response = carsTarget.request().get()
    assertThat(response.status).is(OK)
    cars = response.readEntity(List<Car>)
    if (cars.stream().anyMatch(c -> c.getId().equals(id)))
        fail("Car with ID '" + id + "' existed before")

    // create car X123A345
    JsonObject json = Json.createObjectBuilder()
            .add("identifier", id)
            .add("engine-type", engine.name())
            .add("color", color.name())

    response = carsTarget.request().post(Entity.json(json))
    assertThat(response.status).is(CREATED)
    assertThat(response.header(LOCATION)).contains(id)

    // verify car X123A345
    response = carsTarget.path(id).request().get()
    assertThat(response.status).is(OK)
    car = response.readEntity(Car)
    assertThat(car.engine).is(engine)
    assertThat(car.color).is(color)
```

```
    // verify car X123A345 existent

    // ... similar invocations as before

    if (cars.stream().noneMatch(c -> c.getId().equals(id)))
        fail("Car with ID '" + id + "' not existent");
}
```

Readers might have noticed that it requires quite some effort to comprehend the test case. The inline comments provide some help, but comments like these are in general rather a sign of poorly constructed code.

The example, however, is similar to the system test example crafted previously.

The challenge with test cases like these is not only that they're harder to comprehend. Mixing multiple concerns, both technically and business motivated into a single class, or even a single method, introduces duplication and rules out maintainability. What if the payload of the car manufacture service changes? What if the logical flow of the test case changes? What if new test cases with similar flow but different data need to be written? Do developers copy and paste all code and modify the few aspects then? Or what if the overall communication changes from HTTP to another protocol?

For test cases, the most important code quality principles are to apply proper abstraction layers together with delegation.

Developers need to ask themselves which concerns this test scenario has. There is the test logical flow, verifying the creation of a car with required steps. There is the communication part, involving HTTP invocations and JSON mapping. There might be an external system involved, maybe represented as a mock server that needs to be controlled. And there are assertions and verifications to be performed on these different aspects.

This is the reason why we crafted the previous system test example with several components, all of them concerning different responsibilities. There should be one component for accessing the application under test, including all communication implementation details required. In the previous example, this was the responsibility of the car manufacturer delegate.

Similar to the assembly line delegate, it makes sense to add one component for every mock system involved. These components encapsulate configuration, control, and verification behavior of the mock servers.

Verifications that are made on test business level are advisably outsourced as well, either into private methods or delegates depending on the situation. The test delegates can then again encapsulate logic into more abstraction layers, if required by the technology or the test case.

All of these delegate classes and methods become single points of responsibility. They are reused within all similar test cases. Potential changes only affect the points of responsibility, leaving other parts of the test cases unaffected.

This requires the definition of clear interfaces between the components that don't leak the implementation details. For this reason it makes sense, especially for the system test scope, to have a dedicated, simple model representation. This model can be implemented simply and straightforward with potentially less type safety than the production code.

A reasonable green field approach, similar to the previous system test example, is to start with writing comments and continuously replacing them with delegates while going down the abstraction layers. This starts with what the test logically executes first, implementation details second. Following that approach naturally avoids mixing business and technical test concerns. It also enables simpler integration of test technology that supports writing tests productively, such as **Cucumber-JVM** or **FitNesse**.

# Test technology support

Some test technology also support crafting maintainable tests. AssertJ, for example, provides the possibility to create custom assertions. In our test case the car needs to verify the correct engine and color encapsulated into car specifications. Custom assertions can decrease overall duplication in the test scope.

The following shows a custom `AssertJ` assertion for verifying a car:

```
import org.assertj.core.api.AbstractAssert;

public class CarAssert extends AbstractAssert<CarAssert, Car> {

    public CarAssert(Car actual) {
        super(actual, CarAssert.class);
    }

    public static CarAssert assertThat(Car actual) {
        return new CarAssert(actual);
    }

    public CarAssert isEnvironmentalFriendly() {
        isNotNull();
```

```
        if (actual.getSpecification().getEngine() != EngineType.ELECTRIC) {
            failWithMessage("Expected car with environmental friendly
engine but was <%s>",
                    actual.getEngine());
        }

        return this;
    }

    public CarAssert satisfies(Specification spec) {
        ...
    }

    public CarAssert hasColor(Color color) {
        isNotNull();

        if (!Objects.equals(actual.getColor(), color)) {
            failWithMessage("Expected car's color to be <%s> but was <%s>",
                    color, actual.getColor());
        }

        return this;
    }

    public CarAssert hasEngine(EngineType type) {
        ...
    }
}
```

The assertion is then usable within the test scope. The correct static import of the CarAssert class has to be chosen for the assertThat() method:

```
assertThat(car)
        .hasColor(Color.BLACK)
        .isEnvironmentalFriendly();
```

The examples in this chapter showed tests written mainly with Java, JUnit, and Mockito, with the exception of embedded application containers and Gatling. There are dozens of other test technologies that uses different frameworks as well as dynamic JVM languages.

A famous example of this the **Spock Testing Framework** which uses Groovy. The motivation behind this technology was to write leaner, more maintainable tests. Since dynamic JVM languages such as Groovy or Scala are less verbose than plain Java, this idea sounds reasonable.

Test frameworks, such as Spock, indeed result in test cases that require minimal code. They make use of dynamic JVM language features such as less-constraint method names such as `def "car X123A234 should be created"()`. Spock testing also provides clear readability with low effort.

However, readable tests are achievable with all test technologies if test code quality is minded. Maintainability, in particular, is rather a question of well-crafted test cases and proper abstraction layers than of the technology being used. Once test cases become quite complex, the impact of the technology on maintainability becomes less relevant.

When choosing test technology, the team's familiarity with the technology should also be considered. At the time of writing, enterprise Java developers are usually less familiar with dynamic JVM languages.

However, the test code quality should be more important than the used technology. Applying good practices of software engineering to tests should be considered as mandatory, using other test frameworks as optional. Refactoring test cases frequently increases the maintainability and reusability of test components and ultimately the quality of the software project.

# Summary

Tests are required to verify software functionality in simulated environments. Software tests should run predictably, isolated, reliably, fast, and in an automated way. In order to enable productive project life cycles, it's important to keep tests maintainable.

Unit tests verify the behavior of individual units of an application, mostly single entity, boundary, or control classes. Component tests verify the behavior of coherent components. Integration tests fulfill the need to verify the interaction of the Java EE components. Database integration tests use embedded databases together with standalone JPA to verify the persistence mapping. System tests verify deployed applications that run on actual environments. Container orchestration heavily supports running system test environments with potential mock applications.

In order to verify functionality before it is pushed to the central repository, engineers need the ability to run tests on their local environment. Changes that contain careless mistakes disturb other teammates by unnecessarily breaking the build. Docker, Docker Compose, and Kubernetes can run on local environments as well, enabling developers to verify behavior upfront. It's advisable to craft simple automation scripts that include the required steps.

In order to achieve a constant development velocity, it's required to develop maintainable test cases. In general, test code should have a similar quality to production code. This includes refactoring, proper abstraction layers, and software quality in general.

These approaches are, in fact, more helpful than introducing sophisticated test frameworks using dynamic JVM languages. Whereas frameworks such as Spock certainly enable readable, minimal test cases, the benefits of using proper practices of software craftsmanship have a more positive impact on the overall test code quality, especially once test scenarios become complex. No matter what testing technology is being used, software engineers are advised to mind the test code quality in order to keep test cases maintainable.

The following chapter will cover the topic of distributed systems and microservices architectures.

# 8
# Microservices and System Architecture

The previous chapters covered how to develop a single enterprise application with Java EE. Modern applications contain infrastructure and configuration definitions as code, making it possible to create environments in automated ways, either on premises or in cloud platforms. Continuous Delivery pipelines together with sufficient, automated test cases make it possible to deliver enterprise applications with high quality and productivity. Modern zero-dependency Java EE approaches support these efforts.

Enterprise systems rarely come with single responsibilities that could be reasonably mapped into single enterprise applications. Traditionally, enterprise applications combined multiple aspects of the business into monolithic applications. The question is, whether this approach to crafting distributed systems is advisable.

This chapter will cover:

- The motivations behind distribution
- Possibilities and challenges of distributed systems
- How to design interdependent applications
- Application boundaries, APIs, and documentation
- Consistency, scalability, challenges, and solutions
- Event sourcing, event-driven architectures, and CQRS
- Microservice architectures
- How Java EE fits the microservice world
- How to realize resilient communication

# Motivations behind distributed systems

One of the first questions should ask for the need for distribution. There are several technical motivations behind designing distributed systems.

Typical enterprise scenarios are in essence distributed. Users or other systems that are spread across locations need to communicate with a service. This needs to happen over the network.

Another reason is scalability. If a single application reaches the point where it cannot reliably serve the overall load of clients, the business logic needs to be distributed to multiple hosts.

A similar reasoning aims toward a system's fault tolerance. Single applications represent single points of failure; if the single application is unavailable, the service won't be usable by the clients. Distributing services to multiple locations increases availability and resilience.

There are also other less technology-driven motivations. An application represents certain business responsibilities. In Domain-Driven Design language they are contained in the application's **bounded context**. Bounded contexts include the business concerns, logic, and data of the application and differentiate it from external concerns.

In the same way as engineers cluster code responsibilities into packages and modules, it certainly makes sense to craft contexts on a system scale as well. Coherent business logic and functionality is grouped into separate services as part of separate applications. The data and schema is also part of a bounded context. It can therefore be encapsulated into several database instances, which are owned by the corresponding distributed applications.

# Challenges of distribution

With all these motivations, especially technical ones such as scalability, why shouldn't engineers distribute everything then? Distribution comes with certain overheads.

In general, the overall overhead that comes on top of the system's distilled business logic will be multiplied by the number of applications involved. For example, a single, monolithic application requires a monitoring solution. Distributing this application will cause all resulting applications to be monitored as well.

# Communication overhead

In distribution, first of all, there is an overhead cost in communicating between systems.

Technology is very effective in communicating within a single process. There is effectively no overhead in calling functionality that is part of the application. As soon as inter-process or remote communication is required, engineers have to define interface abstractions. Communication protocols such as HTTP have to be defined and used in order to exchange information.

This requires certain time and effort. Communication between applications has to be defined, implemented, and maintained. Within a single application, the communication is reflected in method invocations.

The required communication also becomes a concern of the business use case. It can no longer be assumed that certain functionality or data can be just used without any overhead. Communicating with the distributed system becomes a responsibility of the application.

# Performance overhead

Distributing applications at first decreases performance of the overall systems. Computer networks are slower than communication within a single host. Therefore networking will always come with a certain performance overhead.

The overhead in performance is not only caused by the communication itself, but also the need to synchronize. Synchronization within a single process already consumes certain processing time, and this impact is much bigger when distribution is involved.

However, despite this overhead in performance, distribution eventually increases the overall performance of the system as its applications scale out. Scaling horizontally always comes with a certain performance overhead compared to a single instance.

# Organizational overhead

Distributed systems containing several applications certainly need more organizational effort than a single one.

Multiple applications imply multiple deployments that need to be managed. Deploying new versions may have an impact on dependent applications. Teams need to ensure that versions of deployed applications work together well. Single, monolithic applications are not affected by this since they are consistent within themselves.

Besides that, multiple applications are developed in several projects and repositories, usually by multiple development teams. In particular, having multiple teams requires communication, not necessarily technically, but human-related communication. In the same way as for deploying applications, responsibilities, system boundaries, and dependencies need to be agreed upon.

# How to design systems landscapes

With all of these challenges and overheads involved, a lot of scenarios still require distribution. It's important to mention, that there must be enough motivation behind distributing systems. Distribution comes with costs and risks. If it's not necessary to distribute, building monolithic applications is always to be preferred.

Now, let's look into how to design reasonable system landscapes, tailored for business requirements.

## Context maps and bounded contexts

**Bounded contexts** define the application's responsibilities in business logic, behavior, and data ownership. So-called **context maps**, as described in Domain-Driven Design, represent the entire system landscape. It shows the individual responsibilities, contexts, and belongings of its applications. Bounded contexts therefore fit within a context map to show how they exchange information among each other.

The following shows the context map of the *cars* domain, including two bounded contexts:

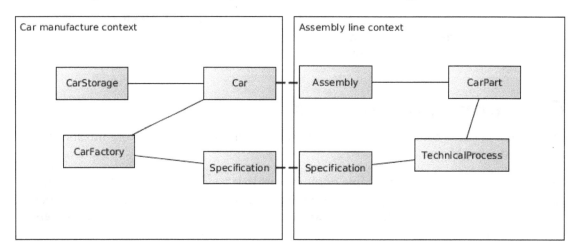

It's advisable to consider the different responsibilities of the system before designing and carving out applications. Lack of clarity on an application's responsibilities usually emerges quickly as soon as the system's context map is recorded.

Context maps are not only helpful during the initial project definition, but also during revisiting and refining responsibilities once business functionality changes. In order to prevent the boundaries and belongings of distribution applications from drifting apart, it's advisable to reflect on them from time to time.

# Separation of concerns

The application's responsibilities should be clearly defined and differentiated from other applications.

In the same way as with code level, the concerns of several applications should be separated. The single responsibility principle holds true here as well.

The application's concerns include all business concerns, application boundaries, and owned data. As the business logic evolves and changes over time, these concerns should be revisited from time to time.This may result in applications that split up or get merged into single ones. The responsibilities and concerns that emerge from the context map should be reflected in the system's applications.

Data and data ownership is an important aspect of distributed applications. The business processes, being part of the bounded context defines the data involved in the use cases. Owned data are a concern of the specific applications and are only shared via the defined boundaries. Use cases that require data that is under the responsibility of another, remote application need to retrieve the information by remotely invoking the corresponding use cases.

# Teams

Teams and organizational structure are other important aspects to consider when designing distributed systems, since, as of writing this book, software is developed by humans. Considering Conway's law, that the organization's communication structure will eventually leak into the constructed system, teams should be defined similarly to the applications in the system.

Or, in other words, it makes sense for a single application to be developed by only a single team. Depending on the responsibilities and sizes, a single team can potentially craft multiple applications.

Again, comparing to the project code structure, this is a similar approach as horizontal versus vertical module layering. Similar to business motivated module structures, teams are therefore organized vertically, representing the structure of the context map. For example, rather than having several expert teams on software architecture, development, or operations, there will be teams for *car manufacture*, *assembly line*, and *order management*.

## Project life cycles

With individual teams being involved in developing distributed systems, applications will have independent project life cycles. This includes the way teams operate, for example, how they organize their sprint cycles.

The deployment cycles and schedules also emerge from the project life cycle. For the overall system to stay consistent and functional, potential dependencies on deployments of other applications need to be defined. This does not only target the application's availability.

Deployed application versions need to be compatible. In order to ensure this, applications that are dependent need to be clearly represented in the context map. Teams will have to communicate when dependent services introduce changes.

Again, painting a clear context map containing the bounded contexts helps define the interdependent applications and their responsibilities.

## How to design system interfaces

After the responsibilities of the system landscape have been defined, the boundaries of dependent systems need to be specified.

In previous chapters, we have seen various communication protocols and how to implement them. Besides the actual implementation, the question is now: how to design the interfaces of applications? Which aspects need to be considered, especially in distributed systems?

# API considerations

The applications within a system are carved out based on their business responsibilities.

Similarly, the application's API should represent that business logic as well. The exposed API represents the business use cases a certain application comprises. This implies that a business domain expert can, without any further technical knowledge, identify the exposed business use cases from an API.

The business use cases are ideally offered in clear, lean interfaces. Invoking a use case should not require more technically-motivated communication steps or details than being part of the business logic. For example, if the *create a car* use case could be invoked as a single operation, the API of the *car manufacture* application should not require multiple invocations providing technical details.

An API should abstract the business logic in a clear, lean interface.

The API should therefore be decoupled from the application's implementation. The interface implementation should be independent from the chosen technology. This also implies that a communication format is chosen that doesn't set many constraints on the used technology.

It therefore makes sense to prefer technology that sets on standard protocols such as HTTP. It's more likely that engineer have knowledge in commonly used protocols, as that are supported by various technologies and tools. Creating application interfaces in HTTP web services allows clients to be developed in every technology that supports HTTP.

Abstracting the business logic in clear, lean interfaces that use standard protocols also enables change in used implementations, technologies, and platforms. Java Enterprise applications that only expose HTTP services could replace their technology with other implementations, without requiring dependent clients to change.

# Interface management

Application interfaces are often subject to change during the development process.

New business use cases are included and existing one refined. The question is, how are these changes reflected in the API?

It depends on the nature and environment of the enterprise application how stable the API needs to be. If the project team is both in charge of the service, all clients and their life cycles, the API can introduce arbitrary changes that are reflected in the clients at the same time. The case is the same if for some reason the life cycles of involved applications are identical.

Usually, life cycles of distributed systems aren't that tightly coupled. For any other client/server model, or applications that have different life cycles, the APIs must not break existing clients. This means that the APIs are fully backwards-compatible, not introducing breaking changes.

# Change-resilient APIs

There are certain principles in designinginterfaces that prevent unnecessary breaks. For example, introducing new, optional payload data should not break the contract. Technology should be resilient as far as it can continue to work if all necessary data is provided. This matches the idea of *being conservative in what you do and liberal in what you accept*.

Therefore adding new, optional functionality or data should be possible without breaking clients. But what if existing logic changes?

# Breaking the business logic

The question to be asked here is what a breaking change in the API means for the business use case. Is the application's past behavior not valid anymore? Should the client have to stop working from now on?

This is equivalent to, for example, a vendor of a widely-used smartphone app that decides to break existing versions and to force the users to update the installations to its latest version. There is arguably no need in doing so for existing functionality to continue.

If for some reason the existing use cases can't be used *as is* anymore, some additional, compensating business logic should be considered.

# Hypermedia REST and versioning

Hypermedia REST APIs can bring some relief with this issue. In particular, Hypermedia controls provide the ability to evolve the API by dynamically defining resource links and actions. The clients of the REST service will adapt to the changes in accessing the services and considerately ignore unknown functionality.

A quite often suggested possibility is to version the API. This means introducing different operations or resources, such as `/car-manufacture/v1/cars`, with the version as the identifying part of the API. Versioning APIs, however, contradicts the idea of clean interfaces.In particular, since REST APIs resources represent domain entities, introducing several *versions* of a car doesn't make sense in business terms. The car entity is identified by its URI. Changing the URI to reflect changes in the business functionality would imply a change to the car's identity.

Sometimes several, different representations, or versions, of the same domain entities are required, for example, JSON mappings containing different sets of properties. Via HTTP interface this is achievable via **content negotiation**, by defining content type parameters. For example, different JSON representations for the same car can be requested via content types such as `application/json;vnd.example.car+v2`, if supported by the corresponding service.

Managing interfaces is a relevant topic for distributed systems. It's advisable to carefully design APIs upfront, with backwards-compatibility in mind. Extra efforts, such as additional operations that prevent an API from breaking existing functionality, should be preferred over clean interfaces that disrupt clients.

# Documenting boundaries

Application boundaries that define APIs to invoke the application's business logic need to be made public to its clients, for example, other applications within the system. The question is, what information needs to be documented?

The application's bounded context is part of the context map. Therefore, the domain responsibilities should be clear. The application fulfills certain business use cases within its context.

This domain information needs to be documented first. Clients should be aware of what the application offers. This includes the use cases as well as the exchanged information and data ownership.

The responsibility of the *car manufacture* application is to assemble cars due to provided, exact specifications. The status information of manufactured cars is owned by the application for the whole process of assembling, until the car reaches the end of the production line and is ready for delivery. The application can be polled to provide status updates about the creation process of a car.

The application's domain description should contain the information the clients require, be precise in responsibilities, but not too verbose, only exposing what clients *need to know*.

Besides the business domain, there are technical aspects that need to be documented. Client applications need to be programmed against a system's API. They require information about the communication protocols, as well as data formats.

We covered several communication protocols and how to implement them in the second chapter of this book. At the time of writing, one of the most used protocols is HTTP, together with JSON or XML content types. With the example of HTTP, what needs to be documented?

HTTP endpoints, especially those following the REST constraints, represent the domain entities as resources, locatable by URLs. The available URLs need to be documented first. Clients will connect against these URLs in order to perform some business use cases. For example, the `/car-manufacture/cars/<car-id>` URL will refer to a particular car specified by its identifier.

The content type with detailed mapping information needs to be documented as well. Clients need to be aware of the structure and properties within the used content type.

For example, a car specification that is provided in order to create a car contains an *identifier*, an *engine type*, and a *chassis color*. The JSON format will look as follows:

```
{
    "identifier": "<car-identifier>",
    "engine-type": "<engine-type>",
    "color": "<chassis-color>"
}
```

The types and available values need to be documented as well. They will point to the business domain knowledge, the semantics behind an engine type. This is important, that both the content types as well as the semantics of the information are documented.

In the case of HTTP there will be more aspects to be documented such as potentially required header information, status codes provided by the web service, and so on.

All this documentation certainly depends on the used technology and communication protocol. The business domain, however, should also be part of the documentation, providing as much context as required.

The application's API documentation is part of the software project. It needs to be shipped together with the application in a particular version.

In order to ensure that the documentation matches the application's version, it should be part of the project repository, residing under version control as well. Therefore, it's highly advisable to use text-based documentation formats instead of binary formats such as Word documents. Lightweight markup languages such as **AsciiDoc** or **Markdown** have proven themselves well in the past.

The benefit of maintaining the documentation directly in the project, next to the application's sources, is to ensure the creation of documentation versions that are consistent with the developed service. Engineers are able to perform both changes in one step. Doing so prevents the documentation and service version from diverging.

There is a lot of tool support in documenting application boundaries depending on the communication technology. For HTTP web services for example, the **OpenAPI Specification** together with **Swagger** as a documentation framework are widely used. Swagger outputs the API definition as browsable HTML, making it easy for developers to identify the offered resources together with their usages.

Using Hypermedia REST services, however, gets rids of the biggest necessity of service documentation. Providing the information of which resources are available in links removes the need for documenting URLs. In fact, the server gets back the control of how URLs are constructed. Clients only enter an entry point, for example `/car-manufacture/`, and follow the provided Hypermedia links based on their relations. The knowledge what a car URL consists of solely resides on the server side and is explicitly not documented.

This is especially true for Hypermedia controls, not only directing the client to resources, but providing information on how to consume it. The *car manufacture* service that tells a client how to perform the `create-car` action: A POST request to `/car-manufacture/cars` is needed, including a request body in JSON content type with properties `identifier`, `engine-type`, and `color`.

The client needs to know the semantics of all relations and action names as well as the properties and where they originate. This is certainly client logic. All information on how to consume the API becomes part of the API. Designing REST services then eliminates the need for a lot of documentation.

# Consistency versus scalability

Certainly it's necessary for distributed system to communicate. Since computer networks cannot be considered as reliable, even not in company-internal networks, reliable communication is a necessity. Business use cases are required to communicate in a reliable way, in order to ensure correct behavior.

Earlier in this book, we introduced the so-called CAP theorem that claims that it's impossible for distributed data stores to guarantee at most two of the three specified constraints. Systems can effectively choose whether they want to guarantee consistency or horizontal scalability. This highly affects the communication in a distributed world.

In general, enterprise systems should be consistent in their use cases. Business logic should transform the overall system from one consistent state to another, different consistent state.

In distributed systems, an overall consistent state would imply that use cases that communicate to external concerns would have to ensure that the invoked external logic also adheres to consistency. This approach leads to distributed transactions. Use cases that are invoked on a system would execute in an *all-or-nothing* fashion, including all external systems. This implies a need for a lock on all involved, distributed functionality until every single distributed application successfully performed its responsibilities.

Naturally, this approach doesn't scale. The fact that the system is distributed requires this transaction orchestration to be performed over the potentially slow network. This introduces a bottleneck, which results in a locking situation, since involved applications have to block and wait a relatively large amount of time.

Generally speaking, synchronous, consistent communication is only advisable for applications that don't involve more than two applications at a time. Performance tests as well as production experience indicate whether a chosen communication scenario scales well enough for the given use case and environment.

Using asynchronous communication is motivated by scalability. Distributed systems that communicate asynchronously won't, by definition, be consistent at all times. Asynchronous communication can happen on a logical level, where synchronous calls only initiate business logic without awaiting a consistent result.

Let's have a look into the motivations and design behind asynchronous, eventually consistent communication in distributed applications.

# Event sourcing, event-driven architectures, and CQRS

Traditionally, enterprise applications are built using a model approach that is based on the atomic **Create Read Update Delete (CRUD)**.

The current state of the system, including the state of the domain entities, is reflected in a relational database. If a domain entity is updated, the new state of the entity including all of its properties is put into the database and the old state is gone.

The CRUD approach requires applications to maintain consistency. In order to ensure the state of the domain entity is reflected correctly, all use case invocations have to be executed in a consistent manner, synchronizing modifications to the entities.

# Shortcomings of CRUD-based systems

This synchronization is also one of the shortcomings of CRUD-based systems, the way that we typically build applications.

## Scalability

The required synchronization prevents the system from scaling infinitely. All transactions are executed on the relational database instance, which eventually introduces a bottleneck if the system needs to scale out.

This ultimately becomes a challenge for situations with huge amounts of workloads or huge numbers of users. For the vast majority of enterprise applications, however, the scalability of relational databases is sufficient.

## Competing transactions

Another challenge that comes with CRUD-based models is to handle competing transactions. Business use cases that include the same domain entities and operate simultaneously need to ensure that the resulting state of the entities is consistent.

Editing a user's name and at the same time updating its account credit limit should not result in lost updates. The implementation has to ensure that the overall result of both transactions is still consistent.

Competing transactions that rely on optimistic locking usually result in failing transactions. This is definitely not ideal from a user's perspective, but at least maintains consistency, rather than suppressing that a transaction has been lost in space.

Following this approach, however, potentially leads to unnecessary locking. From a business theory perspective it should be possible to simultaneously edit the user's name and account credit limit.

## Reproducibility

Since the application only stores its current state, all historical information about previous states is gone. The state is always overwritten by the new updates.

This makes it hard to reproduce how an application got into its current state. If a current state was miscalculated from its originating use case invocations, there is no possibility of fixing the situation later on.

Some scenarios explicitly require reproducibility for legal terms. Some applications therefore include audit logs that permanently write certain information as soon as they happen to the system.

## Event sourcing

Event sourcing is an approach that tackles reproducibility as a shortcoming of CRUD-based systems.

Event sourced systems calculate the current state of the systems from atomic events that happened in the past. The events represent the individual business use case invocations, including the information provided in the invocations.

The current state is not permanently persisted, but emerges by applying all events one after another. The events themselves happened in the past and are immutable.

To give an example, a user with its characteristics is calculated from all events related to it. Applying `UserCreated`, `UserApproved`, and `UserNameChanged` one after another creates the current representation of the user up to its recent event:

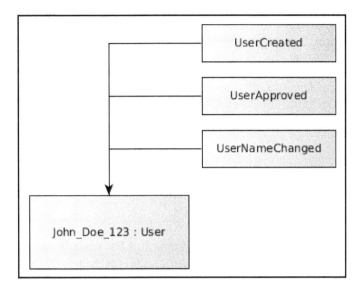

The events contain self-sufficient information mostly concerning the corresponding use case. For example, a `UserNameChanged` event contains the time stamp and the name the user was changed to, not other, unrelated information about the user. The event's information is therefore atomic.

Events are never changed nor deleted. If a domain entity is removed from the application, there will be a corresponding deletion event such as `UserDeleted`. The current state of the system then won't contain this user anymore after applying all events.

## Benefits

An event-sourced application contains all of its information in atomic events. Therefore, the full history and context, how it got into its current state, is available. In order to reproduce the current state for debugging purposes, all events and their individual modifications to the system can be regarded.

The fact that everything that happened to the system is stored atomically has a couple of benefits, not only for debugging purposes.

Tests can make use of this information to replay everything that happened to a production system in system tests. Tests are then able to re-execute the exact business use case invocations that happened in productions. This is an advantage especially for system and performance tests.

The same is true for statistics that use the atomic information to gather insights about the usage of the application. This enables use cases and insights that are designed after an application has been deployed.

Assuming a manager wants to know how many users were created on a Monday, after the application has been running for two years. With CRUD-based systems that information would have had to explicitly been persisted by the time the use case was invoked. Use cases that were not explicitly requested in the past can only be added as new features, and will add value in the future.

With event sourcing these functionalities are possible. Since information about whatever happened to the system is stored, use cases that are developed in the future are able to operate on data that happened in the past.

These benefits, however, are certainly possible without the need for distributed systems. A monolithic, independent application can base its model on event sourcing, gaining the same benefits from it.

# Eventually consistent real world

Before we go further into distributed systems in regard to consistency and scalability, let's look at an example of how consistent the real world is. Enterprise applications are typically built with the aspiration to provide full consistency. The real world, however, is highly distributed and not consistent at all.

Imagine you're hungry and you want to eat a burger. So you go to a restaurant, sit at a table, and tell the waiter that you would like to have a burger. The waiter will accept your order. Now, although your order has been accepted this doesn't necessarily mean that you will receive your meal. The process of ordering a meal is not fully consistent.

A lot of things can go wrong at this point. For example, the chef may tell the waiter that unfortunately the last burger patty was just used and there won't be more burgers for the day. So although your order has transactionally been accepted, the waiter will come back and tell you that the order won't be possible.

Now, instead of asking you to leave, the waiter might suggest to you an alternative dish. And if you're hungry and fine with the substitute you might eventually receive a meal.

This is how the highly distributed real world handles business use case transactions.

If the restaurant would be modeled in a fully consistent way the scenario would look different. In order to guarantee that an order is only accepted if it will be possible to provide the prepared meal, the whole restaurant would need to be locked down. The customers would have to wait and hold the conversation while the waiter goes into the kitchen and orders the meal from the chef. Since many other things can go wrong after ordering, the whole order transaction would actually have to block until the meal is fully prepared.

Obviously, this approach would not work. Instead, the real world is all about collaboration, intentions, and eventually dealing with issues if the intentions can't be fulfilled.

This means that the real world operates in an eventually consistent way. Eventually, the restaurant system will be in a consistent state, but not necessarily at all times, which leads to initially accepting orders that are actually not possible.

Real-world processes are represented as intentions or **commands**, such as ordering a burger, and atomic outcomes or **events**, such as that the order has been accepted. Events will then cause new commands that result in new outcomes or failures.

# Event-driven architectures

Now back to the topic of distributed systems. In the same way as for a restaurant, distributed systems that communicate in a consistent way, via distributed transactions, won't be able to scale.

Event-driven architectures solve this issue. The communication in these architectures happens via asynchronous events that are published and consumed reliably.

By doing so, consistent use case transactions get split up into multiple, smaller-scaled transactions that are consistent in themselves. This leads the overall use case eventually being consistent.

Let's see an example of how the use case of ordering a burger is represented in an event-driven architecture. The restaurant system consists of at least two distributed applications, the *waiter* and the *chef*. The restaurant applications communicate by listening to each other's events. The client application will communicate with the waiter in order to initiate the use case:

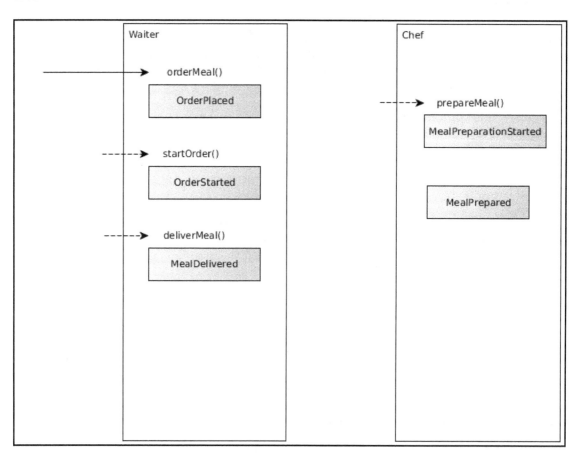

The client orders a meal at the waiter application, which results in the OrderPlaced event. Once the event has been published reliably, the orderMeal() method's invocation returns. The client therefore is able to perform other work in parallel.

The chef system receives the `OrderPlaced` event and validates whether the order is possible with the currently available ingredients. If the order wouldn't be possible, the chef would emit a different event, such as `OrderFailedInsufficientIngredients`. In that case, the waiter would update the order status to failed.

When initiating the meal preparation was successful, the waiter receives the `MealPreparationStarted` event and updates the status of the order, what results in `OrderStarted`. If the client would ask the waiter about the status of their order, it could respond appropriately.

At some point the meal preparation would have been finished, resulting in a `MealPrepared` event, which notifies the waiter to deliver the order.

## Eventual consistency in event-driven architectures

The use case of ordering a meal is eventually consistent. Publishing the events reliably still ensures that all clients *eventually* know about the status of their order.

It is somewhat fine if processing the order doesn't happen immediately or if the order will fail for some reason. However, it must not happen that an order gets lost in the system due to unavailable applications. This needs to be ensured when publishing the events.

There are still transactions involved here, but on a much smaller scale and not involving external systems. Doing so enables distributed systems to cover transactional use cases while still enabling horizontal scalability.

The fact that some reliability is required for approaches like event-driven architectures is an important aspect in distributed systems, and should be considered when designing solutions and choosing technology.

## Enter CQRS

Now let's combine the motivations behind event-driven architectures and event sourcing.

Event-driven architectures communicate by atomic events. It makes sense to piggyback on this approach and build the system using event sourcing, by using the events as the system's source of truth. Doing so combines the benefits of both approaches, enabling horizontally scalable, event-sourced systems.

The question is how to model event-driven applications that base their domain model on events? And how to efficiently calculate and return the current state of domain entities?

The **Command Query Responsibility Segregation (CQRS)** principle describes how to model these applications. It is a consequence of event-driven architectures and is based on event sourcing.

# Principles

As the name suggests, CQRS separates the responsibilities for commands and queries, namely writes and reads.

A command changes the state of the system by ultimately producing events. It is not allowed to return any data. Either the command succeeds, which results in zero or more events, or it fails with an error. The events are produced reliably.

A query retrieves and returns data, without side effects on the system. It is not allowed to modify state.

To give an example in Java code, a command acts like a `void doSomething()` method, which changes state. A query acts like a getter `String getSomething()`, which has no impact on the system's state. These principles sound simple, but have some implications on the system's architecture.

The responsibilities of the commands and queries are separated into several concerns, allowing CQRS applications to emerge in fully independent applications that either write or read. Now, how to design and implement this approach?

# Design

Following event-driven architectures, the write and read systems communicate solely via events. The events are distributed via an event store or event hub. There is no other coupling than the write systems that produce events and both write and read systems that consume for events to update their internal state.

The following snippet shows the architecture of a CQRS system:

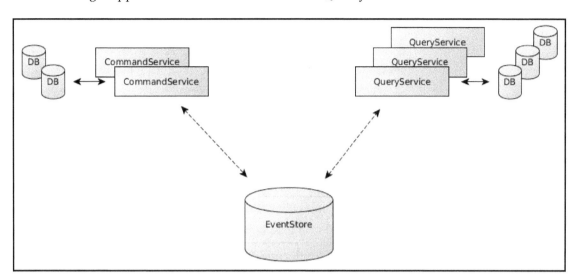

The command and query services consume events from the event store. This is the only way for communication between them.

All services maintain a current-state representation that reflects the state of the domain entities. Entities are, for example, *meal orders* or *cars*, including the latest state of their properties. This state is kept in memory or persisted in databases.

These representations just enable the systems to contain a current state. The golden source of truth is the atomic events contained in the event store.

All application instances individually update their state representations by consuming and applying the events from the event store.

The command services contain the business logic that initiates changes to the systems. They produce events via the event store after potential command verification using their state representations.

In order to make the flow of information clear, let's go through an example meal order:

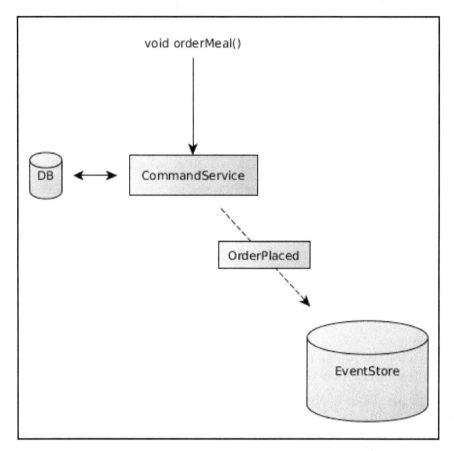

The client orders the meal at a command service instance. After a potential verification against its representation, the command service produces the `OrderPlaced` event to the event store. If publishing the event was successful, the `orderMeal()` method returns. The client can proceed with its execution.

The command service can create a meal identifier for later retrieval, for example, as a universally unique identifier:

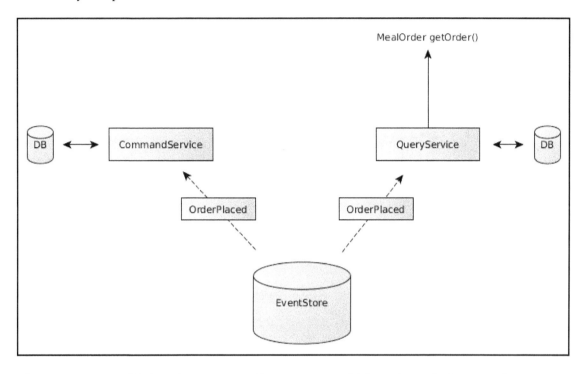

The event store publishes the event to all consumers, which updates their internal representation accordingly. The client can access the status of the meal at the query service using its identifier. The query service will respond with its latest representation of the order.

In order to proceed with the order processing, an authority that invokes potential subsequent commands will handle the event as well:

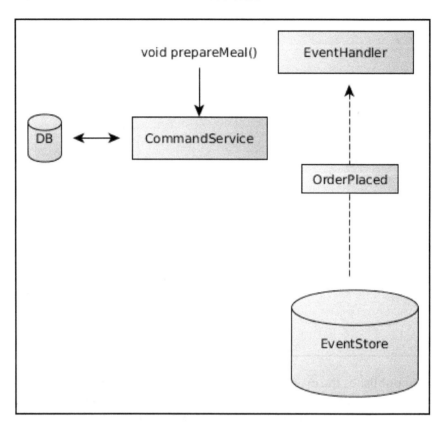

An event handler will listen to the `OrderPlaced` event and invoke the `prepareMeal()` use case of the chef system. This subsequent command will then potentially result in new events.

The section *Implementing microservices with Java EE*, covers how to implement CQRS among other things.

# Benefits

CQRS enables distributed applications to not only scale horizontally, but independently in their write and read concerns. The replicas of query service, for example, can be different from the number of command services.

The read and write load in enterprise applications is usually not evenly distributed. Typically the read operations highly outperform the number of writes. For these cases the number of read instances can be scaled out independently. This would not be possible in a CRUD-based system.

Another benefit is that each service can optimize their state representations accordingly. For example, persistently storing the domain entities in a relational database might not be the best approach for every situation. It's also possible to just store the representation in memory and to recalculate all events at application startup. The point is that both the write and read instances are free to choose and optimize their representations according to the circumstances.

A side effect of this approach is also that CQRS provides read-side failover availability. In case of the event store being unavailable no new events can be published, therefore no use cases that modify state can be invoked on the system. In CRUD-based systems this would correspond to the database being down. In CQRS systems, however, at least the query services can still provide the latest state from their representations.

The state representations of CQRS systems also solve the scalability issue of event-sourced systems. Event-sourced systems calculate the current application state from the atomic events. Executing this each and every time an operation is invoked will over time become slower and slower as more events arrive. The representations of the command and query services eliminate this need by continuously applying the recent events.

# Shortcomings

Building CQRS systems not only has benefits, it also has shortcomings.

Probably one of the biggest shortcoming of constructing these systems is that the majority of developers are not familiar with the concept, design and implementations. This will introduce difficulties when this approach is chosen in enterprise projects. Unlike CRUD-based systems, CQRS would require additional training and know-how.

Like any distributed system, there are naturally more applications involved in a CQRS system compared to the CRUD approach. As previously described for distributed systems in general, this requires some extra effort. Additionally, an event store is required.

Unlike the figures demonstrated, it is not mandatory to have the command and query sides in two or more independent applications. As long as the functionalities only communicate via events published by the event store, both can reside within the same application. This would, for example, result in a single waiter and chef application that still scales out horizontally. This is a reasonable trade-off, if individually scaling the write and read sides is not required.

# Communication

Building CQRS systems is one approach to realizing asynchronous, eventually consistent communication. As we have seen previously in this book, there are many forms of communication, synchronous as well as asynchronous.

In order to enable scalable applications, distributed systems should not rely on synchronous communication that involves several systems. This leads to distributed transactions.

One approach to realize scalability with technology-agnostic, synchronous communication protocols is to model logically asynchronous processes. For example, communication protocols such as HTTP can be used to trigger processing that happens asynchronously while the caller immediately returns. This introduces eventual consistency, but enables the system to scale.

This also involves the consideration of whether the applications that made the distributed system make a difference in system-internal, and external communication. CQRS uses this approach by offering external interfaces, for example, using HTTP, to the clients, whereas the services themselves communicate via the event store. Modeling asynchronous processes that are accessed via uniform protocol doesn't distinguish here.

In general, it's advisable to prefer availability, that is, scalability, over consistency when designing distributed systems. There are many approaches possible, CQRS is one of them, combining asynchronous communication with event sourcing.

The following section covers the necessity of self-sufficient applications.

# Microservice architectures

We saw the motivations, challenges, and benefits of distributed systems, as well as some approaches to handle communication and consistency. Now we will focus on the architecture of distributed applications.

# Sharing data and technology in enterprises

A common idea in enterprises is to share and reuse technology as well as commonly used data. Earlier we looked at sharing Java modules and the shortcomings with that. What about sharing common technology or data models in distributed systems?

Multiple applications that form an enterprise system are often implemented using similar technology. This comes naturally with applications that are built by a single team or teams that work closely together. Doing so very often raises the idea of sharing technology that is being reused in the applications.

Projects could use commonly used modules that remove duplication in the overall system. A typical approach for this is shared models. There could be only one module within the organization that is being reused in all projects.

Sharing models leads to the question whether potentially persisted domain entities or transfer objects are being reused. Domain entities that are persisted in a database could then even be directly retrieved from the database system, right?

Commonly used databases stand in total contradiction to distributed systems. They tightly couple the involved applications. Changes in schemas or technology welds the application and project life cycles together. Commonly used database instances prevent applications from being able to scale. This eliminates the motivations behind distributed systems.

The same is true for sharing technology in general. As shown in previous chapters, commonly used modules and dependencies introduce technical constraints in the implementations. They couple the applications and limit their independence in changes and life cycles. Teams will have to communicate and discuss modifications, even if they would not affect the application's boundaries.

Looking at the domain knowledge and the responsibilities in the context map of the system, sharing data and technology makes little sense. There are indeed points of contact between the systems that are subject to be shared in technology.

However, the point is to implement applications, which only depend on their business responsibilities on the one side and documented communication protocols on the other side. It's therefore advisable to choose potential duplication and independence rather than coupling in technology.

Sharing other concerns rather than points of contact in the system's context map should alert engineers. The application's different responsibilities should make it clear that commonly used models or data reside in different contexts. The individual applications are exclusively responsible for their concerns.

# Shared-nothing architectures

With these thoughts in mind it's advisable to craft applications that share no common technology or data. They fulfill the application boundary contract in communication and business responsibilities.

**Shared-nothing architectures** are independent in technology, potentially used libraries, their data and schemas thereof. They are free to choose implementations and potential persistence technology.

Changing the implementation of an application within a distributed system from Python to Java should have no impact on the other applications, if the contract of its HTTP interface is still met.

If data is required within other applications, this needs to be defined explicitly in the context map, requiring the application to expose data via its business logic interfaces. Databases are not shared.

Shared-nothing architectures enable applications with independent life cycles that depend on nothing more than the explicitly defined contracts. Teams are free to choose technology and the project life cycles. The technology, as well as the data including databases, is owned by the application.

# Interdependent systems

Shared-nothing architectures eventually have to collaborate with other applications. The defined contracts have to be met, documented, and communicated.

This is the point, that shared-nothing architectures are only dependent on the defined contracts and responsibilities. In case of changes in the business logic the contracts are redefined and communicated. Solely the application's team is responsible for how to implement the contracts.

Interdependent systems are made up of several shared-nothing applications with well-defined interfaces. The used interfaces should be technology-agnostic to not set constraints on the used implementation.

This is the idea behind microservice architectures. Microservices consist of several interdependent applications that realize their individual business responsibilities and, combined together, solve a problem.

The name microservice doesn't necessarily say anything about the size of the application. An application should be built by a single team of developers. For organizational reasons team sizes should not grow too big. There is an often-cited notion by Amazon that the whole team should be able to survive on two pizzas.

The motivations behind distributed systems should be considered before crafting microservices. If there is no actual need to distribute a system, it should be avoided. Sticking to monolithic applications with reasonable responsibilities is to be preferred.

Usually the approach to craft microservice architectures is to slice up monolithic applications that grow too large in responsibilities, or diverged in teams and life cycles. This is comparable with refactoring approaches. Refactoring a class that grew too big into multiple delegates works well more often than trying to introduce a perfect scenario from the beginning.

In general, it's always advisable to consider the business requirements, context map of the system with their development teams and life cycles.

# 12-factor and cloud native applications

Chapter 5, *Container and Cloud Environments with Java EE*, introduced the approaches of 12-factor and cloud native applications. They heavily support microservice architectures.

In particular, the shared-nothing approach of having interdependent, distributed applications is well realizable with the principles of containerized, stateless, and scalable enterprise applications.

The 12-factor principles and the effective nature of cloud and container environments support teams in developing microservices with manageable overhead and high productivity.

However, an enterprise system doesn't not have to be distributed in order to comply with the 12-factor or cloud native principles. The approaches are certainly advisable for building monolithic applications as well.

# When to use and when not to use microservices

In the recent years microservice architectures have seen some hype in the software industry.

As always with hypes, engineers should ask themselves what is behind certain buzzwords and whether implementing them makes sense. It's always advisable to look into new technology and methodologies. It's not necessarily advisable to apply them immediately.

The reasons for using microservices are the same as for using distributed systems in general. There are technical reasons, such as applications that need independent deployment life cycles.

There are also reasons that are driven by the business requirements and situations in teams and project working modes.

Scalability is an often-cited motivation behind microservice architectures. As we have seen in event-driven architectures, monolithic applications aren't able so scale infinitely. The question is whether scalability is effectively an issue.

There are big companies that handle business logic for huge amounts of users using monolithic applications. Before considering distribution as a relief for scaling issues, performance insights and statistics should be gathered.

Engineers should avoid to use microservice architectures solely because of believing in a *silver bullet* approach. It can easily happen as a result of *buzzword-driven* meetings and conversations, that solutions are chosen based on limited or no evidence supporting the requirement. Microservices certainly provide benefits, but also come with a price in time and effort. In any way, the requirements and motivations whether to split up responsibilities into multiple applications should be clear.

# Implementing microservices with Java EE

Now on to the question of how to build microservices with Enterprise Java.

In various discussions and meetings, Java EE has been considered as *too heavyweight* and cumbersome for microservices. Whereas this is certainly the case for J2EE technology and approaches, Java EE offers modern, lean ways of developing enterprise applications. Chapter 4, *Lightweight Java EE* and Chapter 5, *Container and Cloud Environments with Java EE* covered these aspects, especially in regard to modern environments.

Java EE is indeed well suited for writing microservice applications. Container technologies and orchestration support the platform, particularly since Java EE separates the business logic from the implementation.

# Zero-dependency applications

Microservices with Java EE are ideally built as zero-dependency applications.

Thin WAR applications are deployed on modern enterprise containers that can be shipped in containers. This minimizes deployment time.Java EE deployment artifacts should only contain provided dependencies, if there is a reasonable need for adding third-party dependencies, they should be installed in the application server. Container technologies simplify this approach.

This also matches the idea of shared-nothing architectures. The team is responsible for the application-specific technology, in this case the application server installation including libraries. Infrastructure as code definitions such as Dockerfiles, enable the development team to accomplish this in effective ways.

# Application servers

Following this approach, the application server is shipped in a container, containing only a single application. The *one application per application server* approach also matches the idea of shared-nothing architectures.

The question is whether application servers introduce too much overhead if a single server instance only contains a single application. In the past, the storage and memory footprint certainly was significant.

Modern application servers considerably improved in this area. There are container base images of servers such as **TomEE** that consume 150 MB and less, for the server including the Java runtime and operating system, mind you. The memory consumption also significantly improved due to dynamically loading functionality.

In enterprise projects installation sizes are usually not an issue to be concerned with, especially if they're not exceeding all bounds. What's much more important is the size of the built and shipped artifacts. The application artifact, which in some technologies contains megabytes of dependencies, is built and transmitted many times. The runtime is only installed once per environment.

Container technologies such as Docker make use of layered file systems that encourage the moving parts to be small. Zero-dependency applications support this approach.

Making each and every Continuous Delivery build only shipping kilobytes of data is far more advisable than saving a few megabytes in the base installation.

If the installation size still needs to be shrunk down, some application vendors offer possibilities to tailor the container to the required standards, especially the MicroProfile initiative, which includes several application server vendors, and defines slimmed profiles.

Java EE microservices don't need to be shipped as standalone JAR files. On the contrast, applications shipped in containers should leverage the use of layered file systems and be deployed on enterprise containers residing in the base image. Standalone JAR files oppose this principle.

There are possibilities to combine standalone JAR files with thin deployments, by so-called hollow JAR. This approach, however, is not required when using containers.

# Implementing application boundaries

Let's move on to the implementation of the application boundaries with Java EE. This is, in fact, a more system-architectural question than an implementational one.

Communication between microservices should use technology-agnostic protocols. As seen previously, Java EE heavily supports HTTP, for both HTTP and REST services use Hypermedia.

The next sub-chapter will cover asynchronous communication in CQRS systems, using publish/subscribe messaging implemented with Apache Kafka.

# Implementing CQRS

Earlier in this chapter we have seen the motivations and concepts behind event sourcing, event-driven architectures, and CQRS. CQRS offers an interesting approach to creating distributed applications that implement scalable, eventually consistent business use cases.

At the time of writing, there is a lot of interest in CQRS, yet little knowledge within companies of how to use it. Some frameworks and technologies have emerged that aim to implement this approach. Yet CQRS is an architectural style, and specific frameworks are not necessary to develop CQRS systems.

Let's have a close look at an approach that uses Java EE.

# System interfaces

The CQRS system interfaces are used from outside the system to initiate business use cases. For example, a client accesses the waiter system to order a burger.

These interfaces are used externally and ideally implemented using a technology-agnostic protocol.

For REST-like HTTP services, this implies that the command services implement HTTP methods that modify resources, such as POST, DELETE, PATCH, or PUT. The query services usually only implement resources queried by GET.

In our example, this means that the client POSTs a new meal order to a command service resource. Similarly, meal orders are retrieved via GET resources from query services.

These HTTP interfaces concern the external communication. Internally the application communicates via events that are published using an event hub.

# Example scenario using Apache Kafka

In this example, I will use Apache Kafka as a distributed message broker, offering high performance and throughput. It's one example of a messaging technology, supporting a publish/subscribe approach, among others.

At the time of writing, Apache Kafka doesn't implement all JMS semantics. The following examples will use the Kafka's vendor-specific Client API.

Apache Kafka's publish/subscribe approach organizes messages in topics. It can be configured to enable transactional event producers and in-order event consumption, which is what event-driven architectures need to ensure in order to create reliable use cases.

Kafka brokers are distributed and use so-called consumer groups to manage message topics and partitions. Examining Kafka's architecture is beyond the scope of this book and it's advised to go further into its documentation when choosing this technology.

In short, a message is published to a topic and consumed once per consumer group. Consumer groups contain one or more consumers and guarantee that exactly one consumer will process the messages that have been published using transactional producers.

A CQRS system needs to consume messages in multiple locations. The applications that are interested in a specific topic will consume the message and update their internal representations. Therefore, all these updating consumers will receive an event. There are also event handlers who use the event to process the business logic further. Exactly one event handler needs to process the event per topic, otherwise processes would run multiple times or not at all.

The concept of Kafka consumer groups is therefore used in such a way, where there is one update consumer group per application and one event handler group per topic. This enables all instances to receive the events, but reliably one command service to process the business logic. By doing so, the instances are able to scale without affecting the overall system's outcome:

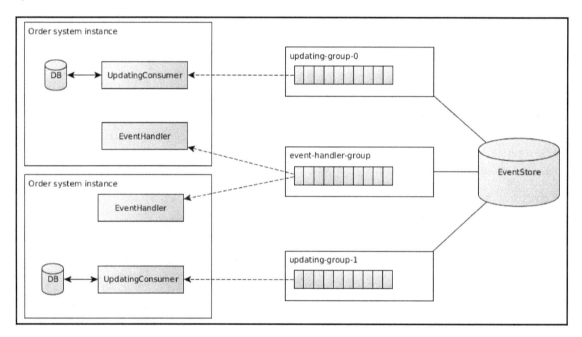

# Integrating Java EE

In order to integrate the Apache Kafka cluster into the application this example will use Kafka's Java API.

The applications connect to Kafka to consume messages in their updating consumers and event handlers. The same is true for publishing events.

The used technology should be encapsulated from the rest of the application. In order to integrate the events, developers can use a functionality that naturally fits this scenario: CDI events.

## CDI events

The domain events contain the event specific data, a timestamp, and identifiers that reference the domain entity.

The following snippet shows an example of an abstract `MealEvent` and the `OrderPlaced` event:

```java
public abstract class MealEvent {

    private final Instant instant;

    protected MealEvent() {
        instant = Instant.now();
    }

    protected MealEvent(Instant instant) {
        Objects.requireNonNull(instant);
        this.instant = instant;
    }

    ...
}

public class OrderPlaced extends MealEvent {

    private final OrderInfo orderInfo;

    public OrderPlaced(OrderInfo orderInfo) {
        this.orderInfo = orderInfo;
    }

    public OrderPlaced(OrderInfo orderInfo, Instant instant) {
        super(instant);
        this.orderInfo = orderInfo;
    }

    ...
}
```

Domain events like these are the core of the application. The domain entity representations are calculated from these events.

The integration into Kafka ensures that these events are fired via CDI. They are observed in the corresponding functionality that updates the state representations, or invokes subsequent commands, respectively.

## Event handlers

The following snippet shows an event handler of the chef system, invoking functionality of a command service:

```
@Singleton
public class OrderEventHandler {

    @Inject
    MealPreparationService mealService;

    public void handle(@Observes OrderPlaced event) {
        mealService.prepareMeal(event.getOrderInfo());
    }
}
```

The event handler consumes the event and will invoke the boundary of the subsequent meal preparation use case. The prepareMeal() method itself will result in zero or more events, in this case either MealPreparationStarted or OrderFailedInsufficientIngredients:

```
public class MealPreparationService {

    @Inject
    EventProducer eventProducer;

    @Inject
    IngredientStore ingredientStore;

    public void prepareMeal(OrderInfo orderInfo) {

        // use ingredientStore to check availability

        if (...)
            eventProducer.publish(new
    OrderFailedInsufficientIngredients());
        else
            eventProducer.publish(new MealPreparationStarted(orderInfo));
    }
}
```

The event producer will reliably publish the events to the Kafka cluster. If the publication fails, the whole event processing has to fail, and will be retried later.

## State representation

The consumers that update the state representation consume the CDI events as well. The following snippet shows the bean that contains the meal order state representations:

```
@Stateless
public class MealOrders {

    @PersistenceContext
    EntityManager entityManager;

    public MealOrder get(UUID orderId) {
        return entityManager.find(MealOrder.class, orderId.toString());
    }

    public void apply(@Observes OrderPlaced event) {
        MealOrder order = new MealOrder(event.getOrderInfo());
        entityManager.persist(order);
    }

    public void apply(@Observes OrderStarted event) {
        apply(event.getOrderId(), MealOrder::start);
    }

    public void apply(@Observes MealDelivered event) {
        apply(event.getOrderId(), MealOrder::deliver);
    }

    private void apply(UUID orderId, Consumer<MealOrder> consumer) {
        MealOrder order = entityManager.find(MealOrder.class,
orderId.toString());
        if (order != null)
            consumer.accept(order);
    }
}
```

This simple example represents the state of the meal orders in a relational database. As soon as a new CDI event arrives, the state of the orders is updated. The current state can be retrieved by the get() method.

The meal order domain entity is persisted via JPA. It contains the status of the order that is updated via observed CDI events:

```
@Entity
@Table("meal_orders")
public class MealOrder {

    @Id
    private String orderId;

    @Embedded
    private MealSpecification specification;

    @Enumerated(EnumType.STRING)
    private OrderState state;

    private MealOrder() {
        // required for JPA
    }

    public MealOrder(OrderInfo orderInfo) {
        orderId = orderInfo.getOrderId().toString();
        state = OrderState.PLACED;

        // define specifications
    }

    public void start() {
        state = OrderState.STARTED;
    }

    public void deliver() {
        state = OrderState.DELIVERED;
    }

    ...
}
```

## Consuming Kafka messages

The part that consumes the messages encapsulates the message hub from the rest of the application. It is integrated by firing CDI events on arriving messages. This certainly is specific to the Kafka API and should be considered as an example solution.

The updating consumer connects to a specific topic via its consumer group. The startup singleton bean ensures the consumer will be initiated at application startup. A container-managed executor service runs the event consumer in its own thread:

```
@Startup
@Singleton
public class OrderUpdateConsumer {

    private EventConsumer eventConsumer;

    @Resource
    ManagedExecutorService mes;

    @Inject
    Properties kafkaProperties;

    @Inject
    Event<MealEvent> events;

    @PostConstruct
    private void init() {
        String orders = kafkaProperties.getProperty("topic.orders");

        eventConsumer = new EventConsumer(kafkaProperties,
                ev -> events.fire(ev), orders);

        mes.execute(eventConsumer);
    }

    @PreDestroy
    public void close() {
        eventConsumer.stop();
    }
}
```

The application-specific Kafka properties are exposed via a CDI producer. They contain the corresponding consumer groups.

The event consumer performs the actual consumption:

```
import org.apache.kafka.clients.consumer.KafkaConsumer;
import java.util.function.Consumer;
import static java.util.Arrays.asList;

public class EventConsumer implements Runnable {

    private final KafkaConsumer<String, MealEvent> consumer;
    private final Consumer<MealEvent> eventConsumer;
```

```
        private final AtomicBoolean closed = new AtomicBoolean();

        public EventConsumer(Properties kafkaProperties,
                Consumer<MealEvent> eventConsumer, String... topics) {
            this.eventConsumer = eventConsumer;
            consumer = new KafkaConsumer<>(kafkaProperties);
            consumer.subscribe(asList(topics));
        }

        @Override
        public void run() {
            try {
                while (!closed.get()) {
                    consume();
                }
            } catch (WakeupException e) {
                // will wakeup for closing
            } finally {
                consumer.close();
            }
        }

        private void consume() {
            ConsumerRecords<String, MealEvent> records =
                    consumer.poll(Long.MAX_VALUE);
            for (ConsumerRecord<String, MealEvent> record : records) {
                eventConsumer.accept(record.value());
            }
            consumer.commitSync();
        }

        public void stop() {
            closed.set(true);
            consumer.wakeup();
        }
    }
}
```

Kafka records that are consumed result in new CDI events. The configured properties use JSON serializers and deserializers, respectively, to map the domain event classes.

Events that are fired via CDI and consumed successfully are committed to Kafka. The CDI events are fired synchronously, to ensure that all processes are finish reliably before committing.

## Producing Kafka messages

The event producer publishes the domain events to the message hub. This happens synchronously to rely on the messages being in the system. Once the transmission is acknowledged, the `EventProducer#publish` method invocation returns:

```java
import org.apache.kafka.clients.producer.KafkaProducer;
import org.apache.kafka.clients.producer.Producer;

@ApplicationScoped
public class EventProducer {

    private Producer<String, MealEvent> producer;
    private String topic;

    @Inject
    Properties kafkaProperties;

    @PostConstruct
    private void init() {
        producer = new KafkaProducer<>(kafkaProperties);
        topic = kafkaProperties.getProperty("topics.order");
        producer.initTransactions();
    }

    public void publish(MealEvent event) {
        ProducerRecord<String, MealEvent> record = new
ProducerRecord<>(topic, event);
        try {
            producer.beginTransaction();
            producer.send(record);
            producer.commitTransaction();
        } catch (ProducerFencedException e) {
            producer.close();
        } catch (KafkaException e) {
            producer.abortTransaction();
        }
    }

    @PreDestroy
    public void close() {
        producer.close();
    }
}
```

Going into the details of the Kafka producer API is beyond the scope of this book. However, it needs to be ensured that the events are sent reliably. The event producer bean encapsulates this logic.

These examples demonstrate one possibility for integrating Kafka.

As mentioned earlier, the **Java EE Connector Architecture (JCA)** is another possibility for integrating external concerns into the application container. At the time of writing, there are vendor-specific container solutions that integrate messaging via JCA. Existing solutions for integrating message hubs such as Kafka are an interesting alternative. However, application developers are advised to encapsulate technology specifics into single points of responsibilities and use standard Java EE functionality within the application.

## Application boundaries

The applications of a CQRS system communicate via events internally. Externally, other protocols such as HTTP can be provided.

The query and command functionality of, for example, the waiter system, is exposed via JAX-RS. The command service offers functionality to place meal orders. It uses the event producer to publish the resulting events:

```java
public class OrderService {

    @Inject
    EventProducer eventProducer;

    public void orderMeal(OrderInfo orderInfo) {
        eventProducer.publish(new OrderPlaced(orderInfo));
    }

    void cancelOrder(UUID orderId, String reason) {
        eventProducer.publish(new OrderCancelled(orderId, reason));
    }

    void startOrder(UUID orderId) {
        eventProducer.publish(new OrderStarted(orderId));
    }

    void deliverMeal(UUID orderId) {
        eventProducer.publish(new MealDelivered(orderId));
    }
}
```

The `orderMeal()` method is called by the HTTP endpoint. The other methods are called by the waiter system's event handler. They will result in new events that are delivered by the event hub.

The reason for not directly firing events or calling functionality internally here is that this application resides in a distributed environment. There might be other instances of the waiter system consuming the event hub and updating their representation accordingly.

The command service contains a JAX-RS resource that is used to order meals:

```
@Path("orders")
public class OrdersResource {

    @Inject
    OrderService orderService;

    @Context
    UriInfo uriInfo;

    @POST
    public Response orderMeal(JsonObject order) {
        OrderInfo orderInfo = createOrderInfo(order);
        orderService.orderMeal(orderInfo);

        URI uri = uriInfo...

        return Response.accepted().header(HttpHeaders.LOCATION,
uri).build();
    }

    ...
}
```

The query service exposes the meal order representations. It loads the current state of the domain entities from the database as seen in the `MealOrders`. The JAX-RS resources of the query service use this functionality.

If the waiter system is shipped as a single instance, containing both the command and query services, these resources can be combined. It needs to be ensured though that the services don't cross-communicate, except via the eventing mechanism. The following code snippet shows the query service endpoint:

```
@Path("orders")
public class OrdersResource {

    @Inject
    MealOrders mealOrders;

    @GET
    @Path("{id}")
    public JsonObject getOrder(@PathParam("id") UUID orderId) {
```

```
        MealOrder order = mealOrders.get(orderId);

    if (order == null)
        throw new NotFoundException();

    // create JSON response
    return Json.createObjectBuilder()...
    }
}
```

These examples are not exhaustive, but are meant to give the reader an idea of integrating CQRS concepts and message hubs into Java EE applications.

# Integrating further CQRS concepts

One of the benefits of event-sourced systems is that it's possible to take the full set of atomic events and replay them, for example, in test scenarios. System tests verify against the actual use cases that happened in production. Audit logging comes for free as well, being part of the core of the application.

This approach also enables us to change business functionality and replay some events, either to fix bugs and to correct behavior, or to apply the event information to new functionality. This makes it possible to apply new features on events as if they were part of the application since day one.

If the chef system adds functionality to continuously calculate the average time of meal preparation, the events can be redelivered to re-calculate the representations. Therefore the database contents will be reset and the events redelivered, only to the updating consumer, which results in new representation being calculated and persisted. Kafka can explicitly redeliver events.

The events, however, are solely used to update the status representations, not triggering new commands during replays. Otherwise, the system would end up in an inconsistent state. The demonstrated example realizes this by defining a dedicated Kafka consumer group for event handlers, which is not reset to redistribute events to the event handlers. Only the updating consumers re-consume the events, to recalculate the internal state representations.

The point is, that CQRS systems enable many more use cases, due to event sourcing being used. The possibilities of capturing and replaying events, as well as the contained context and history information, enable extensive scenarios.

# Java EE in the age of distribution

Microservice architectures and distributed systems naturally require communication that involves more than a single, monolithic application. There are many ways how to implement communication with Java EE, depending on the chosen protocols and communication technologies.

There are some aspects to be considered when realizing communication. External applications that take part of the microservice system, for example, require discovering the service instances. In order to not tightly couple applications and configuration, looking up services should be dynamic, rather than configuring static hosts or IP addresses.

The cloud native principle of being resilient also concerns communication. Since networks can potentially fail anytime, application health should not be impacted when connectivity decelerates or goes down. The application should guard itself from potential errors propagating into the application.

# Discovering services

Service discovery can happen in various ways, from DNS lookup to more sophisticated scenarios where the lookup is part of business logic, providing different endpoints depending on the situation. It generally encapsulates addressing external systems from the application's concerns. Ideally, the application logic only names the logical service it needs to communicate with, and the actual lookup is performed externally.

It depends on the used environments and runtime which possibilities enterprise developers have. Container technologies offer functionality to link services by names, taking away work and responsibility from the application. The clients connect against the link or service names as hostnames, which are resolved by the container technology.

This approach works both for Docker containers and container orchestration such as Docker Compose, Kubernetes, or OpenShift. All communication concerns solely use logical service names and ports to establish connections. This matches the 12-factor principles as well.

Since the lookup work is performed in the environment, the applications will only specify the desired service names. This is true for all outward communication, such as HTTP connections, databases, or message hubs. Chapter 5, *Container and Cloud Environments with Java EE* demonstrated examples for this.

# Communicating resiliently

Network communication is not reliable and can potentially break in all sorts of ways. Connections may timeout, services may be unavailable, respond slowly, or deliver unexpected answers.

In order to not let errors propagate into the application, the communications need to be resilient.

## Validating responses

First of all, this implies client-side validation and handling errors. Irrelevant to the communication technology in use, applications can't rely on external systems to provide responses that are not malformed or not simply wrong.

This doesn't mean that clients immediately have to reject all responses that are not perfect in the application's understanding. Responses that contain more information or slightly different formats than expected, but are still understandable, should not lead to immediate errors. Following the principle to *be conservative in what you do and liberal in what you accept*, messages that contain just enough for the application to do its job should be accepted. For example, additional, unknown properties in JSON responses should not lead to refusing to map the object.

## Breaking timeouts and circuits

Clients that perform synchronous calls to external systems block the subsequent execution until the external system responds. Invocations may fail, slow down the execution, or in the worst case effectively bring the whole application down. It's crucial to keep this fact in mind when implementing clients.

First of all client connections should always set reasonable timeouts, as shown similarly in Chapter 3, *Implementing Modern Java Enterprise Applications*. Timeouts prevent the application from deadlock situations.

As seen before, Java EE interceptors can be used to prevent potential runtime exceptions from propagating into the business logic.

So-called **circuit breakers** take this approach of preventing cascading failure further. They secure client invocations by defining error or timeout thresholds and prevent further invocations in case of failure. The circuit breaker approach comes from the model of electrical engineering, circuit breakers built into buildings, that intercept the connection by opening their circuits to prevent further damage.

A client circuit breaker similarly opens its circuit, that is, preventing further invocations, to not *damage* the application or the external system. Circuit breakers usually allow errors and timeouts to happen up to a certain degree and then cutting the connections for a certain time, or until the circuit is manually closed again.

Java EE applications can implement circuit breakers via interceptors. They can add sophisticated logic on when and how to open and close their circuits, for example, measuring the number of failures and timeouts.

The following demonstrates one possible circuit breaker approach in pseudo code. The interceptor behavior is annotated to a client method, similarly to client interceptor examples demonstrated earlier in this book:

```java
@Interceptor
public class CircuitBreaker {

    ...

    @AroundInvoke
    public Object aroundInvoke(InvocationContext context) {

        // close circuit after recovery time

        if (circuit.isOpen())
            return null;

        try {
            return context.proceed();
        } catch (Exception e) {

            // record exception
            // increase failure counter
            // open circuit if failure exceeds threshold

            return null;
        }
    }
}
```

Similarly, the circuit breaker could measure the service time and open its circuit if the service becomes too slow, additionally to HTTP client timeouts.

There are some open source Java EE libraries available for this purpose, for example **Breakr** by Java EE expert Adam Bien. It depends on the technical requirements and the complexity of the logic, when to open and close the circuit, and whether third-party dependencies are required.

In order to build zero-dependency applications, potential libraries should be installed into the container and not shipped with the application artifacts.

## Bulkheads

Ships contain bulkheads that divide the vessel into several areas. If the ship hull gets a leak in some locations, only a single area is filled with water and the whole ship is likely still able to float.

The **bulkhead** pattern takes this idea to enterprise applications. If some component of the application fails or is working to capacity due to workload, then the rest of the application should still be able to fulfill its purpose. This, of course, highly depends on the business use case.

One example is to separate the thread execution of business processes from HTTP endpoints. Application servers manage a single pool of request threads. If, for example, a single business component fails and blocks all incoming requests, all available request threads will eventually be occupied. The result is in no other business uses cases is being able to be invoked, due to unavailable request threads. This could be the case if used clients don't implement proper timeouts, connect against a system that is down, and block the execution.

Using asynchronous JAX-RS resources together with dedicated managed executor services can relieve this issue. As seen earlier in this book, JAX-RS resources can invoke the business functionality in separate, container-managed threads to prevent the overall execution utilizing a request thread. Multiple components can use independent thread pools, which prevent failures from spreading.

Since the application server is responsible for managing threads, this approach should be implemented following Java EE standards. The idea is to define dedicated executor services that are injectable at the required positions.

The open source library **Porcupine** by Adam Bien uses this approach to create dedicated executor services that use `ManagedThreadFactory` to define thread pools with container-managed threads. The dedicated executor services can be configured and instrumented appropriately.

The following snippet shows one example of the bulkheads pattern, combining asynchronous JAX-RS resources with dedicated executor services:

```
import com.airhacks.porcupine.execution.boundary.Dedicated;
import java.util.concurrent.ExecutorService;

@Path("users")
```

```
@Produces(MediaType.APPLICATION_JSON)
public class UsersResource {

    @Inject
    @Dedicated("custom-name")
    ExecutorService executor;

    @GET
    public CompletionStage<Response> get() {
        return CompletableFuture
                .supplyAsync(this::getUsers, executor)
                .thenApply(s -> Response.ok(s).build());
    }

    ...
}
```

The business use case is executed in a managed thread provided by the executor service, in order to allow the request thread to return and to handle other requests. This enables other functionality of the application to still function, even if this part is overloaded, and utilizes all threads of the `custom-name` executer.

The following examines how the custom executor service is configured.

## Shaking hands and pushing back

Another approach of communicating in a resilient way is **handshaking** and **backpressure**. The idea is that the communication partner being under load notifies the other side, which then backs off and eases the load. Handshaking here means that the calling side has a way of asking the service whether it can handle more requests. Backpressure reduces the load on a system by notifying clients when the limit is reached or pushing back requests.

The two approaches combined form a resilient and effective form of communication.

Information about the current load state of the application can be provided in HTTP resources or via header fields. The clients then take this information into account.

A more direct way is to simply reject a client request when the server's resources are fully utilized. Developers are advised to pay attention to the behavior of pooling such as in executor services, and how they handle situations with full queues. Exceptionally, it's advisable to abort the client request to not unnecessarily run into timeouts.

The following example shows a scenario using the Porcupine library. A business functionality is executed using a dedicated executor service, which will be configured to abort rejected executions. The clients will immediately receive a `503 Service Unavailable` response, indicating that currently the service is not able to serve requests.

The JAX-RS resource is similar to the previous example. The `custom-name` executor is configured to abort rejected executions via a specialized configurator. The `ExecutorConfigurator` is part of the Porcupine library. The following shows the custom configuration:

```java
import com.airhacks.porcupine.configuration.control.ExecutorConfigurator;
import com.airhacks.porcupine.execution.control.ExecutorConfiguration;

@Specializes
public class CustomExecutorConfigurator extends ExecutorConfigurator {

    @Override
    public ExecutorConfiguration defaultConfigurator() {
        return super.defaultConfigurator();
    }

    @Override
    public ExecutorConfiguration forPipeline(String name) {
        if ("custom-name".equals(name)) {
            return new ExecutorConfiguration.Builder().
                    abortPolicy().
                    build();
        }
        return super.forPipeline(name);
    }
}
```

Executions that are rejected due to full queues will then result in a `RejectedExecutionException`. This exception is mapped via JAX-RS functionality:

```java
import java.util.concurrent.RejectedExecutionException;

@Provider
public class RejectedExecutionHandler
        implements ExceptionMapper<RejectedExecutionException> {

    @Override
    public Response toResponse(RejectedExecutionException exception) {
        return Response.status(Response.Status.SERVICE_UNAVAILABLE)
                .build();
    }
}
```

Client requests that would exceed the server limits immediately result in an error response. The client invocation can take this into account and act appropriately. For example, a circuit breaker pattern-like functionality can prevent the client from immediate subsequent invocations.

Backpressure is helpful when crafting scenarios with multiple services that need to meet **service level agreements** (**SLA**). `Chapter 9`, *Monitoring, Performance, and Logging* will cover this topic.

# More on being resilient

Besides resilience in communication, microservices also aim to improve service quality and availability. Applications should be able to scale and self-heal in cases of failures.

The use of container orchestration technology such as Kubernetes supports this approach. Pods that back logical services can be scaled up to handle more workload. The services balance the load between the containers. There are possibilities to auto-scale instances up or down based on the current workload on the cluster.

Kubernetes aims to maximize service uptime. It manages liveness and readiness probes to detect failures and potentially start new containers. In case of errors during deployments, it will leave currently running services untouched, until the new versions are able to serve traffic.

These approaches are managed by the runtime environment, not part of the application. It's advisable to minimize the non-functional, cross-cutting concerns within the enterprise application.

# Summary

There a multiple motivations behind distributing systems. Despite certain introduced challenges and overheads in communication, performance, and organization, distribution is often necessary.

In order to design the system landscape, the system's context map that represents the individual responsibilities needs to be taken into consideration. It's advisable to design application APIs in clear, lean interfaces, ideally implemented with standard communication protocols. Before introducing breaking changes, engineers as well as business experts need to ask themselves whether it is necessary to force client functionality to stop working. In the same way, APIs should be designed in a resilient way, preventing unnecessary breaks, in other words: *be conservative in what you do and liberal in what you accept.*

Engineers that build distributed applications need to be aware of the trade-off between consistency and scalability. The majority of applications that use synchronous communication involving an external system will likely scale well enough. Distributed transactions should be avoided.

In order to communicate asynchronously, application can be based on event-driven architectures. The CQRS principle combines the motivations behind event-driven architectures and event sourcing. Whereas CQRS certainly offers interesting solutions, it only makes sense if there is a need for distributing application.

Microservice architectures don't share common technology or data with each other. Shared-nothing architectures are free to choose implementations and persistence technology. Zero-dependency Java EE applications shipped in containers are a reasonable fit for microservices. The *one application per application server* approach matches the idea of shared-nothing architectures. There are many aspects in which Java EE applications running in container orchestration frameworks support developing microservice architectures, such as service discovery, resilient communication via timeout, circuit breakers or bulkheads.

The following chapter covers the topics of performance, monitoring and logging.

# 9
# Monitoring, Performance, and Logging

We have now seen how to craft modern, scalable, and resilient microservices with Java EE. In particular, the part about adding resilience as well as technical cross-cutting to microservices is a topic that we want to pursue further.

Enterprise applications run on server environments remote from the users. In order to provide insights into the system, we need to add visibility. There are multiple ways to achieve this aspect of telemetry that includes monitoring, health checks, tracing, or logging. This chapter covers the reasoning behind each of these approaches and what makes sense for enterprise applications.

In this chapter we will cover the following topics:

- Business and technical metrics
- Integrating Prometheus
- How to meet performance needs
- Java Performance Diagnostic Model
- Monitoring and sampling techniques
- Why traditional logging is harmful
- Monitoring, logging, and tracing in a modern world
- Suitability of performance tests

# Business metrics

Visibility in the business processes is crucial to business-related persons in order to see and interpret what is happening inside an enterprise system. Business-relevant metrics allow to evaluate the effectiveness of processes.Without visibility into the processes, the enterprise application acts as a black box.

Business-related metrics are an invaluable asset to business experts. They provide domain-specific information as to how the use cases perform. Which metrics are of interested obviously depends on the domain.

How many cars are created per hour? How many articles are purchased and for what amount? What is the conversion rate? How many users followed the email marketing campaign?These are examples of domain-specific key performance indicators. The business experts have to define these indicators for the specific domain.

The enterprise application has to emit this information which originate from various points in the business processes. The nature of this information depends on the actual domain. In many cases, business metrics arise from domain events that occur during performing the business processes.

Take the number of cars that are created per hour as an example. The car creation use case emits a corresponding `CarCreated` domain event, which is collected for future statistics. Whereas calculating the conversion rate involves much more information.

The business experts have to define the semantics and origin behind key performance indicators. Defining and collecting these indicators becomes part of the use case. Emitting this information is a responsibility of the application as well.

It's important to distinguish between business-motivated and technically-motivated metrics. Although business metrics provide insights of high value, they are directly impacted by technical metrics. An example of a technical metric is the service response time which is, in turn, affected by other technical metrics. The sub-chapter *Technical metrics* will examine this topic further.

Business experts, therefore, must not only care about the business aspects of monitoring but also the technical impact of an application's responsiveness.

# Collecting business metrics

Business-relevant metrics allow business experts to evaluate the effectiveness of the enterprise system.The metrics provide helpful insightsinto specific parts of the business domain. The application is responsible for gathering business-relevant metrics as part of it's use cases.

The *car manufacture* package, for example, performs business logic that can emit certain metrics, such as the number of cars created per hour.

From a business perspective, the relevant metrics usually originate from domain events. It's advisable to define and emit domain events, such asCarCreated, as part of the use case, as soon as a car has been successfully manufactured. These events are collected and being used to derive further information in the form of specific business metrics.

The CarCreated event is fired in the boundary as a CDI event and can be observed in a separate statistics collector. The following code snippet shows a domain event fired as part of a use case:

```java
@Stateless
public class CarManufacturer {

    @Inject
    CarFactory carFactory;

    @Inject
    Event<CarCreated> carCreated;

    @PersistenceContext
    EntityManager entityManager;

    public Car manufactureCar(Specification spec) {
        Car car = carFactory.createCar(spec);
        entityManager.merge(car);
        carCreated.fire(new CarCreated(spec));
        return car;
    }

}
```

The boundary fires the CDI event that notifies about a successful car creation. The corresponding handling is decoupled from the business process and no further logic is involved in this place. The event will be observed in a separate application scoped bean. Synchronous CDI events can define to be handled during specific transaction phases. The following transactional observer therefore ensures that only successful database transactions are measured:

```java
import javax.enterprise.event.TransactionPhase;

@ApplicationScoped
public class ManufacturingStatistics {

    public void carCreated(@Observes(during =
            TransactionPhase.AFTER_SUCCESS) Specification spec) {
        // gather statistics about car creation with
        // provided specification
        // e.g. increase counters
    }
}
```

The event information is collected and processed further in order to provide the business metrics. Depending on the situation, more business-relevant data could be required.

Modeling the relevant information as domain events matches the business definition and decouples the use case from the statistics calculation.

Besides defining domain events, the information can also be collected via cross-cutting components, such as interceptors, depending on the situation and requirements.In the simplest case, the metrics are instrumented and collected in primitives. Application developers have to consider bean scopes in order not to throw away collected data with incorrect scopes.

# Emitting metrics

Metrics are usually not persisted in the application but in another system that is part of the environment, such as external monitoring solutions. This simplifies the implementation of metrics; the enterprise application keeps the information in memory and emits the specified metrics. External monitoring solutions scrape and process these metrics.

There are several techniques that can be used to emit and collect metrics. For example, measures can be formatted into custom JSON strings and exposed via HTTP endpoints.

A monitoring solution that is part of the Cloud Native Computing Foundation, and, as of today, has huge momentum, is **Prometheus**. Prometheus is a monitoring and alerting technology that scrapes, efficiently stores, and queries time series data. It gathers data that is emitted by some service over HTTP in a specific format. Prometheus is powerful in scraping and storing data.

For graphs and dashboards for business-related information, other solutions can be built on top of this. A technology that works well with Prometheus and provides many possibilities for appealing graphs is **Grafana**. Grafana doesn't store time series itself but uses sources such as Prometheus to query and display time series.

The following screenshot shows an example of a Grafana dashboard:

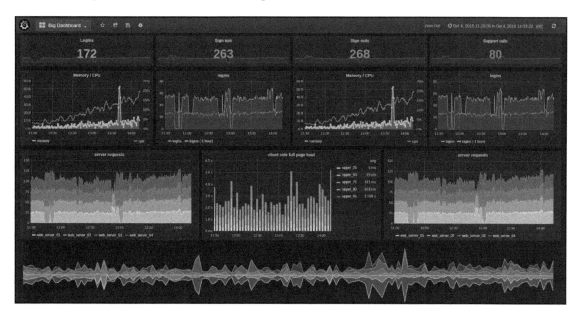

The idea of dashboards provides visibility for business experts and combines relevant information. Depending on the requirements and motivations, coherent information is combined into graphs that provide overviews and insights. Dashboards provide the ability to query and customize time series representations based on the target group.

# Enter Prometheus

The following examples show how to integrate Prometheus into Java EE. This is one possible monitoring solution and aims to give the readers an idea of how to slimly integrate business-related metrics.

The application will emit the gathered metrics in the Prometheus output format. The Prometheus instances scrape and store this information, as demonstrated in the following diagram:

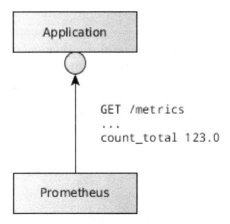

Developers can implement custom functionality to collect and emit information, or use Prometheus' Client API which already ships with several metric types.

There are multiple Prometheus metric types as follows:

- The one mostly used is a **counter** which represents an increasing numeric value. It counts the occurred events.
- A **gauge** is a numeric value that goes up and down. It can be used for measuring values such as conversion rates, temperatures, or turnover.
- **Histograms** and **summaries** are more complex metric types used to sample observations in buckets. They typically observe metrics distribution. For example, how long does it take to create a car, how much do these values vary, and how are they distributed?

A Prometheus metric has a name and labels, which are sets of key-value pairs. A time series is identified by the metric's name and a set of labels. The label can be seen as parameters, sharding the overall amount of information.

An example of a counter metric representation using labels is `cars_manufactured_total{color="RED", engine="DIESEL"}`. The `cars_manufactured_total` counter includes the total number of manufactured cars that are specified by their color and engine type. The collected metrics can be queried for the provided label information later on.

# Realization with Java EE

The following statistics implementation observes the domain event specified earlier and stores the information in the Prometheus counter metric:

```
import io.prometheus.client.Counter;

@ApplicationScoped
public class ManufacturingStatistics {

    private Counter createdCars;

    @PostConstruct
    private void initMetrics() {
        createdCars = Counter.build("cars_manufactured_total",
                "Total number of manufactured cars")
                .labelNames("color", "engine")
                .register();
    }

    public void carCreated(@Observes(during =
            TransactionPhase.AFTER_SUCCESS) Specification spec) {

        createdCars.labels(spec.getColor().name(),
                spec.getEngine().name()).inc();
    }

}
```

The counter metric is created and registered to the Prometheus Client API. Measured values are qualified by the car `color` and `engine` type, which are taken into account when scraping the values.

In order to emit this information, the Prometheus servlet library can be included. This outputs all the registered metrics in the correct format. The monitoring servlet is configured via `web.xml`.It's also possible to include a JAX-RS resource to emit the data by accessing `CollectorRegistry.defaultRegistry`.

The emitted output will look similar to the following:

```
...
cars_manufactured_total{color="RED", engine="DIESEL"} 4.0
cars_manufactured_total{color="BLACK", engine="DIESEL"} 1.0
```

Java EE components, such as CDI events, support developers in integrating domain event metrics in a lean way. In the preceding example, the `ManufacturingStatistics` class is the only point that depends on the Prometheus API.

It's highly advisable to include the Prometheus Client API as a separate container image layer and not in the application artifact.

The monitoring solution scrapes and further processes the provided information, in order to gather the required business metrics. Scraping the counter of manufactured cars over time leads to the number of created cars per hour. This metric can be queried for the total number of cars as well as for specific color and engine combinations. The queries that define the business metrics can also be adapted and refined due to the requirements. The application ideally emits the needed atomic business-relevant metrics.

# Integrating the environment

The application emits the business-relevant metrics via HTTP. The Prometheus instance scrapes and store this data and makes it available via queries, graphs, and external solutions, such as Grafana.

In a container orchestration, the Prometheus instance runs inside the cluster. This removes the necessity to configure externally accessible monitoring endpoints. Prometheus integrates with Kubernetes in order to discover the application instances. Prometheus needs to access every application pod individually, since every application instance emits its monitoring metrics separately. Prometheus accumulates theinformation of all instances.

The Prometheus configuration is either stored in a config map or part of a base image. The instance is configured to access the applications and exporters every $n$ seconds in order to scrape the time series. For configuring Prometheus, refer to its current documentation.

This is one possible solution for integrating business monitoring into a cloud native application.

Business-related metrics are advisably represented by domain events that emerge as part of the business use case. Integrating the chosen monitoring solutions should happen transparently from the domain logic, without much vendor lock-in.

# Meeting performance requirements in distributed systems

Responsiveness is an important non-technical requirement of an enterprise application. The system only provides business value if client requests can be served within a reasonable amount of time.

Meeting performance requirements in distributed systems requires to take all participating applications into account.

Enterprise application are often required to meet a **service level agreement** (**SLA**). SLAs usually define thresholds for availability or response times, respectively.

## Service level agreements

In order to calculate and meet SLAs, it's important to consider which processes and applications are included in business use cases, especially in regard to synchronous communication. The performance of applications that synchronously call external systems directly depend on the performance of these calls. As mentioned before, distributed transactions should be avoided.

As per its nature, SLAs can only be met if all applications perform and work well together. Every application affects the SLAs of dependent systems. This not only concerns the slowest application in a system but all participating services.

For example, meeting an uptime of 99.995% per definition is not possible if it includes synchronous calls to two applications with each of them guaranteeing 99.995%. The resulting SLA is 99.99%, the values of each participating system multiplied.

The same is true for guaranteed response times. Every involved system slows down the overall response, resulting in a total response time that is the sum of all SLA times.

## Achieving SLAs in distributed systems

Let's see an example how to achieve SLAs in distributed systems, assuming the enterprise application resides in a high performance scenario where it's crucial to meet guaranteed response times. The application synchronously communicates with one or more backend systems that provide necessary information. The overall system needs to meet an SLA response time of 200 milliseconds.

In this scenario the backend applications support in meeting the SLA time by applying backpressure and preventively rejecting requests that won't meet the guaranteed SLA. By doing so the originating application has the chance to use another backend service that may respond in time.

In order to appropriately configure pooling, the engineers need to know the average response time of the backend system, here 20 milliseconds. The corresponding business functionality defines a dedicated thread pool by using a dedicated managed executor service. The thread pool can be configured individually.

The configuration is achieved by following some steps: The engineers configure the maximum limit of the thread pool size plus the maximum queue size, so that the SLA time is $n$ times the average response time. This $n$, here $10$, is the maximum number of requests the system will handle at a time, consisting of the maximum pool size and maximum queue size limit. Any request that exceeds this number is immediately rejected by a service temporarily unavailable response. This is based on the calculation that the new request will likely exceed the calculated SLA time of 200 milliseconds, if the current number of handled requests exceeds $n$.

Immediately rejecting requests sounds like a harsh response, but by doing so, the client application is given the opportunity to retry a different backend without consuming the whole SLA time in vain in a single invocation. It's a case example for high performance scenarios with multiple backends where meeting SLAs has a high priority.

The implementation of this scenario is similar to the backpressure example in the previous chapter. The client uses different backends as a fallback if the first invocation failes with an unavailable service. This implicitly makes the client resilient since it uses multiple backends as fallback. The backend service implicitly applies the bulkhead pattern. A single functionality that is unavailable doesn't affect the rest of the application.

# Tackling performance issues

Technical metrics, such as response time, throughput, error rates oruptimeindicate the responsiveness of the system. As long as the application's responsiveness is in acceptable ranges, there is arguably no other metric to consider. Insufficient performance means that the system's SLAs are not being met, that is, the response time is too high or client requests fail. Then the question arises: what needs to be changed to improve the situation?

# Theory of constraints

If the desired load on the system increases, the throughput ideally increases as well. The theory of constraints is based on the assumption that there will be at least one constraint that will throttle the system's throughput. The constraints or bottlenecks therefore cause a performance regression.

Like a chain that is only as strong as its weakest link, the constraining resource limits the overall performance of the system or certain functionality thereof. It prevents the application from handling more load while other resources are not fully utilized. Only by increasing the flow through the constraining resource, that is, removing the bottleneck, will the throughput be increased. If the system is optimized *around the bottleneck* rather than removing it, the responsiveness of the overall system won't improve and, ultimately, it may even decrease.

It's therefore crucial to identify what the bottleneck is. The overall performance won't improve, before the limiting bottleneck gets targeted.

For example, throwing more CPU power at an application with high CPU utilization probably won't help to achieve better performance. Maybe the application isn't performing well because of other root causes than insufficient CPU.

It's important to mention here that the limiting constraint likely is external to the application. In a single, monolithic application, this includes the hardware and the operating system, with all running processes. If other software running on the same hardware heavily utilizes the network adapter, the application's network I/O and overall performance will be affected as well, even if the root cause, the limiting constraint, isn't the in responsibility of the application.

Inspecting performance issues therefore needs to take more into account than just the application itself. The whole set of processes running on the same hardware can have an impact on the application's performance, depending on how the other processes utilize the system's resources.

In a distributed environment, performance analytics also involves all interdependent applications, that interact with the application, and the communication in between. In order to identify the constraining resource, the overall situation of the system has to be taken into account.

Since the applications are interconnected, improving the responsiveness of a single system will affect others and can potentially even decrease the overall responsiveness. Again, trying to improve the wrong aspect, such as optimizing around the bottleneck, will not improve rather than most likely even downgrade the overall performance. An application that connects to an external system that represents the bottleneck , puts certain pressure on the external system. If the application's performance is tuned, rather than the external application, the load and pressure on the latter is increased which ultimately leads to overall worse responsiveness.

In distributed systems, the situation with all interdependent applications involved vastly complicates solving performance issues.

# Identifying performance regression with jPDM

The**Java Performance Diagnostic Model**(**jPDM**) is a performance diagnostic model that abstracts the complexity of systems. It helps interpreting the*performance counters*of the system and thus understanding the root cause of why we experience performance regression.

The challenge with identifying performance regression is that a specific scenario is the result of innumerable influences, many of them*external*to the application. jPDM and the resulting methodologies helps dealing with that complexity.

In terms of responsiveness, there is an infinite number of things that can go wrong, but they will go wrong in a finite number of ways. Performance regression can therefore be categorized into different manifestations. There will be a few typical forms of issues, emerging in innumerable, varying scenarios, and root causes. In order to identify the different categories, we will make use of the diagnostic model.

jPDM identifies important subsystems of our system, their roles, functions, and attributes. The subsystems interact with each other. The model helps to identify tools to measure levels of activity and interactions between the subsystems. Methodologies and processes that help to study and analyze systems and situations in regard to performance, fall out of this model.

## Subsystems

The subsystems in a Java application environment are: the operating system, including hardware, the Java Virtual Machine, the application, and the actors. Subsystems utilize their corresponding, underlying subsystem to perform their tasks.

The following diagram shows how the jPDM subsystems interact with each other:

## Actors

The actors are the users of the system in a broadest sense. This includes end users, batch processes, or external systems, depending on the use case.

By using the system, the actors will generate work load. The properties of the actors include the load factor, that is how many users are involved, as well as the velocity, that is how fast user requests are processed. These properties influence the overall situation similar to all other subsystem's properties.

The actors themselves don't represent a performance issue, they simply use the application. That said, if the system's performance isn't met, the limiting constraint is not to be searched for within the actors; the actors and the load they generate are part of the circumstances the system has to deal with.

## Application

The enterprise application contains the business logic algorithms. Part of the business use cases is to allocate memory, schedule threads, and use external resources.

The application will use framework and Java language functionalities to fulfill this. It ultimately makes use of JVM code and configuration, directly or indirectly. By doing so, the application puts a certain load on the JVM.

## JVM

The **Java Virtual Machine** (**JVM**) interprets and executes the application byte code. It takes care of memory management--allocation as well as garbage collection. There are vast optimization techniques in place to increase the performance of the program, such as **Just-In-Time** (**JIT**) compilation of the Java HotSpot Performance Engine.

The JVM utilizes operating system resources to allocate memory, run threads, or use network or disk I/O.

## Operating system and hardware

A computer's hardware components such as CPU, memory, disk and network I/O, define the resources of a system. They contain certain attributes, such as capacities or speed.

Since the hardware components represent non-shareable resources, the operating system provisions hardware between the processes. The operating system provides system-wide resources and schedule threads for the CPUs.

For this reason, the model considers the overall system, including hardware. The enterprise application potentially doesn't run alone on the system's hardware. Other processes utilize hardware components and thus influence the application's performance. Multiple processes that simultaneously try to access the network will result in poorer responsiveness than running each of them independently.

# jPDM instances - production situations

Specific situations in a production system, are instances of the jPDM model. They contain all their properties, characteristics, and specific bottlenecks.

Any change in one of the subsystems would result in a different situation with different properties and characteristics, thus in a different instance of the model. For example, changing the load on the system could result in a totally different bottleneck.

This is also the reason why performance tests in environments other than production will result in potentially different bottlenecks. The different environment has at least a different OS and hardware situation, not necessarily in the hardware and configuration being used, but in the whole condition of OS processes. Simulated scenarios such as performance tests therefore don't allow conclusions about bottlenecks or performance optimizations. They represent a different jPDM instance.

Since we use the model to ultimately analyze performance issues, the following approaches only make sense when there are actual performance issues. If there is no issue, that is, the defined SLAs are met, there is nothing to investigate or act upon.

## Analyzing the jPDM instances

jPDM is used to assist in investigating performance regression. Methodologies, processes and tools that fall out of the model help to identify limiting constraints.

Each subsystem with its distinct set of attributes and resources plays a specific role in the system. We use specific tools to both expose specific performance metrics and monitor interactions between subsystems.

Looking back at the theory of constraints, we want to investigate the limiting constraint of a production situation, an instance of the jPDM. The tooling helps with investigating.It's important for the investigation to take the overall system into account. The hardware is shared by all operating system processes. The dominance, therefore, may be caused by a single process or the sum of all processes running on that hardware.

First, we investigate the dominating consumer of the CPU and how the CPU is utilized. The CPU consumption pattern will lead us to the subsystem that contains the bottleneck.

In order to investigate the dominating consumer, we make use of a decision tree. It indicates where the CPU time is spent - in kernel space, user space, or idling. The following diagram shows the decision tree:

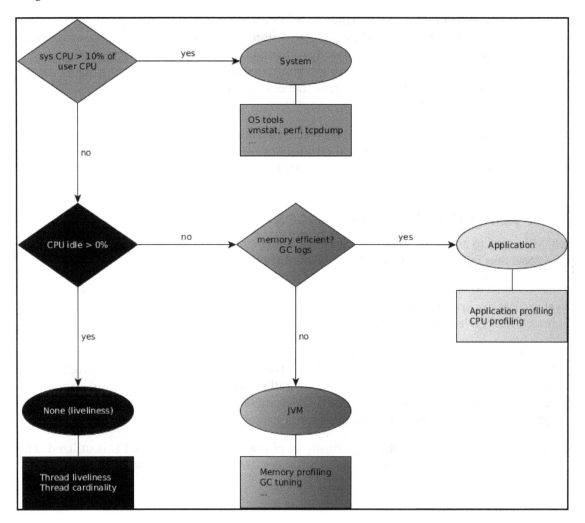

The round nodes in the graph represent the dominant consumers of the CPU. The colors represent the jPDM subsystems. Following the decision tree leads us to the subsystem that contains the bottleneck. Identifying the subsystem narrows down the performance regression to a specific category. We then use further tooling to analyze the instance of jPDM, the actual situation.

Since performance issues can originate from an infinite number of things, we need to follow a process to narrow down the causes. If we would not follow a process but blindly *peek and poke* or guess, we would not only waste time and effort but potentially wrongly identify symptoms as actual dominating constraints.

The dominant consumers of the CPU represent where the CPU time is spent. This is an important information to investigate the situation. It's not sufficient to solely look at the overall amount of CPU utilization. This information alone neither gives us much evidence of the existence of a bottleneck or how much headroom there is, nor does it lead to the dominating consumer. A CPU usage of 60% doesn't tell us whether the CPU is the constraining resource, that is whether adding more CPU would improve the overall responsiveness. The CPU time needs to be analyzed in greater detail.

First, we look at the ratio between CPU user and system time. This indicates whether the CPU time is spent in the kernel for longer than expected and thus whether the operating system is the dominating consumer of the CPU.

## Dominating consumer - OS

The operating system dominates the CPU consumption when it's asked to work harder than it usually should. This means that too much CPU time is spent on resource and device management. This includes network and disk I/O, locks, memory management, or context switches.

If the CPU system time is more than a certain percentage value of the user time, the operating system is the dominating consumer. The jPDM identified 10% as a threshold value, based on the experience of analyzing innumerable production situations. That means if the CPU system time is more than 10% of the user time, the bottlenecks are contained in the OS subsystem.

In this case, we investigate the issue further using operating system tools, such as `vmstat`, `perf`, `netstat`, and others.

For example, an enterprise application that retrieves database entries with a huge number of individually executed queries puts lots of pressure on the operating system in managing all these database connections. The overhead spent on establishing each and every network connection will eventually dominate the overall system and represent the constraining resource in the system. Investigating this situation thus shows a big share of CPU time spent in the kernel where the network connections are established.

## Dominating consumer - none

If the CPU time didn't identify the OS to be the dominating consumer, we follow the decision tree further and analyze whether the CPU is idling. If that is the case, it means there is still CPU time available that cannot be consumed.

Since we are analyzing a situation where the SLA is not met, that is, the overall system is in a situation where it doesn't perform well enough for the given load, a well-saturated situation would fully utilize the CPU. Idling CPU times thus indicates a liveliness issue.

What needs to be investigated is why the threads are not scheduled by the operating system. This can have multiple causes, such as empty connection or thread pools, deadlock situations, or slow responding external systems. The state of the threads will indicate the cause of the constraint. We again use operating system tooling to investigate the situation.

An example for this category of issues is when an external system that responds slowly is accessed synchronously. It will lead to threads that are waiting for network I/O and can't run. This is the difference to dominating OS consumption, that the thread is not actively executing work but waiting to get scheduled.

## Dominating consumer - JVM

The dominating consumers so far weren't contained in the application or JVM subsystems. If the CPU time is not overly spent in the kernel or idling, we start investigations in the JVM.

Since the JVM is responsible for memory management, its performance will indicate potential memory issues. Mainly **Garbage Collection** (**GC**) logs, together with **JMX** tooling help investigate scenarios.

Memory leaks will lead to increasing memory usage and excessive garbage collector runs that occupy the CPU. Inefficient memory usage will equally lead to excessive garbage collections. The GC executions ultimately cause the JVM being the dominating consumer of the CPU.

This is another example of why it's important to follow the process of the jPDM decision tree. The performance issue arises in high CPU usage, although the actual bottleneck in this case is the memory leak.

As of today, the main cause of performance issues are related to memory, mostly from application logging that results in extensive string object creation.

### Dominating consumer - application

If the JVM analysis didn't indicate a memory issue, finally the application is the dominating consumer of the CPU. This means that the application code itself is responsible for the bottleneck. Especially applications that run sophisticated algorithms excessively utilize the CPU.

Application-related profiling will lead to conclusions where in the application the issue originates and how the issue might be resolved. This means that the application either contains suboptimal code or reached the possible limit with the given resources, and ultimately needs to be scaled horizontally or vertically.

# Conclusion

The approach of solving performance issues is to try to characterize the regression first by investigating the situation by following a specific process. After the constraining resource has been identified, further steps to resolve the situation are applied. After potentially fixing the situation, the measurement in production needs to be repeated. It's important to not change behavior or configuration without the verification that the changes in fact provide the expected results.

The jPDM approach investigates performance regression without considering the application's code, by applying a uniform solving process.

What tools and metrics are needed to apply this approach?

Depending on the system in production, tools that ship with the operating system, as well as Java Runtime-related tools, are useful. Since all aspects consider the overall system at the operating system level rather than just the application alone, operating system tools and lower-level metrics are more helpful than application-specific ones.

However, the technical metrics of the application, such as response time or throughput, are the first place of focus that indicate the application's quality of service. If these metrics indicate a performance issue, then it makes sense to investigate using lower-level metrics and tools.

The next section examines how to gather the application's technical metrics.

# Technical metrics

Technical metrics indicate the load and responsiveness of the system. Prime examples for these metrics are the response time, as well as the throughput, often gathered as requests or transactions per second, respectively. They provide information about how the overall system currently performs.

These metrics will ultimately have an impact on other, business-related metrics. At the same time, as we have seen in the previous section, these metrics are just indicators and themselves affected by a lot of other technical aspects, namely all properties of jPDM subsystems.

Therefore, an application's performance is impacted by a lot of technical influences. Thus, the question is, which technical metrics besides response time, throughput, error rates, and uptime should reasonably be collected?

# Types of technical metrics

Technical metrics are primarily concerned with the quality of the application's service, such as response times or throughput. They are the indicators that represent the application's responsiveness and may point out potential performance issues. The information can be used to create statistics about trends and application peaks.

This insight increases the likelihood of foreseeing potential outages and performance issues in a timely manner. It is the technical equivalent of business insights into the otherwise black box system. These metrics alone allow no sound conclusions about the root cause or constraining resources in the case of performance issues.

Lower-level technical information includes resource consumption, threading, pooling, transactions, or sessions. It's again important to mention that this information alone does not direct the engineers to potential bottlenecks.

As shown previously, it's necessary to inspect the overall situation with everything running on specific hardware. The operating system information provides the best source of information. In order to solve performance issues, the operating system, as well as application tools, are required to take this into account.

This doesn't mean that the technical information emitted by the application or the JVM runtime has no value at all. The application-specific metrics can assist in solving performance issues. It's important to keep in mind that these metrics alone will lead to potentially wrong assumptions about what the constraining resources are when a system needs to be performance-tuned.

# High frequency monitoring versus sampling

Often, monitoring aims to collect technical metrics with a high frequency of many collections per second. The problem with this high frequency collection is that it heavily impacts the performance of the system. Metrics often get collected even if there is no performance regression.

As mentioned, application-level metrics, such as resource consumption, alone don't help much in identifying potential performance constraints. In the same way, the collection disrupts the responsiveness of the system.

Instead of monitoring with a high frequency it's advisable to sample metrics with lower frequency, such as for only a few times per minute. The theory behind statistical populations shows that these few samples represent the population of data well enough.

Sampling the information should have as little impact on the application's performance as possible. All subsequent investigations, or metrics querying or calculations should happen out-of-band; that is, outsourced to a system that does not impact the running application. The concerns for sampling the information from storing, querying, and displaying it, are thus separated.

# Collecting technical metrics

The application is a good place to gather the technical metrics, ideally at the system boundaries. It's equally possible to collect these in a potential proxy server.

The application server already emits technically-relevant metrics such as information about resource consumption, threading, pooling, transactions, or sessions. Some solutions also provide Java agents that sample and emit technically-relevant information.

Traditionally, application servers are required to make technically relevant metrics available via JMX. This functionality is part of the Management API, but has never been used much in projects. One of the reasons for this is that the model and API are quite cumbersome.

However, it's helpful to mention that Java EE application servers are required to gather and provide data about its resources. The container emits this information via JMX. There are several ways to scrape this information.

There are so-called exporters available, applications that either run standalone or as **Java agents**, that access the JMX information and emit it via HTTP. The Prometheus JMX exporter, which exports the information in a similar format as shown previously, is an example of this. The benefit of this approach is that it doesn't add dependencies into the application.

The installation and configuration of Java agents is done in the application server, in a base container image layer. This once again emphasizes the principle that containers should not couple the application's artifact with implementation details.

# Boundary metrics

Technical metrics that are application-specific, such as response times, throughput, uptime, or error rates can be gathered at the system boundaries. This can happen via the interceptors or filters, depending on the situation. HTTP-relevant monitoring can be collected via a servlet filter for any technology that builds upon servlets, such as JAX-RS.

The following code snippet shows a servlet filter that gathers the response time and throughput in a Prometheus histogram metrics:

```java
import javax.servlet.*;
import javax.servlet.annotation.WebFilter;
import javax.servlet.http.HttpServletRequest;

@WebFilter(urlPatterns = "/*")
public class MetricsCollectorFilter implements Filter {

    private Histogram requestDuration;

    @Override
    public void init(FilterConfig filterConfig) throws ServletException
{
        requestDuration = Histogram.build("request_duration_seconds",
                "Duration of HTTP requests in seconds")
            .buckets(0.1, 0.4, 1.0)
            .labelNames("request_uri")
            .register();
    }

    public void doFilter(ServletRequest req, ServletResponse res,
            FilterChain chain) throws IOException, ServletException {
```

```
        if (!(req instanceof HttpServletRequest)) {
            chain.doFilter(req, res);
            return;
        }

        String url = ((HttpServletRequest) req).getRequestURI();
        try (Histogram.Timer ignored = requestDuration
                .labels(url).startTimer()) {
            chain.doFilter(req, res);
        }
    }

    @Override
    public void destroy() {
        // nothing to do
    }
}
```

This metric is registered similarly to the business-related example previously, and emitted via the Prometheus output format. The histogram buckets collect the time in four buckets, with the specified times from 0.1, 0.4, or 1.0 seconds, and everything above. These bucket configurations need to be adapted to the SLAs.

The servlet filter is active on all resource paths and will collect the statistics, qualified by each path.

# Logging and tracing

Historically, logging had quite high importance in enterprise applications. We have seen a lot of logging framework implementations and supposedly best practices on how to implement reasonable logs.

Logging is typically used for debugging, tracing, journaling, monitoring, and outputting errors. In general, all information that developers consider somewhat important, but not made apparent to the users, is been placed into logs. In almost all cases, this includes logging to files.

# Shortcomings of traditional logging

This approach, which is way too common in enterprise projects, comes with a few problems.

# Performance

Traditional logging, especially extensively used logging invocations, creates a lot of string objects. Even APIs such as **Slf4J** that aim to reduce unnecessary string concatenation will result in high memory rates.All these objects need to be garbage collected after their use, which utilizes the CPU.

Storing log events as string messages is a verbose way of storing information.Choosing different formats, mainly binary formats would drastically reduce the message size and result in more efficient memory consumption and higher throughput.

Log messages that are stored in a buffer or directly on disk need to be synchronized with other log invocations. Synchronous loggers ultimately cause a file to be written within a single invocation. All simultaneous log invocations need to be synchronized in order to ensure that logged events appear in the right order.This presents the issue that synchronization indirectly couples functionality that otherwise is completely unrelated. It decreases the parallelism of intrinsically independent functionality and has a negative overall performance impact. With a high number of log messages being written, the probability of blocking threads due to synchronization increases.

Another issue is that logging frameworks usually don't write the log messages to disk directly; rather, they use several layers of buffering. This optimization technique comes with certain management overhead involved that does not improve the situation either. Synchronous file operations advisably work with the least overhead layers as possible.

Log files that reside on NFS storage decrease the overall performance even more, since the write operation hits the operation system I/O twice, with both file system and network calls involved. In order to manage and persist log files, network storage is an often chosen solution, especially for container orchestration that needs persisted volumes.

In general, experience shows that logging has the biggest impact in an application's performance. This is mostly due to the memory impact on string log messages.

# Log levels

Logging solutions include the ability to specify the importance of a log entry via log levels, such as *debug, info, warning,* or *error*. Developers might ask themselves which log level to choose for specific invocations.

The approach of having several layers certainly sounds reasonable, since production systems can specify a higher log level than development runs, so as not to produce too much data in production.

The challenge with this situation is that in production there is usually no debug log information available when it's needed. Potential error situations that could need additional insights don't have this information available. Debug or trace log levels that include tracing information are switched off.

Choosing log levels is always a trade-off regarding what information should be included. Debugging in development is done best using actual debug tools which connect against running applications, potentially remotely. Debug or trace logs are usually not available in production and therefore provide little benefit.

Whereas defining multiple log levels may have emerged from a good intention, the practical use in production systems adds little value.

# Log format

Traditional logging solutions specify particular log layouts that format the log messages in the resulting log file. The application needs to manage the creation, rolling, and formatting of log files that are not relevant for the business logic.

Quite a few enterprise applications ship with third-party logging dependencies that implement this functionality, but provide no business value.

Choosing particular plain text log formats is another decision that needs to be made by the application developers. There is a trade-off between a log entry format that is readable by both humans and machines. The result is usually the worst compromise for both parties; string log formats that are both hardly readable and have a tremendous impact on the system's performance.

It would be more reasonable to choose binary formats that store information with the highest density. Humans then could use tooling to make the messages visible.

# Amounts of data

Extensive logging introduces a huge amount of data that is contained in log files. In particular, logs that are used for debugging and tracing purposes result in big files that are cumbersome and expensive to parse.

Parsing log formats in general introduces an avoidable overhead. Information that is potentially technically-relevant is serialized in a specific format first, just to be parsed again later when inspecting the logs.

Later in this sub-section, we will see what other solutions there are.

# Obfuscation

Equal to unreasonably checked exception handling, logging obfuscates business logic in the source code. This is especially the case for boilerplate log patterns that are common in many projects.

Log statements take up too much space in the code and especially draw the developer's attention.

Some logging technology, such as Slf4j, provides functionality to format strings in readable ways while avoiding immediate string concatenation. But still, log statements add obfuscating invocations that are unrelated to the business problem.

This is obviously less the case if the debug log statements are added in a cross-cutting component, such as an interceptor. However, these cases mostly add logging for tracing purposes. We will see in the next sub-section that there are more suitable solutions for this.

# The concerns of applications

As we have seen in 12-factor applications, it is not an application's concern to choose log files and message formats.

In particular, logging frameworks that promise simpler logging solutions add technically-motivated third-party dependencies to the application; dependencies that have no direct business value.

If there is business value in events or messages, then the use of another solution should be favored. The following shows how traditional logging is misused for these other applications' concerns.

# Wrong choice of technology

Traditional logging, and how it is used in the majority of enterprise projects, is a suboptimal choice for concerns that are better handled using different approaches.

The question is: what do developers want to log, anyway? What about metrics, such as the current resource consumption? Or business-related information, such as *car manufactured*? Should we log debugging and tracing information such as *request with UUID xy originated from application A, and called subsequent application B*? What about occurring exceptions?

Attentive readers will see that most of the use cases for traditional logging are far better handled using other approaches.

If logging is used for debugging or debug tracing applications, the approach with using trace or debug levels doesn't help much. Information that will not be available in production can't reproduce a potential bug. Logging a huge amount of debug or trace events in production, however, will affect the application's responsiveness due to disk I/O, synchronization, and memory consumption. Debugging concurrency-related errors may even lead to a different outcome, due to the modified order of execution.

For debugging functionality, it's much more advisable to use actual debugger features during development, such as IDEs that connect against a running application. Logging that is used for business-motivated journaling is better accomplished via a proper journaling solution, as we will see later in this chapter. The plain text log messages are certainly not the ideal solution. The chosen technology should minimize the performance impact on the application.

Another approach to realize the same motivations behind journaling is to introduce event sourcing. This makes the domain events part of the application's core model.

Business-motivated tracing, this should be part of the business use case as well, implemented using an adequate solution. As we will see in the next sub-section, there are more suitable tracing solutions that require less parsing and have a smaller performance impact. Tracing solutions also support the consolidation of information and requests across microservices.

Monitoring information that is stored in log messages is better managed via the use of proper monitoring solutions. This approach is not just much more performant, it is also a more effective way of emitting the information in proper data structures. The examples we have seen earlier in this chapter illustrate monitored data and possible solutions.

Logging is also traditionally being used to output exceptions and errors that cannot properly be handled in the application otherwise. This is arguably the only reasonable use of logging. Together with other potential metrics that may capture the error, such as error rate counters at the system boundary, the logged exception may support developers in investigating errors.

However, errors and exceptions should only be logged if they in fact concern the application and represent an error that can be resolved by developers. With monitoring and alerting solutions in place, the need to look into logs should indicate a serious problem with the application.

# Logging in a containerized world

One of the 12-factor principles is to treat logging as a stream of events. This includes the idea that handling log files should not be a concern of the enterprise application. Log events should simply output to the process' standard output.

The application's runtime environment consolidates and processes the log streams. There are solutions for unified access over all participating applications that can be deployed into the environment.The runtime environment where the application is deployed takes care of processing the log streams.**fluentd**, which is part of the Cloud Native Computing Foundation unifies the access to log events in a distributed environment.

Application developers should treat the used logging technology as simply as possible. The application container is configured to output all server and application log events to standard output. This approachsimplifies matters for enterprise developers and enables them to focus more on solving actual business problems.

As we have seen, there is not much information left that application developers reasonably can log in a traditional way. Monitoring, journaling, or tracing solutions, as well as event sourcing, can solve the requirements in more suitable ways.

Together with logging to standard output without the need for sophisticated log file handling, there is no need for sophisticated logging framework. This supports zero-dependency applications and enables developers to be able to focus on business concerns instead.

It's therefore advisable to avoid third-party logging frameworks, as well as writing to traditional log files. The need to manage log rotations, log entry formats, levels, and framework dependencies, as well as configuration, becomes no longer necessary.

However, the following might seem antithetical to enterprise developers.

The straightforward, 12-factor way to log the output is using the standard output capabilities of Java via `System.out` and `System.err`. This directly writes the synchronous output without needless layers of buffering.

It's important to mention that outputting data via this approach will not perform. The introduced synchronization, again, ties otherwise independent parts of the application together. If the output of the process is grabbed and emitted by a video card, the performance will further decrease.

Logging to console is only meant to emit errors that are, as the name of the Java type indicates - an exception. In all other cases, engineers must ask themselves why they want to output an information in the first place, or whether other solutions are more suitable. Therefore, logged errors should indicate a fatal problem that requires engineering action. It should not be expected to receive this log output in production; in this fatal error case, performance can be disrespected.

In order to output fatal error information, Java EE applications can use CDI features as well as Java SE 8 functional interfaces to provide a uniform logging functionality:

```
public class LoggerExposer {

    @Produces
    public Consumer<Throwable> fatalErrorConsumer() {
        return Throwable::printStackTrace;
    }
}
```

The `Consumer<Throwable>` logger is then injectable in other beans, and it logs using the `accept()` method of the consumer type. If a more readable interface is desired, a thin logger facade type which is injected via `@Inject` can be defined as follows:

```
public class ErrorLogger {

    public void fatal(Throwable throwable) {
        throwable.printStackTrace();
    }
}
```

This approach will seem antithetical to enterprise developers, especially logging without using a logging framework. Using a sophisticated logging framework, which is used to direct the output to standard out again, introduces overhead, which ultimately ends up in the same result. Some developers may prefer to use JDK logging at this point.

However, providing sophisticated log interfaces and thus giving application developers the opportunity to output all kinds of information, especially human-readable strings, is counterproductive. This is why the code examples only allow to output throwable types in fatal error situations.

It's important to notice the following few aspects:

- Traditional logging should be avoided and substituted with more-suited solutions
- Only fatal error cases that are the exception, and are expected to ideally never happen, should be logged
- Containerized applications are advised to output log events to standard out
- Application logging and interfaces should be as simple as possible, preventing developers from excessive use

# Journaling

If journaling is needed as part of the business logic, there are better ways than using logging frameworks. The requirements for journaling could be auditing regulations, such as is the case for trading systems.

If the business logic requires journaling, it should accordingly be treated as such - a business requirement. There is journaling technology available that synchronously persists the required information with higher density and lower latency than traditional logging. An example of these solutions is **Chronicle Queue**, which allows us to store messages with high throughput and low latency.

The application domain could model the information as a domain event and directly persist it into a journaling solution. As mentioned previously, another way is to base the application on an event sourcing model. The auditing information is then already part of the application's model.

# Tracing

Tracing is used to reproduce specific scenarios and request flows. It's already helpful in retracing complex application processes, but it's especially helpful when multiple applications and instances are involved.

However, what's important to be pointed out is that there needs to be a business, not technical, requirement for tracing systems, similar to journaling.

Tracing is a poor technique for debugging or performance tracing systems. It will have a certain impact on performance and doesn't help much in resolving performance regression. Interdependent, distributed applications that need to be optimized in their performance advisably solely emit information about their quality of service, such as response times. Sampling techniques can sufficiently gather information that indicate performance issues in the applications.

However, let's have a look at business-motivated tracing to track the components and systems involved.

The following diagram shows a trace of a specific request involving multiple application instances and components thereof:

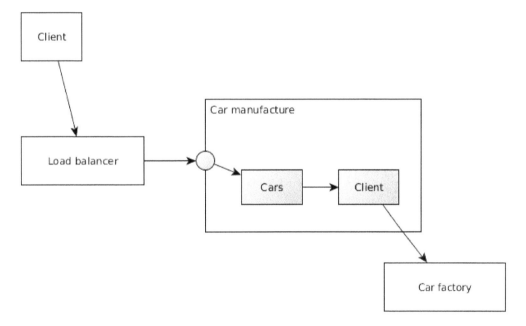

The trace can also be displayed in a timeline to show the synchronous invocations as demonstrated in the following diagram:

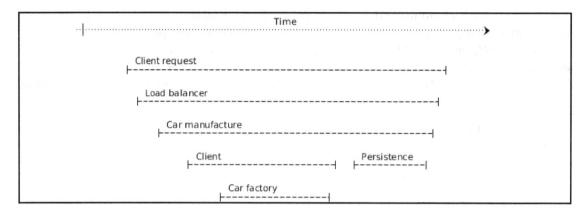

Tracing includes information about which applications or application components have been involved and how long the individual invocations took.

Traditionally, log files have been used for this, by logging the start and end of each method or component invocation including a correlation ID, such as a thread identifier. There is the possibility of including correlation IDs into logs that are used from a single originating request and are reused and logged in subsequent applications. This results in traces that also span multiple applications.

In the case of logging, the tracing information was accumulated from multiple log files; for example, using solutions such as the **ELK** stack. Trace logs are usually implemented in cross-cutting ways; for example, using logging filters and interceptors so as not to obfuscate the code.

However, using log files for tracing is not advisable. Even enterprise applications that experience a moderate load introduce a lot of log entries that are written to files. Many log entries are needed for each and every request.

File-based I/O and the needed log format serialization generally is too heavy for this approach and greatly affects the performance. Tracing to log file formats introduces a lot of data that needs to be parsed again afterwards.

There are tracing solutions that provide a much better fit.

# Tracing in a modern world

In the past months and years, multiple tracing solutions have originated that aim to minimize the performance impact on the system.

**OpenTracing** is standard, vendor-neutral tracing technology that is part of the Cloud Native Computing Foundation. It defines the concepts and semantics of traces and supports tracing in distributed applications. It is implemented by multiple tracing technologies such as **Zipkin**, **Jaeger**, or **Hawkular**.

A hierarchical trace consists of several spans, similar to the ones shown in the previous figures. A span can be a child of, or follow, another span.

In the previous example, the car manufacture component span is a child of the load balancer span. The persistence span follows the client span since their invocations happen sequentially.

An OpenTracing API span includes a time span, an operation name, context information, as well as optional sets of tags and logs. The operation names and tags are somewhat similar to Prometheus metric names and labels described earlier in the *EnterPrometheus* section. Logs describe information such as span messages.

An example for a single span is `createCar` with the tags `color=RED` and `engine=DIESEL`, as well as a log `message` field `Car successfully created`.

The following code snippet shows an example of using the OpenTracing Java API in the *car manufacture* application. It supports Java's try-with-resource feature.

```java
import io.opentracing.ActiveSpan;
import io.opentracing.Tracer;

@Stateless
public class CarManufacturer {

    @Inject
    Tracer tracer;

    public Car manufactureCar(Specification spec) {
        try (ActiveSpan span = tracer.buildSpan("createCar")
                .withTag("color", spec.getColor().name())
                .withTag("engine", spec.getEngine().name())
                .startActive()) {

            // perform business logic

            span.log("Car successfully created");
```

```
        }
    }
}
```

The created span starts actively and is added as a child to a potentially existing parent span. The `Tracer` is produced by a CDI producer that depends on the specific OpenTracing implementation.

Obviously, this approach obfuscates the code a lot and should be moved to cross-cutting components, such as interceptors. Tracing interceptor bindings can decorate methods and extract information about method names and parameters.

Depending on the desired information included in tracing spans, the interceptor binding can be enhanced to provide further information, such as the operation name.

The following code snippet shows a business method decorated with an interceptor binding that adds tracing in a lean way. Implementing the interceptor is left as an exercise for the reader:

```
@Stateless
public class CarManufacturer {

    ...

    @Traced(operation = "createCar")
    public Car manufactureCar(Specification spec) {
        // perform business logic
    }
}
```

The traced information is carried into subsequent applications via span contexts and carriers. They enable participating applications to add their tracing information as well.

The gathered data can be extracted via the used OpenTracing implementation. There are filter and interceptor implementations available for technology such as JAX-RS resources and clients that transparently add the required debug information to the invocations, for example, using HTTP headers.

This way of tracing impacts the system's performance way less than traditional logging. It defines the exact steps and systems that instrument the business logic flow. However, as mentioned before, there needs to be a business requirement to implement a tracing solution.

# Typical performance issues

Performance issues come with typical symptoms, such as response times, that are slow or become slower over time, timeouts, or even completely unavailable services. The error rates indicate the latter.

When performance issues arise, the question to be asked is what the actual constraining resource, the bottleneck, is. Where does the issue originate? As shown earlier, engineers are advised to follow an investigative process that considers the overall situation, including hardware and operating systems, in order to find the constraint. There should be no guessing and premature decisions.

Performance problems can have a huge number of root causes. Most of them originate in coding errors or misconfiguration rather than actual workload exceeding the available resources. Modern application servers can handle a lot of load until the performance becomes an issue.

However, experience shows that there are typical performance issue root causes. The following will show you the most serious ones.

Engineers are instructed to investigate issues properly, without following supposedly best practices and premature optimizations.

# Logging and memory consumption

Traditional logging, such as writing string-formatted log messages to files, is the most common root cause for poor performance. This chapter has already described the issues and advisable solutions for them.

The biggest reason for poor performance is the extensive string object creation and resulting memory consumption.High memory consumption, in general, represents a major performance issue. This is not only caused by logging but by high memory rates in caching, memory leaks, or extensive object creation.

Since the JVM manages the garbage collection of memory, these high memory rates result in garbage collector runs, trying to free unused memory. The garbage collection utilizes the CPU. The situation is not resolved by a single collection run, what results in subsequent GC executions and thushigh CPU usage. This happens if not sufficient memory can be freed either because of memory leaks or a high workload with high consumption. Even if the system doesn't crash with `OutOfMemoryError`, the CPU usage can effectively stall the application.

Garbage collection logs, heap dumps, and measurements can help with investigating these issues. JMX tools provide insights about the memory distribution and potential hot spots.

If business logic is implemented in a lean, straightforward way using short-lived objects, memory issues are far less likely.

# Premature optimization

It regularly happens in enterprise projects that developers try to prematurely optimize applications without proper verification. Examples for this are the usage of caching, configuring pools, and application server behavior, without sampling sufficient measurements before and after tweaking.

It's highly advisable to not consider to use these optimizations before there is an identified performance problem. Proper performance sampling and measurements in production, as well as investigating the constraining resource, are a necessity before changing the setup.

In the vast majority of cases, it's sufficient to go with convention over configuration. This is true for both the JVM runtime as well as the application server. If developers take a plain Java EE approach with the default application server configuration, they won't likely run into issues with premature optimization.

If technical metrics indicate that the current approach is not sufficient for the production workload, only then is there a need to introduce change. Also, engineers should validate the necessity of the change over time. Technology changes and an optimization that provided remedy in previous runtime versions might not be the best solution anymore.

The approach of convention over configuration and taking the default configuration first also requires the least amount of initial effort.

Again, experience shows that a lot of issues originated from prematurely introducing change without proper verification beforehand.

# Relational databases

Typical scapegoats for insufficient performance are relational databases. Usually, application servers are deployed in multiple instances that all connect against a single database instance. This is a necessity to ensure consistency due to the CAP theorem.

The database as a single point of responsibility, or failure, is predestined to become a bottleneck. Still, engineers must consider proper measurements to verify this assumption.

If metrics indicate that the database response is slower than acceptable, again the first approach is to investigate the root cause. If the database query is responsible for causing the slow response, engineers are advised to take a look at the performed queries. Is a lot of data being loaded? If yes, is all this data necessary or will it be filtered and reduced by the application later on? In some cases, the database queries load more data than required.

This is also a question relevant to the business, especially for retrieving data, whether everything is required. More specific database queries that pre-filter results or size limits, such as pagination, can help in these cases.

Databases perform exceptionally well when joining and filtering data. Performing more complex queries directly in the database instance usually outperforms loading all required data into the application's memory and executing the query there. It's possible to define complex, nested SQL queries in Java and to execute them in the database. However, what enterprise applications should avoid is to define business logic queries directly in the database, using stored procedures. Business-related logic should reside in the application.

A typical configuration mistake is also neglecting to index relevant database columns that are used in queries. There were many cases in projects where the overall performance could be improved by several factors just by defining proper indexes.

In general, the insight measurements of specific use cases usually provide good insights on where the issue might originate from.

In some scenarios, queries that update data often result in optimistic locking errors. This originates from domain entities simultaneously being updated. Optimistic locking is rather a business issue than a technical one. The service error rate will indicate such issues.

If the business use case requires that entities are often changed simultaneously, development teams can consider changing the functionality to an event-based model. Similarly, as shown previously, event sourcing and event-driven architectures get rid of this situation by introducing eventual consistency.

If the performance issues purely originates from workload and concurrent accesses, then ultimately a different data model is required, such as event-driven architectures realized with CQRS. However, usually the situation is solvable in another way. The vast majority of enterprise applications scale well enough using relational databases.

# Communication

The majorityof communication-related performance issues aredue to synchronous communication.Most issues in this area emerge from missing timeouts that lead client calls to block infinitely and cause deadlock situations. This happens if no client-side timeouts are configured and the invoked system is unavailable.

A less critical but similarly imperfect situation occurs if the configured timeouts are too large. This causes systems to wait for too long, slowing down processes and blocking threads.

Configuring timeouts for client invocations, as described earlier, provides simple but effective relief from this issue.

High response time and low throughput can have multiple origins. Performance analysis provides insights into where the time is spent.

There are some other potential bottlenecks, such as payload sizes. Whether data is sent as plain text or binary data can make quite some difference in payload sizes. Serialization that uses imperfect algorithms or technology can also decrease the responsiveness. Still, these concerns are usually negligible unless the application resides in high performance situations.

If multiple, synchronous invocations are required, they should happen in parallel if possible, using container-managed threads; for example, provided by a managed executor service. This avoids unnecessarily making the application wait.

In general, use cases that span multiple transactional systems, such as databases using distributed transactions, should be avoided. As described previously, distributed transactions won't scale. The business use case should be considered to effectively process asynchronously instead.

# Threading and pooling

In order to reuse threads as well as connections, application containers manage pools. Requested threads don't necessarily have to be created but are reused from a pool.

Pooling is used to control the load on specific parts of the system. Choosing appropriate pool sizes allows the system to be saturated well, but prevents it from overloading. This is due to the fact that empty pools will lead to suspended or rejected requests. All threads and connections of that pool are then being utilized already.

The bulkhead pattern prevents different parts of the system from affecting each other by defining dedicated thread pools. This limits the resource shortage to a potentially problematic functionality. In some cases, functionality such as a legacy system might be known to cause issues. Bulkheads, implemented as dedicated thread pools, and timeout configuration help preserve the application's health.

Empty pools either originate from the current load on that pool being exceptionally high, or resources that are acquired for much longer than expected. In any case, it's advisable not to simply increase the corresponding pool size but to investigate where the issue originates from. The described investigation techniques as well as JMX insights and thread dumps will supports you in finding bottlenecks, as well as potential programming errors, such as deadlocks, misconfigured timeouts, or resource leaks. In the minority of cases will a shortage in pooling actually originate from a high workload.

Pool sizes and configuration is made in the application container. Engineers must perform proper performance sampling in production before and after reconfiguring the server.

# Performance testing

The challenge with performance testing is that the tests run in a simulated environment.

Simulated environments are fine for other kinds of tests, such as system tests, since certain aspects are abstracted. Mock servers, for example, can simulate behavior similarly to production.

However, unlike in functional tests, validating the system's responsiveness requires to take everything in the environment into account. At the end of the day, applications are running on actual hardware, thus the hardware, as well as the overall situation, impacts the application's performance. The system's performance in simulated environments will never behave equally in production. Therefore, performance tests are not a reliable way of finding performance bottlenecks.

There are many scenarios where an application can perform much better in production compared to performance tests, depending on all the immediate and imminent influences. The HotSpot JVM, for example, performs better under high load.

Investigating performance constraints therefore can only happen in production. As shown earlier, the jPDM investigation processes, together with sampling techniques and tools applied to the production system, will identify the bottleneck.

Performance and stress tests help in finding obvious code or configuration errors, such as resource leaks, serious misconfiguration, missing timeouts, or deadlocks. These bugs will be found before deploying to production. Performance tests can also capture performance trends over time and warn engineers if the overall responsiveness decreases. Still, this may only indicate potential issues but should not lead the engineers to premature conclusions.

Performance and stress tests only make sense in the whole network of interdependent applications. This is because of dependencies and performance influences of all the systems and databases involved. The setup needs to be as similar to production as possible.

Even then, the outcome will not be the same as in production. It's highly important that engineers are aware of this. Performance optimizations that follow performance tests are therefore never fully representative.

For performance tuning, it's important to use investigative processes together with sampling on production instead. Continuous Delivery techniques support in quickly bringing configuration changes to production. Then engineers can use the sampling and performance insights to see whether changing the setup has improved the overall solution. And again, the overall system needs to be taken into account. Simply tuning a single application without considering the whole system can have negative effects on the overall scenario.

# Summary

Business-related metrics can provide helpful insights into the enterprise application. These metrics are a part of the business use case and therefore should be treated as such. Business metrics are ultimately impacted by other, technical metrics. It's therefore advisable to monitor these metrics as well.

The theory of constraints describes that there will be one ore more limiting constraints that prevent the system from infinitely increasing its throughput. In order to improve the application's performance the limiting constraint therefore needs to be eradicated. jPDM helps identifying the limiting constraints by finding the dominating consumer of the CPU first and using appropriate tooling to further investigate performance issues. It's advisable to investigate potential bottlenecks by following this process, which takes the overall situation into account, rather than to blindly *peek and poke*.

Rather than using high-frequency monitoring, engineers are advised to sample technical metrics with low frequency and to query, calculate, and investigate out-of-band. This has tremendously less impact on the application's performance. Distributed applications will need to meet SLAs. The backpressure approach as well as the bulkhead pattern can help achieve highly responsive, resilient enterprise systems.

Traditional logging should be avoided for a number of reasons, especially the negative performance impact. Enterprise applications are advised to only output log events in case of fatal, unexpected errors, which are written to standard output in a preferably straightforward way. For all other motivations, such as debugging, tracing, journaling, or monitoring, there are more suitable solutions.

Performance and stress tests running in simulated environments can be used to find obvious errors in the application. The environments should be as close to production, including all applications and databases involved. For any other reasoning, especially statements about an application's expected performance, bottlenecks, or optimizations, performance tests are not helpful and might even lead to wrong assumptions.

The next chapter will cover the topic of application security.

# 10
# Security

So far, most of the topics covered in this book haven't dealt with the topic of security. This is an often overlooked topic that in some real-world projects only gets interest when it's already too late.

Developers as well as project managers see security as a necessary evil rather than as something providing big benefits to the business. Still, it's a topic that stakeholders must be made aware of.

Quite a few requirements have changed in the age of the cloud and distributed applications. This chapter will look into the situation of the past, as well as today's requirements. It will cover how security is realized using modern Java EE:

- Security lessons learned from the past
- Enterprise security principles
- Modern security solutions
- How to realize security using modern Java EE

## Lessons learned from the past

In today's world IT security is quite an important aspect. Most people have realized that information technology can cause a lot of harm if misused.

The last half-century of computing contained a lot to learn from, in terms of security, and not only for enterprise software.

Let's look into a few lessons learned from the past of enterprise application development. In previous years, the biggest security issues were encryption and approaches on how to manage credentials.

Encrypting and signing data is an incredibly safe way of keeping secrets, if applied correctly. It solely depends on the used algorithms and the key lengths.

There were quite a few encryption and hashing algorithms that turned out to not be secure enough. **DES** is an example, as well as the often-used **MD5** hashing algorithm. As of writing this book, **AES** with 192- or 256-bit key lengths is considered secure. For the hashing algorithm, **SHA-2** or **-3** with at least 256 bits is advised.

User credentials that are stored as part of the application must not be stored in plain text. There have been too many security breaches in the past that especially targeted databases where the passwords resided. Also, simply hashing passwords without providing proper passwordsaltsis discouraged.

In general, it's highly advisable for enterprise developers not to implement security functionality themselves if they can avoid it. The idea of companies was to create their own security implementations that weren't used anywhere else and, therefore, provide*security by obscurity*. This, however, turns out to have had the opposite effect, and, unless security experts are involved, in fact leads to, less secure solutions.

The vast majority of enterprise security demands don't require their own, custom implementations. Enterprise frameworks and the implementations thereof already ship with corresponding functionality that has been well-tested in numerous use cases. We will have a look at these APIs for Java Enterprise later in this chapter.

If the application requires the custom use of encryption, then implementations provided by runtime or third-party dependencies must be used. The Java platform offers the**Java Cryptography Extension(JCE)** for this reason. It provides implementations for modern encryption and hashing algorithms.

In general, applications should only process and store secure information when it's absolutely required by the business use case. In particular, for authentication and authorization, there are ways that avoid storing user credentials in multiple systems.

# Security in a modern world

More distribution of applications leads to higher demand in securing communication. The integrity of exchanged information needs to be ensured. Similarly, people are aware of the necessity of encryption, especially when it comes to encrypting communication.

What possibilities do engineers have in today's enterprise world? What principles should they follow when realizing security?

# Security principles

There are some basic principles that should be followed when implementing security in enterprise applications. The following list aims to give the basic ideas, and is not intended to be exhaustive.

## Encrypt communication

First of all, it's important to mention that external communication that happens over the internet must be encrypted. The usual way of doing this is via TLS using trusted certificates. This is possible for HTTP as well as for other communication protocols.

The authenticity of the certificates used must be verified at runtime by the implementation. They have to be assured by a trusted internal or external certificate authority.

Insecurely accepting any certificates in the application should be avoided, for production as well as other environments. This implies that properly signed certificates are being provided and used for the communication.

## Delegate security concerns

In terms of storing user information, today's approach is to delegate authentication and authorization to security providers if possible. This means that an enterprise application doesn't store security information, but asks a third-party, a trusted security provider.

This is especially interesting in distributed environments, where multiple applications offer potential endpoints to the outside world. The secure information moves to a single point of responsibility.

Security concerns are usually not a part of the core business logic. The application will ask the trusted security provider system to validate the security of user requests. The security provider acts as a secure single point of responsibility.

There are decentralized security protocols, such as **OAuth** or **OpenID**, that implement this approach.

Delegating the responsibility to a trusted security provider eliminates the need to share passwords within enterprise systems. Users identify directly against security providers. Applications that require security information about a user will be provided session tokens that do not directly contain confidential data.

This principle, however, mainly targets communication that includes application users as persons.

## Treat user credentials properly

If for some reason the application manages user authentication itself, it should never permanently store passwords and tokens in plain text. This introduces a severe security risk. Even if an application or database has sufficient protection from the outside world, it's important to protect the credentials from internal leaks.

Passwords that need to be managed within the application must be stored only via appropriate hashing algorithms and approaches such as **salting**. Doing so prevents any malicious attack, from both the inside as well the outside of the coorporation. It's advisable to consult security information organizations such as **Open Web Application Security Project** (**OWASP**). They provide the modern advice for security approaches and algorithms.

## Avoid storing credentials in version control

For the same reason that you should not treat secure credentials poorly, developers shouldn't store clear credentials in the version-controlled project repository. Even if the repository is hosted company-internally, this introduces a security risk.

The credentials will be visible permanently in the repository's history.

As shown in Chapter 5, *Container and Cloud Environments with Java EE,* there are features of cloud environments that inject secret configuration values into applications. This functionality can be used to provide secret credentials that are configured externally.

## Include tests

The security mechanisms that are a responsibility of the application need to be system-tested properly. Any included authentication and authorization must be verified as part of the Continuous Delivery pipeline. This means that you should verify the functionality in automated tests, to not only verify it once, but continuously, after changes in the software.

It's especially important for security-relevant tests to include negative tests. For example, the test must verify that incorrect credentials or insufficient permissions do not allow you to perform specific application functionality.

# Possibilities and solutions

After a few basic but important security principles, let's have a look at the possible security protocols and solutions.

## Encrypted communication

Encrypted communication usually means that the communications are encrypted using **TLS encryption**, as part of the communication protocol in the transport layer. Certificates are used to encrypt and sign the communication. Of course, it's crucial to be able to rely on the certificates.

Companies often operate their own certificate authorities and pre-install their**root CA**in their computers and software. This certainly makes sense for internal networks. It reduces overhead and potential costs compared to requesting certificates for all internal services from an official authority.

Certificates that are*publicly trusted*are required to be signed by one of the official certificate authorities that come pre-installed with operating systems or platforms.

Encrypted communication does not authenticate users, unless individual client certificates are being used. It lays the foundation for a secure, trusted communication.

## Protocol-based authentication

Some communication protocols come with authentication capabilities, such as HTTP with basic or digest authentication. These functionalities are part of the communication protocol and are usually well-supported in tools and frameworks.

They usually rely on the communication being already securely encrypted, otherwise this would make the information accessible for parties that can read it, should they intercept the communication. This is important to mention to application developers to ensure that protocol-based authentication is provided via encrypted communication.

The credentials for protocol-based security are usually provided directly in every message. This simplifies client calls as there is no need for several authentication steps, such as in exchanging tokens. The first client invocation can already exchange information.

# Decentralized security

Other approaches that do not directly include credentials in the client invocations will fetch security tokens first and issue the actual communication with the token being provided afterwards. This goes in the direction of decentralized security.

In order to decouple security from the application, enterprise systems can include identity providers as a central point for authentication or authorization, respectively. This delegates the security concerns from the application to a provider.

The identity providers authorize third parties, such as enterprise applications, without directly exchanging the credentials with them. The end users are redirected to the identity providers and don't hand the secure information to the enterprise application. Third-parties only receive the information when the access has been permitted, contained in tokens that they can verify.

This three-way authentication avoids concerning the enterprise application with security responsibilities. The responsibility to verify whether the information that the user provides was correct moves to the identity provider.

One example of this method is **single sign on** (SSO) mechanisms. They're used quite often in bigger companies to require users to authenticate only once and reuse the information in all services that are secured by an SSO. The SSO system authenticates the user and provides the required user information to the corresponding applications. Users just need to log in once.

Another approach is to use decentralized access delegation protocols, such as OAuth, OpenID, and OpenID Connect. They represent three-way security workflows to exchange security information between clients, third-party applications, and the identity provider. The idea is similar to single sign on mechanisms. However, these protocols enable users to decide which individual application will receive the user's information. The applications receive user access tokens, for example, in the form of **JSON Web Tokens**, that are validated via the identity provider, instead of the actual credentials.

The decentralized access delegation protocols and their implementation are beyond the scope of this book. The responsibility for enterprise systems is to intercept and redirect the user authentication to the identity provider. Depending on the system architecture, this is the responsibility of a proxy server or the application itself.

There are open source solutions out there that implement decentralized security. An interesting technology is**Keycloak**which is an Identity and Access Management solution. It ships with various client adapters and supports standard protocols, such as OAuth or OpenID Connect, what makes it easy to secure applications and services.

# Proxies

Proxy servers that encapsulate communication with enterprise applications can add security aspects, such as encrypting the communication. Web proxy servers, for example, support TLS encryption over HTTPS.

The question is whether engineers want to make a difference between network, internal and external communication. Communication in an intranet network is often unencrypted. Depending on the nature of the exchanged information, internet communication should, in most cases, be encrypted.

Proxy servers can be used to terminate the encryption at the network boundaries, so-called**TLS termination**. The proxy server encrypts all outgoing information and decrypts all incoming information, respectively.

It's equally possible to re-encrypt the communication using different certificates for different networks.

# Integration in modern environments

Modern environments aim to support today's security needs. Container orchestration frameworks offer the provisioning of software proxy servers and gateways that expose the service; for example, Kubernetes`ingress`resources, as well as OpenShift`routes`support TLS encryption for cluster-external traffic.

In order to provide secret values such as credentials or private keys, orchestration frameworks offer the functionality of`secrets`. As seen previously, this enables us to separately provide secret configurations into the environment.`Chapter 5`,*Container and Cloud Environments with Java EE*examined how this is realized.

This enables applications, as well as the configuration in general, to use secret values. The secrets can be injected into the container runtimes, if needed.

# Implementing security in Java EE applications

After seeing the most common security approaches of today's world, let's have a look into how security is implemented using Java EE.

Of all the Java versions, Java EE version 8 aimed to address security aspects. It contains a security API that simplifies and unifies the integration for developers.

## Transparent security

In the simplest way, security in web applications can be implemented by proxy web servers, such as **Apache** or **nginx**. In that case, the security responsibilities are transparent to the application.

This is often the case if the enterprise application doesn't have to deal with users as domain entities.

## Servlets

In order to secure web services offered by the Java EE application, usually security on the servlet layer is used. This is the case for all technology that is built on top of servlets such as JAX-RS. Security features are configured using the servlet deployment descriptor, that is, the web.xml file.

This can happen in several ways such as form-based authentication, HTTP basic access authentication, or client certificates.

Similarly, security solutions such as Keycloak ship their own implementations of adapters and servlet filters. Developers usually just need to configure these components to use the security provider.

## Java principals and roles

Java security principals and roles represent identities and authorization roles, respectively. Principals and roles are usually configured in the application server in vendor-specific ways. Authenticated requests are bound to a principal during the execution.

One example of using the associated roles within the execution workflow is by using common security annotations such as@RolesAllowed. This declarative approach checks whether the principal is authorized correctly and will otherwise result in a security exception:

```
import javax.annotation.security.RolesAllowed;

@Stateless
public class CarManufacturer {

    ...

    @RolesAllowed("worker")
    public Car manufactureCar(Specification spec) {
        ...
    }

    @RolesAllowed("factory-admin")
    public void reconfigureMachine(...) {
        ...
    }
```

Besides vendor-specific solutions, users and roles can be extended to contain domain-specific information. ThePrincipalsecurity type is enhanced in order to do so.

It is possible to inject the principal that is identified by its name and to provide a specialization. The container takes care of the user identification, for example, by using form-based authentication.

This approach was especially advised prior to Java EE version 8. However, modern applications will likely use identity stores to represent domain-specific user information.

# JASPIC

The**Java Authentication Service Provider Interface for Containers**(JASPIC) is a standard that defines authentication service providers' interfaces. It comprises so-called **Server Authentication Modules** (SAM), pluggable authentication components, which are added to the application server.

This standard offers powerful and flexible ways how to implement authentication. Server vendors can ship their own implementation of SAMs. However, implementing authentication modules using the JASPIC standard is seen as quite cumbersome by a lot of developers. This is why the JASPIC standard is not widely used in enterprise projects.

# Security API

The Security API 1.0 is shipped with Java EE 8. The idea for this standard was to provide modern security approaches that are simpler to use for developers. These are implemented in vendor-independent ways, without the need to lock in to specific solutions.

Let's have a look into what the Security API includes.

## Authentication mechanisms

First of all, the Security API includes `HttpAuthenticationMechanism`, which provides the features of the JASPIC standard with much less development effort needed. It's specified to be used in a servlet context.

Application developers are only required to define a custom `HttpAuthenticationModule` and to configure the authentication in the `web.xml` deployment descriptor. We will have a look at a custom security implementation later in this chapter.

The Java EE container already ships with predefined HTTP authentication mechanisms for basic, default, and custom form authentication. The developers can use this predefined functionality with minimal effort. Before we see an example, let's see how to store the user information.

## Identity stores

The concept of identity stores was also added with the Security API. Identity stores provide the authentication and authorization information of users in lightweight, portable ways. They offer a unified way to access this information.

The `IdentityStore` type validates a caller's credentials and accesses its information. Similarly to HTTP authentication mechanisms, the application containers are required to provide identity stores for LDAP and database access.

The following shows an example using the container-provided security functionality:

```
import javax.security.enterprise.authentication.mechanism.http.*;
import
javax.security.enterprise.identitystore.DatabaseIdentityStoreDefinition;
import javax.security.enterprise.identitystore.IdentityStore;

@BasicAuthenticationMechanismDefinition(realmName = "car-realm")
@DatabaseIdentityStoreDefinition(
        dataSourceLookup = "java:comp/UserDS",
        callerQuery = "select password from users where name = ?",
        useFor = IdentityStore.ValidationType.VALIDATE
)
public class SecurityConfig {
    // nothing to configure
}
```

Application developers only need to provide this annotated class. This approach provides simple and straightforward security definitions for test purposes.

Usual enterprise projects arguably require more custom approaches. Organizations usually have custom ways of authentication and authorization that need to be integrated.

# Custom security

The following shows a more sophisticated example.

In order to provide custom authentication, application developers implement a custom HttpAuthenticationMechanism, especially the validateRequest() method. The class only has to be visible to the container as a CDI bean. The rest is done by the application container. This simplifies the security integration for developers.

The following shows a basic example, with *pseudo code* representing the actual authentication:

```
import javax.security.enterprise.AuthenticationException;
import javax.security.enterprise.authentication.mechanism.http.*;
import javax.security.enterprise.credential.UsernamePasswordCredential;
import javax.security.enterprise.identitystore.CredentialValidationResult;
import javax.security.enterprise.identitystore.IdentityStoreHandler;

@ApplicationScoped
public class TestAuthenticationMechanism implements
        HttpAuthenticationMechanism {

    @Inject
```

```
        IdentityStoreHandler identityStoreHandler;

        @Override
        public AuthenticationStatus validateRequest(HttpServletRequest request,
                HttpServletResponse response,
                HttpMessageContext httpMessageContext)
                throws AuthenticationException {

            // get the authentication information
            String name = request.get...
            String password = request.get...

            if (name != null && password != null) {

                CredentialValidationResult result = identityStoreHandler
                        .validate(new UsernamePasswordCredential(name,
                        password));

                return httpMessageContext.notifyContainerAboutLogin(result);
            }

            return httpMessageContext.doNothing();
        }
    }
```

The`validateRequest()`implementation accesses the user information contained in the HTTP request, for example via the HTTP headers. It delegates the validation to the identity store using the`IdentityStoreHandler`. The validation result contains the result that is provided to the security HTTP message context.

Depending on the requirements, a custom identity handler implementation is required as well. It can provide custom authentication and authorization methods.

If decentralized security protocols, such as OAuth, are being used, a custom identity handler will implement the security access token validation.

The following shows a custom identity store:

```
    import javax.security.enterprise.identitystore.IdentityStore;

    @ApplicationScoped
    public class TestIdentityStore implements IdentityStore {

        public CredentialValidationResult validate(UsernamePasswordCredential
                usernamePasswordCredential) {

            // custom authentication or authorization
```

```
        // if valid

        return new CredentialValidationResult(username, roles);

        // or in case of invalid credentials

        return CredentialValidationResult.INVALID_RESULT;
    }
}
```

The `web.xml` servlet deployment descriptor is used to specify the secure resources. The application container takes care of the integration:

```
<security-constraint>
    <web-resource-collection>
        <web-resource-name>Protected pages</web-resource-name>
        <url-pattern>/management</url-pattern>
    </web-resource-collection>
    <auth-constraint>
        <role-name>admin-role</role-name>
    </auth-constraint>
</security-constraint>
```

An HTTP authentication mechanism provides a straightforward, yet flexible, way to implement JASPIC security. Its implementation is simpler compared to a plain JASPIC approach.

It provides the possibility of intercepting communication flows and can integrate the application with third-party security providers.

# Accessing security information

Enterprise applications sometimes need the functionality to access information about the user authorization as part of the business logic. The Security API enables us to retrieve this information in a uniform way.

It contains the `SecurityContext` type that provides a programmatic way to retrieve information about the caller principal and its roles. The `SecurityContext` is injectable into any managed beans. It also integrates with the servlet authentication configuration and provides information about whether the caller is allowed to access a specific HTTP resource.

The following shows an example usage of the`SecurityContext`:

```
import javax.security.enterprise.SecurityContext;

@Stateless
public class CompanyProcesses {

    @Inject
    SecurityContext securityContext;

    public void executeProcess() {
        executeUserProcess();
        if (securityContext.isCallerInRole("admin")) {
            String name = securityContext.getCallerPrincipal().getName();
            executeAdminProcess(name);
        }
    }

    ...
}
```

The idea of the Security API is that it integrates with the existing functionality from previous Java EE versions. This implies, for example, that the`@RolesAllowed`annotation uses the same role information as the`SecurityContext`. Developers can continue to rely on the existing standard functionality.

# Summary

In today's world, IT security is quite an important aspect. In the past, some of the biggest security issues were weak encryption and hashing algorithms, how passwords are persisted, and home-grown security implementations. A few important security principles include encrypting the communication, using external, trusted security providers for authentication and authorization, avoiding keeping credentials under version control, and including test scenarios that verify protection.

Communication is usually encrypted in the transport layer using TLS. Used certificates should be signed correctly, either by a company-internal or official certificate authority. Other approaches includes using security features of the protocol layer, such as HTTP basic authentication on top of encrypted communication.

Decentralized security decouples authentication and authorization responsibilities from the applications by including trusted identity providers. Single sign on as well as decentralized access delegations protocols are examples for this.

Security in Java EE application boundaries is usually realized on top of Servlets. The Security API which was introduced in Java EE 8 aims to provide simpler, uniform approaches on how to tackle security in Java EE applications. HTTP authentication mechanisms are an example that provide easier usage of the powerful JASPIC functionality. Identity stores provide authentication and authorization information of users.

The idea of the Security API is to integrate with existing functionality and offer uniform access mechanisms. The included features should be sufficient to secure enterprise application on the HTTP side.

# 11
# Conclusion

I hope that all that we have learned in this book provides helpful insights into how to build modern, lightweight, business-oriented enterprise applications. Maybe this book could even dissolve some outdated best practices of the past.

We have seen how modern versions of Java EE fit into a new world of software development, embracing container technology, cloud platforms, automation, Continuous Delivery, and more.

## Motivations in enterprise development

As we have seen several times in this book, engineering teams should follow the right motivations when developing software. The main focus of enterprise systems should be on their business motivations. The domain and business use cases of applications need to be clear, before they can deliver value to their customers. At the end of the day, working software that accomplishes business functionality is what generates revenue.

A helpful question that developers can ask themselves over time is: *Is what we're doing helping to solve the business problem?*

Software that aims to meet a customer's demands therefore mainly focuses on fulfilling business uses cases. Technology that fulfills a subordinate necessity, such as communication, persistence, or distribution, comes second. The chosen solutions should aim to solve the business demands first.

Therefore, technology, programming languages and frameworks ideally support the implementation of use cases without too much overhead. The team of engineers is advised to choose technology that they are productive and familiar with, but that also fits this requirement.

# Cloud and Continuous Delivery

We have seen the necessity of moving fast in a fast moving world. It's important to put emphasis on agility and reactiveness towards the customer's demands, the time-to-market, or better, *time-to-production*. The best features don't deliver value, until they are in the customer's hands.

It makes sense to use concepts and technology that help achieve this goal, such as Continuous Delivery, automation, infrastructure as code, and automated software tests.

This is what represents the biggest benefit of modern environments and cloud technology: *the ability to move fast*. Application environments for new projects, features, or test scenarios, can be created in a matter of minutes, using well-defined specifications. In particular, infrastructure as code and container technology support these attempts. Software developers deliver the environment configuration together with the application code, contained in the project's repository.

Defining all contents of enterprise software thus becomes a responsibility of the whole engineering team. Developers, as well as operational engineers, are interested in shipping software that provides value to its users. The whole software team is accountable for achieving this goal.

This also includes the topic of software quality assurance. Delivering features with rapid pace is only possible if proper, automated quality verification mechanisms are in place. Tests that require human intervention and that don't run reliably or fast enough prevent fast processes and keep developers from doing more useful work. It's a necessity to invest effort in automated, sufficient, and reliable test cases that are built with maintainability and code quality in mind.

# Relevance of Java EE

We have seen how Java EE enables all this. The platform supports focusing on business demands by enabling developers to write code without setting too many constraints. Use cases can be designed and implemented by following the domain's demands first.

The technology itself does not *want attention*. In the majority of cases, it's sufficient to annotate business logic which leads the application container to add the required technical necessities. The approaches of Java EE standards, such as JAX-RS, JPA, or JSON-B, accomplish the required technical integration with minimum effort required.

The Java EE platform especially enables engineers to seamlessly integrate multiple standards without configuration work. The JSR specifications that are written with the principles of Java EE in mind, make this possible.

Modern Java EE has to be seen differently to how it was in the old days of J2EE. In fact, the programming model and runtimes have little to do with J2EE.

With the backwards-compatible nature of the platform, outdated approaches are still possible, but the technology has advanced a lot since then. Programming models and design patterns have been revisited and vastly simplified. In particular, the restrictions of past patterns in implementing hierarchies of technology-motivated interfaces, and superclasses, are gone. Developers are able to focus on business domains, not on the technology.

The nature of the Java EE standards allows companies to realize vendor-independent applications. This avoids vendor lock-in on the technology-side. Developers are also not exclusively trained for vendor-specific technologies. We have seen quite a few cases of teams that were solely familiar with vendors that became obsolete.

Java EE technology is not only used on the server-side. Standards such as JAX-RS, JSON-P, or CDI provide valuable benefits for Java SE applications as well. It makes sense to realize certain functionalities, such as HTTP clients, with standards technology that developers are familiar with.

# API updates introduced in Java EE 8

This book focuses on enterprise applications with Java EE 8.

There have been certain standards that have been updated in the course of this version. The following are the most important new features and standards.

# CDI 2.0

Since Java EE 8 and CDI 2.0, events cannot only be handled synchronously. As we have seen previously in this book, CDI natively supports handling events asynchronously. In fact, this was only possible before if the event observer method was a business method of an EJB, annotated with `@Asynchronous`.

In order to emit and handle asynchronous CDI events, the publisher side uses the `fireAsync` method. The observer method parameter is annotated with `@ObservesAsync`.

Another new event functionality the advent of CDI 2.0 included is the possibility to order event observers. Therefore, the @Priority annotation, which is well-known within the Java EE platform, is specified at the event observer method:

```
public void onCarCreated(@Observes @Priority(100) CarCreated event) {
    System.out.println("first: " + newCoffee);
}

public void alsoOnCarCreated(@Observes @Priority(200) CarCreated event)
{
    System.out.println("second: " + newCoffee);
}
```

This approach guarantees that the event observers are called in the specified order, with lower priority numbers first. Developers should consider whether the situation violates loose coupling and the single point of responsibility principle, by needing to order the event handlers.

The biggest feature of CDI 2.0 was the integration outside of an enterprise container, providing the possibility to use CDI in Java SE applications. The idea is that Java SE applications can also use the features of a sophisticated dependency injection standard. This aims to increase the acceptance of CDI outside of the Java EE world.

# JAX-RS 2.1

Version 2.1 of JAX-RS mainly targeted reactive clients, SSE, and better integration into standards such as JSON-B. Besides these, some small improvements have been added.

Reactive programming is used more and more, and, in particular, the client receives new, reactive functionality to make HTTP calls and directly returning so-called reactive types. An example for such a type is the CompletionStage type. This type is supported natively; other types and libraries can be added via extensions.

In order to make reactive calls, the rx() method of the Invocation.Builder is used.

As also shown in this book, JAX-RS 2.1 supports SSE, both on the client and on the server side. The SSE standard represents a lightweight, one-way messaging protocol that uses plain text messages over HTTP.

In order to match the usual approach of the Java EE platform, the JSON-B standard which has been added in Java EE 8 is seamlessly integrated into JAX-RS. This means that, similarly to JAXB, Java types that are used as request or response bodies, respectively, are implicitly mapped to JSON.

Similarly, the new features that are part of JSON-P 1.1 and Bean Validation 2.0 are included in JAX-RS, as well. This is possible since the specifications forward the specific functionality to the corresponding standards.

A smaller update that was incorporated into JAX-RS was the inclusion of the `@PATCH` annotation for the HTTP method of the same name. Although support of HTTP methods other than the provided ones was possible in JAX-RS before, it simplifies the usage for developers who require this feature.

Another small but indeed helpful improvement was to include standardized HTTP timeout methods on the JAX-RS client. The builder methods `connectTimeout` and `readTimeout` handle configured timeouts. A lot of projects require this configuration, which previously resulted in including vendor-specific features.

We have seen the implementation of these features in `Chapter 3`, *Implementing Modern Java Enterprise Applications*.

# JSON-B 1.0

The JSON-B is a new standard that maps Java types to and from JSON structures, respectively. Similarly to JAXB for XML, it provides functionality to declaratively map objects.

The biggest advantage of this standard within the Java EE ecosystem is that applications don't need to rely on vendor-specific implementations anymore. JSON mapping frameworks have typically prevented enterprise applications to be built in a portable way. They increase the risk of breaking runtime dependencies with existing framework versions.

JSON-B solves this issue by providing standardized JSON mapping. Shipping custom mapping frameworks such as Jackson or Johnzon is not required anymore.

# JSON-P 1.1

JSON-P 1.0, which was introduced in Java EE 7, shipped a powerful feature to programmatically create and read JSON structures. The version 1.1 mainly included support for common JSON standards.

One of these IETF standards is **JSON Pointer** (RFC 6901). It defines a syntax to query JSON structures and values. By using pointers such as `"/0/user/address"`, JSON values are referenced, similarly to **XPath** in the XML world.

This feature is included in the `JsonPointer` type, that is created via the `Json.createPointer()` method, similarly to the existing JSON-P API.

Another, newly-supported standard is **JSON Patch** (RFC 6902). RFC 6902 defines so-called patches and modification methods that are applied to existing JSON structures.

JSON 1.1 supports creating JSON patches via `Json.createPatch` or `Json.createPatchBuilder`, respectively. The corresponding JSON-P type is `JsonPatch`.

The third supported IETF standard is **JSON Merge Patch** (RFC 7386). This standard merges existing JSON structures to create new structures. JSON-P supports creating Merge Patches via `Json.createMergeDiff` or `Json.createMergePatch`, respectively, that result in the `JsonMergePatch`type.

Besides these supported IETF standards, JSON-P 1.1 includes a few smaller features that simplify the API usage. One example is the support of Java SE 8 streams via pre-defined stream collectors, such as the `JsonCollectors.toJsonArray()` method. Another small improvement enables the creation of JSON-P values types from Java strings and primitives, via `Json.createValue`.

# Bean Validation 2.0

Java EE 8 updates the Bean Validation version to 2.0. Besides including new, pre-defined constraints, it mainly targets support for Java SE 8.

The Java SE 8 support includes multiple, differently-configured validation constraint annotations. Types of the Java 8 Date and Time API are now supported; for example, via usage such as `@Past LocalDate date`.

Values that are contained in container types can also be validated separately, via parameterized type annotations. Examples for this are `Map<String, @Valid Customer> customers`, `List<@NotNull String> strings`, and `Optional<@NotNull String> getResult()`.

Bean Validation 2.0 includes new pre-defined constraints. For example, `@Email` validates email addresses. `@Negative` and `@Positive` verify numeric values. `@NotEmpty` ensures that collections, maps, arrays, or strings are not empty or `null`. `@NotBlank` validates that strings do not solely consist of whitespace.

These constraints are a helpful default feature that avoids potentially defining this manually.

# JPA 2.2

Java EE 8 updates the JPA specification to version 2.2. This version mainly targets Java SE 8 features.

Similar to Bean Validation, the Java SE 8 support includes the Date and Time API. Types such as `LocalDate` or `LocalDateTime` are now natively supported for entity properties.

Version 2.2 makes it possible to return a query result, not only as `List<T>` but `Stream<T>`, using the `getResultStream()` method as shown in the following code snippet:

```
Stream<Car> cars = entityManager
        .createNamedQuery(Car.FIND_TWO_SEATERS, Car.class)
        .getResultStream();
cars.map(...)
```

What JPA 2.2 also finally added is support to inject managed beans into attribute converters using CDI's `@Inject`. This increases the use and number of scenarios of custom attribute converters. Similar to other standards such as JSON-B, better CDI integration encourages reuse of Java EE components.

Also version 2.2 adds repeatable annotations, such as `@JoinColumn`, `@NamedQuery`, or `@NamedEntityGraph`. Since Java SE 8 allows to repeat the same annotation type multiple times, developers are no longer required to use the corresponding group annotations, such as `@JoinColumns`, for these functionalities.

# Security 1.0

As seen in the last chapter, Security 1.0 aims to simplify the integration of security concerns into Java EE applications. Developers are therefore encouraged to use powerful functionalities such as JASPIC.

We have seen the features and usage of HTTP authentication mechanisms, identity stores, and security contexts in the previous chapter.

# Servlet 4.0

As of writing this book, HTTP/1.1 is the primarily used version of HTTP. HTTP/2 targets the shortcomings of HTTP performance of web applications in the past. In particular, requesting several resources of a web based system could lead to suboptimal performance due to the numerous connections involved. Version 2 of HTTP aims to lower latency and maximize throughput by multiplexing, pipelining, compressing headers, and Server Push.

Most of the changes in HTTP/2 do not affect the engineers' work compared to 1.1. The servlet container deals with HTTP concerns under the hood. The exception to this is the Server Push feature.

Server Push works in such a way that the server directly sends HTTP responses of resources related to a client-requested resource, following the assumption that the client would need these resources as well. It allows the server to send resources which were not explicitly requested by a client. This is a performance optimization technique that in web pages mainly concerns style sheets, JavaScript code, and other assets.

The Servlet API supports Server Push messages by using the `PushBuilder` type that is instantiated with the `HttpServletRequest.newPushBuilder()` method.

# JSF 2.3

Java Server Faces are a traditional way of building server-centric, component-based HTML UIs. Java EE 8 ships with the updated JSF version 2.3.

The main improvements of the version update include better CDI, WebSocket and AJAX integration, class-level Bean Validation, as well as support for Java SE 8.

Since the focus of this book is clearly on the backend-side, it doesn't include much about JSF.

# JCP and participation

The **Java Community Process** (**JCP**) defines the standards that make up the Java SE and EE platforms, including the Java EE umbrella standard itself. The individual standards are defined as **Java Specification Requests** (**JSR**), each forming so-called **Expert Groups**, consisting of experts and companies involved in enterprise software.

The idea is to standardize technology that has proven itself well in real-world projects. The experience of companies and individuals from these real-world projects is brought together to form vendor-independent Java enterprise standards.

It's highly advisable for both companies and individuals to participate in the JCP. It provides the ability to form the standards and the future of Java technology as well as to gain knowledge in this technology. The open processes of the JCP enable developers to get insight about how the future versions of Java EE will look.

Individuals and companies can also follow the standardization processes, even if they don't participate in the JCP. It's possible to review working states of the standards and provide feedback to the Expert Groups.

The Expert Groups indeed welcome constructive feedback while the specifications are being formed. It's very beneficial to receive feedback and experience from real-world projects and helps in crafting standards that suit the needs of the industry better.

I also was involved in shaping Java EE 8, being part of two Expert Groups, namely JAX-RS 2.1 and JSON-P 1.1. I personally gained a lot of knowledge as part of this engagement and can encourage enterprise Java developers to look into the processes within the JCP.

# MicroProfile

The motivation behind the MicroProfile initiative was to build upon the Java EE standards and create smaller-scale profiles that target microservice architectures as well as experiment with features independent from standardization. Multiple application server vendors have been involved in this initiative that forms vendor-agreed de facto standards.

Server applications that support MicroProfile pride the opportunity to run Java EE applications that only require a smaller set of standards, in the first version this includes JAX-RS, CDI, and JSON-P. Similarly, application server vendors provide the ability to strip down runtime to a specific required set of standards.

The advantage of these approaches is that they don't add dependencies to the enterprise project, rather than just optimizes the runtime. Developers still write their applications using the same Java EE standard technology.

# Eclipse Enterprise for Java

In September 2017, just before publishing this book, Oracle, the steward of Java EE and the JCP, announced to move the Java EE platform and its standards to an Open Source Foundation, what emerged in **Eclipse Enterprise for Java** (**EE4J**). The plans aim to lower the barrier for companies and developers who would like to contribute and to ultimately enable to a more open technology.

However the realization of these plans will look, it's important to mention that the plans include the preservation of the nature of the platform. The approaches and techniques presented in this book will hold true in the future of enterprise Java.

I can repeat my message of what I have said in the past about participation within the JCP. However the manifestation of the standardization process of Enterprise Java looks, I encourage engineers and companies to have a look into Eclipse Enterprise for Java and to participate in defining enterprise standards. The collective knowledge and real world experience helped shaping the standards of Java EE, and will help shaping Enterprise Java in the future.

# Links and further resources

Throughout this book, we have covered many topics pertaining to Java EE. There are a few sources that helped me shape the content at various places. To continue your learning journey, you can refer to the following resources and references in the order of their occurrence in the book:

- Java Enterprise Platform: `http://www.oracle.com/technetwork/java/javaee/overview/index.html`

- Java Community Process: `https://jcp.org/en/home/index`

- Clean Code, Robert C. Martin (Uncle Bob)

- Design Patterns: Elements of Reusable Object-Oriented Software, Erich Gamma et al

- Domain-Driven Design, Eric Evans

- Screaming Architecture, Robert C. Martin (Uncle Bob): `https://8thlight.com/blog/uncle-bob/2011/09/30/Screaming-Architecture.html`

- Conway's Law, Mel Conway: `http://www.melconway.com/Home/Conways_Law.html`

- Apache Maven: `https://maven.apache.org`

- Gradle: `https://gradle.org`

- Servlet API 4: `https://www.jcp.org/en/jsr/detail?id=369`

- Entity Control Boundary, Ivar Jacobson

- Java EE 8 (JSR 366): `https://jcp.org/en/jsr/detail?id=366`

- Enterprise JavaBeans 3.2 (JSR 345): `https://jcp.org/en/jsr/detail?id=345`

- Context and Dependency Injection for Java 2.0 (JSR 365): `https://jcp.org/en/jsr/detail?id=365`

- Simple Object Access Protocol (SOAP): `https://www.w3.org/TR/soap/`

- Java API for RESTful Web Services 2.1 (JSR 370): `https://jcp.org/en/jsr/detail?id=370`

- Roy T. Fielding, Architectural Styles and the Design of Network-based Software

- Siren: `https://github.com/kevinswiber/siren`

- Java API for JSON Binding 1.0 (JSR 367): `https://jcp.org/en/jsr/detail?id=367`

- Java API for JSON Processing 1.1 (JSR 374): `https://jcp.org/en/jsr/detail?id=374`

- Java XML Binding 2.0 (JSR 222): `https://jcp.org/en/jsr/detail?id=222`

- Bean Validation 2.0, (JSR 380): `https://jcp.org/en/jsr/detail?id=380`

- Java Message Service 2.0 (JSR 343): `https://jcp.org/en/jsr/detail?id=343`

- Server-Sent Events: `https://www.w3.org/TR/eventsource/`

- WebSocket Protocol (RFC 6455): `https://tools.ietf.org/html/rfc6455`

- Java API for WebSocket (JSR 356): `https://jcp.org/en/jsr/detail?id=365`

- Enterprise JavaBeans / Interceptors API 1.2 (JSR 318): `https://jcp.org/en/jsr/detail?id=318`

- Java Temporary Caching API (JSR 107): `https://jcp.org/en/jsr/detail?id=107`

- MicroProfile: `https://microprofile.io`

- Docker Documentation: `https://docs.docker.com`

- Kubernetes Documentation: `https://kubernetes.io/docs/home`

- OpenShift Documentation: `https://docs.openshift.com`

- Cloud Native Computing Foundation: `https://www.cncf.io`

- The 12-factor app: `https://12factor.net`

- Beyond the 12 Factor App, Kevin Hoffman: `https://content.pivotal.io/ebooks/beyond-the-12-factor-app`

- Jenkins: `https://jenkins.io`

- Using a Jenkinsfile, Documentation: `https://jenkins.io/doc/book/pipeline/jenkinsfile`

- Semantic Versioning: `http://semver.org`

- JUnit 4: `http://junit.org/junit4`

- Mockito: `http://site.mockito.org`

- Arquillian: `http://arquillian.org`

- CDI-Unit: `https://bryncooke.github.io/cdi-unit`

- AssertJ: `http://joel-costigliola.github.io/assertj`

- TestNG: `http://testng.org/doc`

- WireMock: `http://wiremock.org`

- Gatling: `https://gatling.io`

- Apache JMeter: `http://jmeter.apache.org`

- Cucumber-JVM: `https://cucumber.io/docs/reference/jvm`

- FitNesse: `http://fitnesse.org`

- Prometheus: `https://prometheus.io`

- Grafana: `https://grafana.com`

- fluentd: `https://www.fluentd.org`

- Chronicle Queue: `http://chronicle.software/products/chronicle-queue`

- OpenTracing: `http://opentracing.io`

   AsciiDoc: `http://asciidoc.org`

- Markdown: `https://daringfireball.net/projects/markdown`

- OpenAPI: `https://www.openapis.org`

- Swagger: `https://swagger.io`

- Porcupine, Adam Bien: `https://github.com/AdamBien/porcupine`

- Breakr, Adam Bien: `https://github.com/AdamBien/breakr`

- OWASP: `https://www.owasp.org`

- OAuth: `https://oauth.net`

- OpenID: `https://openid.net`

- JSON Web Tokens: `https://jwt.io`

- Java Authentication Service Provider Interface for Containers (JSR 196): `https://www.jcp.org/en/jsr/detail?id=196`

# Index

## 1

12-factor applications
  about 182
  admin/management tasks, executing as one-off
    process 190
  app, executing as more stateless processes 185
  build stage 185
  codebase 182
  config, storing in environment 184
  dependencies, isolating 183
  dependency versions, declaring explicitly 183
  development 188
  logs, treating as event streams 189
  production 188
  robustness, maximizing with shutdown 187
  robustness, maximizing with startup 187
  run stage 185
  scaling out, via process model 186
  services, backing as attached resources 184
  services, exporting via port binding 186
  staging 188

## A

abstract factory pattern 59, 62
ACID transactions (Atomicity, Consistency,
    Isolation, Durability) 125
Apache 386
Apache Maven 23, 28
application
  goals 164
  infrastructure as code (IaC) 165
  installing on application server 159
  lightweight packaging 154, 157
  motivations 164
  production readiness 166
  stability 166

AsciiDoc 295
asynchronous execution
  about 134
  asynchronous CDI events 136
  asynchronous EJB methods 135
  asynchronous JAX-RS 139
  Managed Executor Service 135
  reactive JAX-RS 139
  scopes, in asynchronicity 137
  timed execution 137

## B

Bean Validation 150
business metrics
  about 338
  environment, integrating 344
  monitored metrics, emitting 340
  Prometheus 341
  realization, with Java EE 343

## C

Chronicle Queue 366
Cloud Native Computing Foundation 193
cloud native
  about 192
  benefits 192
cloud
  about 191, 396
  benefits 191
code level integration tests
  shortcomings 257
  versus system tests 257
Command Query Responsibility Segregation
    (CQRS)
  about 303
  application boundaries 326
  benefits 308

CDI events 319
design 304
event handlers 320
example scenario, Apache Kafka used 317
implementing 316
integrating 328
Java EE, integrating 318
Kafka messages, consuming 322
Kafka messages, producing 325
principles 304
shortcomings 309
state representation 321
system interfaces 317
communication
about 310, 330
back-pressure 333
bulkheads 332
circuits, breaking 330
handshaking 333
resilience 335
responses, validating 330
timeouts, breaking 330
component tests
about 245
delegating 248, 250
implementation 245
motivation 245
technology 250
Consistency, Availability, Partition tolerance (CAP)
theorem 125, 296
container orchestration frameworks
about 171, 172
realizing 173, 179
containerd 193
containers 167, 169
Contexts and Dependency Injection for Java (CDI)
50
Continuous Delivery (CD)
about 27, 396
checking in 226
culture 225
enhancements 228
issues, fixing 227
responsibility 225
team habits 225

visilibity 227
Continuous Integration (CI) 27, 199
convention over configuration 144, 151
Create Read Update Delete (CRUD)
about 296
reproducibility 298
scalability 297
shortcomings 297
transactions, competing 297

D

data access object (DAO) 117
DC/OS 171
decorator 64, 68
dependency management 152, 154
design patterns, Java EE
abstract factory 59, 62
decorator 64, 68
facade design pattern 68
factory method 62
object pool 64
observer 70
other patterns 73
proxy 70
singleton 56
strategy 71
development workflows
artifact versions 200
binaries, building 199
configuration 206
containers, building 201, 202
credentials 208
data migration 209
database structures, adding 210
database structures, modifying 211
database structures, removing 212
deployment 206
Java archives 199, 200
metadata, building 216, 217
migration, implementing 212
models, branching 218, 219
pipeline-as-code 220, 224
production 218
quality assurance 202, 204
realizing 197

technology 220
testing 215
version control 198, 199
distributed revision control systems 21
distributed systems
challenges 286
communication overhead 287
motivations 286
organizational overhead 287
performance overhead 287
performance requisites, achieving 345
service level agreement (SLA) 345
SLAs, achieving 345
Docker 167
Docker Compose 171
Domain-Driven Design
about 74
aggregates 76
domain event 77
entities 75
factories 77
repositories 76
services 74
value objects 75
Domain-Specific Language (DSL) 28

# E

Eclipse Enterprise for Java 404
Ehcache 133
Elasticsearch 190
enterprise applications
asynchronous communication 108
asynchronous HTTP communication 108
caching 131
communication technology, selecting 78, 81
communication, with external systems 78
configuring 129
cross-cutting concerns 78, 126
customers demands, meeting 17
database systems 116
database systems, integrating 122
developers focus 16
domain models, mapping 118
enterprise technology, connecting 116
errors, mapping 101

external concerns 78
external systems, accessing 102
HTTP content types, mapping 88
Hypermedia REST services, accessing 106
Java API for RESTful web services 85
message-oriented communication 109
messaging 108
overview 379
purpose 15
RDBMS systems, integrating 117
relational databases, versus NoSQL 125
Representational State Transfer 82
requests, validating 95, 101
server-sent events 110
stability, maintaining 103
synchronous HTTP communication 81
transactions 124
WebSocket 114
enterprise development
motivations 395
Enterprise Information Systems (EIS) 116
Enterprise Java Beans (EJB) 10, 50, 150
enterprise project code structure
about 35
business driven structure 37
horizontal layering, versus vertical layering 36
over-enforce architecture, avoiding 46
package structure, realizing 40
reasonable modules, searching 38
scenarios 36
enterprise systems
development approach 9
features 7
Entity Control Boundary
about 43
package access 45
packages 44
event sourcing
about 296, 298
benefits 299
event-driven architectures
about 296, 301
eventual consistency 303
Expert Groups 403

## F

facade design pattern  68
factory method  62
flow of execution
  about  133
  asynchronous execution  134
  synchronous execution  134

## G

Garbage Collection (GC)  354
Gradle  23, 30
Grafana  341

## H

Hazelcast  133
horizontal layering
  versus vertical layering  36

## I

Infinispan  133
Infrastructure as a Service (IaaS)  191
infrastructure as code (IaC)  165
integration tests
  about  251
  embedded containers  251, 253
  embedded databases  253, 256
  executing  256
inversion of control (IoC)  143

## J

Jackson  152
Jaeger  369
Java API for JSON Binding (JSON-B)  10, 86
Java API for JSON Processing (JSON-P)  91
Java API for RESTful web services (JAX-RS)  85
Java API for WebSocket  114
Java Architecture for XML Binding (JAXB)  89
Java Archive (JAR)  22
Java Authentication Service Provider Interface for
  Containers (JASPIC)  387
Java Community Process (JCP)  11, 403
Java Cryptography Extensions (JCE)  208, 380
Java EE 8
  API updates  397

Bean Validation 2.0  400
CDI 2.0  397
JAX-RS 2.1  398
JPA 2.2  401
JSF 2.3  403
JSON-B 1.0  399
JSON-P 1.1  400
roadmap  10
security 1.0  402
servlet 4.0  402
Java EE application servers  158, 159
Java EE Connector Architecture (JCA)  116, 326
Java EE standards
  using  150
Java EE
  about  182
  Apache Maven  28, 30
  approaches  12
  build systems  27
  CDI producers  53
  communication, implementing  329
  core domain components  50
  dependency management  152, 154
  deploys  183
  design patterns revisited  56
  domain events, emitting  53
  Domain-Driven Design  74
  EJB, integrating with CDI  51
  EJB, versus CDI  51
  external services, connecting  179
  Gradle  30
  in orchestrated containers  179
  integrating  318
  microservices, implementing  314
  orchestrated applications, configuring  180
  overview  396
  patterns  56
  relevance  9
  roadmap  11
  scopes  55
  services, discovering  329
  update  10
  workflows  224, 225
Java Message Service (JMS)  110
Java Performance Diagnostic Model (jPDM)

actors 349
  application 350
  constraints, identifying 348
  hardware 350
  operating system 350
  subsystems 348
Java Persistence API (JPA) 117
Java Specification Requests (JSR) 11, 403
Java Temporary Caching API (JCache) 133
Java Virtual Machine (JVM) 22, 350
JavaDoc 149
Jenkins 27
JFrog Artifactory 199
journaling 366
JSON Patch (RFC 6902) 400
JSON Web Tokens 384
Just-In-Time (JIT) 350

## K

Keycloak 385
Kibana 190
Kubernetes 171, 173, 193

## L

layers of abstractions 145
Log4j 24, 152
Logback 24, 152
logging
  about 359
  amounts of data 361
  concerns of applications 362
  in containerized world 364
  log formats 361
  log levels 360
  obfuscation 362
  performance 360
  shortcomings 359
  wrong technology, selecting 363
Logstash 190

## M

maintainable code
  preserving, with high quality 144
Markdown 295
message-oriented middleware (MOM) 109

MicroProfile 404
microservice architectures
  12-factor principle 313
  about 310
  data sharing 311
  interdependent systems 312
  native application 313
  shared-nothing architectures 312
  usage, determining 314
microservices
  application boundaries, implementing 316
  application servers 315
  CQRS, implementing 316
  implementing, with Java EE 314
  zero-dependency applications 315
modern frontend technologies
  JavaScript frameworks, entering 33
  organizing 34, 35
  structuring 33
modern Java EE
  concepts 143
  design principles 143

## N

N-1 compatibility 209
naming 145
nginx 386
NoSQL (non SQL)
  versus relational databases 125

## O

object pool 64
observer design pattern 70
Open Service Gateway Initiative (OSGi) 158
OpenAPI Specification 295
OpenShift 173
OpenTracing 193, 369
outer enterprise project structure
  about 18
  build systems, for Java EE 27
  business 18
  modern frontend technologies, structuring 33
  project artifacts 26
  project per artifact 26
  reusability 24

single module projects, versus multi-module
  projects 23
software projects contents 19
team structures 18

# P

package structures
  Entity Control Boundary 43
  flat module package 42
  horizontal package layering 41
  package contents 40
  realizing 40
performance issues
  about 371
  communication 374
  conclusion 355
  consumer, dominating 353
  dominating consumer 354, 355
  logging 371
  memory consumption 371
  pooling 375
  premature optimization 372
  production situations 350
  relational databases 373
  tackling 346
  threading 375
performance testing 375
performance tests
  insights 273
  key performance indicators 269
  motivation 269
  realization 273
plain old Java objects (POJOs) 24
Platform as a Service (PaaS) 191
Porcupine 332
productive development workflows
  goals 196, 197
project object model (POM) 28
Prometheus 193
proxy 70

# R

relational databases
  versus NoSQL 125
remote procedure calls (RPC) 81

Representational State Transfer (REST) 82
Resource Adapter Archives (RAR) 116
reusability
  considerations 25
  illusion 24
  organizational challenges 25
  technical dependencies 24

# S

salting 382
Security API
  about 388
  authentication mechanisms 388
  custom security 389
  identity stores 388
  security information, accessing 391
security
  about 380
  communication, encrypting 381
  concerns, delegating 381
  credential storage, avoiding in version control
    382
  decentralized security 384
  encrypted communication 383
  implementing, in Java EE 386
  Java principals and roles 386
  modern environment, integration 385
  password, managing 382
  possibilities 383
  principles 381
  protocol-based authentication 383
  proxies 385
  Security API 388
  servlets 386
  solutions 383
  tests, including 382
  transparent security 386
Server-sent events (SSE) 110
service level agreement (SLA) 345
services
  discovering 329
single points of responsibility 145
single sign on (SSO) 384
singleton pattern 56, 59
Slf4J 152, 360

Software as a Service (SaaS) 182
software projects contents
  application source code 19
  binaries 22
  build systems 23
  software structures 19
  version control systems 21
Sonatype Nexus 199
strategy design pattern 71
Swagger 295
system interfaces
  API considerations 291
  boundaries, documenting 293
  business logic, breaking 292
  consistency, versus scalability 295
  designing 290
  hypermedia REST 292
  interface management 291
  resilient APIs, modifying 292
  versioning 292
system tests
  about 259
  conclusion 258
  external concerns, simulating 261
  external mocks, controlling 266
  external mocks, deploying 266
  realizing 262
  shortcomings 258
  test scenarios, managing 260
  versus code level integration tests 257
systems landscapes
  bounded contexts 288
  context maps 288
  designing 288
  project life cycles 290
  separation of concerns 289
  teams 289

## T

TeamCity 27
technical metrics
  about 356
  boundary metrics 358
  high frequency monitoring, versus sampling 357
  obtaining 357

  types 356
test scopes
  component tests 237
  definition 236
  system tests 238
  tests, integration 237
  unit tests 237
tests
  code level integration tests, versus system tests 257
  code quality 280
  component tests 245
  data, maintaining 276
  determining 235
  executing locally 273, 276
  implementing 239
  importance 276
  integration tests 251
  need for 231, 232
  performance tests 238, 268
  scenarios, maintaining 276
  stress tests 239
  system tests 259
  technology support 280
  test code quality 277
  test quality, lacking 277
  unit tests 240
TLS termination 385
tracing 359, 366, 369

## U

unit tests
  about 240
  realization 240
  technology 244
use case boundaries 49

## V

Version control systems (VCS) 21
vertical layering
  versus horizontal layering 36
virtual machines (VMs) 167

# W

Web Application Archive (WAR) 22
WebSocket 114
well-crafted tests
  automation 234
  execution 234
  isolation 233
  maintainability 235
  predictability 233

  reliability 234
  requisites 232
WildFly 170

# X

XDoclet 149

# Z

Zero-dependency applications 315
Zipkin 369

www.ingramcontent.com/pod-product-compliance
Lightning Source LLC
Chambersburg PA
CBHW060647060326
40690CB00020B/4546